OXFORD READINGS IN SOCIO-LEGAL STUDIES

A Reader on Resourcing Civil Justice

A READER ON

Resourcing Civil Justice

EDITED BY

Alan Paterson and Tamara Goriely

OXFORD UNIVERSITY PRESS
1996

Oxford University Press, Great Clarendon Street, Oxford OX2 6DP

Oxford New York

Athens Auckland Bangkok Bogata Bombay
Buenos Aires Calcutta Cape Town Dar es Salaam
Delhi Florence Hong Kong Istanbul Karachi
Kuala Lumpur Madras Madrid Melbourne
Mexico City Nairobi Paris Singapore
Taipei Tokyo Toronto

and associated companies in
Berlin Ibadan

Oxford is a trade mark of Oxford University Press

Published in the United States
by Oxford University Press Inc., New York

British Library Cataloguing in Publication Data
Data available

Library of Congress Cataloging in Publication Data
A reader on resourcing civil justice / edited by
Alan Paterson and Tamara Goriely.
p. cm.
(Oxford readings in socio-legal studies)
Includes bibliographical references.
1. Legal aid. 2. Legal aid—Great Britain.
I. Paterson, Alan. II. Goriely, Tamara. III. Series.
K133.Z9R43 1996 344'.03258—dc20 [342.43258] 96–29004
ISBN 0–19–876462–6
ISBN 0–19–876461–8 (Pbk)

1 3 5 7 9 10 8 6 4 2

Typeset by Hope Services (Abingdon) Ltd.
Printed in Great Britain
on acid-free paper by
Bookcraft Ltd., Midsomer Norton, Somerset

Contents

Introduction: Resourcing Civil Justice

TAMARA GORIELY AND ALAN PATERSON

For the last two hundred years, the notion of equality under the law has been one of the theoretical underpinnings of the democratic state. Yet it remains an unfulfilled aspiration amid legal systems which reward those with wealth, knowledge, and stamina and exclude those unable to pay for lawyers. So what can be done to give some substance to the slogan of 'justice for all'? As presently conceived much Western law requires skilled interpretation, assistance, and advocacy. One strategy has been to argue for simplified laws and procedures so as to reduce the need for external assistance—possibilities which are explored in a companion volume—Genn, *Access to Justice*.[1] Until such time as law is radically reformed, however, a second strategy is also needed—the provision of expert help. This book is about why and how states should subsidize legal services for their citizens.

In Britain, as elsewhere in the developed world, legal aid budgets are coming under increasing scrutiny. Legal aid is seldom out of the news, and the news is usually bad. Governments complain that the budget has risen too fast, and that new measures are needed to limit its growth; the legal profession complain that they are paid too little, too late; while to consumers it often seems that only the very poor or very rich can afford justice. The legal press is full of the latest proposal and the latest crisis.

What contribution can socio-legal scholarship make to these debates? Its best known contribution is in providing empirical data to underpin social policy. Policy-makers are beginning to understand the value of monitoring the existing scheme and testing the effects of their proposals.[2] The role of socio-legal studies, however, goes much wider than this. It is able to raise fundamental questions which are so often ignored in the

---

[1] Hazel Genn, *A Reader on Access to Justice* (forthcoming, Oxford University Press).

[2] Thus in 1987 the Lord Chancellor's Department commissioned a major study of the effects of representation before tribunals, which demonstrated the need for greater assistance for those bringing cases (Genn and Genn 1989). Subsequent studies include analyses of the increase in criminal legal aid bills (Gray and Fenn 1991), the costs of duty solicitor schemes in county courts (Bridges 1991) and testing transaction criteria as a way of measuring the quality of legal work (Sherr *et al.* 1994a). In Scotland research has been commissioned into criminal legal aid (see, for example, Machin *et al.* 1994) and the geographic distribution of specialist legal service providers (Paterson 1995).

immediacy of policy debates. Why should the state provide legal aid? Why do states develop legal aid schemes? And who do they benefit? Answering these questions involves drawing on a wide range of sources. The normative question—why should the state provide legal services?— touches issues of political legitimacy and the role of the state, and needs to draw on political philosophy. Answering the sociological question— why do states develop legal aid?—involves understanding the historical development of welfarism and disputing cultures in different societies. When assessing the benefits of different ways of delivering legal aid, socio-legal studies are able to consider the experience of many different jurisdictions in the developed world.

Here we start by defining our terms: what do we mean by legal services? We then introduce the readings under three headings. The first considers the philosophical, or normative, issue: why should the state subsidize legal services to its citizens? The second (sociological) question considers the development of legal aid in different advanced capitalist economies: how and why have such schemes developed, and who benefits from them? The third section is concerned with social policy. It attempts to analyse the present crisis in legal aid by asking what has gone wrong and what choices are now open to us. At the end we offer our own, tentative, suggestions for the way forward.

Defining legal services

Traditionally, legal services have been thought of as services provided by lawyers. There is a growing understanding, however, that legal services can be provided by a much wider range of people. In 1980 the Hughes Commission on Legal Services in Scotland stated that: 'when we speak of legal services we mean advice, information or assistance involving a knowledge of rights and obligations conferred by law and of legal procedures, whether provided by a lawyer or otherwise' (para. 2.2). Thus legal services might extend to 'the dissemination of information through notices, leaflets, advertisements and booklets' (para. 2.1). Providers included advice centres such as Citizens Advice Bureaux, trade unions, motoring organizations, or social workers. The Hughes Commission thought that citizens needed legal services for two purposes—firstly to identify potential solutions to their problems, and secondly to pursue a legal solution should they choose to do so (para. 2.9). The Legal Action Group suggests an even wider definition: alongside legal education, information, advice, assistance, and representation they would include lobbying and law reform activities (Reading 3 in this volume). In the discussion that follows, 'legal services' and 'legal aid' are used in a wide sense, rather than simply referring to the activities of lawyers.

Why should the state provide legal services to its citizens?

The access argument

The short and classic answer to this question is that, in the adversarial legal system so common in the developed world, legal services are necessary to provide 'equal access to justice'. The view is put clearly by the Legal Action Group (LAG): 'The ultimate policy aim must be that anyone with a legal problem has equal access to its just conclusion so that disputes are determined by the intrinsic merits of the arguments of either party, not by inequalities of wealth and power' (Reading 3).

The reason why a society may wish to achieve equal access to justice is grounded deep in liberal constitutional theory. It is easy to produce a roll-call of philosophers to support equality before the law. As Ross Cranston (1986: 2) points out, 'insistence on the equal application of laws was common to writers as diverse as Rousseau, John Stuart Mill and Dicey' and is now 'probably the most generally respected of all egalitarian ideals'. It is thought to be a crucial element in the rule of law, and necessary to legitimate the state. Of course, in previous centuries, equality before the law was often purely formal in character, so that a nominal, but ineffective, right to go to court was sufficient. This, it is argued, is no longer sufficient.

One of the earliest statements of this view was T. H. Marshall's renowned essay on *Citizenship and Social Class*, given in Cambridge in 1949 as the Legal Advice and Assistance Bill was passing through the British Parliament. Here he gave voice to what he saw as a new social attitude towards equality. He cited the acceptance of state-funded legal aid as completing the project started in the eighteenth century to provide for the full and equal exercise of civil rights. Interestingly, however, he saw little role for law in securing the new social rights to health, education, housing, or welfare. These, he argued, were primarily collective rights, and therefore inappropriate to individual enforcement. Almost thirty years later, Cappelletti and Garth returned to the same theme (Reading 5, below). In the introduction to their world survey, they trace the changing conceptions of access to justice from nineteenth-century formalism towards a twentieth-century recognition that governments must take affirmative action to make rights *effective*, that is *actually accessible to all*. Cappelletti and Garth do not recognize Marshall's distinction between civil rights to be enforced through law and social rights to be enforced collectively. Instead they see the 'right of effective access' as a vital way of enforcing both civil and social rights. Indeed, they argue, access to justice is of 'paramount importance', since 'the possession of rights is meaningless without mechanisms for their effective vindication'.

Luban argues that there is a right to legal services in any country where—as in the USA—political legitimacy is grounded on the notion of 'equality-of-rights-not-fortune' (Reading 1). He does this on the ground that in order to be effective, it is generally agreed, rights must be legally enforceable. He provides a lucid summary of his argument:

1. Access to minimal legal services is necessary for access to the legal system.
2. Access to the legal system is necessary for equality of legal rights—equality before the law.
3. Equality of legal rights is necessary to the legitimacy of our form of government.
4. Whatever is necessary to the legitimacy of a form of government it must grant as a matter of right.
Therefore,
5. Access to legal services is a right under our form of government.

The classic argument in favour of legal aid, therefore, is that without legal assistance one cannot use the legal system effectively. Yet twentieth-century notions of equality demand that all citizens have equal and effective access to justice. It argues that without such a basic foundation, law— and hence the state itself—will not be able to secure legitimacy in the eyes of those it seeks to regulate. It is a clear and succinct argument, founded on a long and respectable pedigree of political philosophy.

The access argument, however, fails to address the question of limited resources. Luban himself recognizes that society cannot afford to give everyone access to the best lawyers, and he argues for minimal rather than equal legal services. The Legal Action Group, however, accepts no such restraint and argues for equal access for all (Reading 3). One may question whether this would ever be possible. As Grossman and Sarat (1981: 128) point out, if everyone had full access to law the legal order would collapse. It is even less conceivable that everyone should have 'equal' access to justice. Abel remarks that 'even within the courtroom equality remains an unattainable chimera' (Reading 7). Galanter (1974) has shown how repeat players have structural advantages, while Garth (1983) argues that in a market for legal services those with more money will always be able to pay for more of a lawyer's time, and will therefore be better prepared. Any serious attempt to create equality would need to impose rigid restrictions on how repeat players use the courts and on how they are represented. Yet restricting access for the powerful is rarely suggested and almost never implemented. If it were, one suspects that it would soon prove ineffective as the powerful learnt how to circumvent the restrictions.

Of course, the proponents of 'equal access to justice' do not see it as a goal to be achieved but as an ideal to strive for. However much equality one has, one should always want more. Unfortunately, funders may see it differently—however many resources they put into legal services pro-grammes, lawyers will always want more. Furthermore, the more resources they spend, the more lawyers there will be to insist that more is spent. Funders may decide that it is best not to start.

The access argument therefore provides administrators with little help in using a limited budget. Yet in a world of limited resources some form of rationing is inevitable. If one believes in 'equal access to justice' how should rationing be conducted? According to Breger (1982), it is better to use chance than bureaucratic fiat.[3] He argues that individuals have a right to legal services which, following Dworkin, cannot be defeated 'by appeal to any of the ordinary routine goals of political administration'. Rights-holders, therefore, cannot be denied a benefit simply because it would not be efficient to grant it on a utilitarian calculation. Furthermore, rights-holders are entitled to equal concern and respect—so all rights-claims for legal help must be treated equally. Even where resources are limited claims must be decided on an equal basis—by chance through a lottery, for example, or through queuing or co-payment. This, however, is an uncomfortable position to hold. Would it really serve to increase respect for the law and the legitimacy of the state if access to law were provided through a lottery?

In fact, contrary to Breger's argument, at a theoretical level 'rights-talk' may be consistent with ranking claims to legal aid. Dworkin (1981) suggests that procedural rights are ancillary: a person who has a right to a particular outcome also has a right to a fair procedure. The level of resources to be devoted to that procedure should be commensurate with the importance of the right. As different rights may be ranked against each other, claims for legal aid can also be ranked, with those protecting fundamental rights given a higher ranking than those protecting lesser rights. On this basis, legal aid to vindicate a right to visit one's children, for example, should be given greater priority than legal aid for compensa-tion for a faulty dishwasher. This is partly reflected within the English

---

[3] For a reply, see Failinger and May (1984).

legal aid scheme, which provides non-means tested help to parents fighting local authorities for custody of their children, and no legal aid for defamation claims. In its submission to the Benson Commission, the Legal Action Group (1977) sought to extend this approach—drawing a distinction between fundamental rights, for which legal aid should be granted on a non-means tested basis, and non-fundamental rights, for which legal aid should continue to be means-tested. Family, housing, dismissal, and personal injury claims were given a high ranking; consumer disputes and defamation were given a low ranking. Unfortunately, the more specific the examples, the more arbitrary the lists became. Personal injury claims may be seen as preserving 'the right to health'—and would therefore score high. However, personal injury claims do not prevent injuries, they only provide compensation after the event and the £2,000 one receives for a small personal injury claim looks very similar to the £2,000 one may receive for a consumer dispute. Tenancy disputes over repairs were ranked as fundamental ('the right to housing') but owner-occupiers fighting builders or surveyors were non-fundamental. Given that most legal disputes are in the end about money, the distinction between a fundamental and non-fundamental right proves difficult to draw in practice.

The courts themselves have recognized a 'rights argument' in relation to criminal legal aid. The US Supreme Court has upheld the right to criminal defence counsel (Luban, Reading 1), while the European Convention on Human Rights requires that where a criminal defendant has insufficient means to pay for legal assistance, he should 'be given it free when the interests of justice so require' (Article 6(3)(c)). When it comes to civil proceedings, however, the courts have been much more hesitant. As Luban shows, the US Supreme Court has been highly reluctant to recognize a right to counsel in civil proceedings (Reading 1). The European Court of Human Rights went some way towards upholding a right to civil legal aid in the case of *Airey* v *Ireland*.[4] Mrs Airey wished to obtain a judicial separation from her husband—proceedings which at the time could only be heard by the Irish High Court. There was no civil legal aid, both law and procedure were complex, she was too emotionally involved to manage by herself, and she was too poor to afford a solicitor. The Court found that she was effectively denied all access to a remedy. This, they held, was a breach of Article 6(1) of the Convention under which everyone is entitled to have their civil rights and obligations determined

---

[4] (1979) 2 EHRR 305.

by 'an independent and impartial tribunal established by law'. As a result, the Irish Government was forced to establish a limited legal aid scheme. Subsequent decisions by the Commission, however, have tended to restrict the effect of *Airey*. The European Commission of Human Rights has found that legal aid may be denied for defamation,[5] for affiliation proceedings,[6] and before industrial tribunals.[7] Furthermore, legal aid may be denied because a case fails a means or merits test[8] (Cousins, 1992).

The instrumentalist view

Many people would disagree with Luban that society should be founded on the 'equality of rights' rather than on 'equality of fortune'. Would not most people prefer to be housed, fed, and educated than to take a case to the Supreme Court? The rhetoric of access to justice has a dangerous tendency to elide two very different concepts—law and justice. Unfair laws are still unfair even when they are strictly enforced through superb legal aid schemes, and fair and harmonious societies may be created through many mechanisms other than law. We now recognize that the health of a nation depends much more crucially on good diet and clean water than on medical intervention. Equally, a just society is much more likely to depend on the fair allocation of jobs, education, housing, and income than on anything a legal aid scheme can deliver. Once one accepts that justice involves issues of substantive rather than purely formal equality, then legal services no longer have a first call on society's resources, but must take their place alongside other welfare expenditure programmes.

For those who believe in substantive equality rather than equality of rights, access arguments are not enough. To justify spending money on legal aid rather than in some other way, one must show that providing legal services to the poor is a cost-effective way of improving their position. In the United States, in particular, there is an influential body of thought which does just that. Instead of taking an access view, it takes an instrumental or 'utilitarian' view, which states that legal aid is important because it provides the poor with material, psychological, or political benefits.

One of the earliest and most influential expositions of this view was written in 1964 by Edgar and Jean Cahn. The previous year, President Johnston had declared 'war on poverty', establishing the Office of Economic Opportunity to direct aid to the poorest neighbourhoods. Jean

---

[5] *Munro v. UK* (1987) 10 EHRR 503.
[6] *Webb v. UK* (1983) 6 EHRR 120.
[7] *S v. UK* (1983) 6 EHRR 136.
[8] *X v. UK* 21 D & R 85.

Cahn had worked as a lawyer for a model programme in New Haven, Connecticut, and was keenly aware of the limitations of the new approach. The Cahns argued that the 'war' metaphor aptly described a system in which an army of professionals planned poverty programmes as problems in logistics. Monopoly providers established donor–donee relationships with the poor, which not only undercut incipient protest but perpetuated apathy and defeatism. The answer was to allow for a 'civilian perspective', through which beneficiaries could express dissent, critical scrutiny, and impatience. Lawyers working in new 'neighbourhood law firms', the Cahns argued, could play a crucial role in championing the views of the poor. People could take their problems to lawyers without fear of stigma. Furthermore, lawyers are trained to be partisan. Using their legal knowledge and skills in advocacy, they could express the opinions of their clients to a wide range of institutions in a wide variety of ways. As well as taking individual cases, they could, for example, advise local organizations, campaign for law reform, and make representations to administrative agencies.[9]

By 1965 the Office of Economic Opportunity had established a Legal Services Programme and appointed its first Director, Clinton Bamberger (Johnson 1974). In the course of numerous speeches—of which Reading 2 is a typical example—Bamberger set out a new radical agenda for legal aid. Lawyers could bring material benefits to poor communities, by challenging landlords, creditors, and welfare providers, and enforcing and reforming the law. However, their role extended beyond this. For Bamberger, it was not only lack of money that makes a man poor: it was also 'ignorance of rights', 'disregard of personal value', 'a conviction of despair'. Lawyers, he thought, could spark a recognition among poor communities that they were citizens and that the law could be used for their benefit. Thus lawyers had a role in promoting a model of active, participative citizenship which was fundamental to the polity of the United States.

There are problems, however, in using lawyers to give a voice to the poor. Richard Titmuss, in particular, argued powerfully against the War on Poverty approach, which singled out the poor for special treatment. As one of the war-time generation who had founded the welfare state in

---

[9] Richard White (1973: 34–5) develops similar arguments by suggesting that lawyers are particularly effective at representing the views of the poor because they are used to taking instructions and entering into conflicts on clients' behalf. When they seek to change a client's behaviour they do so by reference to open and declared norms. Thus the relationship is one of 'essential dignity'.

Britain, he believed passionately in curing poverty through redistributive taxation. Universal benefits, he thought, should be given to all—poor and non-poor alike—without the intervention of lawyers (1970).[10] After a visit to the United States he commented:

In New York and other American cities today it is claimed by some critics of universalism that social welfare is effectively concentrated to aid poor people. Lawyers and social workers are helping them to demand and get their legal 'welfare rights'. It is instructive, however, to visit and observe the welfare offices, waiting rooms, out-patient and casualty departments (as well as the disorderly queues). What does one see? Mostly one sees throngs of black people; poor black people. They may get their 'welfare rights' but I am convinced that the sense of discrimination that results from 'selectivity' cannot be removed however large the legions of helpful lawyers and social workers. In my judgment, the National Health Service in Britain has made a greater contribution to integration and ethnic tolerance than brigades of lawyers and platoons of social workers (1968: 9).

As the Legal Services Programme expanded, even the Cahns began to have doubts. By 1966, they worried that neighbourhood law firms, like other welfare agencies before them, had already 'begun the long road to unresponsiveness' (Cahn and Cahn 1966: 927). Instead of giving a voice to the poor, they could all too easily end up 'expanding retail outlets' for a system of justice which the middle class had already rejected as 'obsolete, cumbersome and too expensive' (929). Neighbourhood law offices should be kept, they said, but made much more responsive to their communities. Furthermore, there was a need to reconstitute and democratize the whole 'Justice Industry'—with more neighbourhood courts, for example, and more functions carried out by non-lawyers. By the end of the decade, commentators were considerably less sanguine about the role of lawyers in poor communities. Lawyers were most effective, it was thought, when they were least like lawyers. Wexler (1970), in particular, made a strong plea that the poverty lawyer's first task should be to help the poor establish organizations, rather than indulging in the legal games for which they were trained.[11]

A mere sop?

Follow these arguments to their logical conclusion and one may conclude that the poor do not really want or need lawyers at all. Perhaps law

---

[10] For a reply, see R. White (1973). White argues that the British system, far from actualizing some universalist ideal, shows many of the same features of 'hostility, desperation, submissiveness etc.' of the American system (25).

[11] See also Galanter (1976).

inevitably serves the interests of capital and has little to offer the poor in terms of substantive justice? Abel (1985: 521) points out that law has a low salience for the poor and oppressed. They have rarely campaigned for legal aid, which may simply routinize and individualize issues of mass struggle. In his 1986 article (Reading 7), he questions whether legal aid really does much to legitimize law in the eyes of the poor, given that familiarity with court proceedings so often breeds contempt. Maybe legal aid is intended to legitimize law not to the oppressed but to the oppressors—perhaps another example of the 'universal desire of oppressors to believe that they are loved by the oppressed'. The suggestion is that legal aid is not only a con, but an ineffective con. One may reply that any society in which the division between oppressors and oppressed is that stark is beyond the help of legal aid. Clearly Abel is being provocative. Even he does not accept the full logic of the argument and eventually concludes that legal aid 'deserves our critical support'.

Nevertheless, as Zemans comments, the critics of access to justice perform a useful function in enforcing limits to the discussion (Reading 6). We can no longer pretend that legal services will bring about 'a legal "nirvana" where all injustice and inequality will miraculously be obliterated'. Law is not the only way of delivering justice. Legal aid must compete with other welfare programmes—education, health, housing, social security—which also play a part in creating the just society.

Why lawyers rather than cash?

In 1977 Griffiths noted the basic fact that use of legal services correlates closely with wealth (Reading 4). So why not 'intervene to redistribute wealth and the distribution of legal services will take care itself'? After all, poor people would almost certainly prefer the cash so that they, like the rich, could enjoy the freedom it offers. Griffiths is talking about widespread redistribution, but given that in 1994–5 the English legal aid scheme cost around £130 a year for every household eligible for help, even redistributing the legal aid budget might make an appreciable difference to those on a tight budget. If people were allowed to choose for themselves whether they spent their £130 on legal expenses insurance or in some other way, one suspects that few would opt for the insurance policy. So why should the state make the decision for them?

One answer to this is that lawyers are good for people, whether they realize it or not. If the poor are too stupid, too ignorant, or too incompetent to understand this, then the state should make the decision for them. Unless one is an extreme paternalist, however, this is difficult to accept.

The evidence is that the poor know more about surviving on a small income than the rich and are able to make better decisions about it. If they would sooner deal with their disqualification for benefit by drowning their sorrows in the pub than by visiting a lawyer it is probably because they have a keener appreciation of the relative merit of each.

An alternative line of argument suggests that what we are dealing with here is not an individual good to those directly involved, but a social good. Although visiting the pub may give more direct pleasure to the individuals concerned than fighting a legal case, a society in which people challenge bureaucratic mistakes is undoubtedly better than a society in which people fatalistically accept injustice. One cannot compel people to bring challenges, but one can assist them to do it. This is not because it will do much direct good to them personally, but because it will contribute to a more procedurally just society—that is, a society in which law is helped to meet its intended goals, is applied more fairly, and achieves greater public support. Griffiths concludes that the argument for providing legal services is:

not that they are a form of wealth, not that they are good for people, not that social change will result from distributing them, but rather that the just operation of the legal system demands a more equal distribution of the use of facilities collectively believed to be important to the realisation of legal entitlements and protections (Reading 4).

Legal aid and equality

As we have seen, one's views on legal aid will depend crucially on one's view of social equality. In the debate, one may discern a rough continuum between purely formal equality at one end and full substantive equality at the other. At one extreme it may be sufficient for citizens to have a purely formal equality before the law: on this basis it does not matter if they can actually use the law and legal aid is unnecessary. Cappelletti, Garth, and Luban, however, move one step up the spectrum and argue for substantive equality of rights. On this basis, being able to use the law is a 'paramount' right of citizenship. The state therefore has a greater responsibility to see that its citizens can use the law than to see that they are fed, housed, or educated. At the other end of the debate, people would deny that rights are more important than subsistence. After all, most homeless families would much prefer a house than an appearance before the Divisional Court. Like Titmuss, one may think that it would be better to establish good universal benefits which can be administered without lawyers. Or one may agree with Abel that a concentration on legal aid is a diversion from the main task of equalizing resources. Rather than giving to the poor lawyers, one should redistribute money.

Our own view, like that of many other commentators in this volume, lies somewhere between Luban's 'substantive equality of rights' and 'equality of fortune'. It can be found in that grey, fuzzy area in which people start to talk of 'equality of participation' or 'equality of citizenship'. In order to participate in society people need some basic level of material well-being, along with health care, education, and job opportunities. Law is not uniquely important, but it is one method by which people express themselves as citizens. It cannot, by itself, produce a just society, but it can ensure that society respects some of the values of procedural justice. Perhaps, as Titmuss argues, it would be better to provide more universal benefits which people can receive without detailed information, advice, and representation. However, as the welfare state breaks down, that is not a choice we are being offered. The choice increasingly seems to be between arbitrary means-tested benefits administered by over-regulated, overworked agencies without legal help, and the same benefits, administered by the same agencies, without some external legal assistance to prevent the worst mistakes. We believe that legal aid can increase procedural justice. It can help laws meet their own goals, can remove the most flagrant breaches, and can mitigate some of the pain. In doing this it can provide a glimmer of hope to the poor and some legitimacy to the state.

How and why do legal aid schemes develop?

In 1975 Cappelletti, Gordley, and Johnson published a classic study of comparative legal aid. In doing so they organized their material according to four models, depending on how the schemes were funded and staffed. These were: the charitable model; the compensated private attorney (or 'judicare') model; the salaried staff attorney model; and the 'combined' or mixed model.[12] In the introduction to their 1978 world survey, Cappelletti and Garth associate each model with a phase of legal aid history. Thus, until the beginning of the twentieth century most schemes relied on the charity of lawyers. These were supplanted by judicare schemes, which paid private lawyers on a case-by-case basis. The rise of salaried lawyers employed in poor areas can be traced to the US 'War on

---

[12] This continues to be the dominant way in which legal aid schemes are classified and has been used extensively by other authors: see Zemans (Reading 6), Denti (1979), and Paterson (Reading 12).

Poverty' in 1965, and a concern to get the maximum effect for the resources used. Finally, the most sophisticated and modern schemes use both salaried and judicare schemes. To this standard analysis Zemans adds another dimension, contrasting the reactive 'service' model, in which professionals respond to clients seeking their assistance, to a proactive 'strategic' model, which attempts 'to develop a long term approach of research, reform and education' to deal with social ills (Reading 6). Although judicare schemes are usually associated with a service approach, salaried schemes can fall anywhere on the spectrum between the 'service' and 'strategic' models.

Cappelletti and Garth's account was marked by an overwhelming optimism, which traces 'the emergence and development of a new and comprehensive approach to access problems in contemporary society' (Reading 5). The world, they suggested, was getting better and better. Furthermore, it was getting better in a uniform way, with similar 'waves' of the access to justice movement producing similar results in different countries. If some states had inadequate schemes it was because they had not yet reformed them. The optimism did not last long. By 1981, when Cappelletti and Garth returned to the same subject, pessimism had set in. In 1983 Zemans commented that 'in nation after nation limitations [are] being placed on the funding of legal services and restrictions imposed on the types of cases for which representation will be provided' (Reading 6). With the curbs on legal aid has come an unease with the Cappelletti and Garth approach. It no longer appears axiomatic that democracies need more legal aid, and it is by no means inevitable that states will strive to make their legal systems accessible to all. We need more detailed and complex explanations of how and why legal aid schemes develop.

Why do schemes develop differently?

It is clear that countries spend very different amounts on subsidized legal assistance to their citizens. According to the French Conseil d'Etat (1990), in 1989 England and Wales spent £9.80 per head of population on legal aid, compared with £6 in the Netherlands, £3 in Germany, and 70p in France. Belgium and Italy spent even less, surviving on largely charitable systems. There are many problems in putting together such figures: exchange rates vary while countries use different definitions, different years, and different tax regimes. After such provisos and cautionary notes, however, the fact remains that Western societies approach legal aid very differently. How do we account for this?

There are no simple explanations, though various theories have been tried and discarded. Blankenburg points out that the easiest, and superficially plausible, explanation is to relate legal aid to the different traditions of Common and Civil Law (Reading 9). Many common law countries—such as England, Australia, and Canada—do have much more developed legal aid schemes than civil law countries, such as France or Italy. It is easy to explain this in the greater emphasis of the common law on oral argument and adversarial forensic skills, which make legal services both more necessary and more expensive. Blankenburg concedes that there is some truth in this argument, especially in the field of criminal trials, where Civil Law traditions rely on the judge to 'seek out the truth'. It does not, however, account for differences in legal advice schemes, which are just as needed in civil law systems. Nor does it explain differences within the civil law world—why for example the Netherlands has a highly developed scheme, with an emphasis on legal advice, and Sweden has a traditional scheme with high eligibility limits, while France and Italy have so little.

A cynical view might relate legal aid to the number of lawyers: the more lawyers per head of population a country possesses, the more public subsidiary they will consume. Again, though, Blankenburg fails to find a link. The high UK expenditure does appear to correspond with a ratio of lawyers to population above the European average, but it does not account for the high expenditure in the Netherlands, where the ratio of lawyers to population is exceptionally low.

A third theory is that legal aid expenditure should differ according to a state's approach to welfare. After all, legal aid is only one small part of general welfare spending. Surely countries with high commitment to welfare spend more, while those with a low commitment spend less? Apparently not. Mel Cousins (Reading 8, below) shows that while spending on health care correlates closely with GDP per head (the richer the country, the more spent on health care), no such correlation exists for legal aid—except that very poor countries spend little on legal aid. Blankenburg points out that while the Netherlands and West Germany have similar levels of economic growth and welfare state development, the Netherlands spends seven times more than West Germany on legal advice (Reading 9). Scandinavian countries, with high welfare spending, have traditionally spent less than the UK on legal aid.

Finally, Abel (1985) draws attention to a religious divide. Protestant countries—Scandinavia, the Netherlands and the Anglo-Saxon countries—give considerably more attention to legal aid than Catholic countries—such as Ireland, Italy, and France. This distinction has some empirical basis, though the theoretical explanation is less clear-cut (see also Cousins, Reading 8). Abel suggest that it is because Protestant countries take a more positive attitude towards assisting divorce. As he states, 'family law dominates all legal aid programmes' (1985: 608). Divorce was the reason why the English civil legal aid scheme was introduced after the second world war and family problems still constitute one of its main areas of work. However, there is no clear link between the divorce rate and legal aid expenditure. Denmark manages to have the highest divorce rate in Europe without significant legal aid expenditure, while the Belgian divorce rate (without legal aid) is now slightly higher than that in the Netherlands (with legal aid) (LCD 1993: 8). Cousins concludes that the most that can be said is that 'a poorly developed, Catholic country with comparatively low levels of marital breakdown and no marked political instability is very unlikely to have a developed legal aid scheme' (Reading 8). It is much less clear which countries will develop legal aid.

A demand-creation exercise?

There is no simple predictor of which societies will develop legal aid schemes. Legal aid is not an historical inevitability, given a certain form of legal system, social structure, or political system. There is a tendency to assume that, in the absence of functionalist explanations, legal aid is a demand-creation exercise by lawyers or, as both Abel and Cousins put it, 'a solution in search of a problem' (Readings 7 and 8). This is a view which resonates with the Social Market Foundation's report (see below) which claims that the recent increases in the legal aid budget may reflect 'supplier-induced demand' (Reading 14).

Yet the history of the English scheme suggests that such a view is overly simplistic. Although the form of the legal aid scheme undoubtedly reflects the self-interest of lawyers, they did not invent legal aid. Instead, as Paterson and Nelken observe, 'the profession's strategy was one of co-option' (Reading 10). The breakdown of the charitable system to deal with poor person's divorces in 1938 led to a clear political 'problem', reflected in the traditional way—letters to and from Members of Parliament, questions in the House of Commons, concern from Army welfare officers and social welfare groups, articles by academics. In 1939, when the Lord Chancellor's Permanent Secretary wrote to the Law Society suggesting a paid scheme, the Law Society vehemently rejected the idea. The Law Society only developed plans for paid legal aid after it became clear that the problem of lack of help for divorce could no longer be ignored. This is not to suggest that legal aid was the only possible solution: in fact, there was an active lobby for divorce reform, which was successfully blocked by the judiciary, the Bar, and the Church. Nor is it to deny that the detailed plans which were eventually implemented reflected successful lobbying by the Law Society in its own interests. The profession's main concern was to co-opt existing pressures for the benefit of the profession, rather than to invent a new area of business. Similarly, during the 1960s and 70s, 'calls for improved legal access came from a disparate variety of groups with widely different motivations'. Finally, as an analysis of why legal aid schemes develop, the demand-creation theory begs as many questions as it answers. Why do some legal professions develop legal aid while other professions, equally powerful, fail to develop it? Why are some governments susceptible to pressure to develop legal aid, while others manage to resist?

From welfare state paternalism to assertive citizenship: new demands on legal aid

One potential explanation for discrepancies in legal aid spending lies in the fact that legal aid schemes, established for one reason, may be used for another. Goriely's history of the English scheme (Reading 11) shows that it has been affected by substantial social change since the Rushcliffe report was published in 1945. At that time legal aid was not expected to help citizens obtain their rights against the welfare state. Its purpose was mainly, if not exclusively, to help with divorce. Marshall (1949: 109) gave voice to the prevailing orthodoxy by stating that the obligation of the state to provide welfare was towards society as a whole, not towards the individual. Thus the 'remedy in the case of default lies in parliament or a local council', not a 'court of law . . . or quasi-judicial tribunal'. The leading architects of the post-war welfare state—Beveridge, Bevan, and Morrison—strove hard to keep lawyers away from involvement with the new social rights. As paternalistic welfare has given way to the age of the assertive citizen, however, the role of individually enforceable rights has become more central. New rights have been enacted in the fields of housing, education, child care, and mental health, a more legalistic approach is taken to social security, and individuals are more prepared to pursue their grievances before dispute-resolution fora. This has led to greater demands being made on the legal aid scheme, with which it is ill equipped to deal.

This suggests that there may be a paradox in the development of legal aid. Collectivist welfare states are those most likely to legislate for generous legal aid provision. Providing state services comes naturally to such societies and, compared with most welfare programmes, legal aid expenditure is small change. However, it is individualistic dispute-oriented cultures which make the greatest use of legal aid. The British schemes, which were established at a time of collectivist provision and now operate within an individually oriented society, are therefore some of the most extensive (and expensive) in the world.

The crisis in legal aid

'Legal aid in crisis' has a journalistic ring, but it is hard to deny that schemes are now facing serious problems. Over the last decade almost every government with a developed programme has come to the same conclusion: legal aid is too expensive.[13] Expenditure has risen faster than the rate of inflation, despite declining eligibility, higher contributions, and reduced scope. 'A worse service at a higher price' is how the Social Market Foundation pithily described it (Reading 14 below). 'Stagflation' is the Legal Action Group's more prosaic description (1992: 3).

Of course, governments have always sought to contain expenditure, but it is only recently that this has been openly declared to be the overriding objective. In the United Kingdom the Government has made a clear commitment towards curbing the rise in expenditure, even if this means striking at the basis of the scheme. In 1992 the Lord Chancellor, Lord Mackay, told the Annual Conference of the Law Society that legal aid could not continue to take an ever-increasing share of public expenditure: 'what is certain, is that the overall cost of legal aid must be made more affordable. It must also be better targeted.' He returned to this theme with his Management Statement for the Legal Aid Board in 1994 which stressed, *inter alia*, that: '. . . the overall cost of legal aid had to be affordable and controllable; and legal aid should be targeted towards those whose need is greatest' (LAB 1994: 1).

The 1995 Green Paper on reforming legal aid repeats these objectives and proposes, for the first time, to introduce a fixed budget for legal aid. Now, it seems, the Treasury and Lord Chancellor's Department are serious. It is not just the Government who accept that legal aid expenditure

---

[13] This is true even in countries such as Australia where the Legal Aid Commissions have a fixed budget. See National Legal Aid Advisory Committee (1993) and Regan and Fleming (1994). In England and Wales legal aid expenditure increased fivefold in real terms between 1979–80 and 1992–93, and net expenditure more than doubled between 1989–90 and 1993–94 (Smith 1995b 21). In Scotland gross, but real, expenditure rose by 60% between 1989–90 and 1992–93. In Canada legal aid expenditure in the five years up to and including 1991–92 rose in real terms by 13% per annum. In the Netherlands, on the other hand, the real rise in the decade between 1981 and 1991 was only 58% (Huxtable 1994).

should be controlled. While some critics have responded vigorously to the threat of capping the budget (Zander 1995), the parliamentary opposition have indicated that if they were to come to power there would be little more money for legal aid.[14] Pressure groups have also started to talk the language of rationing. In its response to the Fundamental Review, the National Consumer Council (1994: 17) stated that 'clearly some form of rationing of legal services paid for out of taxation is inevitable. It takes place either implicitly or explicitly and has always occurred.' Even the Law Society (1994: 7) agrees 'that, at a time of limited resources, legal aid should be concentrated on those cases where it is most needed, and for which no other satisfactory form of funding is available'.

In Australia the realization came earlier. Following the recommendations of a 1985 Task Force, each Legal Aid Commission now operates within a fixed budget, adjusted annually in line with the Consumer Price Index and average earnings (Commonwealth Attorney-General's Department 1985).[15] In 1995 Canadian provinces also began to restrict access to legal aid. The Quebec Government has proposed a package of cuts which would remove legal aid from those appearing before administrative bodies, those faced with summary offences, and those who have been previously convicted of similar offences (Mackie 1995). In Ontario a new rightwing Government was elected with a mandate to reduce the budget by over a third (Smith 1995a). In the USA the Legal Services Commission's budget has become a political football. It was reduced during the Reagan and Bush presidencies, increased briefly under President Clinton, and then reduced again when the Republicans gained control of Congress (Singsen 1995). Clearly, these changes are part of a more general attack on the welfare state, and right-wing governments (in the USA or Ontario for example) have been quicker to attack legal aid than those committed to welfare. However, even states such as Sweden with a strong welfare commitment have begun to impose restraints in the face of recession (Johnsen 1994).

Why has the cost of legal aid risen so rapidly?

According to the Social Market Foundation memorandum, the cause is straightforward—supplier-induced demand (Reading 14, below). The authors assume that professionals behave as economically rational indi-

---

[14] 'Opening the Legal Aid Debate', *Legal Action*, June 1995, 5.
[15] No provision is made for factors which might affect the demand for legal aid to increase the budget e.g. more applications, changes in population, or a greater emphasis on law enforcement.

viduals by seeking to maximize their income. Lawyers do this by exploiting the information asymmetry between themselves and those paying for the service by supplying services which are not strictly needed. This leads to cost escalation as lawyers not only take on new clients but charge more per case. For legal aid work, the problem is compounded by moral hazard, under which clients do not care that they are being over-supplied because someone else is paying. The authors show that the increase in legal aid expenditure is made up partly of increases in the number of cases and partly by real increases in price, a picture which they claim is 'consistent with the hypothesis of supplier-induced demand' (11). The Lord Chancellor, Lord Mackay (1995: 12) has stated that he finds such an analysis 'compelling'.

The Social Market Foundation report should, however, be treated with care. The figures cited have not been adjusted to take into account increases in Value Added Tax or court fees, for example, and it exaggerates the lack of financial checks on legal aid bills.[16] It is very far from proven that supplier-induced demand accounts for the recorded increases. As Alastair Gray (1994: 62) stresses, 'many other explanations would also be consistent with these trends'. There have been major changes in social attitudes and legislation, which mean that people are more prepared to seek help, not only from lawyers but from advice agencies and other helping organizations (Smith 1995b). Goriely (Reading 11) highlights the effect of the Citizen's Charter and the promotion of assertive citizenship. Changes in law can also lead to increased complexity, making each case take longer. Thus studies suggest that citizens advice bureaux now carry out more follow-up interviews, even though they do not get paid by the hour and have little incentive to spin out their work (see Kempson 1989). It is now accepted that the Children Act 1989 has led to more complex and expensive procedures, reflected in rising legal aid expenditure (Hughes 1994). Similarly, increases in magistrates' court criminal legal aid bills during the early 1990s may be explained (at least in part) by the introduction of advance disclosure, increased waiting times, slower court procedures, and inefficiencies in the police and Crown Prosecution Service.[17]

Increases in the propensity to litigate and in the cost per case are by no means confined to judicare legal aid schemes. Salaried schemes in

[16] These include the auditing of legal aid bills by the Legal Aid Board, which is designed explicitly to identify unnecessary expenditure, and the statutory clawback (or 'statutory charge') which gives the client a financial stake in the final bill.

[17] A. Gray and P. Fenn (1991) have carried out an analysis of legal aid bills in this area. This, however, has yet to be related to external factors elsewhere in the criminal justice system.

Australia and Quebec have also experienced increases.[18] So has work paid for privately. The Lord Chancellor's Department's own Eligibility Review confirmed that non-matrimonial civil work increased more sharply among those who were not legally aided than among those who were (LCD 1991: 86),[19] while the Woolf Report (1995) highlights the general tendency of lawyers to add to procedural complexity, whoever is paying the bill.[20]

The Government has carried out surprisingly little work to analyse the different causes, a failure for which they have been persistently criticized.[21] An initial study of matrimonial bills between 1980 and 1989 carried out for the Legal Action Group suggested a mixed picture (Goriely 1991). It found that there was evidence to suggest that divorce was becoming more complex—more couples owned a home to argue about, domestic violence was taken more seriously, and fathers may have been more prepared to dispute custody of their children. However, lawyers were also becoming better at time-recording, which in turn increased their expectations of what it was 'reasonable' to claim. There probably is some element of supplier-induced demand, especially when conveyancing work is slack and firms need to turn to legal aid to fill the gap. However, the available evidence suggests that it is not the primary cause for rises in legal aid expenditure in the UK in recent times.

Government policy: tactics, not strategy

So what has gone wrong? At least some of the blame must lie with successive UK governments, who have lacked a strategic vision of what legal aid should be doing. For many years they intervened only when the Treasury required cost savings, and chose whatever manœuvre would meet the minimum political resistance. Rather than set clear priorities for legal aid, the scheme was rationed in ways that were seldom articulated or desirable.

---

[18] Despite the fixed budgets, the Australian Access to Justice Advisory Committee (1994: para. 9. 42) identified the following factors as affecting demand for legal services there: economic conditions; population changes; shifts in law enforcement practices; legislative changes; social trends (e.g. more marital breakdowns); greater legal aid entitlement (e.g. from court decisions requiring legal representation in all serious criminal cases); legal costs rising faster than inflation.

[19] The figures are based on actions for personal injury, landlord and tenant, contract, and other miscellaneous non-family proceedings.

[20] See esp. the discussion of discovery in ch. 21.

[21] See Public Accounts Committee (1986), National Audit Office (1992), and Home Affairs Committee (1993: para. 11).

Such cost-controls as have been introduced were tactical rather than strategic. The first tactic was to limit the scope of the scheme. Thus, although the Rushcliffe Committee recommended a comprehensive scheme which would extend to courts, tribunals, and inquests, the first civil scheme, introduced in 1950, was limited to the High Court and Court of Appeal. It was slowly extended—for example to county courts in 1956, legal advice in 1959, and domestic proceedings in magistrates' courts courts in 1961. Only very limited extensions, however, have been made to tribunals, and the lack of help with tribunal representation remains one of the most serious gaps in the scheme. From the days of the Franks Committee (1957), there has been a steady stream of bodies recommending the extension of legal aid for such representation, including the Royal Commission on Legal Services in England and Wales in 1979, the Lord Chancellors' Legal Aid Advisory Committee in 1983, and the Legal Aid Efficiency Scrutiny Team in 1986 (Zander 1988: 62). Although there was some opposition to tribunal representation in the early years, the judicialization and formalization of tribunals during the 1970s ensured that there has long been a widespread consensus for the selective extension of legal aid to tribunals.[22] The lack of representation for major tribunals such as industrial tribunals, immigration adjudicators, and social security appeal tribunals severely distorts the scheme by limiting the help legal aid provides in areas of social welfare law.

The second tactic for curbing expenditure has been to reduce the number of people eligible for help. A favoured ploy has been to fail to increase the means test in line with earnings which, although not particularly effective at saving money, is achieved with relative invisibility, and at minimum political cost. The original means test, introduced in 1950, was not uprated until 1960, while the second uprating was delayed until 1970. During the early 1970s rapid inflation meant that the proportion of people eligible for help dropped steeply, so that by 1973 it was half the original level. The advisory committee expressed serious concern, and the Government did take some action. In 1974 the position was stabilized, and in 1979 eligibility was restored to something approaching its original levels. Since then, however, eligibility has declined steeply (Murphy 1992; Smith 1995b: 20). Not only has the means test failed to keep pace with earnings, but in 1986, for the first time, the Government downrated the

---

[22] The consensus was further strengthened by the research commissioned by the LCD from Genn and Genn (1989). This showed that the current formality and complexity of many tribunals is such that specialist representation can considerably enhance one's chances of success.

means test in money terms by reducing dependants' allowances. In 1993 the Government instituted one of the most serious reductions by abolishing the English contributory green form scheme. In England, initial advice and assistance is now only available to the poor. At the same time, the Government raised contributions for full civil legal aid. More people were required to pay contributions, they were required to pay more per month, and contributions were continued throughout the length of the case.[23] This tactic has also distorted the scheme. It has not only limited the help available to middle-income families, but also emphasized matrimonial disputes—where each spouse's income is assessed separately—at the expense of other work.

The third method has been to hold down lawyers' remuneration. Originally, remuneration rates were fixed in relation to normal private rates set by court taxing masters. Over the years the Government has moved to set hourly fees, although the change has not been easy. For matrimonial work, hourly rates were eventually introduced in 1988 after some political difficulties; but as lawyers claimed for more hours, they failed to hold down costs. The Government's next approach was to pay standard fees for each case rather than by the hour.[24] Again there were massive protests from the profession. Although magistrates' court standard fees were originally proposed in the spring of 1989, they were not implemented until July 1993. It is still far from clear whether they will succeed in holding down costs or whether solicitors will learn to manipulate the rules to their advantage.[25] Nor is it clear how standard fees will affect the quality of the work provided.

Re-evaluating delivery systems

Changes to scope, eligibility, and remuneration work within the confines of the existing judicare scheme. It is only relatively recently that the Government has started to move outside these confines and examined

[23] The UK was not alone in this. In January 1994 the Dutch also substantially increased the contributions due from clients. Increases have also been proposed in Quebec (Mackie 1995).

[24] Standard fees are used to control costs in most advanced legal aid schemes (Huxtable 1993: 9). The Netherlands has used this approach more than most and with some considerable effect. Thus between 1981 and 1991 there was a real decline in legal aid remuneration rates for Dutch Advocates of 28% (Goriely 1992).

[25] The rules, for example, allow both green form and standard fees to be claimed, and encourage solicitors to classify different defendants and offences as separate cases. For a full description of how solicitors can make the maximum use of standard fees, see Edwards 1993.

alternative delivery mechanisms. Much of the comparative literature stresses the advantages of a mixed system, in which salaried provision complements private practice (see for example Zemans, Reading 6 and Paterson, Reading 12). Since 1969 pressure groups have been urging the government to fund advice and law centres to provide strategic services in the field of poverty law. British governments, however, unlike their counterparts in Australia, Canada, and the Netherlands, have failed to take salaried centres seriously (Stephens 1991). Such law centres as do exist have been developed as local initiatives and have relied on local authority and charitable funds, supplemented by whatever money as they could earn on a case-by-case basis from the legal aid fund. Meanwhile, other advice centres which did not employ solicitors were regarded as wholly separate from the legal aid scheme. As the Legal Action Group has shown, funding for most is minimal and insecure (Reading 13).

If salaried provision is conceived as an addition to private practice it has little potential to save money. As an alternative to the judicare system, however, it has the potential to control costs, partly because advice agencies are cheaper per case and partly because they work under fixed budgets.[26] One of the first official enquiries to realize this was that of the Scrutiny team (LCD 1986) who proposed that clients should be prevented from using a solicitor under legal aid unless they had attended an advice agency. This suggestion provoked an uproar of protest. Advice agencies feared that they would be used as a rationing device, where the money offered would be insufficient to allow them to cope with the workload. For, as a cost-saving device, advice agencies have a fatal flaw: they are more accessible than private practice and demand for their services is likely to be much greater.

Following the Scrutiny debacle, the emphasis of British legal aid policy shifted from salaried services to finding new ways of controlling private practice. The mood of the times is hostile to extensions in state bureaucracy. Instead, in keeping with the prevailing ethos of market testing and privatization, the emphasis is on 'contracts' with a number of competing private suppliers each subject to their own 'quality' audit. This new language of contracts, competition, and audits has swept through most public services and has reached legal services relatively late.[27] It made a

[26] For a summary of some of the main studies on cost-effectiveness of salaried and judicare models, see Zemans (Reading 6) and Canadian Bar Association (1987). Although many studies, such as that conducted in Quebec in 1981, purport to show that salaried services cost less per case, these findings have been heavily disputed by the private bar.

[27] For a general discussion of contracting for public services see Harden (1992).

cautious beginning with the Legal Aid Board's franchising pilot in Birmingham from 1990 to 1992, followed by the launching of a voluntary 'franchising' scheme in August 1994. The 1995 Green Paper recommends taking this one step further by introducing an exclusive scheme, in which only contract-holders are entitled to carry out legal aid work. Such contracts would be awarded within a fixed budget. Interestingly, the paper also suggests that contracts might be given to advice and law centres.

The proposals raise a host of new questions, some of which have hardly been addressed in the existing literature.[28] How far is it possible to capture the 'quality' of legal work in performance indicators?[29] Will the loss of choice and access points necessarily mean a poorer service? Will the contractual relationships between solicitors' firms and the Legal Aid Board change the nature of professional autonomy?[30] Equally, by placing control in the hands of purchasers, will client autonomy be undermined? How will priorities be set? How can politicians be persuaded to set an adequate budget? In practice, it is likely to prove much easier to cash-limit the civil budget than the criminal budget. The fear is that uncontrolled increases in criminal legal aid will be paid for by cuts in the civil budget.

One of the major problems with judicare schemes is their lack of planning. Key decisions about what service is provided, and where it is situated, are made by individual solicitors' firms. Contracting is intended to change this by allowing these decisions to be taken centrally. Contracts will allow the Legal Aid Board to make broad decisions about what broad type of service to provide from each outlet. They can therefore act as a vehicle for prioritization, allowing resources to be transferred from one part of the country to another, or from traditional areas of work to neglected areas, such as social welfare law. It is particularly encouraging that the Green Paper advocates such a transfer as well as recommending funding for representation before tribunals.

On the other hand, contract terms are clumsy ways of controlling the much finer value judgements about who to accept or reject for help, or about the effort which should be expanded on each individual. The danger is that if these second-order decisions are delegated, suppliers will 'cherry pick'—that is, they will make such decisions in a way which maximizes their own income but subverts the Government's priorities. In

[28] For an analysis of the Green Paper see Goriely (1995).

[29] The Legal Aid Board's approach to quality is set out in Sherr, Moorhead and Paterson 1994a, and summarized in Sherr *et al.* 1994b. For a critique see Goriely (1993 and 1994), Travers (1994), and Smith (1993).

[30] See Summerlad (1995).

order to control how resources are allocated within a type of work (such as which out of the many potential housing problems receive help), the Board will either need to maintain its present bureaucratic paper-based system of merits-testing, or employ its own staff to screen and advise would-be applicants. As Zemans shows (Reading 6), the most developed and planned systems make use of both private practitioners and salaried staff, and the Government would do well to experiment with a salaried element within the English scheme. Salaried staff can offer a more 'strategic' service. They can also act as a blueprint for contractors, enabling the Board to check the service it receives from contracted suppliers against the baseline provided by its own employed advisers.

The way forward

In our view, any discussion of the future of legal aid should start with an examination of its purposes. Earlier we argued that legal aid could play a part in ensuring that all citizens were able to participate in society according to fair procedures. Following Griffiths (Reading 4), we argued that this was a social rather than an individual benefit. From this it follows that legal aid should be used instrumentally to provide the maximum benefit to society rather than to meet any individual claim. Its aim is to maximize procedural justice within society.

Procedural justice: different perspectives

At this point we need to explore a little further what is meant by the term 'procedural justice', which may be used in many different ways. In their 1990 report, the Australian National Legal Aid Advisory Committee made a useful distinction between justifications for legal aid based on benefits to the government and public administration and those based on benefits to the community. The first objective (that of 'Government/Public Administration') is to enable citizens to protect or assert rights as 'an adjunct to the effective and efficient management of the administrative and legal systems, social and economic policy and as an instrument of the social welfare state'. The second ('community') objective is to assist members of the community 'in favourably resolving or preventing conflict in individual-government and inter-personal relations'. The distinction is not rigid or clear cut, but it does reveal two different starting points.

The British Government's many pronouncements in favour of 'alternative dispute resolution' as a replacement for legal aid focus almost exclusively on the second perspective. They see the purpose of legal aid as leading to the orderly resolution of disputes, which has come to be seen as a private matter between the disputants. The present policy of charging litigants the full cost of maintaining the civil courts takes this to its logical extreme. Governments are increasingly asking why the state should subsidize redress mechanisms for those in private disputes, often on the breakdown of family relationships. There are many possible answers—to prevent violence, to help the children of broken marriages, or to stop divorced wives from becoming dependent on state benefits, for example. However, to see law and legal aid as merely a matter of private dispute resolution is to narrow the terms of the debate and to forget the governmental perspective. As the National Legal Aid Advisory Committee (1990) points out, it is governments who create laws and who use law to control society and to implement policies. Governments have a vested interest in ensuring that laws achieve their desired outcomes and are implemented in such a way as to secure public support.

Many judicare legal aid schemes, however, are locked into a private law model of the legal order, which is much more suited to dealing with dispute resolution between two private parties than in ensuring procedural justice within the administrative state. As Galligan (1986) stresses, in a public law model disputes are much more likely to take place within administrative agencies than within courts. In order to achieve procedural justice in such circumstances, individuals need much better information and access to specialist advisers and advocates—though not necessarily lawyers.[31] Both groups and individuals need to have their interests represented, and the appeal will be as much to policy goals as to legal rights (Galligan 1986: 86–8). This involves a shift away from subsidies to private lawyers for the provision of routine, individuated representation in divorce, crime, and personal injury, towards information, education, the representation of group interests, lay advice, and advocacy. At the same time we need to move from an elite to a mass justice system, with a greater emphasis on improved complaints and appeals procedures such as ombudsmen. When courts do hear cases, they need to do so according to cheaper, quicker, and more standardized procedures (Woolf 1995).

---

[31] For practical examples of what is needed, see Coote (1992). Nick Doyle and Tessa Harding (1992) argue strongly for more information for community-care users and improved complaint and appeal procedures: 'without advice and the kind of support provided by advice agencies, procedural rights are likely to be a sham for many people' (76).

Taking information and advice seriously

We live in a world of 'assertive citizenship' where, to quote the British Government's Citizen's Charter, citizens 'can increasingly put pressure upon those responsible for providing services to deliver them to a high service' (Cabinet Office 1992: 1). People are no longer the passive recipients of welfare, but are expected to complain when things go wrong and to fight for their rights. Yet all too often they are lost in the bureaucratic maze, unaware of their rights, or where to take their complaints. As government breaks up into more self-contained agencies, and more alternative dispute resolution systems are established, the information deficit becomes more pronounced. Much can be done through media and public information campaigns, and far greater use could be made of new technology.[32] However, public services are now so complex, and change so rapid, that a 'one-stop shop' is needed to direct people to the right place.

Britain is particularly fortunate in having a well established and well known advice sector. Consistently, survey after survey[33] shows that, when people are asked where they would go with a problem, they name the citizens advice bureau—an institution known to over 90 per cent of the population (BBC 1986). There are deep reservoirs of public goodwill towards CABx and the other advice agencies—which are generally regarded as helpful, dedicated, informative, and friendly. In practice, however, people are well aware that advice centres are 'underfunded', 'shabby', 'run-down', and 'tatty', with restricted opening hours and clogged phone lines (OFT 1991: 137).[34] As the demands on CABx increase, their work is becoming dominated by the chronic problems of the poor—debt, welfare benefits, and housing—and they are less and less able to fulfil the role they once played of offering accessible, one-off information about a broad range of issues to a wide variety of people. This general service is as—if not more—needed than it ever was, and we must find ways of bringing it back.

Where complains systems have been designed well, many people will only need information to be able to use them. However, vulnerable people, or those with serious cases, also need advice, support, and advocacy. McCarthy and Simpson (1993) point out that many users of council

---

[32] See e.g. LAG Reading 3. Interesting examples of public education projects and the use of new technology—including interactive video kiosks—are given in Smith 1995b.

[33] See for example Research International 1992, McCarthy *et al*. 1992, and MORI 1993.

[34] Genn and Genn (1989) also found that many of those appearing before tribunals who could have used CABx did not do so because they were so difficult to contact.

services, particularly social services, are: 'financially poor, are dispirited and unwell; are lonely, isolated and inarticulate; cannot properly read and write; they are sometimes fearful and occasionally angry' (43). Independent support may be needed to overcome years of distrust, if people are to be persuaded that 'they' will listen. Advice services, using either lay people alone or lawyers and lay people together, have demonstrated how much they can achieve. They should play a major part of future legal aid policy. There are hopeful signs that the Government is now taking lay advice more seriously, with the 1995 Green Paper forseeing a much greater role for advice centres. The English pilot project of non-solicitor agencies has shown the potential for the delivery of certain types of legal aid by non-lawyers (Bull and Steele 1995). Much more needs to be done, however, to support and fund advice centres and to build them into the overall strategy for legal aid.

Limiting the cost of litigation

There is now a greater realization that we cannot afford to fund large numbers of routine court cases through ever more expensive and legalistic procedures. Limiting growth in this area, however, has been easier to talk about than to do. Lawyers and judges have a strong vested interest in the status quo. Procedural changes can all too easily be reinterpreted in the light of prevailing lawyers' norms and fail to secure their desired objectives. Sometimes, they can make things worse (Woolf 1995: 176). Furthermore, alternatives to court are not taken seriously by the governmental machine. While courts have their own permanent department, responsibility for improving out-of-court justice is relegated to the occasional committees, whose conclusions—however valuable—are too soon forgotten.

Limiting the cost of litigation needs a serious and sustained effort. First, much more needs to be done to ensure that alternatives are available, and that they work. Secondly, court procedures need to be simplified. The Woolf report into civil procedure is a good start here, but implementing it will need considerable political will and resources, as money will need to be spent before savings appear. The effects of the changes will also need to be carefully monitored. Finally, we need to explore alternative ways of funding litigation. The impact of conditional fees should be investigated, as should the potential for contingency fees, a contingent legal aid fund, and legal expenses insurance (see Paterson, Reading 12).

A new decision-making structure?

Of course, it would be unrealistic to expect such changes to come overnight or without resistance from lawyers. On past form, we cannot expect the legal profession to provide the lead in this field, though we may anticipate that they will endeavour to co-opt what eventually emerges (Paterson and Nelken, Reading 10). The policy lead will need to come from policy-makers, which in the case of England and Wales has traditionally meant the Lord Chancellor and his staff. Given the Department's lamentable record in this field, the question arises whether a new decision-making structure is needed.

The first problem with the Lord Chancellor's Department is that its remit is too narrow. Although it has been concerned with lawyers, it does not take responsibility for advice; although concerned with courts, it does not include alternatives to courts. The second problem is that it is too closed. Traditionally, outsiders played a part in decision-making through the Legal Aid Advisory Committee, but as the emphasis shifted from expansion to cuts the Committee became more and more marginal. In 1995 it was quietly closed. In some ways the Legal Aid Board has brought in outsiders, but its role is limited. As LAG have pointed out, its statutory framework did little more than transfer the administrative responsibilities of the Law Society to an independent body. It has a much more restricted remit than either the legal aid commission in Australia or Quebec's *Commission des Services Juridique* (LAG 1992: 127). LAG argues for a new legal services commission with wide-ranging powers to monitor the effects of law and legal procedures on its clients and to undertake research into all aspects of legal aid.

We agree with LAG that a new approach to prioritizing legal aid expenditure will involve new decision-making structures. The service will need better planning; national and local priorities will need to be set; information should be taken more seriously; and there needs to be a fresh emphasis on research. Like the Australian National Legal Aid Advisory Committee (1990: 125–7), it should examine the merits of a 'solution-oriented' approach to the problems of legally-aided clients. This would entail experimental projects to identify the most cost-effective way of meeting needs—looking at community information and education, support for self-help, advice agencies, mediation, and out-of-court alternatives. Even within legal aid practices we should expect experimentation with the greater use of paralegal staff (Bhagwati 1995). To use Zemans' analysis, the new organisation will need to be more proactive in the pursuit of a 'strategic model' of legal services provision, rather than relying on the traditional demand-led reactive 'service' approach of the legal profession (Reading 6).

The profession's contribution

Finally, what about the role of the profession? Before 1950, the profession bore primary responsibility for ensuring access to the courts, operating the Poor Persons Procedure on a voluntary basis. With the arrival of a paid legal aid scheme, the state implicitly acknowledged that primary responsibility lay with the Government rather than the profession, but the profession was expected to continue to make a contribution. Thus, for example, fees were deliberately set below the market rate. We would argue that there remains a collective obligation on the part of the profession to contribute to the provision of poverty legal services. This is partly because it is the profession who have devised and benefit from the complex procedures which make access to justice such a problem. Also, professionalism can be seen as a tacit concordat between the state and lawyers, whereby the latter's expectations of status, rewards, monopolies, and autonomy have to be balanced against the community's expectations of competence, public protection, and access (Paterson 1996). It was this contractualist argument which underpinned the charitable model of legal aid and which is used today to justify the growth of voluntary and mandatory *pro bono* movements.[35] The profession's contribution to legal aid can therefore be seen as enlightened self-interest pursued in partnership with the state.

A new vision for legal aid?

In short, our main criticism is that current debates over legal aid policy have lacked a consistent and coherent vision of the rationale of legal aid. For the last decade the Lord Chancellor's Department has given the impression of panic, with an ever-increasing spiral of policy initiatives: the Scrutiny Review (LCD 1986), the Stage Payments Review (unpublished), the Eligibility Review (LCD 1991), franchising, the eligibility cuts in 1993, a fundamental review of expenditure on legal services in 1993–94, and a Green Paper (LCD 1995). Several, such as the Scrutiny Report and

[35] See Law Society (1995). In 1925 the Lawrence Committee stated that 'there exists a moral obligation on the part of the profession, in return for the monopoly in the practice of law which it enjoys, to render gratuitous legal assistance to those members of the community who cannot afford to pay for such assistance, provided that no undue burden is thereby cast upon any individual member of the profession'.

Eligibility Review, were abandoned within a couple of years of publication. Indecision on such a scale suggests that the Department lacks clear objectives for the scheme.

An uncomfortable truth in advanced western societies is that individual demand for access to law is infinite, while resources are all too finite. Priorities have to be set, but until now this has been done on a covert and *ad hoc* basis. As the Government has recently accepted, the measures it has used to curb costs have been crude (LCD 1995: para. 3.22). Judicare schemes, relying as they do on the good will of the private profession, tend by their nature to be individuated, reactive, unplanned, and unfocused. The key question for future policy-makers is whether they can move to a planned 'mixed' model of service provision which is more proactive and utilitarian in its approach.

Bibliography

ABEL, R. L. (1985) 'Law without Politics: Legal Aid under Advanced Capitalism', *UCLA Law Review* 474.

AUSTRALIAN ACCESS TO JUSTICE ADVISORY COMMITTEE (1994) *Access to Justice*, Canberra.

BBC (1986) *Citizens advice bureaux: the price of advice*, a survey of 1,736 people carried out Broadcasting Research Department.

BHAGWATI, JUSTICE P. N. (1995) 'Legal Aid Crisis—The Present and the Future', World Legal Aid Conference, Kuala Lumpur.

BREGER, M. (1982) 'Legal Aid for the Poor; A Conceptual Analysis', 60 *North Carolina Law Review* 281–363.

BRIDGES, L. (1991) *The Provision of Duty Advice Schemes in County Courts*, Legal Aid Board.

BULL, G. and STEELE, J. (1995) *Legal Aid Franchising for Non-Solicitor Agencies: Interim Report*, Policy Studies Institute, London.

CABINET OFFICE (1992) *The Citizen's Charter: First Report*, Cabinet Office, London.

CAHN, E. and CAHN, J. (1964) 'The War on Poverty: A Civilian Perspective' 73 *Yale Law Journal* 1317.

—— (1966) 'What Price Justice: the Civilian Perspective Revisited', (1966) 41 *Notre Dame Lawyer* 927.

CANADIAN BAR ASSOCIATION (1987) *Legal Aid Delivery Models: a discussion paper prepared by the CBA National Legal Aid Liaison Committee*, Ottawa.

CAPPELLETTI, M. and GARTH, B. (1981) *Access to Justice and the Welfare State*, Florence.

GAPPELLETTI, M., GORDLEY, J., and JOHNSON, E. Jr. (1975) *Towards Equal Justice: a Comparative Study of Legal Aid in Modern Societies*, Dott. A. Giuffre Ed, Milan.

COMMONWEALTH ATTORNEY-GENERAL'S DEPARTMENT (1985) *Legal Aid Task Force—Final Report*, Canberra.

CONSEIL D'ETAT (1990) *L'Aide Juridique: Pour un Meilleure Accès au Droit et à la Justice*, Section du Rapport et des Etudes, Paris.

COOTE, A. (1992) *The Welfare of Citizens: Developing new Social Rights*, IPPR/Rivers Oram Press, London.

COUSINS, M. (1992) 'Access to the Courts: The European Convention on Human Rights and European Community Law', 14 *Dublin University Law Journal* 51.

CRANSTON, R. (1986) 'Rights in Practice', in C. SAMFORD and D. J. GALLIGAN (eds.), *Law, Rights and the Welfare State*, Croom Helm, London.

EDWARDS, A. (1993) *Standard Fees in the Magistrates' Court: A Survival Guide*, Law Society, London.

DENTI, V. (1979) 'An International Overview on Legal Aid', in F. ZEMANS (ed.), *Perspectives on Legal Aid: a Comparative Study*, Francis Pinter Ltd., London.

DOYLE, N. and HARDING, T. (1992) 'Community Care: Applying Procedural Fairness' in A. COOTE (ed.), *The Welfare of Citizens: Developing new Social Rights*, IPPR/Rivers Oram Press, London.

DWORKIN, R. (1981) 'Principle, Policy, Procedure' in C. F. H. TAPPER (ed.), *Crime, Proof and Punishment: Essays in Memory of Sir Rupert Cross*, Butterworths, London.

FAILINGER, M. A. and MAY, L. (1984) 'Litigating Against Poverty: Legal Services and Group Representation', 45 *Ohio State Law Journal* 1.

FRANKS COMMITTEE (1957) *Report of the Committee on Administrative Tribunals and Enquiries*, Cmnd 218, HMSO, London.

GALANTER, M. (1974) 'Why the "Haves" Come Out Ahead: Speculations on the Limits of Legal Change', 9 *Law and Society Review* 95.

——— (1976) 'Delivering Legality: Some Proposals for the Direction of Research', 11 *Law and Society Review* 225.

GALLIGAN, D. J. (1986) *Discretionary Powers: A Legal Study of Official Discretion*, Clarendon Press, Oxford.

GARTH, B. (1983) 'Rethinking the Legal Profession's Approach to Collective Self-Improvement: Competence and the Consumer Perspective', *Wisconsin Law Review* 639.

GENN, H. and GENN, Y. (1989) *The Effectiveness of Representation at Tribunals*, Lord Chancellor's Department, London.

GORIELY, T. (1991) *Legal Aid for Family and Care Work*, Nuffield Research project, Background Paper I, Legal Action Group, London.

——— (1992) 'Legal aid in the Netherlands: A View from England', 55 *Modern Law Review* 803.

——— (1993) 'Quality of Legal Services: the Need for Consumer Research', 3 *Consumer Policy Review* 112.

——— (1994) 'Debating the Quality of Legal Service: differing models of the Good Lawyer', 1 *International Journal of the Legal Profession* 159.

——— (1995) 'The Government's Legal Aid Reforms', in A. A. S. ZUCKERMAN and R. CRANSTON (eds.), *Reform of Civil Procedure: Essays on 'Access to Justice'*, Clarendon Press, Oxford.

GRAY, A. (1994) 'The Reform of Legal Aid', *Oxford Review of Economic Policy* 51.

—— and FENN, P. (1991) *Costs of Proceedings in Magistrates' Courts: A Research Report for the Legal Aid Board*, Oxford Centre for Socio-Legal Studies, Oxford.

GROSSMAN, J. B. and SARAT, A. (1981) 'Access to Justice and the Limits of Law', 3 *Law and Policy Quarterly* 125.

HARDEN, I. (1992) *The Contracting State*, Open University Press.

HOME AFFAIRS COMMITTEE (1993) *Legal Aid: the Lord Chancellor's Proposals*, HC 517 Session 1992–93, HMSO, London.

HUGHES COMMISSION (1980) Report of the Royal Commission on Legal Services in Scotland, Cmnd 7846, HMSO, Edinburgh.

HUGHES, S. (1994) 'Suffer the Little Children', *Legal Action*, June, 8.

HUXTABLE, P. (1993) *An Examination of Some Foreign Legal Aid Schemes with Implications for Australia*, A Churchill Fellowship Report, Legal Aid Commission of Western Australia, Bunbury.

JOHNSEN, J. T. (1994) 'Nordic Legal Aid', 5 *Maryland Journal of Contemporary Legal Issues* 301.

JOHNSON, EARL Jr (1974) *Justice and Reform: the Formative Years of the American Legal Services Program*, Transaction Books, New Brunswick.

KEMPSON, E. (1989) *Legal Advice and Assistance*, Policy Studies Institute, London.

LAB (1994) *Legal Aid Board Corporate Plan April 1994–March 1997*, Legal Aid Board, London.

LAG (1977), *Legal Services: A Blueprint for the Future*, Legal Action Group, London.

—— (1992) *A Strategy for Justice: Publicly Funded Legal Services in the 1990s*, Legal Action Group, London.

LAW SOCIETY (1994) *A Lottery for Justice: response to the Social Market Foundation Memorandum*, Law Society, London.

—— (1995) *Solicitors Serving Society*, Law Society, London.

LAWRENCE COMMITTEE (1925) *Report of the Poor Persons Rule Committee*, Cmnd 2358, HMSO, London.

LCD (1986) *Legal Aid Efficiency Scrutiny*, Lord Chancellor's Department, London.

—— (1991) *Eligibility for Civil Legal Aid: a Consultation Paper*, Lord Chancellor's Department, London.

—— (1993) *Looking to the Future: Mediation and the Ground of Divorce. A Consultation Paper*, Cm 2424, HMSO, London.

—— (1995) *Legal Aid—Targeting Need*, Cm 2854, HMSO, London.

MACHIN, D. with WARD, S. and MILLAR, A. (1994) *Applications for Criminal Legal Aid*, Central Research Unit, Scottish Office, Edinburgh.

MACKAY, J. (1995) Speech to the Social Market Foundation, 11 Jan.

MACKIE, R. (1995) 'Quebec to force curbs on legal aid despite criticism', *Globe and Mail*, 5 June.

MARSHALL, T. H. (1949) *Citizenship and Social Class*, reprinted in T. H. Marshall, *Sociology at the Crossroads and other essays*, Heinemann, 1963.

MCCARTHY, P. *et al.* (1992) *Grievances, Complaints and Local Government*, Avebury, Aldershot.

McCarthy, P. and Simpson, B. (1993) 'Effective Complaining in Local Government Services', 3 *Consumer Policy Review* 39.

MORI (1993) *Electricity Services: The Consumer Perspective*, OFFER, London.

Murphy, M. (1992) 'Civil eligibility limits 1979–90', in Legal Action Group, *A Strategy for Justice*, Appendix 1.

National Audit Office (1992) *The Administration of Legal Aid in England and Wales*, HMSO, London.

National Consumer Council (1994) *Response to the LCD's Fundamental Review of Expenditure on Civil Litigation and Legal Aid*, NCC, London.

National Legal Aid Advisory Committee (Australia) (1990) *Legal Aid for the Australian Community*, Canberra.

—— (1993) 'The Cost of Legal Aid Commission Referrals', Information Paper, Canberra.

OFT (1991) *Consumer Redress Mechanisms*, Office of Fair Trading, London.

Paterson, A. A. (1995) 'Access, Legal Aid and Rural Scotland', *Judicial Review* 266.

—— (1996) 'Professionalism and the Legal Services Market', *International Journal of the Legal Profession*.

Public Accounts Committee (1986) *Provision of Legal Aid in England and Wales*, HC 330, Session 1985–86, HMSO, London.

Regan, F. and Fleming, D. (1994) 'International Perspectives on Legal Aid', *Alternative Law Journal*, August, 183.

Research International (1992) *The Charterline Service*, Citizen's Charter Unit, Cabinet Office, London.

Sherr, A., Moorhead, R., and Paterson, A. (1994a) *Lawyers: The Quality Agenda*, Legal Aid Board, HMSO, London.

—— (1994b) 'Assessing the Quality of Legal Work: Measuring Process', 1 *International Journal of the Legal Profession* 131.

Singsen, G. (1995) 'Reality Bites: the US Legal Services Commission', in *Shaping the Future*, Legal Action Group, London.

Smith, R. (1993) 'Transaction Criteria: Back to the Future', *Legal Action*, April 7.

—— (1995a) 'Managing in the Down Cycle', *Legal Action*, August, 6.

—— (1995b) *Shaping the Future: New Directions in Legal Services*, Legal Action Group, London.

Stephens, M. (1991) *Community Law Centres: A Critical Appraisal*, Avebury, Aldershot.

Summerlad, H. (1995) 'Managerialism and the Legal Profession: A New Professional Paradigm', 2 *International Journal of the Legal Profession* 159.

Titmuss, R. (1970) 'Welfare "Rights", Law and Discretion', reprinted in B. Abel-Smith and K. Titmuss (eds.), *The Philosophy of Welfare* 1987.

—— (1968) 'The Right to Society Security' in R. Titmuss and M. Zander, *Unequal Rights*, Child Poverty Action Group, London 1968.

Travers, M. (1994) 'Measurement and Reality: Quality Assurance and the Work of a Firm of Criminal Defence Solicitors in Northern England', 1 *International Journal of the Legal Profession* 173.

WEXLER, S. (1970) 'Practicing Law for Poor People', 79 *Yale Law Journal* 1049.

WHITE, R. (1973), 'Lawyers and the Enforcement of Rights' in P. MORRIS, R. WHITE, and P. LEWIS, *Social Needs and Legal Action*, Martin Robertson, London.

WOOLF (1995) *Access to Justice: Interim Report to the Lord Chancellor on the Civil Justice System in England and Wales*, Lord Chancellor's Department, London.

ZANDER, M. (1988) *A Matter of Justice*, Tauris & Co.

—— (1995) 'Twelve Reasons for Rejecting the Legal Aid Green Paper', *New Law Journal*, 21 July, 1098.

PART ONE: PHILOSOPHICAL JUSTIFICATIONS

. . . before the Law stands a door-keeper on guard. To this door-keeper there comes a man from the country who begs for admittance to the Law. But the door-keeper says that he cannot admit the man at the moment. The man, on reflection, asks if he will be allowed, then, to enter later. 'It is possible,' answers the door-keeper, 'but not at this moment.' Since the door leading into the Law stands open as usual and the door-keeper steps to one side, the man bends down to peer through the entrance. When the door-keeper sees that, he laughs and says: 'If you are so strongly tempted, try to get in without my permission. But note that I am powerful. And I am only the lowest door-keeper. From hall to hall, keepers stand at every door, one more powerful than the other. Even the third of these has an aspect that even I cannot bear to look at.' These are difficulties which the man from the country has not expected to meet, the Law he thinks, should be accessible to every man and at all times . . .

Franz Kafka, *The Trial*, 1925 (trans. Willa and Edwin Muir) Penguin Modern Classics, p. 235.

The essentially conservative bench and bar will vehemently deny any suggestion that there is no law for the poor, but, as the legal aid societies know, such is the belief today of a multitude of humble, entirely honest people, and in the light of their experience it appears as the simple truth . . .

In that direction we have imperceptibly, unconsciously and unintentionally drifted. The end of such a course is disclosed by history. Differences in the ability of classes to use the machinery of law, if permitted to remain, lead inevitably to disparity between the rights of classes . . . And when the law recognizes and enforces a distinction between classes, revolution ensues or democracy is at an end.

Reginald Herber Smith, *Justice and the Poor*, Carnegie Foundation, New York, 1919.

Lawyers must be activists to leave a contribution to society. The law is more than a control; it is an instrument for social change. The role of [the Office of Equal Opportunity] program is to provide the means within the democratic process for the law and lawyers to release the bonds which imprison people in poverty, to marshal the forces of law to combat the causes and effects of poverty.

Address by E. Clinton Bamberger, First Director of the USA Legal Services Programme, to the National Legal Aid and Defender Association's Annual Meeting, Scottsdale, Arizona, 18 November 1965.

1. The Right to Legal Services

DAVID LUBAN

To begin, I wish to argue for legal services for the poor. Equal access to legal services can be understood either as minimal access, that is, equal access to minimally competent legal help, or as access to equal legal services, so that if an indigent is facing a client of a major law firm, she must be provided with the assistance of another.[1] The latter is a better interpretation of the meaning of equal access for the following reason: law, unlike many other professions, is adversarial in character, so in practice minimal access may turn out to be no better than no access. Minimally competent, overworked lawyers seldom do well against adversaries with large budgets for the investigation of cases, good law libraries, the ability to tolerate lengthy delays, and connections.[2]

Access to equal legal services, however, would take more money than our society can be expected to provide for its poor, since it often seems barely willing to tolerate their existence at all and treats requests for such amenities as food and shelter for the poor as an affront to the American way. For this reason, I shall be arguing for the more modest ideal of minimal access to legal services for the poor.

The problem

What is a poor person? In 1986, the federally defined poverty level for a family of four was an annual income of less than $11,203. The 1986 poor population totalled 32.4 million people (13.6 per cent of the population), of whom more than half were over twenty-one years of age and more than 60 per cent were over sixteen years of age.[3]

---

[1] By 'minimally competent' legal help I do not mean less-than-competent legal help, but rather legal help that satisfies reasonable professional standards of ability, diligence, preparation, and so forth, without being in any way exceptional. Thus, I mean the minimum of good lawyering, not the minimum of lawyering: 'C + or better' lawyering rather than 'D'.

[2] See, however, Abel (2) and Galanter for arguments about why access to lawyers may not do much to help the poor, even if the poor have access to very good lawyers.

[3] Census Bureau figures as of July 30, 1987, published in Rich.

On an extremely conservative estimate, the over-sixteen poor person encounters an average of one legal problem per year;[4] as one welfare rights lawyer put it, poor people are constantly bumping into sharp legal things.[5] If we suppose that a legal problem requires on the average an hour to solve—some legal problems obviously require much more, some need only a five-minute phone call or a routine form filled out—we arrive at over twenty million hours of necessary legal services that are, by and large, not provided. This is, let me reiterate, a very conservative estimate.

The Legal Services Corporation (LSC) was instituted by Congress in 1974 to provide legal services for poor people (defined as people whose annual income was less than 125 per cent of the poverty line). LSC's initial goal was to provide two lawyers for every ten thousand poor people (the national average, by contrast, is one lawyer for every 470 people); this goal was reached in late 1980. At that time LSC's annual budget was $321 million.

Under the Reagan administration, the LSC has run into hard times. Its budget for fiscal 1982 and 1983 was cut to $260 million, and its board of directors has been stacked with individuals hostile to the goals, indeed to the very existence of the LSC; in February 1987, in fact, LSC Chairman W. Clark Durant III publicly proposed abolishing the corporation.[6] This was in line with the view of the administration, which each year has proposed defunding the LSC entirely. The Reagan administration's hostility to LSC was devastating. In 1983 the Washington Council of Lawyers surveyed sixty-one LSC-funded programs to determine the effects of the cutbacks:

Overall, programs lost 30 per cent of their staff attorneys. 37.7 per cent of the programs reported losing their more experienced attorneys. Of the fifty programs that tried to replace attorneys who left, forty-one responded that their efforts had been substantially impaired . . . and 52 per cent reported they have been unable to replace their experienced attorneys at all.

By 1983, LSC reported a reduction of 25 per cent in the number of offices. The survey confirms that 85 per cent of the programs in the sample had to close full- or part-time offices because of reduced funding.

Thirty-four per cent of the programs reported that these clients [i.e., 'clients no longer served because of office closings'] are now 'virtually unable to get free legal aid.'[7]

---

[4] Association of the Bar of the City of New York, p. 8.
[5] Wexler, p. 1050.   [6] 'LSC Head Suggests Abolishing Agency'.
[7] The Washington Council of Lawyers, *Report on the Status of Legal Services for the Poor, November, 1983*, pp. iii–iv, v.

Eighty per cent of the respondents decreased their caseloads; 86.9 per cent of the programs were forced to reject between five hundred and four thousand potential clients. Twenty-seven programs (with an affected population of 4,131,800) no longer handle divorces; six programs (population 1,179,300) no longer handle cases of abused and neglected children; eleven programs (population 1,673,200) no longer handle custody and visitation cases; fifteen programs (population 2,401,100) no longer do bankruptcies—the list goes on and on.[8]

It's a disaster, and these statistics are already out of date. Moreover, even in its salad days legal service for the poor was severely limited by enormous caseloads that generated chronic problems: inadequate representation, 'triage' dilemmas, rapid attorney burn-out and turnover.[9]

The situation, moreover, is distinctively American (although the situation in other countries is far from paradisiacal). In England, the right to appointed counsel has existed since 1495, even though it was not put on firm financial footing until modern times.[10] The Italian Constitution states that '[d]estitute persons shall, by institutions created for that purpose, by assured the means to plead and defend themselves before any judicial jurisdiction'.[11] The Swiss Federal Court and the German Federal Constitutional Court have both derived the right to counsel from the constitutional guarantees of equality,[12] and France provides legal aid by state compensation of appointed counsel. In Germany, legal aid is provided in 18 per cent of civil cases (and North Rhine-Westphalia, a representative German area, spent 84 per cent of its 1984 legal aid budget on civil cases, as compared with only 14 per cent on criminal cases);[13] since 1980, Germany has also provided free legal advice for the poor.[14] In 1980, 10 per cent of the Dutch bar specialized in legal aid clientele, and 23 per cent gained much of its income from legal aid clients.[15]

In the United States, however, like Mahagonny, it is still 'a fin, gentlemen / To see the wheels of Justice in motion.'[16] Since *Gideon*, and its

---

[8] Ibid., pp. v–vi.   [9] See especially Bellow for a perceptive discussion of these problems.
[10] Johnson, p. 4.   [11] Article 24, para. 3, quoted in Cappelletti and Cohen, p. 461.
[12] Switzerland: 78 *Entscheidungen des Schweizerisches Bundesgerichts (BGE)* I 193 (1952). Germany: 22 BVerGE 83 (1967). Both quoted in Cappelletti and Cohen, pp. 461–3.
[13] Blankenburg, p. 4.
[14] Cappelletti and Cohen, p. 488. The free advice is provided by the 'Advice Aid Act': see Klinge. Perhaps because the Advice Aid Act only went into effect in 1981, Germany lags far behind England and the Netherlands in out-of-court legal advice services: in 1984 North Rhine/Westphalia spent only 2 per cent of its legal aid budget on advice aid, as compared with 20 per cent in England/Wales and 15 per cent in the Netherlands. Blankenburg, p. 4.
[15] Blankenburg, p. 3.
[16] Brecht, p. 130. For a state-of-the-art survey of legal aid worldwide, see Abel (1).

progeny *Argersinger v. Hamlin* and *In re Gault*, persons accused of crimes have had counsel guaranteed them, but that right has never been extended to civil cases. Neither in law nor in fact is there provision made for legal aid to the poor.

I wish to argue for a thoroughly unremarkable thesis: that it is a right of people too poor to afford legal assistance to have it provided for them, because otherwise they are deprived of equality before the law.

The necessity claim

Recourse to law, we hear tell, is the alternative to recourse to force; take away a person's access to law as a way of protecting her vital interests, and she may have to resort to force—legitimately so. If a legal system that won't protect her nevertheless constrains her by punishing her if she resorts to force, it disadvantages and, indeed, oppresses her compared with those who have access to the law. Now in some societies it might generally be believed that people fall into natural classes, with some classes rightly enjoying legal advantages over others, so that the ideal of equal respect for all people before the law is not honoured even in name. If many or most of the people in that society agree with this natural class view, they may consent to such unequal treatment; then, if we believe that a government enjoying the consent of the governed is legitimate (and that the denial of equal respect does not take that legitimacy away), no rights will be infringed by the denial of equal access to the law.

Our society, however, does not fit this description: one of its *legitimation principles* (I shall say) is a principle of equality. Our government loses its legitimacy by denying equal access to the law. On Locke's view, which I endorse in this matter, the illegitimacy of a government generates a right of resistance; this argument then converges with the initial claim that recourse to force is the alternative to recourse to law. Finally, we may believe that a legal regime is defective in which private recourse to force and public resistance to the regime are morally acceptable. It follows that to deny access to our legal system is to incorporate a grave defect into that system.

This is a capsule summary of the argument I intend to offer. To begin, however, I must show that the denial of access to legal services is a form of the denial of access to the legal system, that is, that legal services are necessary for access to the legal system.[17] Let me call this the 'necessity of

[17] I do not mean to assert that people can never take advantage of the legal system without the help of professional lawyers. Particularly in non-courtroom matters, professional

legal services claim,' or, more compactly, the 'necessity claim'. One might, after all, deny this, claiming that as long as a poor person is entitled to represent herself in a court of law, as she is in our legal system, she has sufficient access to the legal system. On the latter view, access to the legal system entails only that a person is not forbidden or prevented from going to court.

It is an obvious fact, however, that all of our legal institutions (except small claims court) are designed to be operated by lawyers and not by laypersons. Laws are written in such a way that they can be interpreted only by lawyers; judicial decisions are crafted so as to be fully intelligible only to the legally trained. Court regulations, court schedules, even court-house architecture are designed around the needs of the legal profession.[18]

Let us make an extravagant supposition. Suppose that a poor person decided to learn the law from scratch so as to be able to represent herself. Suppose that she was able (somehow) to obtain the first-year casebooks and other legal texts; suppose that her educational level allowed her to read them; suppose that she had lots of leisure time for study. Suppose that she understood the principle of *stare decisis*, had the knack of 'thinking like a lawyer', developed a taste for Byzantine reasoning, logic chopping, and casuistry. Even so, without a civil procedure course under her belt, she would almost certainly be unable to make sense of the most basic features of the cases she had read, namely why they were filed in one court rather than another, why the defendants were chosen as they were, and why the particular cause of action was alleged. These are, after all, questions of tactics as much as of legal doctrine. Consider then that legal advice (though usually helpful) is frequently unnecessary in order to utilize legal procedures.

[18] Many people agree that our legal institutions are designed to be operated by lawyers and not laypersons, but they resist the inference that this means people need lawyers. Instead, they argue, people need a drastic simplification of the legal system. The answer to the problem of legal services is not legal assistance but delegalization.

I agree that a certain amount of delegalization is both possible and desirable. I also agree that if a delegalization strategy could substitute for a legal assistance strategy it would be preferable; but I believe that it cannot, for two reasons. The first is that I am skeptical about how simple the law could be made in a society as enormously complex as ours. How much simpler could securities regulations or environmental protection standards be and still do the job? How much could procedure be simplified without opening the possibility of inadvertent denials of due process?

Second, suppose we grant that deep-cutting delegalization is possible. It seems clear that it would be one of the biggest changes our society has ever experienced, bringing with it a turbulent and expensive transition period. (Compared with delegalization, the switch to the metric system is a triviality.) For this reason delegalization seems to be to be much less practical than legal assistance.

our suppositions were utterly fantastic, and note as well that our heroine lacks access to typewriters and photocopy machines—the mechanical hearts needed to get the supply of paper blood flowing. The inescapable conclusion is that her supposed access to the legal system, based on the bare fact that no regulations forbid her from self-representation, is nothing but a joke.

This is clear from the *Gideon* case. Recall that a lawyer who read the transcript of Gideon's lawyerless trial later remarked: 'He did very well for a layman, he acted like a lawyer. But it was a pitiful effort really. He may have committed this crime, but it was never proved by the prosecution. A lawyer—not a great lawyer, just an ordinary, competent lawyer—could have made ashes of the case.'[19]

The point, of course, is not that Gideon was later acquitted; it is that without a lawyer he was utterly incapable of making his own case. He had access only to the court-room, not to the legal system. For the moment, then, I shall take the necessity claim to be adequately demonstrated; I shall return to it in the concluding sections of this chapter in order to rebut certain counterarguments that might be raised.

Now one might reply that it is unfortunate that poor people cannot obtain the services of lawyers, but that that is not the fault of the legal system. It is rather the fault, if fault it is, of the economic system, which allows poverty to exist. The state is not at fault for failing to make up the gap.

But this objection rests on a premise that is patently false, namely that the state has not blocked poor people from having meaningful access to the legal system. The design of a legal system that cannot be operated by laypeople is surely the result of state decisions, indeed of the accretion of hundreds of millions of state decisions. Moreover, the inability of poor people to afford lawyers is also the result of choices made by the state, both formalistically as a matter of law and also as a matter of plain fact.

The level of attorneys' fees is regulated by the ABA Code and Model Rules; these, in turn, are enforced by the highest court in each state. Legalistically, then, the state courts are responsible for the fact that poor people cannot afford counsel, even though they do not as a matter of fact directly regulate lawyers' fees. But courts are often willing to strike down attorneys' fees if they are too high, as in treble-damage private antitrust class actions. Moreover, courts have the power to appoint counsel in cases in which they think it is important, and to deny compensation to

[19] Anthony Lewis, pp. 62–3.

appointed counsel if budgets do not permit compensation; thus, if a poor litigant cannot obtain counsel, this is in a very direct way the result of decisions by the court.

The fact is that these regulatory powers do virtually nothing to mitigate lawyers' fees. To read the regulations is to understand why. The Model Rules say merely that a 'lawyer's fee shall be reasonable' (Rule 1.5(a)), while the Code elaborates this in an astonishing formula: 'A fee is clearly excessive when, after a review of the facts, a lawyer of ordinary prudence would be left with a definite and firm conviction that the fee is in excess of a reasonable fee' (DR 2–106(B)).

Then there is the unauthorized practice of law regulations. In thirty-seven jurisdictions, it is a misdemeanor for a nonlawyer to practice law (and 'practicing law' is construed to include a large number of activities that on the surface do not require legal training, such as assisting people in filling out do-it-yourself divorce forms); seven other jurisdictions have formalized the power of courts to cite unauthorized practitioners for contempt.[20] By restricting the practice of law to members of the bar, of course, a professional monopoly is guaranteed and a higher-than-otherwise level of lawyers' fees is maintained. The situation is exacerbated because courts usually delegate to bar committees the power to investigate and initiate actions against unauthorized practitioners; this striking conflict of interest has resulted in some amazing cases of turf protection against rather innocent (cut-rate) interlopers.[21]

In 1974, two law school deans wrote a report for the US Senate Judiciary Committee suggesting that deregulation would be a plausible way to reduce the costs of legal services;[22] but such schemes have been strenuously (and understandably) opposed by the bar. The official reason for unauthorized practice regulations is to protect consumers from the legal equivalent of Laetrile and orgone boxes. But Rhode's survey of unauthorized practice enforcement showed that in 1979 only 2 per cent of all inquiries, investigations, and complaints about unauthorized practice originated from consumers and involved specific consumer injury; and of these, 19 per cent concerned laymen pretending to be attorneys. In fact, only twenty-two incidents out of 1188 concerned consumer complaints about unauthorized alternatives to lawyers (as opposed to phony

---

[20] Rhode, p. 11.

[21] See, e.g., *Florida Bar v. Brumbaugh, Florida Bar v. American Business and Legal Forms, Inc.,* and *Florida Bar v. Furman.* The Furman case was the subject of a *60 Minutes* episode, and is discussed in Kern.

[22] Ehrlich and Schwartz.

lawyers).[23] Of course, it could be argued that this low figure is the result of the deterrent effect of the unauthorized practice regulations currently in place; but, since 1166 bar-initiated actions were reported, such an argument would be hard to make out, because the deterrent does not seem to be generally effective. The clear conclusion is that unauthorized practice regulations—state actions—prop up legal fees without serving any other significant public interest.

Furthermore, the selective exclusion of the poor from the legal system does not simply fail to confer an advantage of them—it actively injures them. For a legal system does more than protect people from each other: it enormously expands our field of action, allowing us to do things that we couldn't have done otherwise—to draft wills, adopt children, make contracts, limit liability. As people utilize these features of the system, a network of practices—of power and privilege—is set up from which those who have no access to the system are excluded; and this exclusion itself intensifies the pariah status of the poor. It is hard to avoid the conclusion that the state has conferred the advantages of the legal system on those who can afford to use it and built it on the backs of those who cannot. The state has not been an innocent bystander observing the regrettable spectacle of economic inequality and poverty: it shares primary responsibility with the legal profession (and its well-off clients) for the fact that the poor have no meaningful access to justice and are made worse off by the fact.

Is there a moral right to legal services?

All this does not by itself show that poor people have a right to legal services. Suppose we use the term 'moral rights' in a Kantian fashion to single out our claims to goods necessary for expressing our moral personality or, in other words, to those goods the denial of which treats a person as a mere thing and not as a moral agent. If the term is restricted in this way, I do not believe that we have a moral right to legal services.

It is highly debatable what our moral rights are, because it is unclear what the expression of our moral personality involves. Human life can be lived anywhere on a continuum ranging from bare survival to full human flourishing. It seems reasonably clear that for us to express our moral personality, we must live above the level of bare survival; it is also clear that full human flourishing is more than is needed to express moral personal-

---

[23] Rhode, pp. 33–4.

ity. But where do we draw the line? The further we draw it in the direction of full human flourishing, the more rights we will turn out to have. I suspect that the oft-lamented 'multiplication of rights' in contemporary political discourse arises from our tendency to slide the indicator further and further toward the 'flourishing' end of the continuum, perhaps without even noticing that that is what we are doing. I suggest that the radical vagueness of the pointer's location on the continuum means that rights debates will be very hard to resolve. But in the case of legal services, it is hard to believe that we are talking about a service necessary for the expression of moral personality. In many legal cases, it may well be that a person is perfectly able to express her moral personality even without appointed counsel. Let us see why.

When an unrepresented person is forced to deal with the legal system (or to forego recourse to that system) that person's side of the story, her understanding of the law and the facts of the case, may not be presented, simply because she is inarticulate or uneducated. An adjudicatory system respects a person's human dignity (i.e., moral personality) by giving that person the benefit of the doubt, that is, by presuming that she has a side of the story to tell, until proven otherwise. It is the litigant's interest in telling her side of the story—in legal vindication, we might say—that is crucial for respecting her human dignity.

Sometimes this interest is very strong. In the years in which I have been writing about the legal profession, I have occasionally received letters from people who feel that a legal wrong has been done them and who have spent incredible time and energy attempting to get their due; these are moving, sometimes sad, letters from people whose moral personalities are now inextricably tied to the quest for legal vindication.

Normally, however, legal vindication is only an instrument for achieving something else; normally, then, legal services are valuable only because they are useful in getting other needs and rights fulfilled. The legal system is mostly a strategic pathway to other goods. If there is a moral right in question, it is much more plausible that it is a right to those other goods; it is hard to see a morally significant interest in a particular strategic pathway *per se*.

Thus, whether the affront to the unrepresented person's human dignity violates a moral right depends on the strength of the person's interest in legal vindication as such. In the usual case, then, where legal vindication is an instrument to some other end, there is no moral right to counsel.

For this reason, I would like to suggest a different approach to the problem. I am much more confident that poor people have a right to legal assistance within our legal system than I am that it is a moral right in all such systems (or even in the systems of all wealthy societies). I am more confident that this right follows from the notion of equal justice to which our legal system is in principle committed than I am that it follows from any transsystemic moral theory of rights. Our system's notion of equal justice may be a moral notion, of course, but it may be just a rule of the game as we play it; it may be both, or a bit of each. In any case, perhaps we do not have to assume the full burden of proving that the right to equal access to the law is a moral right. Perhaps it is enough to show that it is a right granted by the rules of the game.

Implicit rights

Let me coin the term *implicit rights* to denote rights granted by the rule of the game. Shortly, I will try to explain what I mean by 'the rules of the game'; for the moment, I will leave the term fuzzy and describe more fully what implicit rights are.[24]

Or rather, what they are not. Implicit rights need not be positive legal rights, because they may not be recognized by the law. One paradigm of an implicit right that is not a positive legal right comes into play when we say that a legal case was 'wrongly decided'. To say this is to say that the court has not assigned rights as it should have; it is to say that a right exists implicitly in the law, which is not recognized under positive law. One characterization of implicit rights, then, or rather one sort of implicit right, comes from the fact that they constitute the *criteria of rightness* of legal decisions.

Implicit rights, then, are not necessarily legal rights. They also do not have to be moral rights (though some may be). No one, we may believe, has a moral right to be an absolute hereditary monarch. Imagine, however, such a monarchy in which the king dies and usurping relatives of the prince succeed in an unjust suit to have his succession invalidated. After he has lost the suit, the prince has neither a moral nor a positive legal right to the throne; but, since we are assuming that the suit was wrongly decided, he still has an implicit right—a right granted by the rules of the (existing social) game.

These examples of implicit rights equate the rules of the game with the positive laws of the society, correctly interpreted. But there are also unwritten understandings within a polity, forming the framework of

---

[24] The term 'implicit rights' is Dennis Thompson's suggestion, replacing 'virtual rights', a term I used in an earlier version of this chapter, published separately as Luban.

political legitimacy from which positive law derives its authority, and these too can generate implicit rights. Before the ratification of the Twenty-Sixth Amendment in 1971, no eighteen-year-old in America had a constitutional right to vote. It is plausible to argue that eighteen-year-olds have no moral right to vote (what, after all, is the moral significance of being eighteen years old?) Finally, eighteen-year-olds had no implicit right to vote if implicit rights are the only criteria of correctness for legal decisions: nothing in the framework of constitutional law suggests such a right, and if an eighteen-year-old had litigated for the right to vote and lost, it is hard to see any grounds for saying that the case was wrongly decided.[25]

Nevertheless, public debate over the Twenty-Sixth Amendment centred around the fact that eighteen-year-old men were being drafted to fight in the Vietnam War. To many people, it seemed wrong to demand from eighteen-year-olds the ultimate responsibility of citizenship without granting them the right to participate in the electoral process. The principle that responsibility and participation go hand-in-hand—'no taxation without representation'—was taken as an unwritten part of the country's framework of political legitimacy (a rule of the game), and because of this, an implicit right of eighteen-year-olds to vote was recognized.

It makes sense, then, to distinguish rights implicit in the law (call them *textual rights*) from rights implicit in the political framework that gives the law its authority (call them *legitimation rights*). It is the latter that will concern us here, for I believe that the principle of equal access to the legal system is part of our framework of political legitimacy. The argument, then, is that to deny a person legal assistance is to deny her equality before the law, and that to deny someone equality before the law delegitimizes our form of government.

Political legitimacy

In any form of government other than direct popular democracy, some men and women rule the rest. The question of political legitimacy asks by what right they do this; it asks for a criterion or principle marking off governments that have this right from those that do not. Legitimacy is, for this reason, the basic normative concept of political theory, just as the good and the right are the basic normative concepts of moral theory.

Now we may believe that the only legitimation principle that holds

[25] But see *Oregon v. Mitchell*, where the Court split on this issue.

water is the *consent of the governed*. Whether this is true or not will not concern me here, however, because even if this belief is right, the fact remains that historically many principles have won the consent, or even the support, of the governed. Even if one is an absolute consent theorist, one must be a practicing pluralist, allowing that legitimation principles other than the explicit consent of the governed are valid. (By a 'legitimation principle,' I mean an account of legitimacy offered by a government to its citizens.) It is possible to supplement the traditional taxonomy of regimes, which distinguishes them according to the composition of their ruling groups—the one, the few, the many, the honourable, the rich, the party—with a taxonomy based on legitimation principles. It will be crucial to my argument that forms of government can be characterized according to their legitimation principles. Legitimation principles generate implicit rights, and these differ between societies precisely because of the variety of such principles.

Consider, for example, the European *ancien régime*, a monarchy legitimated by a complex of theoretical beliefs—that the monarch is 'God's deputy, head and soul of the body politic, sole knower of the mysteries of state, father of his subjects, husband of the realm, healer, peacemaker, sovereign lord.'[26] Each of these is a component of the overarching legitimation principle of *divine right*. The various analogies represented theocratic arguments for divine right and were not mere images, because it was believed that we can speak of God only by analogy.[27] Let us now show that certain implicit rights flow from the principle of divine right.

Could a monarch of the *ancien régime* proclaim the truth of atheism and require of his subjects the destruction of all places of worship? Surely this would be like the pope declaring *ex cathedra* that God does not exist! If there is no God, the pope cannot make *ex cathedra* utterances. If atheism is true, then the king is not God's deputy, and his claim to rule by divine right is undercut. His authority to issue the proclamation vanishes, and thus the proclamation is *ultra vires*, void from the outset. It follows that his subjects possess an implicit right to have the king uphold the faith.

These examples suggest a principle of consistency: no government can authorize actions or institutions that violate its own legitimation principles. The logical mechanism by which legitimation rights are generated is therefore this: a legitimation principle, in conjunction with the principle of consistency, demarcates a set of actions and institutions that a govern-

---

[26] Walzer, p. 9.   [27] Ibid., pp. 21–7.

ment cannot authorize, as well as a set that it must authorize. These in turn generate negative and positive rights against the government.

Legitimation in America

Above the entrance to the Supreme Court of the United States one may read the words 'Equal Justice Under Law'. It is a lofty slogan and one in which most of us believe. Is it, however, part of our structure of political legitimacy; that is, is equality before the law a principle of weight similar to popular sovereignty and republicanism (our other legitimation principles)?

Of course one cannot give a knock-down argument that it is: a legitimation principle is an unwritten understanding of how a polity should be run, one which perhaps forms a presupposition of most political discourse, but which will always be denied by some people (it's a big country). It is hard to prove that something is an unwritten understanding. Moreover, American politics has always involved major struggles over the legitimacy of redistributive schemes, that is, schemes meant to promote economic equality. Many of us believe in one or another form of economic egalitarianism, but many of us do not. Furthermore, it would be hard to argue that a country that allowed human slavery for its first two hundred years, and denied the franchise to women for another fifty odd years, has consistently displayed any noticeable fervour for egalitarianism.

Yet the fact remains that even opponents of economic egalitarianism have almost always favoured the equality of legal rights, at least for citizens. Although women could not vote, they could sue in court; and the Civil War amendments that made black Americans citizens allowed them access to the courts. Supreme Court decisions, moreover, allow non-citizens access to American courts. I believe that a fair reading of American political history shows that equality-of-rights-not-fortunes has always been a common denominator of American political life, economic egalitarians holding that equality of rights is not enough, economic inegalitarians asserting that it is enough, but nobody asserting that it is too much.[28]

---

[28] See, for example, the (by and large conservative) political writings collected in Hyneman and Lutz, especially pp. 5, 577, 928–9, 954, 1048, and 1229, all of which argue for equality-of-rights-not-fortunes. A typical example of such an argument appears in James Fenimore Cooper's classic anti-Jacksonian tract *The American Democrat*, pp. 93–5:

That one man is not as good as another in natural qualities, is proved on the testimony of our senses. One man is stronger than another; he is handsomer, taller, swifter, wiser, or braver, than all his fellows. In short, the physical and moral qualities are unequally distributed, and, as a necessary consequence, in none

What follows from this? Nothing, unless we add the premise that the quality of rights spoken of here is taken in American political discourse to imply equality of legal rights, so that 'equal justice under law' is a corollary of equality-of-rights-not-fortunes. Then we are entitled to conclude that 'equal justice under law' is indeed a legitimation principle of American government, and thus that it generates a legitimation right of equal access to the legal system. Add to this the necessity claim (that access to the legal system requires a lawyer), and we have arrived at the conclusion that citizens have a (legitimation) right to legal services.

Does equality of right, however, mean equality of legal right? The early American writers who formulated the principle of equality-of-rights-not-fortune were probably thinking of moral rights, or (more likely) rights given by God in natural law. And it need not be the case that moral rights or natural law are institutionally realized primarily through the adjudicative system: they might be institutionalized primarily through the legislature, or through the executive agencies, or (for that matter) through informal dispute resolution organs—neighborhood councils, family gatherings, churches, or whatever.[29]

The American republican system, however, is justified largely by arguments expressing a mistrust of legislatures and of the executive as rights enforcers. The argument of *The Federalist* is that only the courts can be relied on to protect rights:

The independence of judges is . . . requisite to guard . . . the rights of individuals from the effects of those ill humours which the arts of designing men, or the influence of particular conjunctures, sometimes disseminate among the people themselves . . . [including] the injury of the private rights of particular classes of citizens, by unjust and partial laws.[30]

Hamilton speaks of '[t]hat inflexible and uniform adherence to the rights . . . of individuals, which we perceive to be indispensable in the courts of justice', and argues for the judiciary's role in 'the inviolable maintenance

---

of them, can one man be justly said to be as good as another. . . . But . . . all men have essentially the same rights, an equality, which, so far from establishing that 'one man is as good as another,' in a social sense, is the very means of producing the inequality of condition that actually exists. By possessing the same rights to exercise their respective faculties, the active and frugal become more wealthy than the idle and dissolute; the wise and gifted more trusted than the silly and ignorant; the polished and refined more respected and sought, than the rude and vulgar.

The Hyneman and Lutz excerpts, dating from 1762 to 1802, are all variations on this argument.

[29] This has been the case at various times in American history; see Auerbach.
[30] Hamilton, in Hamilton, Jay, and Madison, Number 78, pp. 469–70.

of that equality of privileges and immunities to which the citizens of the Union will be entitled'.[31]

The Federalist, of course, is just one work on American government (albeit the most influential one); but, I expect, few readers doubt that the standard view of the legitimacy of American government presumes a strong connection between moral or natural rights (if there are such things) and legal rights, so that if the court system claimed that its activities have nothing much to do with respecting moral rights we would view it as seriously defective.

We have now arrived at our conclusion, that *absent* equal access to the legal system (and thus at least minimal access to legal services), our system violates the principle of consistency and its own legitimation principles. What is the upshot of this? At the risk of unduly prolonging our Civics 101 meditation on the principles of American democracy, let me quote from John Locke concerning the dire consequences of a legal system that permits the haves to trench upon the rights of the have-nots (as ours does, if it does not provide the means for the have-nots to utilize the legal apparatus):

[W]here an appeal to Law, and constituted Judges lies open, but the remedy is deny'd by a manifest perverting of Justice, . . . to protect or indemnifie the violence or injuries of some Men, or Party of Men, *there* it *is* hard to imagine anything but a *State of War*. For . . . it is still violence and injury, however colour'd with the Name, Pretences, or Forms of law . . . ; *War is made* upon the Sufferers.[32]

This in turn implies a right to resist:

Whosoever uses *force without Right*, as every one does in Society, who does it without Law, puts himself into a *state of War* with those, against whom he so uses it, and in that state all former Ties are cancelled, all other Rights cease, and every one has a *Right* . . . *to resist the Aggressor*. . . . That it is lawful for people, in some Cases, to *resist* their King, . . . that, since they may in some Cases *resist*, all resisting of Princes is not Rebellion.[33]

It was precisely this argument, of course, that was taken to justify the American revolution against a king who, under color of the 'Name, Pretences, or Forms of Law', entered into a 'state of War' against the colonists by denying them meaningful access to governmental institutions.

This is the proverbial bottom line: without the state of law we are left with the state of war. If have-nots are excluded from access to the legal

---

[31] Ibid., Number 80, p. 478.   [32] Locke, §20, p. 322.   [33] Ibid., §232, pp. 467–8.

system, 'the end whereof being to protect and redress the innocent'[34] (Locke), their alternative is the law of the streets, of resistance that is entirely rightful.

This Lockean argument was well understood by Reginald Heber Smith, who founded the legal aid movement in the United States. I conclude this portion of my argument with his words (written in 1919):

> For the State to erect an uneven, partial administration of justice is to abnegate the very responsibility for which it exists, and is to accomplish by indirection an abridgment of the fundamental rights which the State is directly forbidden to infringe. To deny law or justice to any person is, in actual effect, to outlaw them by stripping them of their only protection. . . .
>
> In that direction we have imperceptibly, unconsciously, and unintentionally drifted. The end of such a course is disclosed by history. Differences in the ability of classes to use the machinery of the law, if permitted to remain, lead inevitably to disparity between the rights of classes in the law itself. And when the law recognizes and enforces a distinction between classes, revolution ensues or democracy is at an end.[35]

Legal services and the Supreme Court

My argument has relied on the claim that the principle I have labelled 'equality-of-rights-not-fortunes' is a legitimation principle of American government, a claim I have defended by suggesting that the principle is a common denominator of political discourse in this country. To this it might be replied that the opponent of state-provided legal services means something quite different by 'equality-of-rights-not-fortunes' than does the supporter of them, and consequently, that merely pointing out the near-universal espousal of the principle does not prove that it is a legitimation principle if it is read so as to imply the right to state-provided legal services. The historical record shows that few of those who espoused equality-of-rights-not-fortunes contemplated the possibility that the government would play any role at all in affirmatively providing for substantive equality. If the principle means different things in the mouths of different people, it is no common denominator—it is not even a single, unequivocal principle.

But I have argued above for the necessity claim that the denial of access to legal services is a form of the denial of access to the legal system. Equality of legal rights surely implies access to the legal system, and by the necessity claim, it therefore implies access to legal services. The bur-

---

[34] Locke, §20, p. 322.   [35] Reginald Heber Smith, pp. 5, 12.

den, therefore, is on the opponent of state-provided legal services to make out an interpretation of equality-of-rights-not-fortunes that is as plausible as the one that acknowledges the necessity claim.

Obviously, there is a variety of approaches the opponent of state-provided legal services might take to finesse the necessity claim, and it would be a tedious and inconclusive exercise to try to anticipate and respond to all of them. What I shall do in the remainder of this chapter, therefore, is to criticize three such arguments that exert a special claim to our attention. Three times in recent history the Supreme Court has begun to delineate a line of decisions that looked as thought it would lead to establishing a constitutional right to counsel in non-criminal cases; each time the Court pulled back from asserting that right. The Court, in effect, has rejected the necessity claim. I shall examine these decisions, and argue that in each case the Court has relied on a principle that is erroneous, arbitrary, or incapable of supporting its conclusion.

The constitutional history of the right to counsel in non-criminal matters is this. Two lines of Due Process Clause cases and one line of Equal Protection Clause cases looked as though they were going to establish a right to legal services in civil matters, but the Supreme Court eventually limited the principles at work in all three so that they did not do so. (It is worth noting that the Due Process Clause is a plausible interpretation of what I have called minimal access to the legal system, as the Equal Protection Clause is a plausible interpretation of equal access.)

Boddie/Meltzer/Kras/Ortwein

The first line of decisions began with *Boddie v. Connecticut*, in which the Court struck down filing fees for divorce courts on the ground that such fees excluded people of limited means from the courts and thus violated due process of law. The reasoning was thoroughly Lockean:

Perhaps no characteristic of an organized and cohesive society is more fundamental than its erection and enforcement of a system of rules defining the various rights and duties of its members, enabling them to govern their affairs and definitively settle their differences in an orderly, predictable manner. Without such a 'legal system,' social organization and cohesion are virtually impossible. . . . Put more succinctly, it is this injection of the rule of law that allows society to reap the benefits of rejecting what political theorists call the 'state of nature' (*Boddie* at 374).

Using this 'theoretical framework' (as the Court calls it), Justice Harlan goes on to infer that ' "within the limits of practicability," a State must afford to all individuals a meaningful opportunity to be heard if it is to fulfill the promise of the Due Process Clause.'[36] This argument suggests that all financial obstacles—including, presumably, the inability to hire counsel—to the meaningful use of the courts violate due process.

Indeed, this was how Justice Black understood *Boddie*. In the same term, the Court refused to grant certiorari in eight cases in which access to the courts was prevented by financial obstacles. In an unusual dissent to the denial of certiorari, Justice Black, who had disagreed with and dissented in *Boddie*, argued that under *Boddie* no indigent should be denied access to civil courts because of an inability to pay fees or hire an attorney.[37]

What followed, however, amounted to an invasion of the *Boddie*-snatchers. In *US v. Kras*, the Court found that a filing fee for bankruptcy proceedings does *not* deny due process. It distinguished *Kras* from *Boddie* because (1) going bankrupt, unlike obtaining a divorce, is not a 'fundamental' interest and (2) in disputes with creditors—from which bankruptcy proceedings are one way out—the courts do not hold a monopoly on dispute resolution mechanisms; whereas going to court is the only way to terminate a marriage. Then, in *Ortwein v. Schwab*, the Court reiterated its narrow reading of *Boddie* by finding that a fee for obtaining an administrative hearing over a cut in welfare payments does not violate due process, for the same two reasons.[38]

Let us examine these two reasons. 'Fundamental interests (or rights)' is a term of art in constitutional adjudication; it signifies those rights that are 'explicitly or implicitly guaranteed by the constitution'.[39] The Court has found that among those interests is a cluster of matters concerning familial relations, which includes the right to divorce (but not to file for bankruptcy or argue welfare payments). And the Court's argument is that fundamental rights deserve greater constitutional protection and a higher level of judicial scrutiny than do rights that are not fundamental.

The problem is that interests can be fundamental to a citizen that are not fundamental in this technical sense. And the social contract argument that forms the *Boddie* decision's 'theoretical framework' is based on the idea that law protects interests that are fundamental to the citizenry, not merely those that are fundamental in the Court: for it is threats to the former that would drive us back into the state of nature. Thus, when *Kras*

---

[36] *Boddie* at 379; citation omitted.   [37] *Meltzer v. C. Buck LeCraw & Co.*, at 955–6.
[38] This case concerned a welfare-recipient who believed his old-age benefits to have been unjustifiably cut and whose appeal had been denied in administrative hearings. He was prevented from taking the case to court because of a filing fee.
[39] *San Antonio Independent School District v. Rodriguez*, at 33–4.

and *Ortwein* limit access to the courts to the latter interests, they undercut the legitimation argument that forms the basis of the rule of law in our system (and that the *Boddie* analysis relies upon). This does not imply, of course, that the *Kras* and *Ortwein* Courts misread the precedents—then the right to legal services would be a textual right—but rather that the principle they are advancing delegitimizes our form of government.

A look at the *Kras* case will clarify what I mean by interests fundamental to the citizen. Kras was an insurance salesman who had a thousand dollars in premiums stolen. He lost his job, owed the insurance company for the premiums, and could not find work because his former employer gave him bad recommendations. He had a dependent mother and wife, and a child with cystic fibrosis. The final blow came when he attempted to declare bankruptcy; the bankruptcy court required a fifty-dollar filing fee, which Kras could not afford to pay, even in the form of $1.28-a-week time payments. It was this filing fee that the Court upheld. Surely Kras's interest in getting into bankruptcy court is as fundamental to him as an interest could be: without it his family's life may be at an end.

I do not see how this is different from a case Smith described in 1919, nor how his conclusion fails to follow:

A woman borrowed ten dollars in 1914, and for two years paid interest at 180 per cent. In 1916 a law was enacted fixing 36 per cent as the maximum rate. The lender, by a device contrary to the statute, compelled her to continue paying 156 per cent interest. The law also provided that if excess interest were charged, the loan would be declared void by a suit in equity. The law was on the books. The court house was open, the equity court in session with its judge on the bench and its officers in attendance. All that was of no avail to her, for the law could not bring its redress until five dollars was paid for service of process and entry fee, and ten dollars to an attorney to draw, file, and present the necessary bill of complaint. Fifteen dollars she did not have and, because of her condition, could not earn. *For her there was no law.*[40]

The Court's second argument is even more mysterious; that argument, again, is that filing fees need not be struck down unless, as in divorce cases, no dispute resolution mechanisms other than the courts are available.

What might these other mechanisms be? Well, for a family dispute that falls short of divorce, they might be other members of the family, or a marriage counselor; for a dispute between neighbors, another neighbor; for a dispute between a shopkeeper and a customer, some third party both of them trust, such as the parish priest. If all else fails, two disputants can simply argue out the issue to the point of compromise.

---

[40] Reginald Heber Smith, p. 11 (emphasis added).

Now, my question is this: what alternative dispute resolution mechanism is available to Mr Kras? Precisely what is he supposed to do?
Following out the line of thought just presented, Krass can attempt to get
his creditors to sit down and talk in the presence of a mutually respected
third party. Perhaps they will give him an extension on his repayments, or
even abrogate the debts. Bankruptcy is not the only method of debt-relief.

This might work if Kras's creditors are his neighbours and acquain-
tances: Mr Whipple might extend his line of credit for three more months
if Kras promises never to squeeze the Charmin. But the idea seem slightly
absurd when the creditors are his absentee landlord, Household Finance,
Tender Mercies Hospital, or various other large institutions that keep a
collection agency on retainer. Indeed, even in the good old ethnic neighborhood—Mean Street, USA—there are creditors known as 'Shylocks'
who will not sit down with Mr Kras and the parish priest. They will hire
adjustors, or 'goons' as they are sometimes called, to break Mr Kras's legs.

I agree with Frank Michelman, according to whom the argument about
alternative dispute resolution

fairly passeth understanding. . . . An indigent insolvent person, for example, has
alternative avenues to relief from debts only on the assumption that his creditors
are not unyielding. But why should they yield, since he is indigent and, by holding
out, they cannot get less than they would get out of bankruptcy?[41]

Similarly, Ortwein's avenues for extra judicial satisfaction from welfare
officials are merely logical possibilities, not practical ones. The officials
have followed their procedures, heard his appeals, and made their decisions; they have many other cases and little time. Even as we speak,
another file is being placed on their desks, someone named Joseph K . . .
The welfare officials uphold their decisions, and Ortwein gets by without
the money as best he can. That is how his dispute is resolved.

I conclude that the Court's arguments in *Kras* and *Ortwein* do not provide grounds for a reasonable alternative interpretation of equality-of-
rights-not-fortunes. The necessity claim stands.

Gideon/Argersinger/Lassiter

The *Gideon* line of cases provided a due-process right to counsel for
people accused of crimes for which imprisonment might be the sentence.
Could this right be extended to civil litigants? In *Lassiter* the Court said no.

Abby Gail Lassiter was sentenced to twenty-five to forty years of
imprisonment for second-degree murder. The Department of Social

[41] Michelman, p. 1179. See Tribe, pp. 1008–10 for a similar criticism.

Services of Durham County, North Carolina, petitioned to have her parental rights regarding her three-year-old son terminated; the petition was granted after a hearing in which Lassiter was not represented by counsel, and Lassiter appealed, averring that the Due Process Clause entitled her to the assistance of counsel.

One noteworthy feature of this case is that Lassiter met both of the *Kras/Ortwein* conditions: parental rights are 'fundamental' even in the technical sense, and, since she was the defendant in the Department of Social Service's case, she had no alternative to the hearing. In rejecting her argument, the Court found a 'presumption that an indigent litigant has a right to appointed counsel only when, if he loses, he may be deprived of his physical liberty'. This presumption is to be rebutted by using a test derived from *Mathews v. Eldridge*, which weighs three factors: the private interests at stake, the government's interest, and the risk that the procedures will lead to erroneous decisions. By requiring such a balancing test, the Court is saying that counsel is not always necessary for due process of law, even if a case goes to adjudication. (Since, moreover, the Court found that Lassiter required no counsel, even though her interest was 'fundamental', we have an inkling of how the Court proposes to balance the private interests at stake against the government's interest in saving money on a lawyer.)

The fallacy in the Court's argument lies in its lopsided emphasis on physical liberty over all other interests. Why is there a 'presumption that an indigent litigant has a right to appointed counsel only when, if he loses, he may be deprived of his physical liberty'? To be sure, physical liberty is of great importance to us; but so are other things. We should not forget that the loss of physical liberty can be slight as well as great; when it is slight, other things can outweigh it. 'Losing one's driver's license', Justices Powell and Rehnquist pointed out in their concurring opinion in *Argersinger*, 'is more serious for some individuals than a brief stay in jail.'[42] I would rather do thirty days in jail than be fined twenty thousand dollars or lose parental rights. Wouldn't you? And once physical liberty is put on the same footing with other important interests, the argument for legal aid in loss-of-liberty cases can be generalized to cases involving those interests as well.

Once again, I am not arguing that the Court misread its precedents, which indeed incorporate the lopsided emphasis on physical liberty over other interests. My inquiry is solely into the question of whether the

---

[42] *Argersinger* at 48, citing *Bell v. Burson*, which requires government to provide persons a hearing before terminating their driver's license.

principles upon which the Court relies provide a plausible interpretation of equality-of-rights-not-fortunes. And it seems clear that a principle that acknowledges the necessity claim only in cases where physical liberty is at stake (no matter how slight the loss of liberty), subjecting it to balancing tests of questionable integrity where any other interests are at stake (even important ones), is simply arbitrary.

Griffin/Douglas/Ross v. Moffitt

In *Griffin v. Illinois*, the Court ruled that to offer equal protection of the laws, a state must provide a free trial transcript to an indigent person appealing his criminal conviction. (A transcript is required for an appeal, and may cost thousands of dollars.) And in *Douglas v. California*, the Court held equal protection to require a state to provide counsel to an indigent person appealing by right from a criminal conviction.

These cases raised the possibility that their principles would be extended to providing the means of litigation for any indigent person having recourse to the courts. But in 1974 the Court scotched that hope: In *Ross v. Moffitt*, it drastically limited the scope of the *Griffin-Douglas* line of cases by finding that there is no denial of equal protection if an attorney is not appointed when an indigent person pursues a merely discretionary appeal of a criminal conviction. By implication, no attorney would be appointed in other, less drastic, cases. Does *Ross v. Moffitt* raise any issues that undercut the necessity claim?

It does not. Justice Rehnquist's reasoning is tailored very narrowly to the facts of the case, and it generates a very narrow holding. Moffitt had lost a first appeal and wished to take a second. For the first appeal, he:

received the benefit of counsel in examining the record of his trial and in preparing an appellate brief on his behalf. . . . We do not believe that it can be said, therefore, that a defendant in respondent's circumstances is denied meaningful access to the North Carolina Supreme Court simply because the State does not appoint counsel to aid him in seeking review in that court. At that stage he will have, at the very least, a transcript or other record of trial proceedings, a brief on his behalf in the Court of Appeals setting forth his claims of error, and in many cases an opinion by the Court of Appeals disposing of his case. These materials, supplemented by whatever submission respondent may make *pro se*, would appear to provide the Supreme Court of North Carolina with an adequate basis for its decision to grant or deny review.[43]

---

[43] *Ross v. Moffitt*, at 614–15.

If you've already had a lawyer provided to you who has done much of the work, and if you possess the work that that lawyer has done, and if you don't need to make an oral argument yourself but need simply to present a written petition, then you've got meaningful access to the courts without being given a second lawyer. More briefly, if you've had the benefit of one lawyer, you needn't be provided with another.

Suppose we agree. This is enough to prove Justice Rehnquist's general point that equal protection doesn't *always* require the appointment of counsel. But it says nothing about what equal protection requires when the highly idiosyncratic circumstances of this case are not met—in particular, when the indigent person has not already had the benefit of one lawyer. Justice Rehnquist in fact carefully limits the principle in *Ross v. Moffitt*:

The Fourteenth Amendment 'does not require absolute equality or precisely equal advantages,' nor does it require the State to 'equalize economic conditions.' . . . The question is not one of absolutes, but one of degrees. *In this case* we do not believe that the Equal Protection Clause, *when interpreted in the context of these cases*, requires North Carolina to provide free counsel for indigent *defendants seeking to take discretionary appeals* to the North Carolina Supreme Court, or to file petitions for *certiorari* in this Court. (Emphasis added.)[44]

Notice the emphasized phrases: they tell the whole story. *Ross v. Moffitt* is irrelevant to the general question of whether indigents have an equal protection right to legal services, for its principle has met the Death By a Thousand Qualifications.

In *Kras* and *Ortwein*, the Court's limitations on the necessity claim were based on an erroneous argument; in *Lassiter*, on an arbitrary principle; and in *Ross v. Moffitt*, on a principle that is too weak to prove the point. I conclude that the necessity claim stands undamaged by these arguments; they have failed to make out an interpretation of equality-of-rights-not-fortunes as plausible as one that implies the right to legal services.

Concluding remarks

Let me summarize the argument. It relies on a simple intuition: whereas egalitarianism in any robust sense of the term is very controversial, effective equality of legal right is not. Equality before the law, like universal suffrage, holds a privileged place in our political system, and to deny equality before the law delegitimizes that system. The argument goes as follows:

---

[44] Ibid., at 612; citations omitted.

1. Access to minimal legal services is necessary for access to the legal system.

2. Access to the legal system is necessary for equality of legal rights—equality before the law.

3. Equality of legal rights is necessary to the legitimacy of our form of government.

4. Whatever is necessary to the legitimacy of a form of government it must grant as a matter of right.

Therefore,

5. Access to legal services is a right under our form of government.

In recent years a large literature has emerged on the subject of welfare rights—that is, rights to be given something, as opposed to rights to be left alone. It is tempting to view the argument of this chapter as just one more product of what critics have labelled 'the rights industry'. The present argument, however, is different in several important respects from arguments for welfare rights, and I would like to conclude by reflecting on the character of the argument I have presented and noting those differences.

First of all, the argument is political rather than distinctively moral in character. I have denied that we have a moral right to legal services, claiming instead that the right derives implicitly from the nature of political legitimacy. Mine is an argument about the presuppositions of a certain form of government, not about the presuppositions of moral life in general.

Second, and as a consequence, the argument is relativistic. I do not claim that anyone, in any society that has an organized legal profession, has a right to legal services. Rather, I have claimed that the right follows from a legitimation principle at work in our society. Although popular support is the ultimate ground of political legitimacy in any system, support can be garnered through the variety of principles to which people yield their allegiance, and thus legitimation rights will differ from system to system.

The argument, however, is not subject to one of the characteristic infirmities of relativism, namely the inability to recommend practices that differ from what is already in place. Although governments are legitimate by various principles, they seldom live up to the implications of those principles, and thus those principles may be used as instruments of what is sometimes called 'immanent critique'—critique from within the extant standards. In particular, I have claimed that the American government is legitimated by a principle of equality of rights that implies a right to legal services, which has not so far been legally or practically recognized.

Third, my argument has this peculiarity: because it proceeds by drawing out the implications of a legitimation principle of equality-of-rights-not-fortunes, it generates a legitimation right to legal services but no legitimation rights to much more valuable goods: food, shelter, education, resources, medical treatment, jobs, control of the conditions of one's labour, and so forth. This does not mean that I do not believe we have rights to these substances (in fact, I do); it means only that such rights must be argued for in a different way. Thus, mine is not an argument for welfare rights in general. In one sense, I suppose, this is a weakness of the argument: it focuses on a good that is unimportant relative to the substances of other welfare rights, and thus it might be taken to endorse a skewed and unacceptable set of priorities. But I do not mean to suggest that legal services are more important than these other substances. Moreover, this weakness of the argument is also a strength. It does not depend on the validity of other arguments for welfare rights, and it appeals to a principle—equality-of-rights-not-fortunes—that is accepted even by people who are hostile to the general idea of welfare rights. It does not take a position on where the rights pointer should be located on the 'bare survival/full human flourishing' continuum, and it is for that reason impervious to the usual objections based on that controversy. It is not, I think, a controversial argument at all.

Finally, it connects directly with a view of rights that I find plausible, namely that rights are claims to goods that are presuppositions of significant institutions and aspects of life. Legitimation rights are claims to goods that form presuppositions of a people's common political life; when these rights are denied, the expectation that the affronted parties should continue to respect the political system—in other words, the expectation that they should continue to treat it as a legitimate political system—has no basis. It is for this reason that I have emphasized Locke's argument that an illegitimate system generates a right of resistance: for resistance is the ultimate sanction when a political system undermines the premises of its own claim to govern a common life.

Bibliography

ABEL, RICHARD L. (1). 'Law Without Politics: Legal Aid under Advanced Capitalism'. *UCLA Law Review* 32 (1985): 474–621.

—— (2). 'Socializing the Legal Profession: Can Redistributing Lawyers' Services Achieve Social Justice?' *Law and Policy Quarterly* 1 (1979): 5–51.

ASSOCIATION OF THE BAR OF THE CITY OF NEW YORK. *Toward a Mandatory Contribution of Public Service Practice by Every Lawyer: Recommendations and Report*

64   *David Luban*

of the Special Committee on the Lawyer's Pro Bono Obligation. 1980.

AUERBACH, JEROLD. *Justice Without Law? Resolving Disputes Without Lawyers.* New York: Oxford University Press, 1983.

BELLOW, GARY. 'Turning Solutions Into Problems: The Legal Aid Experience', *NLADA Briefcase* 1977 (1977): 106–22.

BLANKENBURG, ERHARD. 'Comparing Legal Aid Schemes in Europe'. American Bar Foundation London Symposium. Unpublished typescript, July 1985.

BRECHT, BERTHOLD. *The Rise and Fall of the City of Mahagonny.* Trans. Michael Feingold, in *Collected Plays.* Ed. Ralph Manheim and John Willett. Vol. 2. New York: Vintage Books, 1977.

CAPPELLETTI, MAURO and COHEN, WILLIAM. *Comparative Constitutional Law.* Indianapolis, Ind.: Bobbs-Merrill, 1979.

COOPER, JAMES FENIMORE. *The American Democrat, or Hints on the Social and Civic Relations of the United States of America* Indianapolis, Ind.: Liberty Classics, 1956.

EHRLICH, THOMAS and SCHWARTZ, MURRAY L. 'Reducing the Costs of Legal Services: Possible Approaches by the Federal Government'. A Report to the Subcommittee on Representation of Citizen Interests, US Senate Committee on the Judiciary, 93d Congress, 2nd Session.

GALANTER, MARC. 'Why the "Haves" Come Out Ahead: Speculations on the Limits of Legal Change'. *Law and Society Review* 9 (1974): 95–124.

HAMILTON, ALEXANDER, JAY, JOHN, and MADISON, JAMES. *The Federalist Papers.* Ed. Clinton Rossiter. New York: Mentor Books, 1961.

HYNEMAN, CHARLES S. and LUTZ, DONALD S. *American Political Writing During the Founding Era, 1760–1805.* Indianapolis, Ind.: Liberty Press, 1983.

JOHNSON, EARL, Jr. *Justice and Reform: The Formative Years of the OEO Legal Services Program.* New York: Russell Sage Foundation, 1974.

KERN, LEILA R. 'The Northside Secretarial Service: Unauthorized Practice'. Harvard Law School Case Study PLP–83–004. Typescript, 1982.

KLINGE, ERICH. *Das Beratungshilfegesetz: Kommentar zum Gesetz über Rechtsberatung und Vertretung für Bürger mit geringem Einkommen.* Neuwied: Luchterhand, 1980.

LEWIS, ANTHONY. *Gideon's Trumpet.* New York: Vintage Books, 1964.

LOCKE, JOHN. *Second Treatise of Government,* in *Two Treatises of Government.* Cambridge: Cambridge University Press, 1960.

LUBAN, DAVID. 'Political Legitimacy and the Right to Legal Services'. *Business and Professional Ethics* 5 (1985): 43–68.

MICHELMAN, FRANK I. 'The Supreme Court and Litigation Access Fees: The Right to Protect One's Rights—Part I'. *Duke Law Journal* 1973 (1973): 1153–215.

RHODE, DEBORAH L. 'Policing the Professional Monopoly: A Constitutional and Empirical Analysis of Unauthorized Practice Prohibitions'. *Stanford Law Review* 34 (1981): 1–112.

RICH, SPENCER. 'Percentage of Poor Americans At Lowest Level Since 1980'. *Washington Post,* July 31, 1987.

SMITH, REGINALD HEBER. *Justice and the Poor.* In *Carnegie Foundation for the Advancement of Teaching Bulletin.* Vol. 12. New York: Scribner's Sons, 1919.

TRIBE, LAURENCE H. *American Constitutional Law*. Mineola, NY: Foundation Press, 1978.

WALZER, MICHAEL. *Regicide and Revolution: Speeches at the Trial of Louis XVI*. Cambridge: Cambridge University Press, 1974.

THE WASHINGTON COUNCIL OF LAWYERS. *Report on the Status of Legal Services for the Poor, November, 1983*.

WEXLER, STEPHEN. 'Practicing Law for Poor People'. *Yale Law Journal* 79 (1970): 1049–67.

2. The Legal Services Program of the Office of Economic Opportunity

E. CLINTON BAMBERGER, JR.*

> Laws grind the poor; and rich men rule the law.
>
> *Oliver Goldsmith*

Speakers coming before distinguished forums such as this symposium to speak about some aspect of the War on Poverty—now, a year and half after the passage of the Economic Opportunity Act[1]—face audiences of mixed sophistication in terms of what and where the poverty effort is. We risk boring the more sophisticated with fundamental statements of Office of Economic Opportunity (OEO) policy. If to satisfy this group we start with a set of implicit assumptions we risk underinforming— or worse, misinforming—the less sophisticated. I confront something of a Hobson's choice, but I choose a restatement of the fundamentals.

The OEO Legal Services Program is, in simplest terms, a program to enable local communities to offer free legal assistance to the poor as part of community action in the War on Poverty. The OEO does not render legal services or furnish lawyers. It does not initiate or conduct programs for free legal assistance. Neither does it send federal attorneys to offer such assistance. Essentially, it is a source of funds with certain fundamental objectives to be pursued.

To date, too few communities have sought OEO funds, but the number has increased significantly in the last four months. By 30 June [1966] the OEO expects to have funded nearly 125 projects totalling at least twenty million dollars. The President of the American Bar Association and the National Advisory Committee have recommended to Congress that fifty million dollars be allocated for the conduct of programs in fiscal 1967. Approximately half of the present grants have gone to existing legal aid societies, with the remainder to bar associations or bar association sponsored groups, to law schools, or simply to groups of lawyers who

---

* Director, Legal Services Program, Office of Economic Opportunity.
[1] 78 Stat. 508 (1964), 42 USC §§ 2701–981 (1964).

have developed a component agency to affiliate with a community action program.

The money is being used to provide legal assistance to the poor. It means national recognition that the least affluent members of our society have at least as many legal problems as the rest of us, and probably more. It means national recognition that the poor are least equipped with the resources and resilience to obtain fair treatment and, accordingly, least able to cope with the landlord, the merchant, the welfare official, the policeman—people you and I handle with relative ease in the unlikely event we ever see them—and that competent advocacy in the form of a lawyer—an articulate friend—can improve the lot and dignity of the poor. The OEO seeks the achievement of some greater approximation of equal justice for the poor—equal significance as human beings and citizens— than has ever been achieved before. The lawyer's actions can be formidable in a number of arenas: substandard housing, retaliatory evictions, evictions without notice, unconscionable adhesion contracts, usurious loans, foreclosures and repossessions, irrational administrative agency action denying or terminating statutory benefits, invasions of privacy, anachronistic treatment of juveniles and, simply, economic force out of balance. These are facts of the lives of the poor—the city slum dweller, the mountaineer, the racial outcast—effects and causes of their destitution and the deprivation of that decency and dignity we find so casually in our daily lives. Lawyers can change this scene. They are already doing so in New York where the courts finally destroyed the odd administrative presumption, by which thousands had been denied public assistance, that a person coming to a city without employment must have come for the purpose of receiving welfare in violation of the statute. They are changing the scene in Washington, where a court ruled as valid a defense to a landlord's possessory action that the landlord's sole purpose for seeking the eviction was to punish the tenant for informing the government of unlawful housing conditions on the leased premises. In Oakland, where a lawyer stopped a campaign of unreasonable harassment by creditors and obtained a just settlement for a family of five under serious financial pressure, the family was then referred to another service of the community action agency for family and debt counselling.

This kind of service will become increasingly commonplace as more and more community action programs add the skills of lawyers to their arsenals. Perhaps the arsenals image suggests something which cannot be emphasized enough, that we are engaged in giving arms, not alms, to the poor. Service in thousands upon thousands of additional individual cases is of course inevitable. Certainly the individual client's case and his need must always be the focal point of the lawyer's work. Legal service in the context of the War on Poverty, however, must mean something more as well. Defending the poor against the evils from which lawyers regularly insulate the rest of us is only part of the job. Lawyers must excise the evils that prey on the poor—challenge that minority of disreputable and unethical businessmen until their values and their actions conform to the high standards of the remainder of the commercial community and pierce the complacency of those federal and state bureaucrats who administer benefit programs arbitrarily on the premise that what the statute calls a right is really only a privilege subject to their Olympian discretion. By educational efforts in schools, churches, and neighborhood groups, lawyers must speak a recognition in the low-income community that just because you are poor doesn't mean you aren't a human being or a citizen, doesn't mean that you haven't any rights, doesn't mean that your rights can be disregarded, doesn't mean that the law is, as Marx told us, the instrument of the landed gentry alone.

It is not that lawyers must now join the picket lines but simply that lawyers for the poor must do no less for their clients than does the corporation lawyer checking the Federal Trade Commission for sloppy rulemaking, the union lawyer asking Congress for repeal of 14(b), or the civil rights lawyer seeking an end to segregation in bus stations. The dormant meaning of unconscionability must obtain widespread recognition among merchants; the building code must be made a rule for landlords; the legislatures must be persuaded to end irregular presumptions governing the administration of public assistance. I speak of results with long-range significance for large numbers of people, not just individual service of limited impact.

If we are in agreement as to what has to be done, let me proceed to discuss how it is to be done. First, there is no standard national model promulgated by OEO for the offering of legal services to the poor. The *Guidelines for Legal Services Programs*[2] and the OEO booklet on how to apply for a grant[3] stress that local communities should use ingenuity and local initiative to design programs. Needs will obviously vary from locale to locale. Washington, DC has ten neighborhood law firms established with a full complement of thirty-five attorneys, but the OEO has also funded a one-attorney operation for harvest-season service to migratory workers in Ulysses, Kansas. The differences between urban and rural set-

[2]   OEO, Guidelines for Legal Services Programs (1966).
[3]   OEO, How to Apply for a Legal Services Program (1966).

tings obviously require variety in approach. The applications received reflect an understanding of this principle.

Most of the programs funded to date have been in cities and have followed, with some variations, the form adopted in part here in South Bend, the neighborhood law office. Although the neighborhood law office possesses the key characteristics of accessibility and visibility to the low-income community, it may not always be the most suitable vehicle for service. Accessibility to the low-income group is one key characteristic of the structure of a legal services program. There are numerous other important aspects of a program's form and substance which are examined with each application. The program should offer a full range of service, in every type of civil case for which a private attorney cannot be obtained, and the service should range from advice to trial and appeal. The poor must have the same kind and degree of legal help as the non-poor.

Eligibility standards should be set in terms of weekly or monthly income for an individual, with appropriate additions for each dependent. Such standards should be administered flexibly, with debts and assets considered in determining whether service can be offered. Persons just above the income eligibility standard should not be turned away if their total financial portrait makes it plain that counsel will be unobtainable elsewhere; conversely, persons below the standard should occasionally be referred to private sources when an ability to pay in fact exists.

Certain segments of the bar have felt threatened by the expansion of free legal assistance for the poor. It is not the object of this program to deprive practitioners of clients, however. It will provide assistance for a part of the population of which only a tiny fraction has ever been served before. If this program even approaches general success, it will inspire such an appreciation of law in the community that people moderately able but previously unwilling to employ a lawyer will do so—to the obvious benefit of the same lawyers who now perceive an economic threat.

I have spoken primarily about service being offered by full-time salaried lawyers. This system is preferable to the proposed alternatives for providing legal services to the poor, specifically, the so-called 'English system' or its variations. Under the English system a branch of the state or local government or some other organization certifies the indigency of a potential client, who may then consult the private attorney of his choice. The private attorney is then compensated, in whole or in part, directly by the government.

At first glance, such a system seems attractive. It would involve the whole bar. With only a relatively minor change in our present system of legal representation, it might permit more people to consult a lawyer. It would also make every lawyer in the community available to the poor, instead of the few practicing in the legal services office, giving clients a 'freedom of choice'. Finally, the lawyers who perform services for the poor are guaranteed payment, a virtue which needs no further explanation.

Despite these attractive features, there are several inescapable doubts. The cost of the English system, given the level of OEO funds available for legal services, seems prohibitively high. The OEO roughly estimates that free legal services would cost at least two to three times more under an English system than with salaried full-time lawyers. Another disadvantage of an English system is that the procedure for certifying indigency would probably be administered by another bureaucracy for the poor to combat. This might well cause many prospective clients to shy away. It is as important to the poor as to the bar that legal services are not regarded as just another arm of a welfare department. In addition, the procedure for certification is bound to conflict with the ability of lawyers to give, and clients to obtain, fast emergency legal assistance—the kind of help that is usually required in situations common to the poor, such as arrests, evictions, repossessions, and attachments.

The most important reason why full-time lawyers offer the best vehicle for rendering effective legal assistance to the poor is that they will provide the poor with the full scope of services that a lawyer renders in our society. The poor should have lawyers who will be able to devote the time, achieve the perspective, and accumulate the knowledge to attack the legal problems of the poor on a broad and deep scale. This is what lawyers do for other groups in our society. The law has been the instrument for orderly social change throughout our nation's history, and lawyers have always been more than mere agents directed by others. They have been the architects as well as the artisans of social reform—redesigning, reforming, and creating not only legal institutions but social, economic, and political institutions as well. Wearing a wide variety of hats in American life, lawyers are not only counselors to our large corporations, business councils and cooperatives, trade unions and suburban neighborhood improvement associations, but more often, policy-makers and strategists as well. Lawyers are our most effective public servants in all areas of government, in foundations, and in other institutional public service. Lawyers are our lobbyists. Lawyers are our legislators. Lawyers sat in more than sixty per cent of the seats of the Congress which passed the Economic Opportunity Act. In each of these functions, lawyers do more than handle a particular legal matter bounded by a particular isolated set of facts. They take the common threads of social, economic, and political problems affecting large groups of people and weave the test case, remedial statute, or administrative reform to solve the pervasive problems and eliminate the cause for the future.

Similarly, the poor must be represented on a broad and deep scale. An English system which parcels out the legal problems of the poor to lawyers—however dedicated to the resolution of the case at hand—will not so easily focus upon the issues, produce the research, and marshal the facts to give this kind of representation. Twenty lawyers selected by twenty poor clients on twenty different days to defend eviction notices may never realize that each eviction was in retaliation for the tenant's complaint of housing code violations and so may never solve the underlying problem and eliminate the cause of the repeated legal difficulties.

Some have cried that group representation and broad research looking to law reform—at least when done by attorneys in legal services programs—are sinister and a departure from the accepted role of lawyers. They call it 'social reform'. It is social reform in the sense that all changes in the law are social reform, and it is social reform in the sense in which lawyers have historically advocated and effected changes—reform in the law—for every interest or segment of our society except that of the poor.

The OEO will approve some limited English system grants, evaluate the costs and results, and assess their comparative success. It has received several such proposals already. I doubt that it will approve all of them, and there is little likelihood that any additional applications will be approved, except possibly in sparsely populated areas where there is no other feasible method to provide free legal assistance. My attitude about the English system is best described by the remark a judge once made about my argument before him: 'Mr Bamberger, I have an open mind about that point—but not necessarily an empty one'.

There is another aspect of representation of the poor for which the OEO looks in applications. Section 202 of the Economic Opportunity Act calls for the development and administration of community action programs 'with the maximum feasible participation of residents of the areas and members of the groups served'.[4] In the legal services setting this means participation of the poor or their representatives as members of a program's policy-making board as well as on closely related advisory committees. No fixed percentage of a board or committee is required;

[4] 78 Stat. 516 (1964), 42 USC § 2782(a)(3) (1964).

there must simply be meaningful representation—representation which will bring to the councils of charity voices angry with the failures of charity and which will produce a fruitful dialogue between groups that may have never talked to one another before. The agency should have a responsible, informed, and active governing body selected from the community as a whole, a majority of which should be practicing lawyers. The governing body should meet at regular intervals, at least quarterly. To the extent feasible and for the purpose of establishing community participation, representation of the areas covered and people served should be included on the agency's governing body or on a separate community advisory group.[5]

This principle of participation is not a conversation piece; it has been applied. Residents of the area and members of the groups to be served or their representatives constitute a significant proportion of the policy-making bodies of all legal services programs funded to date. The American Bar Association and the National Legal Aid and Defender Association have formally adopted the principle as a guide in the creation of legal aid society boards.

The poor are also participating at the employment level. New jobs, such as those of investigative aides, secretaries, and registrants, have been filled by community residents in legal services programs. The Missouri Bar Association has submitted a proposal for the training of legal technicians to provide attorneys with assistance analogous to that offered physicians by nurses and laboratory technicians. Participation here and at the policy-making level is more than therapeutic for the participants. It can add a positive contribution to the process of community education in the law—preventive legal education—which is another key aspect of every program. Participation can open new lines of communication to the low-income population.

Much of this article assumes a final major point of legal services development. To the maximum extent possible these services are to be coordinated with general community action agency activity in a given locale. 'Community action' under Title II of the Act means concerted action against all the features of poverty—from malnutrition and disease to limited education and employment skills—and it means interrelated action by many different disciplines. Thus, a legal services program, typically a delegate agency of the central organization, must make every effort to co-

[5] Standards and Practices for Civil Legal Aid, Adopted by the National Legal Aid and Defender Association Delegate Assembly, Nov. 19, 1965, and approved by the American Bar Association.

ordinate with other services being offered in the community. This effort presupposes no compromise of the traditional independence of lawyers. That independence must be preserved—indeed, this program would be useless without it. No program lawyer will suffer the direction of an outsider; the client is his, the service is his, the judgment must always be his. This independence will not be abandoned by cooperation with the multitude of other people in the community whose help the client may need.

The law is more than rules of rights and repressions. The law is a dynamic force for social change. Lawyers must be not only advocates for individuals trapped by poverty but also the articulate spokesmen for the fifth of our population which suffers from being poor—invisible, inarticulate, unrepresented, depressed, and despairing—living the emasculating contradiction of poverty in an affluent society.

It is not only the lack of money that makes a man poor. The shackles that bind to poverty are ignorance of rights, disregard of personal value as a human being, a sense of being abandoned, a conviction of despair as an object manipulated by a system. Lawyers committed to the finest traditions of the bar can speak for the inarticulate, can challenge the systems that generate the cycle of poverty, can arouse the persons of power and affluence. The OEO program marshals the forces of law and the power of lawyers in the War on Poverty to defeat the causes and effects of poverty.

3. The Scope of Legal Services

LEGAL ACTION GROUP

Legal aid in England and Wales remains dominated by the narrow frame-work in which it was originally conceived. Other jurisdictions, as we have seen, have developed a broader view. For instance, in the Australian state of Victoria, legal aid has been statutorily defined to mean not only 'any legal services that may be provided by a legal practitioner', but also 'education, advice and information in and about the law' and a range of other legal services specified in the legislation.[1] LAG argues for a similarly wide view of legal services in this country. The traditional concept of providing advice, assistance, and representation should be seen as only one element in publicly funded legal services. Along with the broadening of the definition, there is a need for greater planning in how those services are delivered.

The role of legal services

The unifying theme in legal services policy must be the acceptance of an overall objective against which success or failure can be measured. For LAG, that objective is the attainment of equal access to justice for all members of society. This firmly shifts the emphasis from the means by which publicly funded legal services are delivered to their intended result.

The addition of 'equal' to the usual 'access to justice' phrase is deliberate. The promotion of access to justice is now almost a cliché. The basic approach encouraged by its early academic promoters was to place legal services in the context of 'the full panoply of institutions, procedures and persons that characterise our judicial system'.[2] People excluded from justice not only need accessible lawyers but also accessible procedures, adjudication, and laws. Even the early proselytizers saw the potential problems: 'The risk is that the use of rapid procedures and inexpensive

---

[1] S. 2 Legal Aid Commission Act 1981 (Vic).
[2] M. Cappelletti and B. Garth, *Access to Justice: a world survey* Sitjhoff and Noordhoff, 1978, Vol. 1, p. 49.

personnel will produce cheap and unrefined products. This risk must be kept continually in mind.'[3]

The risk was real. The language of 'access to justice' has been eagerly taken up by governments wishing to save money on publicly funded legal services. For instance, the final report of the Civil Justice Review in 1988 contained a chapter entitled 'Access to Justice', but made only one general recommendation about legal aid: 'As a matter of priority the Legal Aid Board should take early action to reduce the time taken to handle applications for civil legal aid.'[4] Yet its main proposal was for greater devolution of cases throughout the court system from High to county court and from the county court to the small claims procedure. Such moves have profound legal aid implications. The report omitted to consider, or even mention, the consequence that legal aid would no longer be available for those cases deemed suitable for transfer to the small claims procedure. Only subsequently was there any recognition that personal injury cases can pose severe difficulties for litigants without representation.

The ultimate policy aim must be that anyone with a legal problem has equal access to its just conclusion so that disputes are determined by the intrinsic merits of the arguments of either party, not by inequalities of wealth or power. To achieve this, legal aid policy alone provides too narrow a focus. It is necessary to consider a more comprehensive range of policies relating to the totality of publicly funded legal services. We have called this the 'legal services approach'.

The legal services approach provides three means by which equal access to justice may be attained. In addition to the provision of advice, assistance, and representation (defined as the statutory goals of legal aid in the Legal Aid Act 1988), it stresses the importance of both education and information and the reform of law and procedure.

For twenty years LAG has been critical of the lack of strategic planning in relation to legal services. In its evidence to the Royal Commission on Legal Services in 1977 the Group repeated its concern that 'there is no national policy for the provision of publicly financed legal services'.[5] This remains the case today. Legal aid rates of eligibility and remuneration are, it is true, set nationally. However, their levels lack any logic and the actual provision of services is determined by the vagaries of market forces on individual practitioners. Similarly, the distribution of law centres and

---

[3] Ibid., p. 124.

[4] Civil Justice Review *Report of the Review Body on Civil Justice* Cm 394, HMSO, 1988, recommendation 56, p. 159.

[5] Legal Action Group *Legal Services: a blueprint for the future* LAG, 1977, p. 4.

advice agencies is independent of any national assessment of need, depending instead on the varying attitudes and financial health of local authorities. We now consider the principles that should underlie the provision of all publicly funded legal services.

Education and information

Equal access to justice requires all members of society to be aware of their rights and obligations. Acceptance of an educational role for publicly funded legal services is closely linked to the currently fashionable idea of 'citizenship'. The British are, in law, more subjects of the Crown than citizens of the country. British citizenship is so legally insubstantial that it does not even give an automatic right of residence. What is required is a fundamental transformation in the status of all members of British society, whereby they will be able to exercise real rights.

Vital to this process is knowledge of the law. This is as true in relation to general provisions of the law as it is to the consumer rights which have been the focus of a range of current citizenship initiatives.

The need for information in relation to the rights and obligations of citizens has been stressed by many commentators. The Speaker's Commission on Citizenship recommended 'a review and codification of the law relating to legal rights, duties and entitlements of the citizen in the United Kingdom and the dissemination of this information in a clear way to all citizens', and urged 'the Lord Chancellor to invite the government and other appropriate individuals and institutions to consult on the best way of ensuring these objectives'.[6]

The government's commitment to citizenship carries a similar emphasis: 'openness', 'information', and 'accessibility' are key elements of the 'principles of public service' in its Citizen's Charter.[7] These are as relevant for legal services as for public services; indeed, much of the government's description of basic principle is directly transferable. For instance, just as 'full, accurate information should be readily available, in plain language' on the public services that the citizen may choose to use, so it should be on the law that imposes on a citizen.

The Legal Aid Board and, before it, the Law Society have accepted responsibility for some measure of information about legal aid. The Legal Aid Act 1988 gives the board specific power 'to promote or assist in the

[6] Commission on Citizenship *Encouraging Citizenship* HMSO, 1990, recommendation 10, p. xix.
[7] *Citizen's Charter* HMSO, 1991, p. 5.

promotion of publicity'.[8] Although the board has produced a very good range of leaflets and forms, its commitment to advertising has, over time, been uneven. In fact, it was recently critized for its lack of adequate publicity in a National Audit Office report. The statutory power should be converted into a positive duty to inform those likely to be eligible of the services available to them. Furthermore, the effectiveness with which this duty is carried out should be monitored by annual surveys of the target population.

The adoption of a legal services approach entails, however, a much wider commitment to education and information than simply more advertising for legal aid. Such a commitment can be seen in the examples of education work undertaken by the *Commission des Services Juridiques* in Quebec and by the Australian legal aid commissions. Furthermore, the Office of Fair Trading, with a range of clear and attractive material on the subject of consumer rights, provides a domestic example of what can be done. There needs to be an institution which takes on a similar role in relation to the rights of citizens more generally, a function widely known abroad as 'public legal education'. Such a responsibility might extend as far as encouraging legal education in school. Some work in this field has already been done: the Law Society established an imaginative 'Law in schools' project which has now been taken over by the Citizenship Foundation. The Legal Aid Board is ideally placed to take on this public legal education function.

This sort of initiative ought to be encouraged if a commitment to citizenship by government is to have any real meaning. The very act of establishing a national body with an express responsibility for legal education and awareness would be a catalyst to further development. Such a project could have a considerable effect without a very large budget. Developments like the 'Courtguide' programme in New South Wales even offer the potential to save money, at least in terms of court and tribunal staff time. Using interactive technology—whereby a clip of film can be shown as the answer to a question—it is possible to guide people undertaking their own cases through courts and tribunals.

Within a legal services approach, education can also provide an alternative method of dealing with people's problems. Some of the Australian legal aid commissions, for instance, provide classes for women going through divorce or seeking child support, deliberately substituting a 'do-it-yourself' approach within an educational framework for traditional

---

[8] S. 4(2)(e) Legal Aid Act 1988.

lawyer–client casework. Some clients might actually prefer this alternative, as it may be a less isolating experience. The same might be true for those seeking advice on debt. With money saved in legal aid costs, such classes could be offered to all on a non-fee paying basis.

Another example is already provided by law centres. They, and their equivalents in other jurisdictions, have developed a variety of imaginative educational approaches in order to help people facing a common problem work towards a common solution. This is often known as community action or community work. It is, however, perhaps best described by the phrase 'community legal education'.

Law reform

Law reform, to a British observer, may not seem an immediately obvious aim for publicly funded legal services. It is, in fact, crucial for the following reasons.

First, a legal services approach requires consideration of what services are to be provided within the context of the reform of law and procedure. The divorce reforms proposed in 1976, which removed the need for court hearings in undefended divorces and thereby shifted the balance of legal aid expenditure, stand as a model of what can be done. In contrast, an integrated consideration of legal procedure and legal aid was lacking from the Civil Justice Review, the Legal Aid Board's multi-party action proposals and the Lord Chancellor's Department suggestion for a 'safety net' system for civil legal aid. Compartmentalizing discussions on legal aid and on court procedures does not allow for the development of coherent, integrated policies.

Mechanisms must be developed whereby proposals to reform law and procedure are accompanied by a consideration of the likely effects—either negative or positive: what legal services will need to be provided and what their cost will be. In Australia, for instance, proposed commonwealth legislation is accompanied by a 'legal aid impact statement' to encourage this approach. Such a requirement should be introduced in this country.

Second, it must be recognized that traditional forms of litigation taken by individuals are not always the best way of handling disputes. There are various alternatives: some cases can be removed from the courts and resolved by alternative means, such as by tribunals or through conciliation; certain disputes require the development of collective procedures, such as multi-party personal injury litigation, and some rights may be better enforced through third parties, such as the Health and Safety Executive or the Commission for Racial Equality.

Third, it follows that the Legal Aid Board, or any future administrator of publicly funded legal services, should play a much larger role in promoting the links between legal services, substantive law, and procedure. The board cannot function properly within a remit confined to legal aid. Its limited approach to multi-party actions made this very apparent. Yet the problems in the Opren case illustrate just how much these issues of law and procedure need tackling.

The board should both initiate, and respond to, proposals for law reform—for instance, by making published submissions to suggestions for reform from the Law Commission. This would introduce the legal services approach into public debate. Current concern about the overall level of legal aid expenditure, which is largely determined by the cost of criminal cases, provides an example of what is required. A narrow approach to this problem has led the government to advocate fixed fees for solicitors in magistrates' courts, to keep down unit costs. This may curtail the rise in expenditure, but the effect is likely to be relatively marginal. A proper solution requires consideration of whether so many cases need to be brought before the court in the first place, and whether magistrates need such extensive powers of imprisonment. Either or both might allow savings to the legal aid budget, but they require a far more integrated approach to reform than seems possible under the present circumstances.

Fourth, the contribution that experienced legal aid practitioners could make to law reform should be recognized. The remit of publicly funded legal services should include an aim similar to that of the CAB service: to 'exercise a responsible influence on the development of social policies and services, both locally and nationally'. This role for the CABx was explicitly accepted by a government-sponsored review in 1984: 'Not only do we think that such exercises are proper and useful, but that the CAB Service would be open to criticism if it did not undertake them.'[9]

The Legal Aid Board should foster ways in which the practitioners it funds could contribute, as legal aid providers rather than as Law Society members, to responsible policy discussion. An obvious method would be to fund groups of practitioners in particular fields, such as criminal defence, so that they could put forward distinctive views on how the system of justice might be improved. In furtherance of this approach, the Board should take over the functions of the Lord Chancellor's Advisory Committee of Legal Aid, as a stimulator of debate within and outside government.

[9] *Review of the National Association of Citizens Advice Bureaux* (the 'Lovelock report'), 1984, Cmnd 9139, para. 6.3.

Advice, assistance, and representation

It is fundamental to a legal services approach that legal aid should be seen as only one component in a broad range of provision. A comprehensive view of legal services must include all legal advice, assistance, and representation, ranging from preliminary advice with a legal component provided by agencies like the CABx to the specialized advocacy services of Queen's Counsel. A more integrated approach, where such functions are not looked at, or funded, completely separately, is essential to LAG's model of how publicly funded legal services should be delivered.

Furthermore, the definition of representation needs to be expanded. Legal aid has been dominated by the need for services related to litigation. A committee of the Canadian Bar Association showed itself open to a broader approach: ' "Legal services" need not be narrowed to standard litigation orientated services. For the private client, the lawyer offers the full range of advocacy on behalf of his or her client, not just individual representation before the courts, but also preventive legal advice, non-adversarial representation, representation before tribunals, client legal education, formal and informal efforts to change laws affecting clients. If legal aid plans have an avowed goal of providing equal access to legal services for their clients, then they too should obtain the benefit of the full range of a lawyer's services, constrained only by the demands of the client's case.'[10]

Publicly funded legal services must be made accessible to those that need them. The Legal Aid Board must be responsible for planning where and how services are to be delivered. There must also be a coherent policy in relation to eligibility, constructed upon a set of clearly expressed principles. In LAG's view, the form of provision should reflect several important considerations.

First, there should be a tier of publicly funded legal services to provide immediate diagnostic advice and information. This should be free to any enquirer and highly accessible. The traditional perception of this frontline function as separate from 'proper' legal services is unhelpful. The need for such general advice services must be recognized as national; though how that need is met may vary around the country. Advice agencies may continue to have other functions, but their basic role is to be an information and referral point on which much of the edifice of publicly funded legal services is based.

Second, some areas of legal need should be given priority and assistance

[10] National Legal Aid Liaison Committee of the Canadian Bar Association *Legal Aid Delivery Models: a discussion paper* 1987, p. 181.

with them should be free of charge, regardless of means. LAG has long argued that some services must be regarded as essential and delivered on this basis, though tests of sufficient merit may be retained. In 1986 we listed these as including services that deal with 'disputes over residential accommodation, settlement of disputes about custody of children, compensation of those suffering bodily injury, protection of persons in fear of attack and assault, protection against dismissal or exclusion from employment or occupation, defence of persons accused of any crime punishable by imprisonment, protection against wrongful imprisonment, and protection of rights of entry and residence in the United Kingdom'.

The Government has made some recent moves towards its own prioritization: legal aid is available without a means test in relation to certain disputes about children, and advice in the police station is also seen as sufficiently important to be given without charge.

LAG stands by its concept of 'essential legal services' meriting free provision, though recognizing both that attainment of this is a long-term goal and that, in practice, the detail of the list of essential services is open to discussion.

Third, greater priority must be given to the field of social welfare law, including providing representation at tribunals. At present, legal services in this area are inadequate. A number of the matters in LAG's list of essential services relate to landlord and tenant, immigration, and employment law. Immigration and employment are also areas of law in which the lack of tribunal representation clearly puts people at a disadvantage. Representation by specialists in the relevant area of law and procedure— who may not themselves need to be qualified lawyers, but should have easy access to them—must be made available.

Legal aid, as currently conceived, is not well suited to deliver such a service. For instance, the statutory charge is generally inappropriate in tribunal proceedings: costs are not usually available from the losing side in tribunal cases, so that the expense cannot be offset in the same way as is possible in court-based litigation. In any event, expertise in social welfare law has been fostered by law centres and advice agencies, and should be built upon. Such bodies already deliver free services. Clients in landlord and tenant cases, employment, immigration, debt, and social security cases are, on the whole, sufficiently likely to be poor as to merit the withdrawal of an individual means test (relatively wealthy people with problems in these areas are likely to consult private solicitors). Financial eligibility can, therefore, be defined by subject matter rather than by the means of individual clients.

4. From 'The Distribution of Legal Services in the Netherlands'

JOHN GRIFFITHS*

This extract is taken from a book review, in which John Griffiths discusses a major empirical investigation of legal services in the Netherlands carried out by K. Schuyt, K. Groenendijk, and B. Sloot and published as *De Weg Naar Het Recht* (The Road to Justice) (Deventer: Kluwer 1976). The study found that the more money a person had, the more likely they were to use a lawyer, and the authors argued strongly for an improved legal aid scheme. Griffiths summarizes the book's main findings and policy implications. At the end, however, he takes the authors to task for not considering *why* the state should intervene to provide a more equal distribution of legal services to its citizens.

What is missing from most discussions of the redistribution of legal services is any serious confrontation with the most basic question of all: *why* should there be intervention to secure redistribution? I certainly do not want to be taken as arguing against such intervention, but I do regard the matter as a good deal more problematic than seems usually to be assumed. Unequal distribution of various goods, when associated with other important kinds of inequality (especially wealth), seems often to be regarded as calling, in and of itself, for redistributive intervention. For me, the connection between fact and policy is more complex than that.

This and other studies abundantly demonstrate that the distribution of legal services varies with the distribution of wealth. Very well, one might say, let us intervene to redistribute wealth and the distribution of legal services will take care of itself. One might even regard concentration upon the latter symptom as obscurantist—distracting attention and energy from the disease itself. One might also ask: do the poor prefer intervention in the form of specific services or might they prefer cash (and the consequent freedom of choice which the rich presently enjoy)? One should also wonder whether the inequalities associated with unequal distribution of wealth will not reappear, in different forms, despite redistrib-

* Professor of Sociology of Law, University of Groningen.

utive efforts directed at an effect (distribution of legal services) instead of at a cause (distribution of wealth).

I can think of only four basic sorts of argument for intervention to redistribute legal services:

1. Legal services *are* a kind of wealth, so giving them to the poor *is* redistribution of wealth. True, but giving the poor cash seems more sensible (from the point of view of freedom and of efficiency) in all but one state of affairs: the existence of a pool of otherwise unemployable legal professionals, whose services the state can give to the poor for not much more than it costs to maintain them on public assistance. In that case alone, one might concede that it makes sense to kill two birds with one stone (redistribution of wealth to the poor as well as fulfilment of welfare obligations). It is interesting that one offhand argument made by Schuyt *et al.*, in favour of intervention in the distribution of legal services is that it will reduce the number of unemployed lawyers.[1]

2. Legal services are a merit-good, one which is good for people even if they don't have the sense to buy it for themselves (in a class with culture, knowledge, health, etc.) Redistribution of legal services, independently of redistribution of wealth, is desirable because it ensures that the poor get what is good for them, not merely what they would pay for. This argument is perhaps slightly less patronizing if to it is added the supposition that it is ignorance, lack of 'competence', or the like which keep some people from buying what they otherwise would: the present book is rife with suggestions to that effect.

Why, however, is it assumed that legal services are a merit-good? That idea is associated with a certain legalist ideal of the good citizen (and the good of the citizen), in which emphasis is put upon knowing and asserting one's *legal rights*. It is good for people to insist upon, and to vindicate, those rights. All sorts of words can be used to express this value: one can speak of autonomy, self-respect, dignity and the like. But it all comes

---

[1] The authors pay, on this and other points, too little attention to various latent functions of legal assistance programs. Jobs for unemployed lawyers are not unimportant. Nor is taking the *pro bono* pressure off the private practice Bar at public expense. Among the most prominently mentioned considerations in support of the Law of 1957 was the necessity to lighten the burden of non-paying cases being borne by the Bar. It is no accident that the Bar has, on the whole, been receptive to legal assistance programs, so long as they do not draw away potential paying clients. The tolerant attitude of the Dutch Bar to the advent of such phenomena as the 'law shops' seems to me better explained as enlightened self-interest than as enlightenment *per se*. Fundraisers for various legal services organizations in the United States prey upon the *pro bono* vulnerability of large law firms in seeking to exact contributions from them; one hears that the strategy is successful.

down to a vision of a social order in which social relationships are carried on according to legal rules. I don't find anything intuitively attractive about such a conception of the good society. I find myself particularly suspicious when I notice that this kind of merit-good approach to the distribution of legal services comes mostly from the mouths and pens of lawyers, who naturally tend to exaggerate the actual importance and the value of legalism in social relationships. Legalism is an important social *variable*, to be sure, but I am unconvinced that it is always and everywhere an unqualified *value*.

The present authors more or less implicitly disagree. They insist that what is to be redistributed is the specifically '*adversary*' kind of service which legal assistants are supposed to render, not the less formal, less rule-bound, and less partisan help of a social worker or the like. They expect that with an increase and wider distribution of legal services will come an increased legalization of relationships, and they apparently regard this as desirable. Indeed, they apparently regard legalism as synonymous with law. What is missing from their analysis is any critical reflection upon legalism, its causes and effects, its desirable and undesirable aspects, and its connection (which is perhaps not a *necessary* one) with the redistribution of legal services. In all of this they merely reflect a default which is general in the literature on the subject of legal services.

Not only is the value of legalism an undiscussed premise of much of what the authors write, but attorneys seem often, in their book, to be the only persons capable of delivering that value. There is, on this point, an acute ambivalence throughout the book. On one hand, the authors explore, as we have seen, the range of kinds of assistance that are in fact used by persons who think they have a 'legal problem'—from self help, through specifically legal agencies, to attorneys in the narrow sense. They approve of this variegated state of affairs. They expressly approve of self-help, and consider increase in the capacity for self-help an important focus of political action. Within the sphere of legal assistance more narrowly conceived (restricted to specifically legal agencies), the authors insist that the existing pluriformity be maintained. Nowhere, when policy is being considered, do the authors suggest that legal assistance should be the preserve of attorneys. On the other hand, in their empirical investigation of the existing state of affairs, and especially in their analysis of the distribution of legal services, the focus of attention narrows drastically and inexplicably: most of the time, it is only attorneys (in the narrow sense) who occupy the authors' attention. Thus, in their definition of 'legal problem', there is first a built-in bias toward the sort of problems for which legal assistance is sought, since 'problem-laden' situations are considered by the authors to involve 'legal problems' only in such cases (and not when self-help is used). Second, there is a further built-in bias toward the sort of help that attorneys give, by contrast with that given by notaries: divorces are treated as 'problem-laden', while real estate transactions and the making of wills are not, although the two situations seem on the surface practically identical.[2] In the presentation of their data on contacts with legal services, the authors include only specifically legal agencies; they focus among these very heavily on attorneys (e.g., in correlating income and wealth with legal contacts) and they nowhere discuss the distribution of the *sum* of legal services (let alone those, plus para-legal services, plus non-legal help, plus self-help). To an unfortunately large extent, therefore, their book really only considers the distribution of *attorneys'* services, not legal services more generally, and gives almost no systematic attention to the distribution (by wealth, among other things) of the *totality* of possible sources of help available to those with 'legal problems'. Given the fact, which their book richly demonstrates, that attorneys constitute but a limited part of the total picture, I do not believe that either satisfactory empirical understanding of the distribution of legal services, or sound political policy concerning the redistribution of legal services, can emerge from such a one-sided emphasis on attorneys.

In short, if I think there is room for scepticism about the idea that legalism is desirable, I think there is even more room for scepticism about the idea that the help of attorneys and other specifically legal assistants in dealing with 'legal problems' is desirable in itself. I remain, therefore, dubious about the merit-good approach to the redistribution of legal services.

3. Legal services are a potential instrument for social change, and if redistributed toward the poor will help to secure an ultimate redistribution of wealth in their favour. The authors are, in my opinion, quite right to be sceptical about this argument for the redistribution of legal services.

---

[2] The assistance of an attorney is legally required in the first case, that of a notary in the second. The authors believe that divorce cases more frequently escalate—but they seem to have only their lawyers' intuitions to go on, and even if they are right they cannot know whether it is not the nature of attorneys' help, rather than the nature of clients' problems, that makes the difference.

The author's built-in bias toward the sort of problems which lawyers have traditionally handled is typical of the legal 'need' (or 'access') literature.

[3] Early Legal Aid reformers in the United States saw themselves as staving off the Bolsheviks. (Page 15, citing J. S. Auerbach, *Unequal Justice* (1976 Oxford U.P., New York), 61.) It has also been supposed that there is a connection between civic violence and lack of legal assistance. (Page 339, citing S. A. Scheingold, *The Politics of Rights* (1974 Yale U.P., New Haven), 207 and 218.)

It rests, so far as I know, on little more than the naïve faith of lawyers in the importance of what they do. I take with similar scepticism the supposition of both revolutionaries and conservatives that redistribution of legal services is counter-revolutionary.[3]

4. More widespread use of legal services is required in the name of a public good: justice. If you want soap you can buy it or have it made, pretty much regardless of whether anyone else does too; within limits imposed by the costs of transacting, you can buy clean air if you want it (by bargaining jointly with like-minded neighbours to bribe your local air polluter to stop). Even military defense could, in the abstraction of theory, be organized in the same way; it is only high transaction costs (especially the problem of 'free-loading') which make defense a 'collective good' and justify (supposedly) coerced participation in its purchase.[4] A 'just' legal system is, by contrast, a *purely* 'public good': it could not, even in theory, be purchased by individuals acting on their own or in concert. The problem is not that 'free-loaders' are difficult to exclude from the benefits of justice, but that they, too, must be treated justly by a just legal system. Justice requires us to treat people justly whether they value justice or not. There is no way to reduce the value of justice to the sum of individual decisions to purchase a bit of it. It is an attribute of the way *we* (as society) treat people, not a matter of what is good for (or *a* good for) them. Because justice is a property of the behaviour of a public, decisions about what is necessary in its name *must* be public decisions.

The 'public good' argument for redistributing legal services, then, is not that they are a form of wealth, not that they are good for people, not that social change will result from redistributing them, but rather that the just operation of the legal system demands a more equal distribution of the use of facilities collectively believed to be important to the realization of legal entitlements and protections. If we, as a society, are to treat people justly in their dealings with *our* legal system, they must have legal assistance (or at least have it available to them free from various sorts of obstacles such as cost)—whether *they* want it (or want it free) or not. If we

---

[4] Cf., for the elements of the argument sketched here, M. Olson, *The Logic of Collective Action* (1965 Harvard UP, Cambridge); Coase, 'The Problem of Social Cost' (1960) 3 *J. Law and Econ.* 1; Calabresi, 'Transaction Costs, Resource Allocation and Liability Rules—a Comment' (1968) 11 *J. Law and Econ.* 67. In general, I follow Olson's analysis, except that the distinction between individual and collective goods seems to me, in light of Coase' and Calabresi's analysis of transaction costs, to be a continuum rather than the disjunction which Olson supposes. The concept of a purely 'public' good, not reducible to a sum of individual goods which cannot practically be attained without public action only because of transaction costs, is my own.

don't like legalism the solution is to reduce it—but so long as it character-izes our legal system, that system (if it is to be a just one) must afford to everyone a fair opportunity to deal with it, and that entails the help of lawyers.

There are fragments and suggestions of an argument along these lines in the present book, for example, in its insistence on the importance of the (asserted) fact that individuals increasingly confront organized oppo-nents, not other individuals, in their legal dealings; but on the whole the authors' argument for redistribution proceeds from the standpoint of what the individual wants or ought to want. It would be very difficult to justify redistribution in those terms, I believe.[5]

In short, is there the 'gap' in legal services which the authors suppose? I do not think that any of their political argument establishes that there is. Given their preference for pluriformity and their acknowledgement of the importance of self-help, and my additional observation that resignation is frequently good social and personal policy and should be encouraged, I cannot see that they have argued convincingly that their ideal is not now being realized: cases may now be going to the very sorts of legal assis-tance (from resignation and self-help, through 'law shops', and up to attorneys) to which, according to the authors, they ought to go. A policy of pluriformity demands, as a basis for further intervention, an explicit argument for a *different pattern* of solutions from that which now takes place. It would have to be a rather subtle argument to be convincing, con-fronting above all the sociological and philosophical complexities of the role of legalism in modern society, by way of persuading the reader that if public intervention is called for, it should take the form of *legal* services. This the authors have not done. While I admire their research, and while I happen to agree with the political lessons they draw from it, I am disap-pointed by their political argument: because I see nothing in it which would tend to persuade the unconverted.

---

[5] The four kinds of arguments for redistribution set out here are, of course, only sketches of possible arguments for the redistribution of legal services. Each of them introduces prob-lematic elements requiring further consideration. Nor are they as separable from each other as my treatment suggests. But my purpose here has been a limited one: primarily, just to canvass the range of possible types of arguments for redistribution and to note the essential characteristics of each type. Although my own view is that only the argument from justice is likely ultimately to be a persuasive one, evaluation of their strengths is less important here than typology.

PART TWO: THE DEVELOPMENT OF LEGAL AID

It would be idle to establish a system whereby every person upon whom a County Court plaint was served had access to free legal assistance. The result would be, amongst other things, to render the whole business of the Court so cumbrous and expensive that the credit system would break down . . .

. . . the wise man does not have recourse to litigation, either in attack or in defence, except as a last resort and it is desirable in the interests of the State that the path to litigation, while not encumbered with unnecessary expense or delay, should not be so smoothed and eased that litigation can be made an instrument of oppression. It may as easily become such an instrument in the hands of the poor as of the rich. Indeed more so, for the rich man who is quarrelsome and litigious knows that he goes to his warfare at his own risk. The poor man, if excused court fees and fees for counsel and solicitor, is at no such risk and his operations may bring ruin upon persons who, though not technically poor, are in no position to stand prolonged and costly litigation.

Sir Claud Schuster, Permanent Secretary to the Lord Chancellor, giving written evidence to the Finlay Committee on Legal Aid for the Poor, 1925.

The object of the [legal aid] scheme is to provide assistance in a more effective form in the conduct of civil proceedings and legal advice for those of slender means and resources, so that no one will be financially unable to prosecute a just and reasonable claim or defend a legal right, and to allow counsel and solicitors to be remunerated for their services.

Legal Aid and Advice Bill 1948: Summary of the Proposed New Service, Cmd 7563, HMSO, London, November 1948.

The 1949 Act, while based on a recognition that legal services should be more widely available, was, as we have seen, conservative in style. Its approach was that the state should pay towards the legal costs of all who, according to accepted notions, need a lawyer, cannot afford him, and ask for assistance. It assumed that the traditional private structure of the profession was adequate in composition, training, attitudes and customs to provide legal services to the poorest and worst educated sections of the community, and that the individual would initiate proceedings where he has need of legal aid or advice under the scheme. Such a system was bound to work ineffectively where the individual did not succeed in identifying his own need for a lawyer because of ignorance, or did not seek a lawyer's help because of despair or fear, or could not find a lawyer because few worked in his neighbourhood or were not available after his working day had ended; or did not get a lawyer who was truly competent to advise him on his particular problem.

Society of Labour Lawyers, *Justice for All*, Fabian Research Pamphlet 273, 1968.

5. From 'Access to Justice: The Worldwide Movement to Make Rights Effective'

MAURO CAPPELLETTI and BRYANT GARTH

No aspect of our modern legal systems is immune from criticism. Increasingly it is asked how, at what price, and for whose benefit, do these systems really work; and this type of fundamental question, already discomforting to many lawyers, judges, and legal scholars, is made all the more unsettling by an unprecedented invasion into the legal profession's traditional preserve by, among others, sociologists, anthropologists, economists, political scientists, and psychologists. We must not, however, resist our invaders; rather, we must respect their insights and respond to them creatively. By revealing the actual workings of our legal systems, critics in the social sciences can in fact be our allies in the most recent phase of a long historical battle—the struggle for 'access to justice'. It is this struggle, as reflected in modern legal systems,.that is the basic focus of this General Report and the comparative Access to Justice Project which produced it.

The words 'access to justice' are admittedly not easily defined, but they serve to focus on two basic purposes of the legal system—the system by which people may vindicate their rights and/or resolve their disputes under the general auspices of the state. First, the system must be equally accessible to all, and second, it must lead to results that are individually and socially just. Our focus here will be primarily on the first component, access, but we will necessarily bear in mind the second. Indeed, a basic premise will be that social justice, as sought by our modern societies, *presupposes* effective access.

The task in this Report is to trace the emergence and development of a new and comprehensive approach to access problems in contemporary societies. This approach, it will be seen, goes much beyond the earlier ones. Originating, perhaps, in the breakdown of the traditional faith in the soundness of our legal institutions, and inspired by the desire to make the rights of ordinary people real, and not merely symbolic, it calls for far-reaching reforms and for new creativity. It refuses to accept as immutable any of the procedures and institutions that characterize our machinery of justice. Reformers, in fact, have already accomplished much with this approach. Their basic accomplishments, ideas, and proposals, as well as the risks and limits of this necessary but daring method of legal reform, are discussed in this Report.

The changing theoretical conception of access to justice

The concept of access to justice has been undergoing an important transformation, corresponding to a comparable change in civil procedural scholarship and teaching. In the liberal, 'bourgeois' states of the late eighteenth and nineteenth centuries, the procedures for civil litigation reflected the essentially individualistic philosophy of rights then prevailing. A right of access to judicial protection meant essentially the aggrieved individual's *formal* right to litigate or defend a claim. The theory was that, while access to justice may have been a 'natural right', natural rights did not require affirmative state action for their protection.[1] These rights were considered prior to the state; their preservation required only that the state did not allow them to be infringed by others. The state thus remained passive with respect to such problems as the ability, *in practice*, of a party to recognize his legal rights and to prosecute or defend them adequately.

Relieving 'legal poverty'—the incapacity of many people to make full use of the law and its institutions—was not the concern of the state. Justice, like other commodities in the *laissez-faire* system, could be purchased only by those who could afford its costs, and those who could not were considered the only ones responsible for their fate. Formal, not effective, access to justice—formal, not effective, equality—was all that was sought.

Until recent years, with rare exceptions, legal scholarship was similarly unconcerned with the realities of the judicial system: 'Such factors as differences among potential litigants in practical access to the system or in the availability of litigating resources were not even perceived as problems.'[2] Scholarship was typically formalistic, dogmatic, and aloof from the real problems of civil justice. Its concern was frequently one of mere exegesis or abstract system-building; even when it went beyond this concern,

---

[1] For a more detailed treatment of this theme, see Cappelletti, 'General Report', in *Fundamental Guarantees of the Parties in Civil Litigation* 659, 726–40 (Milan/Dobbs Ferry, NY, Giuffrè/Oceana, M. Cappelletti and D. Tallon eds. 1973).

[2] Chayes, 'The Role of the Judge in Public Law Litigation', 89 Har. L. Rev. 1041, 1048 (1976).

its method was to judge the *rules* or procedure on the basis of historical validity and their operation in hypothetical situations. Reforms were suggested on the basis of this theory of procedure, rather than on actual experience. Scholarship, like the court system itself, was removed from the real concerns of most people.

As the *laissez-faire* societies grew in size and complexity, the concept of human rights began to undergo a radical transformation. Since actions and relationships increasingly assumed a collective rather than an individual character, modern societies necessarily moved beyond the individualistic, *laissez-faire* view of rights reflected in eighteenth- and nineteenth-century bills of rights. The movement has been toward recognizing the *social rights and duties* of governments, communities, associations, and individuals.[3] These new human rights, exemplified by the Preamble of the French Constitution of 1946, are above all those necessary to make *effective*, *i.e., actually accessible to all*, the rights proclaimed earlier.[4] Among such rights typically affirmed in modern constitutions are the rights to work, to health, to material security, and to education.[5] It has become commonplace to observe that *affirmative* action by the state is necessary to ensure the enjoyment by all of these basic social rights.[6] It is therefore not surprising that the right of effective access to justice has gained particular attention as recent 'welfare state' reforms have increasingly sought to arm individuals with new substantive rights in their capacities as consumers, tenants, employees, and even citizens.[7] Indeed, the right of effective access is increasingly recognized as being of paramount

[3] See, e.g., M. Cappelletti, *Processo e Ideologie* 511–24 (Bologna, Il Mulino, 1969); L. Scarman, *English Law—The New Dimension* 28–50 (London, Stevens and Sons, 1975); Häberle, 'Grundrechte im Leistungsstaat', in 30 *Veröffentlichungen der Deutschen Staatsrechtslehrer* 76, 90, 99 (Berlin/NY, de Gruyter, 1972).

[4] The Preamble of the French Constitution of 1946, which was explicitly incorporated in the Preamble of the present Constitution of 1958, acknowledges that the addition of new 'social' and 'economic' rights to the traditional civil rights is 'particularly necessary in our time'. See also, e.g., art. 3 para. 2 of the Italian Constitution of 1948; arts. 20, 28 of the Fundamental Law of the Federal Republic of Germany (*Grundgesetz*).

[5] See, e.g., the Preamble of the French Constitution of 1946.

[6] See, e.g., P. Calamandrei, 3 *Opere Giuridiche* 183–210 (Naples, Morano, M. Cappelletti ed. 1968); and Claude, 'The Classical Model of Human Rights Development', in Comparative Human Rights 6, 32 (Baltimore, Johns Hopkins University Press, R. Claude ed. 1976), stating that 'positive rights generally presuppose an affirmative commitment from the state'.

[7] Probably the first explicit recognition of the duty of the state to insure equal access to justice (at least once the parties were in court) came with the Austrian Code of 1895 and its provision of an active judge to equalize the parties. See Cappelletti, 'Social and Political Aspects of Civil Procedure—Reforms and Trends in Western and Eastern Europe', 69 Mich. L. Rev. 847, 854–5 and n. 38 (1971).

importance among the new individual and social rights, since the possession of rights is meaningless without mechanisms for their effective vindication.[8] Effective access to justice can thus be seen as the most basic
requirement—the most basic 'human right'—of a modern, egalitarian
legal system which purports to guarantee, and not merely proclaim, the
legal rights of all.

The focus on access—the means by which rights are made effective—
now also increasingly characterizes modern civil procedural scholarship.
Theoretical discussion, for example, of the various rules of civil procedure
and how they can be manipulated in various hypothetical situations, can
be instructive, but hidden within such neutral descriptions is the frequently unrealistic model of two (or more) equal sides in court, limited
only by the legal arguments that the skilled advocates can muster.
Procedure, however, should not be placed in a vacuum. Scholars must
now recognize that procedural techniques serve social functions,[9] that
courts are not the only means of dispute resolution that must be considered,[10] and that every procedural regulation, including the creation or
encouragement of alternatives to the formal court system, has a pronounced effect on how the substantive law operates—how often it is
enforced, in whose benefit, and with what social impact. A basic task of
modern civil procedure scholars is to expose the substantive impact of
various dispute processing mechanisms. They must, therefore, broaden
their focus beyond simply the courts; they must utilize the insights of
sociological, political, psychological, economic, and other analyses; and

More recently, a modern trend has been to develop the 'social right' of access out of the fundamental rights of action and defense. See, e.g., art. 3 para. 2 and art. 24 para. 3 of the Italian
Constitution of 1948; art. 6 of the European Convention for the Protection of Human
Rights and Fundamental Freedoms. See, e.g., Constitutional Court, Decision of Dec. 22,
1961, no. 70, [1961] *Giur. Ital.* III 1282.

[8] As Professor Richard Claude observes, 'the enforcement or procedural protection is
merely another side of the content of the right'. Claude, 'Comparative Rights Research:
Some Intersections Between Law and the Social Sciences', in *Comparative Human Rights*,
supra note 6, at 383, 395.

[9] As the great Austrian scholar Franz Klein observed perceptively in 1906: 'the squalid,
arid, neglected phenomenon of civil procedure is in fact strictly connected with the great
intellectual movements of peoples: and . . . its varied manifestations are among the most
important documents of mankind's culture.' F. Klein, *Zeit- und Geistesströmungen im Prozesse*
8 (Frankfurt am Main, Klostermann, 2d ed. 1958). See also P. Calamandrei, *Procedure and
Democracy* 76 (New York, New York University Press, 1956).

[10] Of course, the activities of courts help to determine what other means of dispute resolution are available, how they are utilized, and what the results will be. See, e.g. Galanter,
'Why the 'Haves' Come Out Ahead: Speculation on the Limits of Legal Change', 9 Law &
Soc'y Rev. 95 (1974).

they must learn from other cultures. 'Access', therefore, is not only an increasingly recognized fundamental social right; it is also necessarily a central focus of modern procedural scholarship. Its study presupposes both a broadening and deepening of the aims and methods of modern legal science.

...

The first wave: legal aid for the poor

Appropriately, the first major efforts to improve access to justice in Western countries focused on providing legal services to the poor.[11] In most modern societies the help of a lawyer is essential, if not mandatory, to decipher increasingly complex laws and arcane procedures encountered in bringing a civil claim to court. Methods of providing legal representation for those who cannot afford it are therefore vital. Until very recently, however, the legal aid schemes of most countries were fundamentally inadequate. They relied, for the most part, on services provided by the private bar without compensation (*'munus honorificum'*).[12] The right to access was thus recognized and given some support, but the state undertook no affirmative action to guarantee it. Predictably, the result was that such legal aid systems were ineffective.[13] Lawyers in market economies, particularly those who were more experienced and highly skilled, tended to devote their time to remunerative work rather than to gratuitous legal aid. Moreover, in order to avoid having to provide too much charity, program sponsors tended to erect steep barriers to qualifying for free legal aid.

The flaws in these programs became increasingly apparent. Reforms were introduced relatively early in Germany and England, in both cases under a social democratic or labour regime. In 1919–23, Germany began a system of state compensation for private attorneys providing legal aid, and the aid was given as a matter of right to all eligible persons.[14] In

[11] See generally M. Cappelletti, J. Gordley and E. Johnson, Jr., *Toward Equal Justice* (Milan/Dobbs Ferry, NY, Giuffrè/Oceana, 1975).

[12] The French, German, Italian, and a number of other statutory schemes of the second half of the nineteenth century placed a duty on private attorneys to provide legal services, gratuitously to the poor. See generally Cappelletti, 'The Emergence of a Modern Theme', *id.* 3, 18–21.

[13] *Id.* 23–7.

[14] The 1919 German statute allowed attorneys to recover their actual disbursements— not attorneys' fees—from the state. 'Gesetz über Teuerungszuschläge zu den Gebühren der Rechtsanwälte und Gerichtsvollzieher' of December 18, 1919, [1919] RGB1. I 2113; Hagelberg, *Zur Reform des Armenrechts*, 49 Juristische Wochenschrift 876 (1920). A 1923

England, the major reform began with the 1949 statute creating the Legal Aid and Advice Scheme and entrusting it to the Law Society, the national association of solicitors.[15] This Scheme recognized the importance of compensating private attorneys for providing legal consultation ('legal advice') as well as assistance in litigation ('legal aid'). These approaches were limited in several ways, but they commenced the move beyond the anachronistic, semi-charitable, *laissez-faire* legal aid programs.

The dramatic activity in reforming legal aid has taken place in the last twelve years. The social consciousness which reawakened especially in the mid and late 1960s placed legal aid at the top of the law reform agenda. The contradiction between the theoretical ideal of effective access and the totally inadequate legal aid systems became more and more intolerable.[16]

Reform began in 1965 in the United States with the Legal Services Program of the Office of Economic Opportunity (OEO)[17] and continued throughout the world in the early 1970s. In January 1972, France replaced its nineteenth-century legal aid scheme, based on gratuitous service rendered by the bar, with a modern *sécurité sociale* approach in which the cost of compensation is borne by the state.[18] In May 1972, Sweden's innovative new program was enacted into law.[19] Two months later the English Legal Advice and Assistance Act greatly expanded the reach of the system

---

statute allowed attorneys to recover their full fees from the state, although the amount was limited later in the same year. 'Gesetz über die Erstattung von Rechtsanwaltsgebühren in Armensachen' of February 6, 1923, [1923] RGB1. I 103; Küster, 'Erstattung von Rechtsanwaltsgebühren in Armensachen', 52 Juristische Wochenschrift 676 (1923).

[15] Legal Aid and Advice Act 1949, 12 and 13 Geo. 6, c. 51. This Act was rewritten and its provisions consolidated in the Legal Aid Act 1974, c. 4.

[16] Several countries even experienced judicial challenges to archaic legal aid schemes. In Austria, the decision of the Constitutional Court on December 19, 1972, declared invalid the Austrian scheme on the ground that it did not provide adequate compensation to lawyers acting for indigents. See Judgment of Dec. 19, 1972, Supplement (*Beilage*), [Feb. 1973] Österreichisches Anwaltsblatt. Other examples of such judicial review can be found in Cappelletti, *supra* note 12, at 70–6.

[17] Title I of the Economic Opportunity Act 1964 (42 USC §§ 2701–981 (1970), *repealed in part*, Act of Dec. 28, 1973, Pub. L. No. 93–203, 87 Stat. 833) authorized grants of federal funds to approved 'community action' programs. The OEO decided that legal services programs qualified as community action programs, and this interpretation was given clear statutory recognition in 1965. See Economic Opportunity Amendments of 1965, Act of Oct. 9, 1965, Pub. L. No. 89–253 § 12, 79 Stat. 973, *amending* Economic Opportunity Act 1964, § 205 (a), 42 USC § 2785 (a) (1970).

[18] Law of Jan. 3, 1972, no. 72–11, [1972] *Journal Officiel de la République Française* [hereinafter JO] 167. The law went into effect on September 16, 1972.

[19] Public Legal Aid Law of May 26, 1972, [1972] *Svensk Författningssamling* 429.

set up in 1949, especially in the area of legal advice,[20] and the Canadian Province of Quebec established its first government-financed legal aid progam.[21] In October 1972, the Federal Republic of Germany improved its system by increasing the compensation paid to private lawyers for legal services to the poor. And in July 1974, the long-awaited Legal Services Corporation—an effort to preserve and extend the gains of the by-now-disbanded OEO program—was established in the United States.[22] Also during this period both Austria and the Netherlands revised their legal aid programs to compensate private attorneys more adequately; there were several major reforms enacted in Australia; and Italy came close to changing its own anachronistic system, which was similar to the pre-1972 French scheme.[23]

The legal aid systems of much of the modern world were thus dramatically improved. A movement was unleashed that has continued to grow and, as we shall see, has even overflowed the categories and constructs of legal aid reform. Before exploring further dimensions of the movement—and indeed to help clarify the logic of these further dimensions—we must survey the major accomplishments as well as the limits of this first great wave of reform.

1. *The judicare system*

The major accomplishment of the Austrian, British, Dutch, French, and West German legal aid reforms was the bolstering of what has been termed the 'judicare' system of legal aid. Judicare is a system whereby legal aid is established *as a matter of right* for all persons eligible under the statutory terms, with *the state paying the private lawyer* who provides those services. The goal of judicare systems is to provide the same representation for low income litigants that they would have if they could afford a lawyer. The ideal is to make a distinction only with respect to the billing: the state, rather than the client, is charged the cost.

In the modern English program, for example, an applicant meeting the financial and merit tests for his claim may choose his attorney from a list of lawyers who have agreed to provide such services.[24] The list is a long one, since the compensation for the legal aid attorney is sufficient to

---

[20] Legal Advice and Assistance Act 1972, c. 50, rewritten and consolidated in the Legal Aid Act 1974, c. 4.

[21] Legal Aid Act, 21 Eliz. 2, c. 14 (Quebec, 1972).

[22] Legal Services Corporation Act 1974, Pub. L. No. 93–355, 88 Stat. 378 (1974).

[23] See Cappelletti, *supra* note 12, at 33–9.

[24] Legal Aid Act 1974, c. 4, § 12.

attract almost all practitioners.[25] Since legal assistance is often necessary to demonstrate formal qualification for legal aid, the 1972 reform enables the applicant to obtain up to £25 of legal services without the need for any formal authorization;[26] these services can then include helping to prepare the application for legal aid. The system thus goes far to provide the poor with the financial means to obtain a lawyer. While it has been criticized because its standard of need is too restrictive and because it does not provide assistance for proceedings before most special tribunals—where, in fact, many of the 'new rights' must be asserted[27]—its results have been impressive: aid over the years has been given to steadily increasing numbers of persons.[28]

The French system, as introduced in 1972 and modified by enactments of 1974 and 1975, also moves a long step toward an effective judicare system.[29] A particularly important feature of the French system since 1972 is that it is constructed to reach not only poor people, but also some people above the poverty level. Decreasing levels of aid are now available to persons with monthly incomes of up to 2950 francs (about US $460) for a family of four.[30] In addition, also since 1972, legal aid may be granted for a

---

[25] Legal Aid Act 1974, c. 4, Schedule 2. An American study ten years ago found that 98% of English attorneys felt the fees to be adequate: Utton, 'The British Legal Aid System', 76 Yale LJ 371, 376 (1966).

[26] Legal Advice and Assistance Act 1972, c. 50, rewritten and consolidated in the Legal Aid Act 1974, c. 4, § 3. For divergent evaluations of this reform, see Samuels, 'Legal Advice and Assistance Act 1972; The Scheme and an Appraisal', 122 New LJ 696, 697 (1972); Pollock, 'Legal Advice and Assistance Act 1972; The Scheme and a Mis-appraisal', 122 New LJ 807 (1972).

[27] See, e.g., First Report of the Legal Aid Legislation Working Party, in 25th Legal Aid Annual Reports [1974–75], at 55 (London, HMSO, 1975); S. Pollock, Legal Aid—the First 25 Years 110–15, 117–19 (London, Oyez, 1975); E. Moeran, Practical Legal Aid 12–14 (London, Oyez, 1969); Dworkin, 'The Progress and Future of Legal Aid in Civil Litigation', 28 Modern L. Rev. 432, 444–6 (1965).

[28] See S. Pollock, supra note 29, at 104–5. Also: 'It has been estimated that about half the work dealt with by the Courts which could in principle fall within the scope of legal aid (i.e., excluding company litigation and the like) is conducted under the provisions of the Scheme, either free so far as the assisted person is concerned or on the basis of a contribution by him.' Id. 103. Unfortunately, however, for a variety of reasons, including inflation, the eligibility standards have been becoming stricter since the Scheme's beginning so that fewer people are now eligible for legal aid than in the past. See 26th Annual Report of the Lord Chancellor's Advisory Committee on Legal Aid, in 26th Legal Aid Annual Reports [1975–76] at 60–1 (London, HMSO, 1976).

[29] Law of Jan. 3, 1972, no. 72–11, [1972] JO 167, [1972] DL 69; Financial Law (loi de finances) of Dec. 30, 1974, no. 74–1129, JO (Dec. 31, 1974); Decree of May 14, 1975, no. 75–350, [1975] JO 4909, modifying the Decree of Sept. 1, 1972, no. 72–809, which applied the Law of Jan. 3, 1972. The initial reform was analyzed in Herzog & Herzog, 'The Reform of the Legal Professions and Legal Aid in France', 22 Int'l & Comp. LQ 462 (1973).

[30] Decree of May 14, 1975, no. 75–350, [1975] JO 4909, arts. 4, 5, modifying the Decree of Sept. 1, 1972, arts. 66–8. Financial Law (loi de finances) of June 22, 1976, no. 76–539, [1976] JO 3739.

particularly important case regardless of the litigant's income.[31] The main problem with the French system is that despite a one-third increase in 1974 in the compensation paid to attorneys, the amount is still inadequate. Nevertheless, France now provides an important model of a modern judicare system.

Despite the significant accomplishments of judicare schemes such as those in England and France, however, the judicare system itself has faced substantial criticism. It has become almost commonplace to observe that the attempt to treat poor persons like regular clients creates difficulties. Judicare solves the costs barrier, but it does little to affect the barriers caused by other problems typically encountered by the poor. For one thing, it relies on the poor to recognize legal claims and seek assistance;[32] it fails to encourage or even allow for efforts by individual practitioners to help the poor understand their rights and identify the areas where they may be entitled to legal remedies. It is indeed highly suggestive that the poor tend to utilize judicare systems mainly for legal problems with which they are already familiar—criminal and divorce matters—rather than to pursue their new rights as consumers, tenants, and the like.[33] Moreover, even if they recognize their claims, poor people may be intimidated from pursuing them by the prospect of going to a law office and discussing them with a private lawyer. Indeed, in societies where the rich and poor live apart, there may be geographical as well as cultural barriers between the poor and the private bar. Further, it is clear that representation by private practitioners does not counter the disadvantages of a poor person *vis-à-vis* organizational litigants. Most important, judicare treats the poor as individuals to the neglect of the poor as a class. Neither the English, the French, nor the German judicare system, for example, provides aid for 'test cases'[34] or group actions on behalf of the poor unless

[31] Law of Jan. 3, 1972, no. 72–11, § 16, [1972] JO 167.

[32] The shortcomings of this reliance are suggested by the findings in B. Abel-Smith, M. Zander and R. Brooke, *Legal Problems and the Citizen* (London, Heinemann, 1973) at 219: 'In total our 1,651 respondents told us of 1,022 cases where, in our view, legal advice was needed. Advice of any kind had been taken in only 450 cases and in only 270 cases was a lawyer the main adviser . . .'

[33] Under the English judicare system, for example, about 60% of the cases are matrimonial, and about 15% are criminal. See *Report of the Law Society*, in 26th Legal Aid Annual Reports [1975–76] at 18 (London, HMSO 1976). For Australia, see Commission of Enquiry into Poverty, Second Main Report, Law and Poverty in Australia 41 (Canberra, Australian Govt. Printing Office, 1975).

[34] As stated for England by Seton Pollock, former Secretary of the Law Society for Legal Aid and a leading authority in this field: '[test] cases are . . . only supported where the applicant for legal aid has himself a case which, in relation to his own personal circumstances, is reasonable and one which he would be expected to take in his own interests if he were

they can be justified by the interests of each individual involved. Given that the poor encounter many legal problems as a group, or class, and that the interests of any one individual may be too small to justify legal action, merely individual remedies are inadequate. Judicare systems, however, are not equipped to transcend individual remedies.

2. *The public salaried attorney model*

The public salaried attorney model of legal aid has a different objective than the judicare model, one which reflects its modern origin in 1965 with the Legal Services Program of the United States Office of Economic Opportunity—the vanguard of a 'War on Poverty'.[35] Legal services were to be provided by 'neighborhood law offices', staffed with attorneys paid by the government, and charged with furthering the interests of the poor as a class.[36] As one commentator observed: 'The objective was to use taxpayers' money in the most cost-effective way—to obtain, in Department of Defense terminology, "the most bang for the buck." '[37] To be sure, this goal did not preclude helping individual poor persons settle their grievances. In contrast to existing judicare systems, however, this system tends to be characterized by major efforts to make poor people aware of their new rights and willing to use lawyers to help pursue them. In addition, offices were small and typically located in poor communities to facilitate contact with the poor and to minimize the barriers of class. Attorneys were supposed to learn at first hand about these barriers and thus be able to attack them more effectively. Finally, and perhaps above all, the staff attorneys sought to extend the rights of the poor by test cases, lobbying, and other law reform activities on behalf of the poor as a class. Indeed,

wealthy enough to do so on his own account.' S. Pollock, *supra* note 29, at 136. Klauser and Riegert have made the following observation about judicare systems, particularly in Germany: 'Probably the most cogent objection to the judicare approach to legal aid is that judicare does nothing except give service to the individual client. It does not effectively provide for law reform, for community action, or for community education.' Klauser & Riegert, 'Legal Assistance in the Federal Republic of Germany', 20 Buffalo L. Rev. 583, 604 (1971). See also Johnson, 'The Prospect of Future Themes', in M. Cappelletti, J. Gordley and E. Johnson, Jr., *supra* note 11, at 133, 184–94.

[35] See note 17 *supra*. See generally, E. Johnson, Jr., *Justice and Reform: The Formative Years of the OEO Legal Services Program* (New York, Russell Sage Foundation, 1974) for a detailed history of the early years of the Legal Services Program.

[36] See, e.g., Cahn and Cahn, 'The War on Poverty: A Civilian Perspective', 73 Yale LJ 1317 (1964); Note, 'Neighborhood Law Offices: The New Wave in Legal Services for the Poor', 80 Harv. L. Rev. 805 (1967).

[37] Huber, 'Thou Shalt Not Ration Justice: A History and Bibliography of Legal Aid in America', 44 George Wash. L. Rev. 754, 760 (1976).

attorneys often helped to organize the poor to present their interests more effectively inside and outside the courts.

The advantages of this approach over that of judicare are obvious. It clearly attacks other barriers to individual access besides costs, particularly the problems of the personal legal competence of the poor. Further, it can support the diffuse class interest of poor people. Staff attorney offices can secure for themselves the advantages of organizational litigants by acquiring expertise and experience with the problems which are typical of the poor. Private attorneys charged solely with servicing individuals are generally unable to secure such advantages. In sum, besides just handling the individual claims of the poor that are brought to lawyers, as in the judicare system, this American model (1) reaches out to the poor to help them vindicate their rights and (2) creates an effective advocate for the poor as a class.

The disadvantages or limits of the staff attorney approach stem mainly from its very aggressiveness and ability to create such advocates. It is apparent, first, that the more glamorous and seemingly cost-effective nature of test cases and law-reform actions can in practice lead the staff attorney to neglect the interests of particular clients. Indeed, staff attorneys must every day decide how best to allocate their limited resources between cases important only to individuals and cases important from a social perspective; there is always a chance that individuals will be ignored or given second-rate help. Second, many people feel, with some justification, that the notion of an attorney setting himself up as an advocate for the poor and, in fact, treating the poor as though they were unable to pursue their own interests, is overly paternalistic. Treat the poor, they would argue, simply as normal individuals with less money.

Probably an even more serious problem of the staff attorney, 'War on Poverty' approach to legal aid is that it necessarily relies on government support for activities of an inevitably political nature which often are directed against the government itself. This reliance presupposes that a society has decided that any legal device to help the poor is desirable even if it means challenging governmental action and the actions of dominant groups in the society. The United States, for example, seemed to have committed itself to eradicate poverty, but in fact the American legal aid attorneys, unlike private attorneys in England, France and Germany, have been under continual political attack.[38] Only recently, after a very difficult

---

[38] For instance, Spiro Agnew, then-Vice President of the United States, criticized the system precisely for the reason many supported it: 'We are dealing, in large part, with a systematic effort to redistribute societal advantages and disadvantages, penalties and rewards, rights and resources.' Agnew, 'What's Wrong with the Legal Services Program', 58 ABA J. 930 (1972).

legislative fight involving one Presidential veto, was the Legal Services Corporation made independent of direct governmental influence; but the new law contains many rules intended to forbid or limit law reform activity on the part of legal services attorneys.[39] In the light of this recent history in the United States, it is not surprising that aggressive activity for the poor through staff attorney offices in other countries is exceedingly difficult.[40] While this system can break down many barriers to access, it is far from perfect.

The salaried staff attorney solution, if not combined with other solutions, is further limited in its utility by the fact that it, unlike judicare systems utilizing the private bar, cannot guarantee legal aid as an *entitlement*. Realistically, there simply cannot be enough staff attorneys to give first-rate individual service to all the poor with legal problems. Similarly, and no less importantly, there clearly cannot be enough staff attorneys to extend legal aid beyond the 'poor' to the middle classes, a development which is a distinct, fundamental feature of the most advanced judicare systems.

3. Combined models

A few countries have recently chosen to combine the two major models of legal aid systems, having recognized the limitations which exist in each of them and recognizing that the two can, in fact, be complementary. Sweden[41] and the Canadian Province of Quebec[42] were the first to offer

---

[39]   Legal Services Corporation Act 1974, Pub. L. No. 93–355, § 1007 (a), (b), 88 Stat. 378 (1974). For example, the Act states that no funds may be expended 'to undertake or influence the passage or defeat of any [government] legislation'; no legal service lawyers may engage in 'any political activity'; and no legal service lawyers may engage in activity to organize a group. Indeed, at the present time it is still impossible to be certain about the success of the new Legal Services Corporation as finally established. For some indications that lawyers will retain their aggressiveness on behalf of the poor as a class, see J. Handler, E. Hollingsworth and H. Erlanger, *Lawyers and the Pursuit of Legal Rights* (Madison, Wis., forthcoming).

[40]   The most striking experience with this problem was the Indonesian staff attorney program, the Legal Aid and Public Defender Bureau, which was established in Jakarta in 1970. As a result of its activities on behalf of the poor, the Director of the Bureau, Adnan Buyung Nasution, was imprisoned without charge from early 1974 until near the end of 1975. See Magavern, Thomas, and Stuart, 'Law, Urban Development, and the Poor in Developing Countries', 1975 Wash. ULQ 51, 58–60.

[41]   Public Legal Aid Law of May 26, 1972, [1972] *Svensk Författningssamling 429*. The statute is translated and annotated by professors Bruzelius and Bolding in M. Cappelletti, J. Gordley and E. Johnson, Jr., *supra* note 11, at 525–61.

[42]   Legal Aid Act, 21 Eliz. 2, c. 14 (Quebec, 1972). The statute is set out in M. Cappelletti, J. Gordley and E. Johnson, Jr., *supra* note 11, at 585–613. See also Cooper, 'Report on the Quebec Legal Aid System', in M. Cappelletti, J. Gordley and E. Johnson, Jr., *id.* 614.

clients the choice between representation by staff attorneys or by regular private attorneys, although, it should be noted, the programs do have different emphases. The Swedish system leans more toward the judicare approach since staff attorney offices are supposed to support themselves essentially from attorneys' fees paid by the state on behalf of assisted individuals, while in Quebec the law offices are supported directly by the government regardless of how successfully they compete with private firms. In Quebec, therefore, the legal offices may have less of a tendency to focus only on individual claims, and are more likely to mobilize the poor and to be advocates for them as a group. The important point, however, is that the possibility of choice in both programs has opened up a new dimension in legal aid and advice. Ideally this combined model allows individuals to choose between the individualized services of a regular (private) attorney and the special expertise of staff attorneys closely attuned to the problems of the poor. Also ideally, both poor individuals and the poor as a group can benefit.

Recognizing these advantages, reformers in many areas, including Australia,[43] Holland,[44] and Great Britain,[45] have helped implement systems in which law centres now supplement the established judicare schemes. The increasingly important British 'neighbourhood law centres' are particularly notable. These centres are located in poor areas, mostly around London; their salaried solicitors (and a few barristers) perform

[43] Australia's federal government established a salaried legal services agency in 1973 to supplement state judicare systems. According to the Australian Report, however, the organized bar has sought to and succeeded in severely circumscribing this agency's activities. The status of the federal program is as of this writing at best uncertain, but it appears that the notion of a 'combined model' is still prevailing.

[44] Since 1970 there have been 'law shops' (*Rechtswinkel*) throughout the Netherlands, which in effect supplement the judicare system which has been in place since 1957. These offices are primarily staffed by students, with some assistance by young attorneys, and they also attempt to provide services aimed at improving the position of the poor as a class. There is much discussion now in Holland about, and some experimentation with, more formal state-controlled salaried legal services offices.

[45] There are now nearly 30 Law Centres. The first, in North Kensington, London, began its activities in 1970, and the rest have been formed since 1973. A typical office, as of the date of a recently published survey, had from one to four full-time lawyers, and a few even had a barrister working full time. The centres are funded by various sources, including local authorities, legal aid, private charitable foundations, and the Lord Chancellor's special law centres' fund. In order to reduce competition with solicitors, law centres are prohibited from becoming involved in matrimonial issues or issues involving the buying and selling of houses. See Zander and Russell, 'Law Centres Survey', 73 Law Society's Gazette 208 (1976); M. Zander, 'Who Should Manage Legal Services?', at 12–13 (1978, to be published in Volume III of the Florence Project series). For a history and detailed examination of the law centre movement, see M. Zander, *Legal Services for the Community* 59–115 (London, Temple Smith, 1978).

many of the tasks handled by the staff attorneys in the United States. They have increasingly sought to treat the disputes brought to them not merely as individual matters, but also as community problems. Their work, despite some initial hesitation on the part of the Law Society, has become recognized as 'an integral and essential branch of legal services'.[46]

Sweden has also pioneered further important developments. First, it goes considerably beyond other countries, including France, in extending legal aid to the middle classes. As of mid-1977, for example, a person earning as much as 80,000 Swedish Crowns per year (about US $17,400) is eligible to receive subsidized legal aid.[47] This figure is automatically adjusted to keep up with the cost of living. In addition, the combination of private insurance and legal aid presently available in Sweden has filled a major gap existing in most other European systems. In virtually all countries where the 'winner takes all' system prevails, legal aid generally will not assume the obligation of reimbursing the unassisted winner for his costs, even if the loser is very poor. Thus, unable to recover his costs, the adversary of the poor litigant may incur considerable financial hardship.[48] In Sweden, however, about 85 per cent of the population has legal insurance which covers, *inter alia*, most of the costs of *losing* a lawsuit.[49] Hence the winner can easily recover his costs from a poor adversary, if the latter is insured. Obviously this development has important implications for access to justice in Sweden; indeed, it reflects a move beyond the simple legal aid solution.

4. The legal aid solution: strengths and limitations

Very important measures have been enacted in recent years to improve legal aid systems; as a consequence, access-to-justice barriers have begun to come down. The poor are obtaining legal aid in ever larger numbers, not only for divorces and criminal defense, but also to vindicate their

---

[46] *Twenty-Sixth Annual Report of the Lord Chancellor's Advisory Committee on Legal Aid*, in 26th Legal Aid Annual Reports [1975–76] 57, 71 (London, HMSO, 1976).

[47] This figure, which was applicable for 1977, is reached by multiplying by eight the *basic amount*—a figure defined by law and reconsidered and changed by law each month—of October 1976, which was 10,000 Swedish Crowns (about US $2,250).

[48] This problem, however, is dealt with at least partially by some legal aid systems. In England, for example, according to a 1964 reform now embodied in the Legal Aid Act 1974, s. 13, a prevailing unassisted party may be given his costs out of the legal aid fund if, *inter alia*, it is shown that 'the unassisted party will suffer severe financial hardship unless the order is made'.

[49] The insurance covers expenses both in and out of court except for a deductable charge of 200 crowns (about US $45) plus 10% of costs in excess of that amount. It covers a litigant's own costs plus costs he might pay upon losing.

new, non-traditional rights, whether as plaintiffs or as defendants. It can be expected that the experiments in legal aid that are now taking place will further eliminate those barriers.

Legal aid, however, cannot be the only focus for access-to-justice reform. There are serious limits on the legal aid approach. First, in order for the system to be effective, legal aid schemes require a very large number of lawyers, a number that may exceed the supply, especially in developing countries.

Second, even assuming there are enough lawyers in the country, they must be made available to help those unable to afford their services. This requires funding, which is the basic problem of legal aid schemes. Legal aid relies on the relatively expensive provision of legal services through lawyers who primarily utilize the regular court system. To obtain the services of a highly trained lawyer for litigation is an expensive proposition, whether the compensation is provided by the client or by the state. In market economies, as we have noted, the inescapable fact is that without adequate compensation, legal services for the poor tend to be poor. Few lawyers will provide such services, and those who do tend to perform them in a substandard fashion. In view of the high cost of lawyers, it is not surprising that to date very few societies have even tried to meet the goal of providing an adequate attorney to *anyone* for whom the cost is too heavy an economic burden to bear. Sweden, with relatively little poverty and yet perhaps the most expensive legal aid system *per capita* in the world, has been characterized by one observer as the only nation which has really attempted to offer legal aid to *anyone* who cannot afford legal services in a particular case.[50]

Third, legal aid even at its best can hardly solve the problem of small claims brought by individuals. Not surprisingly, since even an individual who can afford an attorney's services often cannot economically prosecute (or risk losing) a small claim, government-paid attorneys are not usually given the uneconomic luxury of handling such cases.[51] Once again, the problem of small claims calls for special attention.

[50] See Johnson, *supra* note 36, at 233–4. The costs were 120 million SwCrowns (about US $27 million) in 1975, of which about 66 million crowns were for non-criminal legal aid and 895,000 crowns were for legal advice.

[51] For example, legal assistance tends to be unavailable for small claims in the English County Courts and the German *Amtsgerichte*. See Gordley, 'Variations on a Modern Theme', in M. Cappelletti, J. Gordley and E. Johnson, Jr., *supra* note 11, at 77, 105–6 and nn. 65–8. For Australia, see, e.g., Harland, 'Consumer Protection in Australia', 40 Rabels Zeitschrift 631, 645 (1976). The only time legal aid becomes feasible is in systems where it is permitted for 'test cases' or where claims are aggregated in 'class actions', but neither of these approaches could provide remedies for very many individuals with small claims.

Finally, while the staff attorney model addresses the need to vindicate the diffuse interests of the poor as a class, other important diffuse interests, such as those of consumers and environmentalists, may be ignored.

6. Recent Trends in the Organization of Legal Services

FREDERICK H. ZEMANS*

This paper outlines the significant developments in the provision of legal services to low-income persons that have taken place since the First Congress on Civil Procedures, held in Ghent, Belgium, in August of 1977. Although only six years have passed, there have been numerous developments in various parts of the world with respect to legal services, as the legal profession, the judiciary and governments have grappled with civil and criminal procedures in their attempts to make them more accessible to the poor, the unemployed and other groups which have traditionally been excluded from the legal system. This paper carries forward the analysis of Professor Vittorio Denti which was published with the Ghent national reports on this topic in *Perspectives on Legal Aid—A Comparative Survey*, (1979),[1] and relies heavily on the data generated by the 26 responses to a questionnaire designed by the writer which addressed the issues of changes and developments since 1977.

As scholars we are both intrigued by the development of differing models of legal services within particular nations or regions, and also challenged to develop international models of comparative analyses and typologies which consider common factors in procedural developments. Within the broad parameters that are necessitated when one is dealing with a world overview of legal services, I shall focus on these issues. I shall also attempt to give a sense of the nature and state of legal delivery systems in the contemporary world with a special emphasis on new and innovative developments.

A number of national reports suggest that the commitment to social justice and social reform that gave birth to the first wave of legal services

* Professor of Law, Osgoode Hall Law School of York University, Toronto.

[1] Denti, 'An International Overview on Legal Aid', in F. H. Zemans, (ed.) *Perspectives on Legal Aid: A Comparative Survey* (London: Frances Pinter, 1979) 346–61. Also published under the title 'Accessibility of Legal Procedures for the Underprivileged: Legal Aid and Advice' in M. Storme and H. Casman, (eds.) *Towards a Justice with a Human Face: The First International Congress on the Law of Civil Procedure* (Antwerpen: Kluwer, 1978) 167.

in the 1960s is being eroded by inaction and, in some instances, outright hostility on the part of governments in the early 1980s. As well as outlining the developments in legal services over the past five years, this paper will also examine the impact of political, economic, and structural factors that have influenced these developments during the past several decades. Analysis of data received suggests that, currently, the provision of legal services to low-income and underprivileged citizens is not based on the recognition that there exists in the sophisticated legal systems of the latter part of the twentieth century an inherent right of access. Rather, despite the gradual acceptance by many nations that reform-oriented social programmes should include legal assistance, we see in nation after nation limitations being placed on the funding of legal services and restrictions being imposed on the types of cases for which representation will be provided. In some instances, attempts have been made by governments to dismantle schemes which previous governments or regimes had introduced as aspects of state-supported welfare schemes. The issue of the right to legal services and models that will address that right is of primary concern to the writer, as it was to his respondents in this international survey.

Implicitly or explicitly, there has been a single underlying justification for intervention in the legal market-place, whether it be in contemporary North America or earlier periods in Europe. It is the undemocratic nature of the legal system. The twentieth century has seen the recognition of the reality that large segments of the population of all nations are effectively denied entry to or use of the legal system. It is the recognition of the exclusive nature of the legal system that has created the demand for, and the slow evolution of, a plurality of legal services and state supported delivery systems. It is this 'democratization' of the legal system that this writer develops as the main theme in his discussion of developments of legal service schemes. To understand the present situation, it is important to consider the manner in which the contemporary legal system came to be exclusive and undemocratic and to examine the question of whether legal services can possibly ameliorate such fundamental features of our legal culture.

Lawrence Friedman has traced the development of the modern legal system, and discussed the movement for access to justice in a historical context.[2] In essence, Friedman shows the historical trend toward a uniform, central legal system, one which brings all citizens under one

---

[2] Friedman, 'Access to Justice: Social and Historical Context' in M. Cappelletti and Weisner (eds.) *Access to Justice*, vol. II, bk. 1 (Milan: 1978) 3.

regime. The growth of a centralized system of law, he points out, has been at the expense of local and customary rules of social organization. Central authority came to be paramount over customary laws, and eventually succeeded in smothering local diversity. The significant issue for students of the provision of legal services is Friedman's observation of the paradoxical nature of this evolution. At the time when all citizens were being brought within a single legal system, more and more citizens also became effectively excluded from participation in the operation of law:

As the law became more and more 'uniform', it became both more and less accessible: more, in that a lot of medieval, crabbed, technical, obsolete trappings were pruned away; less in that system and uniformity destroyed what was left of popular (and lay) justice.[3]

Such was the evolution of the legal system in the industrialized world during the late eighteenth and nineteenth centuries. Of course, the coincident social force of the time was the entrenchment of the market system of economy. It is crucial to recognize these parallel developments. At the time when the legal system became widely applicable, the basic distributive mechanism was the market place. Not surprisingly then, the legal system and the services of the legal profession came to reflect the ideology of market economics; legal representation was a commodity that could be purchased; legal action could be purchased if the tenacity of the litigant was convertible into the necessary form of monetary exchange.

It is probably most accurate to describe these historical trends as coincident rather than coincidental. The uniformity and rationality of the legal system, and the objectification of social relationships cultivated by a market economy, were part of a matrix of change. As Foucault wrote of the reforms of the criminal law in the eighteenth and nineteenth centuries:

The true objective of the reform movement, even in its most general formulations, was not so much to establish a new right to punish based on more equitable principles, as to set up a new 'economy' of the power to punish, to assure its better distribution, so that is should be neither too concentrated at certain privileged points, nor too divided between opposing authorities; so that it should be distributed in homogeneous circuits capable of operation everywhere, in a continuous way, down to the finest grain of social body. . . . The new juridical theory of penalty corresponds in fact to a new 'political economy' of the power to punish.[4]

Foucault makes the argument that the centralization and rationalization of the criminal law reflected a change in the power base of law in general.

---

[3] *Id*. at 10.   [4] M. Foucault, *Discipline and Punish* (London: A. Lane, 1977) at 80–1.

Power, or the power to punish, in Foucault's words, was rendered 'more regular, more effective, more constant, and more detailed in its effects'.[5] As the legal system became more effective as a medium of general control, then, its monetary expense, according to the market principles in vogue, ensured that access to the formal legal system was limited. Friedman puts it this way:

Somehow, the influential people in society sensed that litigation was an enemy of rapid economic growth. Litigation is inconsistent with a vigorous, active market; the market thrives best when people do not break off commercial relations and sue each other at the least trouble or disagreement; rather, they absorb their losses in the short run and keep on trading.[6]

Not only was the legal system organized along market principles, but it was deliberately made expensive in order to discourage litigation, except by those who had the resources to engage in costly legal proceedings, or those who had interests at sake that sufficiently exceeded the cost of participation in the legal system. The average man was deterred from utilizing the courts of most countries and came to perceive the legal system as another impenetrable aspect of the socio-economic elite.

One should not, however, emphasize the role of the cost barrier to the exclusion of other impediments to participation. Equally significant have been the psychological barriers, those features of legal culture that serve to discourage the approach of tentative claimants. For example, the legal system's success as a system of control lies in its highly formalized procedures and proceedings. In particular, its formal character communicates the weight of authority to legal proceedings, and at the same time generates the commonly perceived image of hostility.

Similarly, formality has significant implications. The opulence of palaces of justice, the garb of court personnel and the appointments of counsel offices all contribute to the intimidating face of the legal system by suggesting power through prestige. The creation of a uniform legal system as a medium of authority founded on market principles achieved limited access by erecting barriers of cost, psychology and class. These issues are often discussed in terms of formality, remoteness, and expense, but ultimately all reflect the barriers to litigation—the principal mode of dispute resolution.

Cappelletti's recent discussions of legal services, particularly his *Access to Justice* study, describe the underprivileged as gradually being allowed to

---

[5] M. Foucault, *Discipline and Punish* (London: A. Lane, 1977) at 80.
[6] *Supra* note 3, at 12.

'enter' the palace of justice—or at least the waiting rooms.[7] The Cappelletti studies, as do the Wurzburg national reports, show that when legal services are provided they are directed, at least in their initial stage of development, to providing advice and assistance in the legal problems experienced by the underprivileged, primarily for litigation; in other words, access to justice has been in most instances exclusively associated with access to the courts. The barriers of cost, an elite profession, and highly formalized court procedures continue to reinforce the remoteness and undemocratic nature of the legal system.

Recently some writers have questioned the legitimacy of the access to justice movement.[8] If the legal system has evolved with the purpose of excluding from participation democratic interests and rather has as its purpose the strengthening of minority and elitist interests, is it not likely that there is little of substance in the law to serve the interests of those who have been excluded from the legal system? One must inquire as to what possible advantages there can be in seeking entry for the poor and powerless to such a hostile place. The usual justification for improved access to justice and the development of legal services programmes is that if the substance of the law has developed by the exclusion of large elements of the community, then there is a possibility that improved access may bring about reform of the legal system or perhaps fundamental changes in the decisions of courts respecting underprivileged persons.

Grossman and Sarat discuss the drawbacks inherent in the simple solution of increasing litigation or improving representation. Neither is, in itself, a sign of progress nor an indication of social justice. They point out that there is no guarantee that increased access implies increased effectiveness. Indeed, they argue that expanded access may be counterproductive, since the capacity of the legal system to deal with the resulting increased burden of cases is often diminished. By overloading the capacity of the system, the value of the system as a deterrent may be undermined.[9]

Such critics of the access to justice movement contend that legal services are merely a device by which legitimization is enhanced. For them,

[7] See generally, Cappelletti and Garth, 'Access to Justice and the Welfare State: An Introduction', in M. Cappelletti, (ed.) *Access to Justice and the Welfare State* (Florence: 1981) 1 and also M. Cappelletti and B. Garth, 'Access to Justice: The Worldwide Movement to Make Rights Effective', in *Access to Justice*, vol. I, bk. 1 (Milan: 1978) 3.

[8] See for example, A. Sarat, 'Book Review' (1981), 94 Harv. L. Rev. 1911 and E. Blankenburg (ed.), *Innovations in Legal Services* (Mass.: Oelgeschlager, Gunn & Hain, 1980).

[9] Grossman and Sarat, *Access to Justice and the Limits of Law* (1981), 3 Law and Policy Quarterly 125 at 138.

access to justice leads to formal adjudication conducted under the idea of 'formal equality', providing the basis for the erroneous equation of 'fair procedure with substantive justice'.[10] Others believe that expansion of access to justice leads to the expansion of state intervention in social affairs, hence amplifying social control by the state in what is perceived to be a repressive manner.[11]

Although discussions of the criticisms of the access to justice movement are helpful and contribute to the examination of developments of the legal services movement, their main value is that they enforce limits to the discussion of access to justice, making it clear that access itself does not lead inevitably to a 'new social order'. Discussion of legal aid and legal services can no longer take place under the belief that adjudication will bring about a legal 'nirvana' where all injustice and inequalities will miraculously be obliterated. Professor Santiago Oñate, the Mexican national reporter, sums up the argument in a brief but considered analysis of the situation:

Notwithstanding the virtues inherent in these critical approaches, they might involuntarily lead to consider legal services as an artful decoy provided by the ruling classes for the perpetuation of their order and as a practice that does not purport significant progress for the underprivileged.

This peril is easily avoided when the roles of adjudication in particular, and of law in general, are carefully considered. Adjudication is certainly not a good in itself, nor is it a general system for the redistribution of power within society. Contemporary legal scholars have clearly stressed that neither the regime of formal nor that of substantive adjudication is able to solve, *per se*, the problem of freedom in our society. Nevertheless, adjudication and dispute processing activities represent a precise mode by which law is created and applied. Broader access to the courts means broader participation in the creation and construction of law. For the under-privileged, generally unrepresented in other law enactment bodies, litigation might prove to be their only instance of participation in activities related to the legal shaping of social structures.[12]

Like Oñate, we recognize the barriers to a more democratic legal system, and we realistically assess the possibility for change inherent in litigation. We are nevertheless unprepared to abandon the movement for access because of these obstacles. The presence of such impediments should rather justify more ambitious access initiatives which will make the movement for legal services more politically sophisticated and viable.

[10] *Supra* note 8, Sarat.
[11] Z. Bankowski and G. Mungham, *Images of Law* (London: Routledge & Kegan Paul, 1976).
[12] Oñate, Mexican National Report (1982) at 4–5.

There appears to be no merit in the argument that access is an unworthy objective merely because there are substantive as well as procedural inequities in the legal system. Either out of supreme optimism, political naïvety, partisan rhetoric, or sound reasoning, some form of model of legal services for the underprivileged can be rationalized. The greater difficulty for the analyst of legal services lies in articulating what the character and the form of these services should be.

The moral argument

Historically, the concern of lack of access to the legal system first emerged in the late nineteenth century in Western European countries, particularly Germany, and in the United States, when members of the legal profession voluntarily chose to donate their services to certain underprivileged persons. As such, only the causes with the greatest moral merit, as perceived by concerned members of the profession, were recipients of service from the public-minded advocates. Although the creation of legal aid societies in New York City and other limited assistance programmes of this period implied recognition that the legal marketplace did not adequately distribute services to all elements of society, there was no significant pressure for reform or change. Rather, the political economy of the Victorian era saw universalism, centralization, and the market system adopted as the values of the legal system in developed, industrial nations. Rules of procedure reinforced these tendencies and any possibility of inexpensive, informal dispute resolution, or class actions were thwarted by the courts and governments. These forces served to exclude the vast majority of society from asserting legal interests and their lack of substantive and procedural rights reinforced their secondary and often impotent role within society. Even the early charitable groups and compassionate lawyers who exhibited concern for attempting to right the imbalance by providing some form of legal services, did so for religious or charitable purposes and not out of a sense that the poor, or for that matter, the working man, had the right to be represented, or to legitimate his substantive legal claims. Quite the contrary. Early legal aid groups applied moral criteria which effectively meant that legal services were not available in the very situations which affected the poor most significantly: bankruptcy, eviction, and divorce lacked the necessary degree of purity or propriety to be given legal assistance.[13]

[13] The first successful legal aid to the poor in the United States was organized by the German Society in New York City in 1876 to provide aid to recent German immigrants who

As Professor Martin Partington has written in his national report on England:

It is against this ideological and socio-economic background that legal services are provided. The rhetoric of the law talks of justice and freedom. But the law which lawyers help to administer, and the services that they therefore provide, are in essence a part of the private enterprise economy in which it is essential that work be done for profit, if business is not to go to the wall.

In protecting their own business interests, lawyers in England (as in other developed countries) have been able to use their knowledge of law and their social organizations to create powerful professional control over legal services provision, and to determine, to a large degree, the nature of the services provided. Although some of the wider manifestations of monopoly power (restrictive practices) have been relaxed in England in recent years, as a result of external pressures on the legal professions to reform themselves, the professional bodies still remain an extremely powerful influence on the scope and quality of legal services provision.[14]

The Wurzburg national reports underline the fact that legal services, even in the most developed programmes, continue to retain their original judgmental qualities. Legal services continue to be allocated frequently on the basis of moral merit,[15] rather than legal right, and controversies continue,

were exploited by merchants and landlords (J. S. Auerbach, *Unequal Justice: Lawyers and Social Change in Modern America* (New York: Oxford University Press, 1976). The second group was formed in Chicago in 1886 as an adjunct to the Women's Club with the 'reform' purpose of protection of women and children (J. Katz, *Poor People's Lawyers in Transition* (New Brunswick, NJ: Rutgers University Press, 1982)). Both of these organizations set the stage for legal aid societies for many years. They were private organizations, financed by private charitable contributions and controlled by boards of directors, virtually indistinguishable from other charitable organizations. Legal services were 'doled' out frequently because of moral merit, rather than legal right, and controversies developed early in prohibiting the provision of divorce services that would split up families and possibly increase the drain of poverty on society. (Menkel-Meadow, 'Legal Aid in the United States: The Professionalization and Politicalization of Legal Services in the 1980's' (1984), 22 OHLJ at 33.

[14] Partington, English National Report (1982) at 4.

[15] 'Moral merit' may be used in some cases as a mere justification for other ends. Recent limitations in the American legal services scheme serve as an example. Legal services are not provided in cases involving school desegregation, abortion, aliens, and homosexuals, and lawyers may not engage in lobbying activities. The arguments of the Reagan administration to exclude aliens from eligibility in the programme were phrased in terms of morality. (See Menkel-Meadow, *supra*, note 13, at 59.) It cannot be ignored, however, that such aliens benefited significantly from Caesar Chavez's farmworker unionization drive in California, when Reagan was governor of that state. This programme was a political thorn in Reagan's side at that time, and was supported by California Rural Legal Assistance. The present restriction of legal services to aliens, and, indeed, Reagan's attacks on the programme as a whole are an outgrowth of these earlier political struggles. (See Menkel-Meadow, *supra* note 13, at 55–63.) It is difficult to distinguish whether exclusion of services is based on moral, political, or cost factors.

particularly within judicare schemes, as to the type of service that should be provided. Legal services remain discretionary with respect to most minor criminal offences and with respect to civil and domestic disputes involving lesser services. Similarly, it is not universal in service-oriented schemes that private lawyers will be paid to represent low-income persons before administrative tribunals determining eligibility for social welfare, unemployment insurance, and workers' compensation. As well, bankruptcy and often divorce are a discretionary area of legal service representation.[16] The relevant criterion in judicare-private lawyer schemes is whether similar services would be provided for a paying client. Criteria with moral overtones are particularly vexatious in periods of economic restraint such as the present where we find legal services curtailed on the basis of selective value judgments.

Professor Menkel-Meadow, the United States national reporter, describes the current American situation:

Furthermore, the early philosophical underpinnings of the Legal Aid movement of providing individual representation for 'deserving' cases continues to affect legal services delivery systems today. With more demands for services than can possibly be met, programs must establish priorities and decide who is to receive some of the available, but limited resources. Some continue to argue that the most 'deserving' should receive aid.

The significance of these legal aid developments in the United States must be underscored in the present climate of attempts to disembowel legal services for the poor.[17]

Despite their individualistic, moralistic, relatively ineffective, and badly funded nature, they did succeed in establishing that the provision of legal services to the poor was a legitimate, if not a necessary function of industrialized nations. And what had developed initially in countries such as Germany and the United States has become, in the last two decades, an aspect of most contemporary legal systems.

It becomes clear that in the western world (and elsewhere), legal services have not grown out of the belief that there is an inherent right to legal representation. Rather, services have tended to be dominated by notions of moral relativity and differential entitlement. But if the fundamental justification for legal services is, as is proposed here, that the legal system is inherently undemocratic, does it not logically follow then that

[16] Access to justice is limited in a number of ways. The most straightforward of these are specific limitations on the types of problems and the individuals eligible for services. Limitation of the types of problems is the most common restriction.

[17] Menkel-Meadow, *supra* note 13, at 35–6.

access to justice can only be meaningful if a right to legal representation is recognized?

It has been seen that, historically, the legal system has deliberately denied access to a definable segment of society. Yet it is the legal system that must be relied upon to give effect to the intention of governments. Legal entitlements approved by parliament can have no meaning if their vindication is dependent upon the holder's pursuit of his or her due, and such pursuit must be carried out by an unaffordable and unapproachable agent. In the organization of the modern polity, the legal system is virtually as prominent an institution as the commons, the executive, or the judiciary itself. The courts and the profession, in practice, bear increasingly the burden of administering the modern state. How, then, can differential access to the machinery of our society be justified?

The issue can be put simply: if the legal system's inherent defect is that it alienates a portion of the population, and if it is recognized that this offends the democratic aspirations of our society, then should not a democratic right to equal participation in the legal process be recognized?

Further, in the context of the legal process alone, equal participation can be considered essential to the adversarial system. Richard Abel, describing the situation in the United States, writes:

Equality in the distribution of legal services has a value beyond that of enhancing the welfare of the unrepresented or underrepresented. The very integrity of the US legal system as an adversary system depends upon equal representation of all parties. The legitimacy of contemporary law rests on the assumption that optimally efficient allocations of scarce resources are produced by parties who freely negotiate with each other on the basis of equal information about the law and equal competence to use it. The adversarial model of litigation . . . is grounded upon the belief that factual truth and fidelity to substantive and procedural rules are best achieved by partisan struggle between equal opponents, which at a minimum means opponents who are equally represented. Moreover, the theory of democratic pluralism assumes that all citizens are equally able to influence the making and application of laws. Given the influence of lawyers in US politics, that assumption requires equal representation by lawyers before both the legislature and the executive at all levels of government.

Virtually every problem in the area of legal services is related to this central issue of equality.[18]

Yet, there is a qualitative difference between the recognition that access to legal representation is an absolute necessity and the characterization of that necessity as a 'right'.

[18] R. Abel, 'Legal Services' in *Handbook of Applied Sociology 1981*, ch. 19.

To elevate the concept of access to justice to the status of 'right' is to view it with symbolism, reverence and, at least, a certain degree of inalienability. This is one argument that has been used to determine an appropriate system of legal delivery. Its proponents argue that this right is protected in the same way as democratic rights, such as the right of a citizen to vote, to assemble, and to speak freely.

The concept of 'rights', though apparently straightforward, is far from unproblematic. Precisely because of their symbolic character, rights are difficult to define. Removed from objective, unimpassioned discourse, they are in fact frequently ignored.

The positive aspect of 'rights' is that they give the person being represented a certain amount of protection from political interference. One of the main objectives of legal services advocates has been to entrench the concept of the entitlement to representation deeply in the public consciousness, in order to place the institutions of legal services on a firmer footing. In the past, the perceived 'charitable' character of legal services has, to an extent, prevented the question of legal needs from being taken seriously in public debate. To seek recognition of an access 'right', then, may well raise the profile of the legal services issue and concomitantly give the access movement a firmer foundation. Difficulties arise in discussing the introduction of the concept of 'access rights', however, since that concept may, in itself, restrict the type of legal services that any particular government, professional organization, or other body may decide to provide.

Rights proponents argue that a juridical model of legal services is the most appropriate delivery mechanism if all citizens are entitled as a matter of right to legal representation. Superficially, the juridical model is attractive to access rights theorists because services are provided on a case by case basis by a wide range of advocates. Such a model is perceived to be a reflection of the independent 'legal system', based on the belief that all litigants can have their cases heard in a comparable fashion and that representation is best accomplished by the 'independent' practitioner.

Opponents of the 'rights' theory condemn its irrational insistence on pursuing individuality over a calculable collective welfare. They argue that a more compelling justification for legal services is a utilitarian approach, recognizing that human existence is enhanced by the provision of such services and that priorities for the development of legal services programmes ought to be determined according to what will generate the greatest benefit for the greatest number of recipients. This approach has

developed in the United States in the last two decades[19] and is an outgrowth of the recognition of many writers that the allocation of scarce
resources to legal services requires careful assessment of their effective
allocation.

We find that in the United States in the 1980s, the utilitarian approach
to legal services is under attack. Professor Marshall Breger is sharply critical of utilitarianism as a guiding principle in legal services delivery.[20]
Breger extols the greater humanity of a legal services delivery model
which is based upon the 'rights' theory, arguing that utilitarianism
requires that value judgments about the legal position of others must be
made arbitrarily by disinterested persons. Only rights theories, he argues,
give primacy to individual dignity. Thus, the debate is far reaching and is
conducted by scholars remote from the usual areas of legal services discourse.[21]

The merits and faults of both theoretical bases for legal services delivery have great implications for the access movement. Utilitarianism is
most compatible with a clinical, public-funded, salaried lawyer model of
delivery, whereas the rights theory suggests a more traditional judicare
system. In fact, an imaginative interpretation of the right to counsel may
well include both the judicare and the community-based delivery models,
although it has been seen that at a theoretical level, rights theory and utilitarianism have been perceived as completely incompatible.

---

[19] The emphasis on broadly based reform, rather than on a case-by-case approach, may
be seen in the uniquely American characteristics of the legal services plan in the United
States, as explained by Professor Menkel-Meadow:

In reviewing trends in the development of legal aid in the United States, it is essential to note those characteristics of legal aid which are peculiarly American. In 1977, Clinton Bamberger, then a member of the
Legal Services Corporation national staff, identified three 'immutable characteristics' of the American
legal aid system: (1) public financing, (2) law reform (rule changes) for the poor, and (3) full-time salaried
staff lawyers, specializing in 'poverty law' (Bamberger, 1977). To these characteristics, I would add two
more. First is the employment of paralegals, who are legal assistants, trained especially to aid in providing
services to the poor, many of whom were drawn from the indigenous poverty community. Second is the
use of explicitly political forms of advocacy to better the conditions under which poor people live. These
include community organizing and lobbying, national research or 'back-up' centres specializing in certain
areas of law affecting the poor, and the use of peculiarly American legal constructs to fight the legal bat-
tles of the poor—the class action, group plaintiffs, and American constitutional theory as a device for
expanding both substantive and procedural legal rights. (Dooley and Houseman, 1982) (Menkel-Meadow,
supra, note 13, at 31–2. Professor Menkel-Meadow's references are to Bamberger, *The American Approach:
Public Funding, Law Reform, and Staff Attorneys* (1977) Cornell Intl. LJ 207–12 and to Dooley and
Houseman, *Legal Services in the 80's and Challenges Facing the Poor* (1982), 15 Clearinghouse Review
104–18).

[20] Breger, 'Legal Aid for the Poor: A Conceptual Analysis' (1982), 60 North Carolina LR
282–363.

[21] See R. Dworkin, *Taking Rights Seriously* (London: Duckworth, 1977), and H. L. A. Hart,
Law, Liberty and Morality (London: Oxford University Press, 1968).

Models of delivery

The most frequently discussed aspect of legal services is the question of delivery models. Although much of the literature has focused on the distinctions between the use of salaried, full time legal services lawyers as opposed to private practitioners, we find a growing recognition that much of what the providers have accomplished, whether working in legal services on a full time basis or on a case-by-case basis, is not only comparable, but in many instances identical. In reviewing recent developments, the writer discerns in the national reports significant developments in the delivery of legal services concerning the types of clients served, the problems handled, the providers of the service, and the service model. All appeared to be in a state of flux. An observable trend in countries with sophisticated social welfare schemes such as the Netherlands, Finland, England, Canada, and the United States, is the movement towards a mixed delivery system—a development that is worthy of careful analysis.

In our search for a typology or framework for analysis of these recent developments in legal services, it is helpful to contrast the 'service' model of delivery with what has been described as the 'strategic' model of legal services.[22] Such a contrast takes the reader beyond the traditional discussions which tended to become mired in debate between the merits of private and public lawyering delivery schemes. Although service schemes and strategic schemes are not mutually exclusive, it is helpful to recognize that models of delivery of service to low income people have developed within a spectrum in which the poles are represented by a purely service orientation and a model dedicated to the strategic approach. Like the philosophical access rights as opposed to utilitarian approach, an analysis of these approaches and their underlying premises will assist in our examination of the mixed delivery models which have recently emerged.

The service model is the traditional and the most common form of legal services. An outgrowth of the juridical and charitable approach,[23] service models confine their attention to discrete claims and problems brought to a programme by an individual with a readily categorized legal

[22] The author wishes to acknowledge the contribution of Marc Galanter of the University of Wisconsin to this section of the paper. Galanter's paper on 'Making Law Work for the Oppressed' (1983), 3 The Other Side 7–15 develops the contrast between 'services' and 'strategic' legal services.

[23] The juridical rights approach to legal aid is contrasted to the welfare rights approach by M. Cappelletti, J. Gordley and E. Johnson, Jr., *Toward Equal Justice: A Comparative Study of Legal Aid in Modern Societies* (Dobbs Ferry, NY: Oceana, 1975) at 26–7 and at 110–12, and 124–8.

problem. This approach grows directly out of the traditional approach to protecting rights which:

. . . has been essentially legalistic and individual; it involves the promulgation of legal standards defining the obligations of the state, the vesting of corresponding legal rights in individuals, and the provision of judicial or quasi-judicial redress if these state obligations are not met. The end of this approach is to assign each individual his proper rights and responsibilities; the means is to provide objective legal standards and to ensure their impartial application . . . The nineteenth century granted legal protection to the right to aid; however, the right remained in good part charity since distrust of affirmative state action and a concern for a purely formal equality led to reliance on the charitable services of the bar. As that distrust subsided in the face of concern for an effective quality, it was only natural to attempt to combine such action with the traditional approach to protecting political rights.[24]

It is important to note that within the service mode, the lawyer (in some instances, the paralegal) can respond only in cases where clients, aware of their problem, have sought out legal assistance. Whether this assistance is provided by the private lawyer or by the salaried lawyer, in bureaux such as those created by the Quebec Commission des Services Juridiques,[25] or the municipal legal aid offices in Sweden, is of little consequence. The results are essentially the same. The role of the scheme is to represent low income persons who can establish that they are economically eligible and that their problems are worthy of a lawyer's time.[26] Inevitably overloaded, service models can expend little time or energy in educating the community or on outreach programmes. Since service models accept the norms of the legal system and provide a service for poor people which, in the opinion of the administrators (inevitably lawyers), is the same for the poor as for the rich, poor people using service schemes face many of the same obstacles that they would encounter within the traditional setting. Such service models offer little recognition of the uniqueness of the poor person's lifestyle. They neither make the service psychologically more accessible, nor do they attempt to handle problems which have not been on the traditional agenda of legal services (e.g. eviction). The service

[24] M. Cappelletti, J. Gordley and E. Johnson, Jr., *Toward Equal Justice: A Comparative Study of Legal Aid in Modern Societies* (Dobbs Ferry, NY: Oceana, 1975) at 109–10.

[25] It is worth remembering that there exists a wide variety of methods for establishing 'worthiness'. It may also be determined in direct response to the caseload and funding of the particular scheme.

[26] For a description of the Quebec Commission des Services Juridiques see F. H. Zemans, *Perspectives on Legal Aid: A Comparative Study* (London: Frances Pinter, 1979). The national report on Canada for the First Congress on Civil Procedure written by Zemans, at 98–103.

model reinforces the distance between the 'recipient' and the 'deliverer' of the service by encouraging clients to assume passive and dependent roles in their relation with the legal aid scheme. Lawyers write briefs, interview witnesses, negotiate settlements, and go to court. The client's perspective is generally of an over-worked, under-paid lawyer who is dealing with the immediate problem and ignoring the fundamental cancer of poverty and poverty-related problems that continue to survive and destroy.[27]

In contrast to the service model of legal services, there is the 'strategic' legal services scheme. Such a programme is oriented to identifying the significant social problems facing the community it is serving. While dealing with the inevitable daily problems, a strategic legal services programme attempts to develop a long-term approach of research, reform, and education to deal with the more fundamental issues. Rather than handling cases which are relevant to the lawyer's experiences, a strategic programme sets priorities in one or several areas of concern to a particular community such as the environment, housing, land-ownership, occupational health, or immigration, to enumerate but a few. In concert with the geographic community or the community of interest, the professional will consider collective issues or the complaints of a class of individuals. (Thus, an emphasis on handling the problems of tenants will lead to an analysis of security of tenure and rent control.) A significant distinction between the service and strategic models is in methodology. While the

[27] The major studies of legal services lawyers have been undertaken in recent years in the United States. These studies are of lawyers working for the Legal Services Corporation which goes beyond the service model and is considered to be the basis for the strategic approach. The major studies to date of legal services programmes include Bellow, 'Turning Solutions Into Problems: The Legal Aid Experience' (1977), 34 *NLADA Briefcase*, 4 at 106; Bellow, 'Legal Aid in the United States' (1980), 14 *Clearinghouse Review* 337; Erlanger, 'Lawyers and Neighbourhood Legal Services: Social Background and the Impetus for Reform' (1978), 12 *Law and Society Review* 253; F. Handler, 'Perspectives on Legal Aid: United States', in *Perspectives on Legal Aid: An International Survey*, ed. Zemans (London: Frances Pinter, 1979); J. F. Handler, E. J. Hollingsworth, and H. S. Erlanger, *Lawyers and the Pursuit of Legal Rights* (New York: Academic Press, 1978); Hosticka, 'We Don't Care About What Happened: We Only Care About What is Going to Happen: Lawyer-Client Negotiations of Reality', 26 *Social Problems* 599; E. Johnson, *Justice and Reform: The Formative Years of the American Legal Services Program*, (NJ: Transaction Books, 1978); Katz, *Poor People's Lawyers in Transition*, (New Brunswick, NJ: 1982); Legal Services Corporation, *Delivery Systems Study*, (Washington: 1980); Menkel-Meadow and Meadow, 'Allocating Legal Resources in a Non-Market Context: The Case of the Legal Services Attorney', paper presented to the Midwest Political Science Assoc. Annual Meeting, (Cincinnati: 1981); Menkel-Meadow and Meadow, 'Resource Allocation in Legal Services: The Limits of Rationality in Attorney Decisions', paper presented to the Law and Society annual meeting (Amhert: 1981); and H. P. Stumpf, *Community Politics and Legal Services: The Other Side of the Law*, (Beverly Hills: Sage, 1975).

service model perceives itself as bound to the court and to litigation, the strategic model views advocacy as only one potential strategy. Other strategies might include tenant organizing, lobbying the legislature, television and media coverage, or community picketing of a particularly abhorrent landlord.

The distinction between the strategic and service models of delivery should not be taken to describe schemes which are mutually exclusive. Most legal service administrators have been attracted to the juridical or service model. The problem inherent in the service approach is that seldom, if ever, are there enough funds available for all needed services to be provided to all persons eligible for the service. As Professor Mary Jane Mossman of Canada has written:

From the perspective of legal aid administrators, moreover, the focus on individual rights prevents decision-making which allocates available funds on the basis of cost-benefit analysis, an eligible client must receive legal aid for a service included by the programme even though, by any objective standards, the funds could provide a greater benefit to an eligible client for services excluded from the programme. Unless funds are available for *all* eligible clients for *any* needed legal services, it is inevitable that legal services will not be 'covered' in a programme using a juridical rights approach.[28]

The attraction of progressive theorists to a utilitarian, welfare, or strategic approach to legal services has grown in large measure from recognition that governments will seldom provide sufficient funds to allow all individual and collective claims to be asserted.

Models of legal services

The discussion of various analytical frameworks for legal services brings us face to face with the significant issues that confront current developments in legal services. The national reports indicate that in all parts of the world an on-going debate is taking place between those committed to developing the welfare rights or strategic approach to legal services and those who are desirous of expanding traditional service models. The national reports clearly indicate that legal services, even in wealthy nations where the welfare state is well developed, remain a fragile movement, frequently lacking direction and unity and existing solely at the whim of government. Unable to distinguish themselves from other social services, legal services have often been the subject of political attack as

[28] Mary Jane Mossman, 'Legal Aid in Canada' (unp., 1983) at 28–9.

governments have become more conservative in the changing political climate of the late 1970s.

The most significant and progressive development in recent years appears to be a movement towards mixed delivery systems which combine aspects of the service and strategic models, and which combine the use of the private bar and salaried lawyers based in clinics to deliver legal services. This move to a mixed system is often a reflection of the political compromises and partnerships necessitated by declining political and financial support for legal aid and the need for political and, in some instances, financial support of the organized legal profession.[29]

In 1977, Professor Vittorio Denti noted the almost exclusive use of a judicare system of legal services in European countries:

The first trend, certainly more homogenous with the laws of civil procedure in liberal countries, can be traced in the legal systems which have maintained practically unchanged the scheme of legal assistance introduced in the second half of the nineteenth century. These were based on: (a) the obligation for the lawyer to render free services to indigent litigants: (b) special committees establishing the requisites to be met for free assistance; (c) a preliminary inquiry into the probability of a favourable outcome.

This view of legal assistance as an honourary duty of the lawyer, has remained practically unchanged in the countries (like Italy, Spain and Belgium) where the legislation is still that of the nineteenth century. On the contrary, in other countries, changes have recently been made, leading to the direct or indirect coverage of lawyers' fees . . . All these reforms provide that fees are paid directly to the lawyer on public funds.[30]

Denti did recognize a somewhat different system operating in both Great Britain and Sweden, but noted as well that these systems did not represent a clear break from the judicare model:

Like the English reform, the Swedish reform of 1973, though one of the most advanced legal assistance laws in Europe, is a compromise between the traditional model of services rendered by private lawyers and the need to organize assistance by means of public offices established for this purpose.[31]

The judicare model must be compared to the community legal services model—the law clinic—which developed in the United States during the

---

[29] The support of the American Bar Association in the face of the unmitigated attack on the Legal Services Corporation in the United States is the most significant example of this phenomenon.

[30] Denti, *supra* note 1, at 175–6 of the Storme and Casman volume and, with editorial revisions, at 351 of the Zemans volume.

[31] *Id.*, Storme and Casman at 177 and Zemans at 353.

1960s. Denti discusses the community clinic model of legal services solely in respect of the United States, although community-based clinics had developed during the 1970s to a greater or lesser extent in the Netherlands, Canada, Finland, the United Kingdom, New Zealand, and Australia.[32]

The contrast between the traditional service-oriented models which exist in varying degrees in most countries of the world and the community-based law clinic with its more strategic welfare-based orientation operating in the United States still prevails. The service model with the private lawyer as the primary deliverer of services represents the major or exclusive delivery system in France, the Federal Republic of Germany, Great Britain, Japan, Israel, Australia, South Africa, the Netherlands, New Zealand, and the Canadian provinces of Alberta, New Brunswick, and Ontario. But despite the recent commitment by the Legal Services Corporation that at least 10 per cent of their funds would be spent on judicare schemes, the United States has retained a legal services model that is predominantly staffed by salaried lawyers and which continues to take a utilitarian reform approach to legal services.

Many countries with judicare models are developing strategically oriented elements in their programmes. The Netherlands is an interesting example of the trend towards a mixed delivery system. Holland introduced a judicare system in 1957 and extended it during the 1970s. The judicare system still absorbs most of the public funds for legal services, but since 1974 Holland has seen the development of a state clinic movement in the *Buro's voor Rechtschulp* (BVRs). These clinics were first established in 1974, out of a desire on the part of the government and the legal profession to become more directly involved in the community clinic movement which had been initiated in Holland by the development of the law shops during the previous five years. Law shops had been opened by Dutch law students as a response to the student unrest in the late 1960s. The first such law shop opened in Tilburg in 1969 and was inspired by the North Kensington Law Centre in London, England. Legal services were freely provided in the law shops by law students who worked as volunteers. The offices were casual, informal, and client-oriented. The concept was contagious in Holland, and within a few years approximately ninety shops operated on a regular basis throughout Holland. As Freek Bruinsma, our Dutch national reporter, writes:

[32] Some of the developments in these countries are discussed in this paper. In Saskatchewan and Nova Scotia American-style community clinics have been adopted as the delivery model.

The political influence on the law shop movement was much more important than their actual market-share in legal services would suggest. The only, rather controversial figure (based on a cumulation and extrapolation of the annual reports of the biggest law shops) is about 60,000 clients in 1974, a top year for the law shops: this amounts to about 5% of the articulated demand for legal services of individuals. The law shop movement derived its political influence from the fact that it put into practice an alternative legal service: the existence of a law shop was a practical criticism of the professional legal services by the private bar. In the first years of their existence, some doubts were raised about the quality of the legal services by law students, but these were not substantiated, while the law shop movement referred convincingly to the accessibility of the law shop, the kind of legal problems the law shops handled, i.e., welfare state law, and the kind of people the law shops serviced, i.e., low income people. At all these points a law shop scored better than the office of a lawyer, at least in the eyes of the public at large.[33]

By the mid 1970s, the Dutch Bar Association came to accept, or at least no longer to oppose, the law shop concept and recognized that such shops did not detract clients or income from the private bar, but rather expanded the market for legal services by providing lawyers and paralegal services to clients who previously found the system inaccessible. As well, the law shops expanded the demand for legal services by generating litigation and referring previously unrepresented clients to the private bar. The Dutch judicare system, in existence for nearly twenty years, theoretically available for both litigation and legal advice, was administratively cumbersome and ill equipped to handle welfare law problems. The Bar Association joined forces with the law shop movement in lobbying the Dutch government to set up the BVRs. After 1974, when the government took over their initiative, some law shops continued to exist, providing sporadic services dependent upon voluntary assistance.

BVRs were funded by the Dutch government and some forty offices have been established between 1974 and 1980, employing approximately 200 lawyers. These offices have the dual purpose of granting legal aid certificates for the judicare scheme and giving readily accessible legal advice. Although the staff lawyers are progressive, their heavy caseloads and conservative management boards have limited the possibility of social action. The use of the *Buros* had grown to 250,000 clients in 1981, approximately five per cent of the Dutch population.[34] *Buros* not only grew in number

---

[33] Bruinsma, Dutch National Report (1982), at 4.

[34] *Id.* at 6. An empirical study conducted in 1979 by the Dutch government examined the distribution of the clients of *Buros* and law shops. The income distribution in the client group matched approximately the income distribution of the population as a whole. Selection of clients is regarded as incompatible with the Dutch constitution (*id.* at 8).

and size, but their budget increased tenfold from 1977 to 1981, when it represented 9 per cent of the total legal services budget.[35]

A significant empirical study of legal services in the Netherlands was conducted by Professor Freek Bruinsma in conjunction with law students. The project adopted the consumer's perspective with respect to the actual access to and quality of public legal services in Holland. A law student went as an undercover client with a self-made problem for advice to different BVRs. The Bruinsma study showed that one-third of the advice given was of a poor quality while one-fifth was considered to be of a really bad quality. According to the law students, they were quite often given incomplete or out-of-date information which would have impaired the client's legal position. The report was critical of both the legalistic attitude of the salaried lawyers and the highly service oriented approach of the Dutch *Buros*.[36] The Dutch mixed delivery system is very much a service scheme with a minimal reform component. As Jeremy Cooper writes:

Access for all, national conformity, lack of local community involvement, bureaucratic thinking on policy: these are the features of the Buro philosophy, and they do not make happy bedmates for the romantic political radicalism that was sought in the early 70s to use lawshops as a spearhead for more fundamental social reforms within the state as a whole.[37]

Finland is another example of a country that expanded its judicare system in the 1970s to include legal services offices staffed with full-time lawyers. A system of 'common legal aid' was created at the commune level. Communes were allowed to establish legal aid *Buros* either alone or with other communes. By 1981 virtually all of the population was included in this *Buro* system wherein one or two communities received service from a full-time lawyer and one clerk. The programme was staffed by young, inexperienced lawyers who were controlled through the Finnish Bar Association. Workers in the common legal aid programme acted in a fashion comparable to lawyers who deal primarily with court matters.[38] The

[35] Expenditures for legal services jumped from 25 million guilders in 1972 to 225 million guilders in 1982 (Bruinsma, Dutch National Report (1982), at 10).

[36] See *id.* at 8–10.

[37] J. Cooper, 'Preserving Justice for the Poor: Can Public Legal Services Survive a Recession?' (unp., 1982) at 22.

[38] The Finnish national report offers a breakdown of their caseload:

Family	30%	Criminal matters	12%
Execution of wills	17%	Administrative matters	11%
Housing rents	5%	Other civil matters	20%

(Nousainen, Finnish National Report (1982) at 15).

Finnish system seems to be another example of the extension of the service model which places little emphasis on aggregating claims or pressing for reform of either the substantive law or the position of underprivileged persons.

A most interesting development in mixed delivery systems has occurred in Canada. Legal aid in Canada has been accepted in the last decade as a joint venture of the legal profession and the federal and provincial governments. Although Canada does not have a nationally administered legal services scheme, as is the case in the United States, there is some level of uniformity in the service delivered by the various provincial schemes because of the federal government's introduction of a cost-sharing scheme for criminal legal aid in 1972. Because the Canadian Constitution places the administration of justice within provincial responsibility, it has allowed Canada to develop twelve different legal aid schemes (in the ten provinces as well as in the Yukon and Northwest Territories). Thus, we see in Canada the full range of legal services from exclusively judicare to combinations of judicare and community clinics, to exclusively community clinics at the other end of the spectrum. Development of provincial schemes rather than a centralized federal scheme has encouraged a number of experiments, as well as an interchange of ideas and experiences between the provinces. The provincial funding base and structure has allowed Canada to avoid the political onslaught of legal services which recently took place in the United States.

The various Canadian approaches can be summarized into three major strands: judicare, salaried lawyers, and the mixed delivery system—which has been labelled the 'Canadian compromise'. The first government funded legal aid scheme to be introduced in Canada was the judicare model, in 1967, in the province of Ontario. This scheme was a service delivery model funded by the government of Ontario and administered by the provincial Bar Association—the Law Society of Upper Canada. Services were delivered on a case-by-case basis by private practitioners to clients who were able to demonstrate eligibility for a legal aid certificate. Today, New Brunswick, Alberta, and the Yukon territories operate exclusively judicare schemes. At the other end of the spectrum we find that Nova Scotia, Saskatchewan, and Prince Edward Island have established salaried lawyer models of legal services. The 'Canadian compromise' of a mixed-delivery system has developed in the provinces of Quebec, Manitoba, British Columbia, Newfoundland, and most recently, in Ontario.

Professor Mary Jane Mossman, our Canadian national reporter, writes:

In Canada, most legal aid programs have adopted what is essentially a juridical rights approach, sometimes with added special programs modelled on the rights approach. The juridical rights approach, with its emphasis on defined 'coverage', is in place in six provinces (Alberta, Saskatchewan, Nova Scotia, New Brunswick, Prince Edward Island, and Newfoundland) and the two territories . . . In three other provinces (Manitoba, Quebec, and British Columbia), the legislation provides essentially for a juridical rights approach but there is some limited scope for a welfare rights approach as well. In Manitoba, for example, neighbourhood legal aid centres created by corporations appear to have encouraged law reform activities by law centres, in addition to the case by case services required by the statute; the Annual Report of the Quebec Commission contains details of the activities of individual regional corporations although, as the report notes:

> 'There is a marked tendency to put more emphasis, in the annual report, on community activities rather than activities pertaining to the individual representation of clients before the Courts. This is not significant with respect to the daily reality of the work implied for each type of activity. In fact, the individual representation of clients counts for the vast majority of efforts . . .'

In British Columbia, the Legal Services Society is organized primarily as a juridical rights model of legal aid services, although it also provides funding (or partial funding) to a few independent organizations which have law reform mandates in the nature of the welfare rights model.[39]

As can be seen from Professor Mossman's report, the Canadian legislation in mixed delivery systems is permissive rather than requiring the implementation of a welfare rights or strategic model of legal services.

Perhaps the most controversial mixed delivery system has been the modified welfare rights system which has evolved in Ontario. As in the Netherlands, the profession has grown to gradually accept the concept of community-based clinics staffed by salaried lawyers. The profession's acceptance of the welfare rights approach was brought about in no small measure by two judicial inquiries which strongly approved the clinic model and encouraged government to fund clinics with a more strategic and community orientation. There are over 45 clinics in Ontario operating with many features of the American welfare rights model of legal services. Some are speciality clinics providing services in specific areas of the law,[40] services to ethnic communities, including Native

---

[39] Mossman, *supra* note 28, at 30–1. The interior quotation is from Commission des Services Juridiques, *Ninth Annual Report*(1981), at 25.

[40] The strength of the community clinic movement in Ontario is its diversity and the specialization of its clinics. The speciality clinics include the Canadian Environmental Law Association (CELA), Metro Tenants Legal Services, Tenant Hotline, Landlord's Self Help—all located in Toronto.

Canadians,[41] or clinics dealing with underprivileged groups in the community such as children and the handicapped.[42] Community-elected boards of directors establish financial eligibility guidelines and service priorities so that the caseload accepted is not solely on the basis of individual merit, but with reference to the likelihood of establishing significant reform for a client group. The boards have full responsibility for allocating limited resources to the areas of service that they determine will be most effective.[43] As an auxiliary of the original judicare scheme, the Ontario clinics have been able to develop a strategic approach to legal services and in most instances move beyond a service model to being involved in community education, community development, and some significant law reform litigation. These clinics are involved in some of the most significant and far reaching projects affecting low-income persons in Canada.

Before concluding our discussion of mixed delivery systems, it is important to briefly consider the development of the British law centre movement. The United Kingdom has, since 1970, seen the development of law centres in England and Wales which have taken a strategic and social change approach to legal services. The first law centre opened in North Kensington, London, in 1970. This office had a high profile from the time of its opening, having involved itself in controversial issues of police harassment of West Indian immigrants and committing itself to the housing issues of the racial minorities who were locating themselves in metropolitan London. Although North Kensington continually fought for its survival, it was eventually able to consolidate its position financially and professionally. By 1974, there were five law centres in England, each of which was operated independently, was publicly funded, had its own community board, and was staffed by a full-time staff of law clerks and solicitors. The English legal professions have given limited support to the law centres and have on occasion joined the public outcry against the termination of funding for several law centres.

---

[41] The Centre for Spanish Speaking People, located in Toronto since 1972, is the oldest ethnic clinic still in existence. There is a growing number of clinics serving Native Canadians, including Kenora Community Legal Clinic and Thunder Bay District Native Legal Counselling Services. Staff in both Native clinics speak Ojibway and include Native paralegals.

[42] Two important clinics are Justice for Children and Advocacy Research Centre for the Handicapped (ARCH).

[43] The clinics are also located in Toronto and concentrate on test-case litigation, lobbying for reform of legislation, community education, and some case-handling for their specific constituency.

By 1980, forty-two law centres were in operation in England and Wales, with the majority located in urban regions. The strength of the law centres has been their local management by members of the client community who have been prepared to join the struggle to sustain the continued existence of their law centre.[44] Funding for the law centres has been diversified and has come primarily from the Department of the Environment, with a stipulation that there be a 25 per cent matching contribution from the local government where the law centre is located. This diversity of funding has allowed the law centres to be resistant to attack, as no one government agency could close all of the centres. Since 1974, a law centre federation has existed and carries out a programme of new centre development, staff training, and publication of an excellent newsletter.

Cooper has written that the short-term strength of the law centre movement in England is its deep community roots, diversity of funding, and developing co-ordination. But he suggests that, in the long term, law centres will probably remain a marginal element to the state provision of legal services to the poor.[45] The marginality of the British law centres may ultimately be perceived as their major strength and allow the law centre movement to flourish as a strategic element within the basic judicare scheme.

The national reports on developments in legal services note the continued concern with the assessment of existing legal services schemes. In common law countries where the judicare model took root in the early 1970s,[46] we find a movement in the early 1980s to broaden these schemes to include programmes with reform components.[47]

National reports also note the caseload pressures on legal services offices. It is these pressures which prevent these offices from responding to their reform agendas and force them to deal only with burgeoning caseloads. Recent studies[48] in the United States indicate that American

---

[44] By comparison, the struggle for the continued existence of the Legal Services Corporation in the United States was waged by staff attorneys and the American Bar Association; the American client community had only limited involvement.

[45] *Supra* note 37, at 36.

[46] For example, Canada, Australia, New Zealand, and England.

[47] Our New Zealand national reporter, Smith, writes of widespread discontent with the existing judicare model of services. The first neighbourhood law office opened in Auckland, in August of 1977. As in other jurisdictions where professionally dominated legal services schemes already existed, the Grey-Lynn Law Centre encountered opposition. Under the supervision and control of the Auckland District Law Society, the project has had only limited community involvement in its administration and must continue to legitimate itself with its two distinct constituencies; its clientele and the legal profession.

[48] *Supra* note 27 for a full listing of recent American studies.

legal services lawyers have become acclimatized to their work and no longer engage on a day-to-day basis in the political struggles against the issues that fundamentally affect their communities.

According to Gary Bellow, former legal services attorney and presently a law professor and teacher of legal services lawyers at Harvard University, the practice of legal services lawyers in the 1970s was characterized by routine handling of cases, low client autonomy and increased client dependence on legal services staff, a tendency to favour settlement over litigation, and a focus on needs as presented by the client rather than as uncovered by the lawyer's broader investigations.[49] Bellow attributed much of this behaviour to the crushing pressure of high caseloads,[50] the complexity of cases that could consume all of the lawyer's time, and the emergency quality of many of the cases. As Bellow has noted:

Increasing amount of regulation and law governing activity in the United States makes the possible number of cases in any given poor population extremely large if not unlimited. Every conflict in the family, at school, at work, or with a vast array of governmental institutions has some legal aspect—that is, it is capable of being handled in whole or in part by a lawyer. Moreover, it is now reasonably well established that demand for legal services increases with supply. The more lawyers that are available, the more clients who will seek their help.[51]

Simply put, our national reports from both Canada and the United States indicate that with the expansion of the caseloads in both the judicare and clinic systems of legal aid the two schemes have become virtually indistinguishable. Judicare schemes have generated some mixed delivery aspects with limited reform elements, while the clinic model has moved away from strategic approach with an inherent social philosophy and responded to the pressures of caseloads and individual client demands.

Mossman, our Canadian national reporter, writes:

In the result, there is remarkable uniformity in the services actually available to legal aid clients across Canada, notwithstanding the difference in models in delivering services. The combination of minimum standard requirements in the cost-sharing agreements with the federal government, and the inevitable limit on provincial spending for legal aid programmes, has resulted in a salaried model which can offer some accessibility and expertise, but which generally

---

[49] See Bellow (1977), *supra* note 27.

[50] Average caseloads hovered between 100 and 400 cases per lawyer per year during this period. *Vide* Auerbach Corporation, *Office of Legal Services Individual Project Evaluation Final Report*, (Washington: 1971).

[51] Bellow (1980), *supra* note 27; see also Bellow and Bellow and Kettleson, 'The Politics of Scarcity in Legal Services Work' (1979), 36 *NLADA Briefcase* 5–11.

cannot provide more than the services traditionally available in the fee-for-service model.[52]

Katz has arrived at similar conclusions regarding the situation in the United States since the creation of the Legal Services Corporation in 1974:

In the seventies, reform activity in Legal Services was treated officially as a professional, apolitical matter. Within the administration of Legal Services, 'anti-poverty' rhetoric passed from being an officially sanctioned routine—Legal Services Programmes originally had to report annually to the OEO-Office of Legal Services with an evaluation of the year's progress in reducing poverty—to an embarrassment to a dimming memory. Ever since its creation in 1974, the Legal Services Corporation has steered clear of indignant commentary on the social reality of poverty in America. The research projects funded by the Corporation have emphasized standard professional and administrative concerns—how to keep the federal courts open to Legal Services litigation, how to reduce staff turnover—not the development of a guiding social philosophy on a relation of the law to the social class justice for the poor.[53]

The fundamental question continues to be: what type of service model should be implemented or, for that matter, retained, in light of the similarity of the services performed? Cost may, unfortunately, become the basis for such a determination. The significant issue of a system's potential is overlooked in its concern with cost effectiveness. In Canada, the cost issue became significant at the end of the 1970s, as government restraint programmes threatened both existing and proposed legal aid services:

When money was more readily available, discussions about legal aid concentrated on meeting needs. Now discussions focus on controlling cost. But the objectives of legal aid have not changed, they still relate to meeting needs. What has changed is the resources available in legal aid. Thus, this, like our newly heightened interest in the cost of justice, is a result of government financial restraint.[54]

Two studies of legal aid costs in Canada are noteworthy. A three-year evaluation was undertaken in the province of British Columbia, to analyse the cost of delivering criminal legal aid services under a salaried, public defender system.[55] This study concluded that there is little differ-

---

[52] *Supra* note 28, at 46.

[53] Katz, 'Legalizing Poverty: Poor People's Lawyers in Transition' (unp., n.d.) at 3.

[54] 'Legal Aid in the Age of Restraint', quoted in Mossman, *supra* note 28, at 48–9.

[55] As there was no public defender system in British Columbia, it was necessary to establish a small project office staffed by three full-time lawyers, a paralegal, and a secretary. The public defense office routinely offered cases to the private bar when it became overloaded or when a conflict of interest arose, but cases were referred in blocks and there was

ence in cost of services whether provided by a salaried lawyer or through a fee-for-service model using lawyers in private practice.[56]

Significantly, related costs within the justice system rose dramatically under the judicare schemes in comparison with the public defender system. The British Columbia study concluded that judicare lawyers pleaded their clients guilty less often than public defense lawyers[57] and that judicare lawyers proceeded to trial more often than public defenders.[58]

Judicare and public defense clients experienced overall similar guilty rates, however, with about 60 per cent of the cases ending with guilty verdicts.[59] There was, however, a significant difference in sentences received: about 30 per cent of public defense clients, compared to 40 per cent of judicare clients, were sentenced to jail terms.[60] The relatively higher number of judicare clients receiving jail terms implies higher costs for correctional institutions for these clients, in addition to the costs of legal representation.

no screening of individual cases prior to referral. The study involved a comparison of data on all cases handled by the public defender lawyers and all cases referred to private practice lawyers during the period of the study.

[56] The average costs per case were as follows:

	Vancouver Judicare	Burnaby Judicare	Burnaby Public Defense
Average cost per case			
With eligibility assessment	$263.66	$225.36	$235.65
Without eligibility assessment	253.07	218.53	227.62

The results of this study may be subject to quite dramatic changes with only small shifts in the variables. The report indicates that, 'If the caseload in the Criminal Defense Office were increased by one case per lawyer per month, the average public defense cost would drop to $223.00, or effectively the same average cost as a judicare case. An increase of four cases per lawyer per month would decrease the average cost for a public defence case to $192.00, thirty-three dollars below the average judicare cost. The determination of accurate cost comparison depends as well on the level of judicare costs which are directly related to judicare staff.' (Patricia Brantingham and Peter Burns, 'The Burnaby, British Columbia Experimental Public Defender Project: An Evaluation' (Dept. of Justice of Canada, and BC Legal Services Society, 1981), Report III. The table is at page 61, and the quotation at 65).

[57] Percentage of cases ending in a guilty plea:
    Vancouver Judicare: 35.9%
    Burnaby Judicare: 38.8%
    Burnaby Public Defense: 51.0%
    (*Id*. Report II at 35.)

[58] Percentage of total cases going to trial:
    Vancouver Judicare: 42.7%
    Burnaby Judicare: 36.4%
    Burnaby Public Defense: 29.1%
    (*Id*. Report II at 36.)

[59] *Id*. Report II at 40.   [60] *Id*. Report II at 46.

While public defense clients obtained more lenient sentences, the fact that more of them pleaded guilty raised the possibility that public defence clients had been denied the opportunity of a fair trial to determine guilt:

However, . . . in order to obtain those sentences, public defenders are entering guilty pleas for clients who would have been acquitted had they been represented by a member of the private bar. This fact goes to the heart of the purpose of defense counsel within that system . . . [If] use of public defenders results in guilty pleas by a statistically significant number of accused persons who have been found not guilty at trial, that alone is a reason for rejecting the public defender system of legal defense.[61]

The British Columbia research does raise questions about the assumption that the salaried service model is necessarily more cost effective. It also forces the legal aid analyst to compare the quality of service provided. Mossman writes: 'The report's value, however, lies in its clear demonstration of the mutability of cost figures for judicare and public defender services, depending on the tariff levels and payment categories for fee-for-service lawyers, compared to case volumes and salary levels for the salaried lawyers.'[62]

It is significant to compare the British Columbian results with cost studies in the Province of Quebec in 1981, where the Commission des Services Juridiques provides both criminal and civil services through both private practitioners and salaried lawyers.[63] In 1980-1, the Quebec Commission operated 142 legal aid offices, of which forty were only open part-time. Three hundred and thirty-one lawyers and 442 other full-time staff were employed through this scheme.[64] Of the 200,332 cases handled in 1980-1, 69.3 per cent were handled by salaried staff and the remaining 30.7 per cent were referred to private lawyers. A cost comparison was undertaken using the methodology of an earlier study.[65] The latter study

[61] 'Brief Presented on Behalf of the British Columbia Section of the Canadian Bar Association concerning the Burnaby Public Defenders Pilot-Project Study' 1982, at 23.
[62] *Supra* note 28, at 56. The 1982 cutback in tariffs in British Columbia would have made the judicare services even most cost effective than the salaried lawyers. Only by significantly increasing case volumes or reducing salaries could the salaried lawyer model retain its effectiveness.
[63] 'Evaluation de l'Aide Juridiques' (1982), at 35-6.
[64] *Id.* at 22-3.
[65] 'Etude des Coutes d'Execution des Dossiers Juridiques' 1977-8, discussed in *id.* at 56 and 80.

confirmed the cost effectiveness of the salaried model demonstrated by the earlier study.[66]

The 1980–1 evaluation report in Quebec indicates that the increase in the cost of salaried legal aid services was less than 14 per cent between 1977–8 and 1980–1, and could be related primarily to the increase in the average years of experience of salaried lawyers working in the Quebec plan.[67] The Quebec study also noted the relevance of the tariff: for example, a tariff increase effective March, 1978 meant large percentage increases in costs for criminal and family legal aid cases handled by private practitioners.

The two Canadian costs studies, in Quebec and British Columbia, arrived at different results with respect to the comparative costs of salaried and private lawyers. Any comparison between the sets of results, however, must take into account certain differences in the scopes of the reports. The Quebec figures are based on a comparison of the delivery of both civil and criminal legal aid services, while the British Columbia study was much more restricted, with a salaried public defender office created specifically for the project. It is difficult to assess the relative effects of the tariff paid to private lawyers in Quebec and British Columbia to determine what, if any, correlation the tariffs would have on the outcome of the studies. The Quebec study attributes the cost effectiveness of the salaried model to the increasing experience of the staff,[68] but also notes that cost effectiveness seems to increase when salaried offices employ three or more lawyers.[69] The Quebec study would appear to be more meaningful than the British Columbia study both because of the larger caseload and the greater number of lawyers, and the length of time that the Quebec legal aid services has been in existence. Although government and bureaucrats continue to become much more concerned with the

[66] *Couts Comparatifs d'Execution des Dossiers d'Aide Juridique*, 1980–1:

1 Nature de Dossier	2 Cout par dossier avocats salaries	3 Cout par dossier pratique privée	4 Variation 3 vs. 2
Séparation, divorce	$267.14	$319.53	19.6%
Autre matrimonial	108.79	133.89	23.1%
Compte en defense	84.12	233.77	166.0%
Autre civil	65.27	142.37	118.1%
Criminel	105.17	214.22	103.7%
Moyenne (Average)	$105.44	$221.58	110.1%

Source: 10th Annual Report Commission des Services Juridiques at 160.

[67] Lawyers had an average of 6.8 years of experience in 1977–8, and 8.5 years in 1980–1 (*supra* note 63, at 81).

[68] *Id*. at 81.   [69] *Id*. at 81.

issue of cost effectiveness, discussions of cost have done little to advance the discussion of legal services to low income people. Since both salaried and private lawyers schemes provide similar services, the cost effectiveness discussions become a digression from the crucial discussion of the democratization of legal services and provision of appropriate legal services to respond to the socio-economic needs of underprivileged and low income persons. Mossman writes in her Canadian report:

As is evident, there has been a major focus on the issue of relative cost in the delivery of legal aid services in Canada in recent years. To an extent, the focus on the cost-effectiveness has detracted from, rather than contributed to, a better understanding of legal aid objectives. Thus, rather than questioning decisions about equality objectives or the approaches to providing legal aid services, most legal aid efforts have been directed to assessing models of delivering such services; and because both salaried and private practice lawyers provide essentially similar services, the focus on cost effectiveness has been directed very narrowly indeed. Moreover, the preoccupation with cost-effectiveness seems to have obscured, for everyone except the administrators and government, the fact that salaried lawyer services provide an opportunity for cost control—potentially a much more significant feature than cost savings even on the scale reported by the Quebec evaluation.[70]

Although I have concentrated my discussion on new developments in models of legal services, particularly the evolution of the mixed delivery system, it is important to recognize that in most countries we find continued limited legal services programmes for low income persons provided by a variety of juridical rights approaches. In western countries, the juridical rights schemes have seen some considerable developments. In Germany, in 1980, the *Prozesskostenhilferecht* (law concerning relief of litigation costs) replaced the traditional *Armenrecht* (poor man's law). The new law retains the basic structure of the German judicare schemes but increases both the numbers of persons who are entitled to legal services, and more importantly, for the first time provides for legal advice outside of a litigation context.[71]

Judicare remains the preponderant model of legal services in France, New Zealand, Italy, Japan, and Australia. Within these countries there is

---

[70] *Supra* note 28, at 59–60.

[71] The German legal aid system is administered by the courts rather than by the legal profession. A potential litigant obtains a certificate of means from the town hall and then approaches a lawyer or court officer. There, the nature of the claim is reduced to its fundamental principles in writing. Application is then made by the litigant or his/her representative to the judge who will eventually try the case. This judge decides whether or not to grant legal aid. The decision is rendered according to the dual test of the reasonableness of the claim and the means of the litigant.

considerable variation in the services provided. Within the European Common Market, no right to counsel for accused persons exists in either Italy or France, despite Article 6 of the European Convention.[72] Although there is a growing awareness even in judicare schemes that services may be a legitimate expectation of tenants, consumers and welfare recipients, such services are often not available. This applies even in wealthy nations such as Japan, where until recently 50 per cent of the legal aid cases were traffic offences.[73] The largest growth area in Japan has been in the provision of legal services for domestic disputes. Similarly, despite the highly sophisticated social welfare scheme in Germany, there has been no development of independent legal representation in non-traditional matters; although advice can be obtained at some social welfare offices, very little representation takes place for basic poverty law problems. In Poland, where there is no private legal practice, costs are exempted in some matters when need is shown. Some assistance is given over and above the cost exemption by the judiciary whose general duty is to assist parties and inform them of their legal rights. As well, Polish social organizations attempt to resolve disputes by conciliation and may provide lawyers in certain limited instances.[74]

In countries where legal aid schemes have been in existence for some time, we note the development of a private legal aid bar which has become specialized in handling, not only domestic and criminal disputes, but also social welfare cases. Judicare administrators are being pressured by the expanding legal aid bar to grant certificates in landlord and tenant disputes, immigration cases, and social welfare matters which were traditionally considered to be outside the orbit of the juridical model. Private

---

[72] Article 6, paragraph 3 of the European Convention for the Protection of Human Rights and Fundamental Freedoms states: 'Everyone charged with a criminal offence has the following minimum rights: . . . (c) to defend himself in person or through legal assistance of his own choosing or, if he has not sufficient means to pay for legal assistance, to be given it free when the interests of justice so require.' (Quoted in Varano, Italian National Report (1982), at 3–4).

In addition, paragraph 1 provides: 'In the determination of his civil rights and obligations . . . everyone is entitled to a fair and public hearing within a reasonable time by an independent and impartial tribunal established by law.' (Quoted in Varano, Italian National Report (1982), at 4.)

In the Airey case of October 9, 1979, the European Court of Human Rights held that the inadequacy of the Irish legal aid system constituted a violation of the 'fair hearing' requirements of this paragraph.

[73] Uchida, Japanese National Report (1982). The statistics refer to the assistance scheme organized by the Japanese Legal Aid Society. Since the Legal Aid Society uses the same criteria to grant aid as the government scheme, it may be assumed that a roughly comparable figure is applicable to the government scheme.

[74] Erecinski, Polish National Report (1982), at 117.

lawyers who have worked in clinics, either as part of their legal education or as staff lawyers, have often chosen to remain involved within the practice of poverty law. Similarly, many young lawyers who are unable to penetrate the corporate law firms or more traditional areas of practice have gravitated to legal services. Thus we note the growth for specialization in poverty law in the private and public sectors. The continued development of both the quality and quantity of poor people's lawyers is dependent on the willingness of governments to allow legal aid funds to grow so that tariffs for private lawyers and salaries for public lawyers can be kept at a relatively tolerable level.

Professionalization of legal services

As this paper has already discussed, the traditional provider of legal services has been and continues to be the lawyer. The professional monopoly has protected the legal professions from intrusion from immigration consultants, divorce advocates, or welfare rights workers by various forms of policing of intruders. The significant development in provision of legal services, particularly in the community legal aid clinic, has been the growing use of paraprofessionals, non-lawyers providing legal services to low-income persons. Non-lawyers are being utilized in the public sector, either directly delivering legal services to low-income citizens or assisting staff lawyers in community legal aid clinics. Since legal aid services schemes have not permitted low-income citizens to retain paralegals directly or indirectly on a fee for service basis, the public sector paralegal or the community legal worker, as they have come to be known in Ontario, is the result of the community legal aid movement in North America and the English law centre. In Poland, where there are no private law firms and where citizens may represent themselves or be represented by a member of their family, most persons are in fact represented by advocates.

Public-sector paralegals bring to their tasks varying degrees of formal training and experience, but they usually have a special awareness of the situation confronting the potential client. In the United States, these workers have been recruited from within the community, sometimes from ranks of formal social security claimants, and are therefore uniquely in tune with the social and legal problems confronting the poor. There are distinct advantages to the familiarity and interest the legal worker brings to a situation. Thorough familiarity with the community and its needs, an ability to communicate easily with members of the community, and the potential for innovative solutions not always apparent to the university-trained professional are all distinguishing features of the legal worker. It has been argued that the paralegal can articulate more effectively the problems of the underprivileged person or community group to government and public agencies which dispense services and monies to the poor.[75]

The use of non-lawyers in the delivery of legal services first arose in the American legal services movement in the 1960s. Initially, community clinics were staffed primarily by salaried lawyers and little use was made of either volunteer members of the bar or paralegals. This situation was severely criticized by Edgar and Jean Cahn. In their article 'What Price Justice: The Civilian Perspective Revisited',[76] they noted the failure of the neighbourhood clinics to use non-professionals on their delivery staff:

Finally, with respect to manpower, we have created an artificial shortage by refusing to learn from the medical and other professions and to develop technicians, non-professionals and lawyer-aides-manpower roles to carry out such functions as: informal advocate, technician, counsellor, sympathetic listener, investigator, researcher, form writer, etc.

At present lawyers are expected to perform all these functions. To so equip them, lawyers are put through an extensive period of formal training and then apprenticeship that limits the number that can be produced. Yet lawyers spend only a small portion of their time performing functions which cannot be performed equally well by less thoroughly trained persons. Nonetheless, the profession has refused tenaciously to delegate any of these functions to anyone else.[77]

Today, paralegals are a significant element in the delivery of legal services in the United States and Canada, both in clinics and in mixed-delivery systems.

The makeup of the staff of clinics and the relationship between the number of legal and non-legal personnel is of particular interest to the study. During the mid 1970s, Ontario clinics employed three paralegals for every lawyer. While the percentage of community legal workers relative to the total number of people employed in the clinics declined between 1976 and 1980, the ratio of community workers to lawyers is still two to one in favour of the paraprofessionals.[78]

We find by comparison that paralegals composed 17.5 per cent of the total staff in American legal clinics in 1974, while attorneys composed 39.4

---

[75] Wexler, *Practicing Law for Poor People* (1970), 79 Yale LJ 1049.
[76] Cahn and Cahn, (1966), 41 Notre Dame Lawyer 927. [77] *Id.* at 934–5.
[78] Zemans, 'The Public Sector Paralegal in Ontario: Community Legal Workers' (1980), *Canadian Legal Aid Bulletin* 30.

per cent.[79] From another perspective, the Ontario clinics employ twice as many paralegals as lawyers, where the American clinics employ half as many paralegals as lawyers. The greater proportion of community workers employed in the public sector in Canada can be explained by the resistance of public-sector lawyers in the United States to both the hiring of and the delegation of responsibilities to paralegals, and the unwillingness to provide adequate funding to paraprofessionals.

In recent years the number of paralegals working in public-sector legal services in countries with a welfare perspective on legal services has increased substantially.[80] Concern has shifted from an initial preoccupation with the creation of the role of the paralegal to an emphasis on specific jobs, standards of performance, quality control, accreditation, and training needs. Functions which public-sector paralegals perform in the delivery of legal services may be characterized as follows:[81] (1) information giving: the paralegal is often called upon to provide information and advice on legal matters ranging from landlord and tenant to criminal law. The client will typically wish to be informed about: what the governing law is, what protection the law grants him in the situation, and which course of action is most advisable in the circumstances. (2) Assistance: this involves identifying and researching the legal problems, collecting and analysing the factual and legal material, providing procedural assistance, and in some instances preparing legal forms. (3) Advocacy: this function can be subdivided into informal and formal advocacy. The paralegal often functions as mediator and conciliator, attempting to negotiate in an informal manner through letters, telephone calls, and discussions with the parties. Where no settlement is possible, the paralegal will take a formal advocacy function. He will prepare his client's case for formal dispute resolution and will represent the client in the designated forum. Paralegals have the capacity in most jurisdictions to appear before administrative tribunals, lower courts, and legislative committees.[82] (4) Public education:

[79]   National Survey of Paralegals in OEO Legal Services Projects, (1974).

[80]   In Jamaica paralegals are employed in the Kingston Legal Aid Clinic, the Mid-Island Clinic and the Montego Bay Clinic and played a significant role in each of these programmes.

[81]   In the development of the paralegal in England, see Michael Zander, *Legal Services for the Community* (London: Temple Smith, 1975) especially at 299–302, and *The Royal Commission on Legal Services, Final Report* (1979), vol. 1, at 406. Canadian developments with respect to paraprofessionals in law are discussed by Zemans in 'The Non-Lawyer as a Means of Providing Legal Services', Chapter 9 *Lawyer and the Consumer Interest: Regulating the Market for Legal Services*, Evans and Trebilcock, (Toronto: Butterworth, 1982).

[82]   The work of Centro Pernanode Estudios (CEPES) is noteworthy and was discussed by Diego Garcia-Sayan at the first Conference on Legal Services in Latin America and the Caribbean in San Jose, Costa Rica in October 1981.

this includes the preparation of booklets, newsletters, and other literature for popular dissemination and the planning of workshops and seminars. These aim at making the general public more aware of their rights and of the remedies available. Educators may also use the mass media such as newspaper columns, radio, and television to bring to the attention of the community their legal rights. This latter function has been used effectively by paralegals in Latin America. Land reform information, for example, has been brought to the attention of peasants in Peru by using comic strips.[83] (5) Community development and law reform: this function includes facilitating the organization of the community into groups that are prepared and able to exercise their rights effectively and press for genuine social change.

Any discussion of the role and functions of paralegals in the provision of legal services must consider the extent to which they are capable of functioning independently. This writer has conducted empirical studies on this topic—studies which conclude that paralegals working in community clinics have been given the freedom to handle a wide assortment of legal tasks with little or no supervision by staff lawyers.[84] Much of the work done by the paralegals has been handled effectively, efficiently, and economically. There are legal services programmes in Canada which are staffed exclusively by paralegals who received limited supervision from either part-time lawyers or private practitioners.[85] Such speciality clinics have tended to work in specific areas of the law such as housing or social assistance.

As funding for legal services becomes more constrained, the need for legal services continues to increase. Legal paraprofessionals allow the delivery of both effective traditional legal services and more innovative and reform-oriented services at a moderate cost and in a responsive

---

[83] Paralegals are allowed to appear at tribunals and before lower courts as 'agents' or 'friends' or at the discretion of the presiding judge or chairman of the administrative body. The non-lawyer is not able to appear in the higher courts.

[84] Zemans, 'Community Legal Clinics in Ontario: 1980: A Data Survey', (1981) I *The Windsor Yearbook of Access to Justice* 230 at 236–8.

[85] Injured Workers' Consultants (IWC) in Toronto, Canada is such a clinic. One of the original legal clinics in Ontario, IWC provides legal assistance to injured workers pursuing claims for the Workmen's Compensation Board of Ontario. In 1980, Injured Workers' Consultants received funding in the amount of $162,982 from the Ontario Legal Aid Plan to employ eight paralegals on its staff, but no full-time lawyers. The day-to-day casework in this clinic is handled by the individual community legal worker who assumes responsibility for over thirty active files and is primarily responsible for the quality of the casework. These paralegals have developed a special expertise and competence equal, if not superior, to that of lawyers in the area of workmen's compensation.

fashion to the client community.[86] Training citizen advocates to represent their own community and to work within their particular areas of interest offers new potential and challenge to the delivery of legal services.

Along with the growing use of paralegals, the last decade has seen the growing professionalization of the lawyers working in salaried legal services programmes. By the late 1970s, legal services lawyers in the United States had become well established and their number grew to the extent that they became a significant force within the American legal profession.[87] As the political climate had changed, so had the lawyers who worked for the Legal Services Corporation. Gone was the radicalism of the sixties and early seventies. Legal services lawyers of the eighties are concerned with job security, limiting caseloads, and rationalizing their professional development. Some legal services lawyers have quite naturally banded together with others and unionized. Legal services lawyers not only had greater security in the late seventies, but they were better trained and more prepared to initiate test-case litigation. Such litigation was encouraged by national training seminars, exchange of pleadings, and the reports of significant victories in reviews and journals. Legal services lawyers began to see themselves as being legitimately able to join their professional colleagues as they moved from fighting for social change in the streets into the courtrooms. Appellate litigation as well as participation in professional activities gave legal services lawyers a level of acceptability with the establishment bar which 'poor people's lawyers' had not previously enjoyed in the United States.

The well-intentioned reform litigation of legal services lawyers began to have a significant impact on the administration of social welfare in the United States in the late 1970s.[88] Writers such as Jack Katz suggest that, in their efforts to rationalize the administration of welfare to the poor in America, legal services lawyers have reformed and rationalized welfare schemes but have, at the same time, effectively legitimated the treatment of poor people as a separate class.[89] Katz argues that much of the reform litigation generated by legal services lawyers is an outgrowth of their need to act like and perform tasks considered to be significant by other lawyers.[90] The effect of this form of practice has been the stabilization, regularization, and insulation of poverty programmes into separate government agencies.

---

[86] Partington, in the English National Report, discusses the issue of the professional monopoly and the position taken by welfare lawyers in the United Kingdom that the legal profession should be nationalized.

[87] *Supra* note 27.

[89] *Supra* note 27.

[88] *Supra* note 13, at 50–5.

[90] *Supra* note 13, at 52.

At the same time that critics of the system like Bellow and Katz raised their criticism concerning the 'insularity' of American legal services lawyers, the Legal Services Delivery Study, conducted by the Legal Services Corporation, concluded that the American staff attorney programme was the most effective form of delivery of legal services, especially with respect to law reform, because of the 'professional expertise' that such offices had developed. Thus, American legal services lawyers, at the end of the seventies, were cost effective, well trained, and sophisticated deliverers of traditional as well as reform litigation. Yet the concern continued to be expressed that the services were becoming too routinized, that poverty was being regulated and legitimized, and not removed, and that the justice system had merely expanded its boundaries slightly to encompass legal services lawyers whom the profession had co-opted.[91] The Reagan administration's attack on legal services in early 1980 has politicized the legal services lawyers if for no other reason than to sustain their programme and their livelihood.[92]

. . .

Conclusion

This paper has examined some of the recent developments in legal services as reflected by the national researchers and the recent literature on legal services. It is difficult within the confines of a short paper to do justice to all the issues and changes which are taking place in twenty-five countries with distinct socio-economic situations. I have attempted to describe some of the significant developments in mixed delivery systems in Europe and North America, which I would suggest as the direction of the future. Whether such mixed delivery systems will develop beyond the provision of legal services and attempt to grapple with more fundamental problems is, at the moment, unclear.

Despite various recent developments in legal services, including the growth of welfare rights schemes in some countries and the continuing development of juridical schemes, we find that not only are legal services open to financial evaluations and government cut-back, but in some countries—notably the United States—the 1980s has witnessed a questioning of their very existence.

Access to justice, or even improved quality of justice, in the eighties appears to be of less significance than the issue of the cost of justice and

---

[91] These developments are discussed in the conclusion of this paper.
[92] *Supra* note 27.

the acknowledgement of the limited political commitment to reform and change. Thus this paper concludes on a note of realism which recognizes the vulnerability of legal services at the present time. We observe that during the recent world-wide recession, legal services have been open to severe government cut-backs in funding, zero-growth funding, and in the United States a sustained attack from the Reagan administration that attempted to totally dismantle the Legal Services Corporation. This abrupt change in attitude in many industrialized countries, as more conservative governments have been elected, not only emphasizes the fragility of the movement towards a more democratic legal system, but underlines how legal services are themselves perceived as an aspect of the political system. The threat posed by liberal governments' encouragement of social change and redistribution of power has been identified by think-tanks such as the Heritage Foundation in the United States and acted upon by the Republican government of Ronald Reagan:

Going to court is a political act, contesting a government action that threatens to terminate benefits is a political act. Demanding that a landlord maintain a home in habitable condition as a condition of being paid is a political act. All of these acts are assertions or expressions of power or of a right to something. Some power or rights can be given or shared without necessarily diminishing other people's enjoyment of them. Other forms of power or rights are necessarily competitive. Thus, providing those without power or resources with the means to attempt to obtain some is as much a political issue as the protection of those with power and resources. The debate surrounding the substantive limitation of what legal services attorneys can do poses this issue at its most extreme. Why else would opponents of class actions or suits against governmental entities fight so hard to prohibit these forms of legal action unless they feared they might just be successful?

So writes Menkel-Meadow about the fight for survival of the most sophisticated and highly funded legal services scheme in the world. Such a political attack as that mounted in the United States cannot be dismissed as merely an outgrowth of the political philosophy of a particular conservative government. The vulnerability of the Legal Services Corporation and the lengthy fight in which it engaged demonstrates that governments will only permit limited incremental change and will ultimately protect those interests which have a power-base and control the financial resources of the community.

Although I have outlined the development of new and more effective models of legal services and recognized the increase in access to the legal system through the use of paraprofessionals, the fundamental question remains: will the access to justice movement be successful only as a procedural exercise which must continuously defend itself against political attack and economic cut-backs? The radicalism of legal services activities in the United States has left it open to political assassination. Legal services are dependent on the political and economic support of government and of the legal profession. As the winds have shifted in the United States in the early seventies and in the early eighties, legal services have found themselves in an extremely vulnerable position.

At a time when funding security is desperately needed to allow legal services to continue to develop stability and attract and retain the best advocates, we note the need to justify its very existence. This is in many ways the contradiction of the eighties: greater needs of low-income citizens and the underprivileged in all parts of the world confronted by less political and economic support of social welfare. We find little hope for the consumers of legal services who continue to be faced with a justice system which remains expensive and isolated from their lives. It is difficult, as legal services proponents well know, to sketch any strategy to enhance access to justice in face of the theoretical–practical paradox discussed in this paper. Developments during the next decade will determine whether the winds of change which began to blow through the legal system a decade ago will have totally subsided or whether government and lawyers will allow at least a breeze of democracy to flow into the justice system.

7. The Paradoxes of Legal Aid

RICHARD ABEL

Legal aid is doubly paradoxical.[1] First, there is the analytic mystery of why the state creates and supports an institution that frequently challenges its actions, constrains its discretion, reveals its ineptitude, and makes vocal and sometimes irresistible demands on its resources. We may be able to resolve this mystery, at least in part, by examining where and when legal aid emerges (and fails to emerge). Secondly, there is the normative puzzle: is legal aid promise or peril? Is it a non-reformist reform that not only offers material gains to its beneficiaries but also permits them to gain control over their lives and to organize for further action? Or is it a mere sop, a diversion from the important tasks of social, political, and economic mobilization? Comparative and historical analysis also may offer insight into this more difficult and more pressing question.

Why Does Legal Aid Emerge When and Where It Does?

One set of explanations takes a functionalist form. Since legal aid is a creation of the state, *raison d'état* is an obvious starting point. Erhard Blankenburg has suggested that legal aid is associated with the appearance of what, in the nineteenth century, would have been called the 'dangerous classes'.[2] These may be a working class or lumpen proletariat created by capitalist industrialization and urbanization, or ethnic and racial minorities who migrate from other regions or countries. Indeed, these two phenomena do seem to coincide. The earliest legal aid associations in the United States, founded at the end of the nineteenth and beginning of the twentieth centuries, were inspired by concern for European immigrants to the major cities—New York and Chicago, for instance (albeit by a category rarely characterized as dangerous—namely women).[3] On the other hand, the passage of legal aid legislation in Britain in 1949 and the Netherlands in 1957 anticipated by more than a decade the wave of immi-

---

[1] The present chapter is based on the conclusion to Abel 1985b.
[2] Blankenburg 1980: 233.　　　　　　[3] Katz 1982: 35.

gration into both countries by inhabitants of their former colonies. However, the growth in the 1970s of law centres in Britain and law shops, legal collectives, and legal aid *Buros* in the Netherlands is roughly contemporaneous with that migration, and the founding of the Office of Economic Opportunity Legal Services Program in the United States in 1965 might be seen as a belated response to the migration to northern cities of blacks from the southern United States and Latinos from the Caribbean and Latin America. A similar relationship may exist between the ethnic diversification of what had been relatively homogeneous populations in Canada and Australia and expansion of legal aid in the 1970s. Nevertheless, large-scale migration does not always stimulate legal aid schemes. Both Germany and Sweden have absorbed large numbers of 'guest-workers' during the last two decades, yet only Sweden created a legal aid programme.[4] And although France experienced a substantial immigration from its former colonies in North and West Africa and Southeast Asia in the 1960s, it introduced only a minimal legal aid programme in 1972.

Migration, and the contemporaneous phenomena of urbanization and incorporation within capitalist relations of production, engender social conflict and disorder. At the same time, capital demands a more disciplined labour force. If the state responds by criminalizing behaviour, increasing the number of prosecutions, and imposing more severe penalties, it may have to legitimate this highly visible expansion of coercion by an equally conspicuous affirmation of due process, one manifestation of which is the provision of legal representation to all accused. However, this correlation is even weaker: Britain's penal system had been experiencing a progressive liberalization for more than a century before the 1949 Legal Aid Act was passed; the Netherlands, with one of the most comprehensive legal aid systems, has one of the least repressive criminal justice systems, whether measured in terms of the number arrested or imprisoned or the length of sentences. If anything, the introduction of legal aid appears to invite more prosecution. Whichever direction the causation, it cannot explain why and when the state begins to offer legal assistance in civil courts and tribunals.

A more promising avenue of inquiry may be recent changes in family structure. The assumption that marriage signified a lifetime union between a male bread-winner and a female home-maker and child-rearer was substantially undermined during World War Two and the decades

---

[4] Blankenburg 1980: 240.

that followed. Although there continues to be disagreement about the cause—the entry of women into employment, an increase in the ratio of women to men, changes in cultural norms—there can be no doubt that divorce laws were liberalized and divorce rates increased.[5] In Britain, at least, this increase was intimately related to the decision by the state to take fiscal responsibility for legal aid to servicemen during the war; family matters have consistently represented the single largest category in most civil legal aid programmes. Furthermore, this centrality of divorce may explain the correlation that Kees Schuyt has noted between the presence of legal aid in Protestant northern Europe (and North America and Australia) and its absence in Catholic southern Europe (and Ireland and Latin America), which, until recently, has not permitted divorce. Perhaps, then, legal aid can be explained in part as a mechanism for ensuring the reproduction of the labour power essential to capitalism by preserving family obligations after divorce, albeit in altered form. Granting custody to women affirms and enforces their continuing responsibility for nurturance. The requirement that an ex-husband support his former wife and children can be seen as an attempt to place the cost of reproduction on labour, rather than allow it to fall entirely on the state.[6] The termination of the marriage following its breakdown frees the parties to enter into new marriages.

It may be possible to generalize this last observation: since World War Two, the welfare states of advanced capitalism have assumed ever greater responsibility for the reproduction of labour: 'informal ways of insuring against life risks are increasingly replaced by formal ones'.[7] One problem with this kind of explanation is the enormous variation in the size and shape of the welfare apparatus in different countries, and the different dates at which the numerous provisions were introduced. A second objection is the fact that legal aid is much less intimately connected with the reproduction of labour than are health, housing, education, nutrition, and the maintenance of unproductive populations.[8] Nevertheless, the relationship between legal aid and the growth of the welfare state cannot be

---

[5] Rheinstein 1972; Guttentag and Secord 1983. However, it is not clear what is cause and what is effect: the divorce rate declined for several years after legal aid was introduced in Britain, before climbing dramatically, and it was declining in the Netherlands at the time of the establishment of its legal aid programme.

[6] Although this has been singularly unsuccessful (Chambers 1979).

[7] Blankenburg 1980: 237.

[8] Thus Sweden has a large elaborate legal aid programme, but Denmark, which otherwise resembles Sweden in its welfare apparatus, does not have a comparable scheme (Blankenburg 1982: 247).

gainsaid. First, once the state assumes some burdens, it invites other demands. The success of the Services Divorce Department in Britain during World War Two made the legal profession reluctant to resume representing indigent clients without payment. The growth of the Legal Services Corporation in the United States has led the organized profession to oppose a proposal by the Reagan administration to devolve the legal problems of the indigent onto *pro bono* activities.[9] Secondly, during the 1960s and early 1970s the welfare apparatus embarked on a period of growth in which it sought new forms of state action through which to wage a war on poverty. Finally, and perhaps most relevant, the state needs ways of controlling and disciplining the sprawling welfare apparatus, especially the peripheral street-level bureaucrats in the local offices of central government and in regional and local government itself. Legal aid is an important regulatory mechanism.

It is also possible to explain the emergence of legal aid using the framework of interest-group pluralism. The legal profession would seem to be the group with the greatest interest in such programmes. However, that interest developed gradually: the profession tended to react to proposals to establish legal aid rather than initiate them, although it was quick to demand a major voice in shaping and controlling the institution. Lawrence Friedman has suggested that changes in the legal system rendering it less accessible to the mass of the population and requiring the intermediation of professionals also contributed to the emergence of legal aid.[10] Yet the decline in access and the professionalization of law antedated the creation of significant legal aid programmes by many decades. A similar lack of chronological correspondence troubles two other possible linkages. I have argued elsewhere that legal aid is one expression of the professional project of creating demand, to which the lawyers turn when their control of supply is significantly eroded. However, legal aid emerged in Britain, the Netherlands, and the United States at times when supply control appeared extremely secure; in Britain in the 1940s and 1950s, in fact, the Law Society was concerned about a shortage of solicitors, not an overabundance, and the number of practising barristers actually diminished in the late 1950s. The enormous increase in the production of lawyers in those countries began only in the late 1960s and the early 1970s,

---

[9] The American Bar Association flirted briefly with a requirement of mandatory *pro bono* services in its recent revision of the Rules of Professional Conduct but quickly substituted a bland and unenforceable exhortation to render 'Public Interest Legal Service' (Abel 1981b: 639).

[10] Friedman 1981: 251.

by which time legal aid was firmly established, although budgets did experience a substantial growth that was roughly contemporaneous with the expansion of the profession. Furthermore, although almost every professional organization ultimately endorsed judicare programmes as a means of stimulating demand, staffed offices create little business for private practitioners (if they do not take it away, as once was feared). Also, though it is possible to argue (as I do below) that legal aid programmes help to legitimate the profession, there is little evidence that lawyers perceived legal aid as a significant source of legitimation *before* the programmes were created or embraced them for that reason.

Two other categories of actors deserve mention, although their roles have been less significant than one might expect. First, capital, in the guise of philanthropy, was instrumental in establishing some of the earliest legal aid programmes in the United States, but its contribution dwindled after World War Two, and its role has been thoroughly eclipsed by that of the state. Secondly, social movements of the oppressed occasionally have turned to law as an instrument of social change: for instance, the Workers' Offices in Germany at the turn of the century,[11] and the National Association for the Advancement of Coloured People in the United States starting in the 1930s.[12] In each instance they have found a committed core of lawyers eager to champion their cause. Once again, though, these activities have been either taken over by the state or rendered relatively marginal to state programmes.

Finally, it is important to stress the critical impact of external events. World War Two was central in the British experience because it undermined family stability and fostered the penetration of the state throughout daily life. The coincidence of the civil rights, anti-war, and feminist movements in the United States in the 1960s helped to create a generation of law students dedicated to social activism. The tenure of particular administrations—democratic in the United States, social democratic in the UK, the Netherlands, and Australia—is closely associated with the rise and fall of legal aid. These concrete historical events help to explain why there is such diversity between nations that otherwise share many common characteristics.

What is the Significance of Legal Aid?

Like all welfare programmes, legal aid is the product of two very different processes. First, it is an object of class struggle. True, legal aid has a lower

---

[11] Reifner 1982: 81.   [12] Council for Public Interest Law 1976: 34.

priority for the poor, the working class, and other oppressed categories than do social services like housing, health, education, or income maintenance, because it is viewed more as an instrumental than an ultimate good. Although lawyers might wish it were otherwise, people are interested less in procedural justice than in what they can win (or avoid) through law.[13] Nevertheless, to the extent that law is viewed as an important, or at least an indispensable, instrument for the achievement of desired ends, legal aid also is valued. Any doubts about the appropriateness of a class analysis are quickly dispelled by the ferocious attacks on legal aid waged by the petit bourgeois and their spokespersons in the legal profession and in politics. Yet this perspective tends to be overshadowed by another that sees legal aid, like other welfare programmes, as essential to the maintenance of capitalism. I adverted to the latter view above when I suggested that criminal legal aid is a necessary concomitant of increased state coercion and that civil legal aid, which is very largely matrimonial, serves to reconstruct the family and thus to ensure the reproduction of labour. In analysing the significance of legal aid below, I will try to sustain the tension between these two perspectives.[14]

One inspiration of legal aid is the implicit presupposition that because legal rights appear to have been instrumental to the rise of capitalism they must be equally salient in subsequent class struggles. The analogy is badly flawed and therefore misleading. Certainly the proletariat has secured important protections through legal guarantees: the regulation of wages, hours and conditions of work, and health and safety, and, most importantly, the right to organize. However, the workers won these gains through collective action, in which they withheld their labour power, formed political parties, and sometimes threatened violence. The primary beneficiaries of legal aid—women, children, the disabled, and the elderly—have no labour power to withhold, have been unable to organize politically, and pose no threat to social order.[15] The analogy is flawed in other ways as well. E. P. Thompson has cautioned radical critics of bourgeois law against derogating the civil rights that were won at enormous cost through the struggles of oppressed classes.[16] Granting the force of this warning, though, we must not assume that because law is an essential shield against the abuses of state power it also can be wielded as a sword to alter fundamental class relationships. This assumption is false not only because of the essential difference between resisting state power

---

[13] Galanter 1976b: 243; Griffiths 1980: 29.   [14] Gough 1979: ix.
[15] Piven and Cloward 1977; Roach and Roach 1978: 160; Katz 1982: 98.
[16] Thompson 1975: 264.

and seeking to mobilize it (which I discuss further below), but also because the form of bourgeois law is not equally appropriate to protect all interests. Charles Reich assumed such universality in his landmark article on the 'new property',[17] and, ever since, legal aid lawyers have been trying to clothe welfare benefits in the same legal protections that the bourgeoisie secured for capital and the proletariat for labour power.

However, as Richard de Friend has forcefully argued, welfare 'rights' are not the equivalent of legal rights in capital or in labour power, and giving them the same name only obscures the fundamental differences.[18] Labour and capital are created by the action of private individuals, welfare benefits by state action; there is a market for the former (hence the need to embody them in legal form) but not for the latter. Whereas capitalism is said to require the certainty and predictability conferred by the legal form,[19] the welfare state requires the greatest possible flexibility.[20] Welfare recipients have no 'rights' to their benefits. The state can grant, modify, and withdraw them at will, as when it denies abortions to poor women. The only recourse available to the latter is collective political action. All the law offers is a guarantee that certain procedures will be followed in determining whether an applicant is entitled to a particular benefit.

One of the ironies of legal aid, therefore, is that it was becoming obsolescent even as it was being established. Legal rights may have served the bourgeoisie well in overthrowing feudalism and still may be salient to the proletariat in its struggle with capital, but legal aid is directed against neither of these adversaries. Instead, legal aid lawyers typically confront the state (when they oppose a class adversary at all, rather than a client's spouse). The importance of this shift in focus cannot be exaggerated. In its early years, legal aid served a still unorganized and relatively impoverished working class, who suffered exploitation by capital in their roles as both workers and consumers. Lawyers pursued wage claims, challenged usurious loans, and fought slumlords.[21] Today, however, most American legal aid recipients (and many in other countries) do not belong to the workforce and, partly for that reason, consume many public rather than private goods—in the areas of health and housing, for instance. The state, however, is a peculiar adversary in that its interests are not opposed to

---

[17] Reich 1964: 733.
[18] de Friend 1979: 43; for an orthodox marxist critique of the legalization of welfare entitlements see Fraser 1976: 3.
[19] Trubek 1972: 3; Kronman 1982.   [20] Luhmann 1982; Teubner 1983: 239.
[21] Jones 1940; Katz 1982: 35.

those of welfare recipients in the way that capital confronts labour. Not only is welfare intended to benefit its recipients (as the name implies), but welfare officials actually may welcome the challenges fited by legal aid, both as a source of political leverage to increase the welfare budget and as a means of disciplining low-level bureaucrats who violate substantive and procedural norms out of incompetence, inertia, local pressure, or lack of sympathy. What the state does demand is efficiency—the lowest possible unit cost per case. Just as the criminal justice system finds it far easier to process accused who are represented by counsel,[22] so legal aid lawyers serve to weed out unqualified welfare claimants, remonstrate with those who cause trouble, and get all the papers in order.[23] Rather than threatening the welfare bureaucracy, legal aid becomes an indispensable adjunct, another instance in the infinite regress of paternalistic institutions created to benefit the powerless. Just as the regulatory agencies established to protect consumers from the economic and physical hazards of capitalism were captured by the industries they regulated, thereby stimulating the emergence of public interest lawyers,[24] so welfare bureaucracies spawn legal aid programmes. In each instance, though, the small cadre of lawyers representing powerless clienteles can extract only marginal concessions from either capital or the state. Like the epicycles of the Ptolemaic universe, the process of adding further layers to the regulatory-cum-welfare state appears endless.

Legal aid is at least consistent with, and arguably supportive of, capitalism in several other respects. Since it necessarily seeks to enforce legal rights, it tends to force grievances into legal, i.e. individual form.[25] Eligibility criteria define the clientele of legal aid as a collection of individuals sharing common characteristics—indigence, residence, perhaps nationality—rather than as a group. Legal aid programmes do create bonds—but among lawyers, not clients.[26] Clients share few experiences except those inherent in the amorphous status of poverty; they are not even united by a visible common enemy. In both respects they contrast markedly with trade unions, ethnic associations, the feminist movement, even environmentalist groups. Although legal aid clients may be treated as a category for purposes of litigation, this does nothing to build an ongo-

---

[22] King 1976: 33.   [23] Katz 1982: 193.   [24] Weisbrod *et al.* 1978.
[25] Citizens' Advice Bureaux keep records of all those against whom complaints are made—retailers, landlords, government agencies, employers etc. However, this information is not made available to the public, and the bureaux make no use of it to launch campaigns; see Bridges *et al.* 1974: 175.
[26] Katz 1982: 114. Gary Bellow (1977: 106) has described how legal aid preserves the atomization of the individual client.

ing collectivity but merely provides a temporary surrogate. Therefore, it is not surprising that efforts to institute community control of legal aid programmes generally fail, for they presuppose precisely what is missing and what legal aid is unable to create—a meaningful community. Indeed, legislators and central administrators often curtail or prohibit efforts to organize groups, although such restrictions seem superfluous since most lawyers lack both the skills and the inclination to attempt that task. In extreme situations the state may consciously use legal aid to undermine collective action by offering individual grievants legal advice designed to foster 'peace through law'—as in Weimar, and later in Nazi Germany.[27]

The clients of legal aid not only are individualized, they also are unusually reluctant and reactive litigants. Of course, no one wants to litigate. Yet whereas most people shun litigation because they can pursue their goals in other ways—through the market or politics—the poor avoid the law for the same reason they take no other action: out of despair, resignation, fatalism, a recognition of their powerlessness, and a fear of retaliation.[28] For instance, when the military offered to review the three million veterans in the United States who hold less than an honourable discharge and consider upgrading the discharge, less than one out of a thousand exercised that right.[29] Marc Galanter's powerful generalization that litigation is typically a claim by a repeat player against a one-shot defendant[30] has been confirmed by studies in other countries that find banks, finance companies, and landlords suing debtors, consumers, and tenants.[31] Although in its early days legal aid represented a significant number of plaintiffs, today it defends most cases.[32] The poor who are its clients apparently feel that law should be not only a last resort but also one to which they will submit only under coercion. Are they wrong? The remedies law offers rarely are responsive to their felt needs. Moreover, they may be in a stronger position as defendants than as plaintiffs, resisting state power rather than mobilizing it. For one thing, the procedural safeguards—which is all that law offers them in most instances—are valuable primarily as obstructions.[33] For another, the very poverty that discourages offensive action itself may be a powerful defence.[34]

The influence of legal aid is circumscribed not only because it must

[27] Reifner 1982.   [28] Abel-Smith *et al.* 1973: 181.
[29] *Legal Services Corporation News* Nov./Dec. 1980.   [30] Galanter 1974: 95.
[31] Wanner 1974: 421; Blankenburg 1975: 307; Jettinghof 1983: 283.
[32] Katz 1982: 40.   [33] Handler 1978; Lazerson 1982: 119.
[34] In Albert Hirschman's (1970) terms, the poor have the option of exit, even if they lack the political strength to voice their grievances or the economic clout to withhold their loyalties as consumers.

respond constantly to crises in the lives of poor individuals, but because that is all it does: it is yet another instance of the segregation of the poor.[35] This is obvious in staffed office programmes, but it is true of judicare as well, for specialization is the inevitable response to the technical complexity of poverty law and the mass processing required to make a profit, given inadequate levels of remuneration. Indeed, the nature of poverty in advanced capitalism segregates legal aid, not only by class but also by race, gender, age, disabilities, date of immigration, and place of origin.[36] State welfare programmes do not *have* to be segregated in this fashion: health care in western Europe is universal, and even in the United States medicare, social security and public education (primary, secondary, and to a lesser extent tertiary) are offered to and taken up by almost everyone. Even law itself has been partly socialized: the state assumed full responsibility for criminal prosecution in the nineteenth century rather than leave it in the hands of the aggrieved individual. Also, of course, the state subsidizes much of the cost of the judiciary.[37] Thus the fact that most legal services are delivered through the market as a private consumer good and a tiny fraction then are provided to the poor in kind through discrete programmes must be seen for what it is—a political choice. Of course the legal needs of the poor differ from those of the rich, but the same can be said of the needs of those categories for health or education. Legal services could be nationalized.[38] The decision not to do so leaves legal aid in an exposed position, politically vulnerable and economically short-changed.

The last few paragraphs can be summarized by saying that legal aid is a social reform that begins with a solution—lawyers—and then looks for problems it might solve, rather than beginning with the problem— poverty, or oppression, or discrimination, or capitalism—and exploring solutions. The early legal-need studies—which assumed that people who are using lawyers less often than others, or for different purposes, had an unfulfilled 'need' for law—are just an extreme example of this perspective. The demand is always for more of the same: more laws,

[35] Katz 1982: 91. The present Conservative Government has declined to act on the recommendations of the Royal Commission on Legal Services to extend legal aid to the entire population (Royal Commission on Legal Services 1979: 121).

[36] Fitzgerald 1977: 6.

[37] A recent American study estimated that state and federal goverments contribute $2 billion a year to the operation of civil courts alone, in addition to the costs borne by the litigants themselves and the costs of operating the criminal justice system (Kakalik and Ross 1983).

[38] Abel 1979: 5.

more lawyers, more courts, and now more alternatives to court.[39] This is merely another illustration of what Ivan Illich has criticized as the creation of false needs.[40] It is not surprising that lawyers should succumb to the temptation, even if they may be driven less by material incentives and more by the desire to feel that their expertise is valuable to society. Regardless of the motivation, however, the result is that lawyers persist in seeking political significance through the legal form. Public interest law perfectly exemplifies this trap. Its theoretical justification is not a concrete social evil but a failure of process: the non-representation of inchoate interests within the regulatory apparatus.[41] The lack of substantive content is proclaimed by the very concept of 'public interest' law, a concept that allows the form to be appropriated by conservative 'public interest law firms', which seek to hide their partisanship beneath a cloak of neutrality by assuming the name of regions rather than interest groups.[42] Criminal defence also illustrates the subordination of substance to form: socially conscious lawyers do such work in the belief that by representing criminal defendants—the most oppressed of all litigants—their work acquires progressive political content, even though they remain wholly confined within the legal form.

That form has severe and inescapable limitations for those who seek to effect social change. To the extent that legal aid alters the balance of power at all, it does so only within the judicial or quasi-judicial arenas (i.e. the administrative agency). It therefore assumes that the most significant conflicts within society have been legalized and ignores those that are not or cannot be.[43] Although substantive rules can give powerless groups and individuals significant leverage within the judicial arena, the latter also are constrained by those rules. More important, they cannot change the rules (except by appealing to higher rules), nor can they resist rule changes sought by others. Even within the court-room, equality remains an unattainable chimera. The criminal prosecution is often portrayed as a setting in which a single courageous dedicated lawyer, by invoking procedural safeguards, can protect the accused against the awesome power of the state. There are several problems with this image. First, even when due process and the rule of law prevail, the state enjoys enormous advantages. Secondly, the accused and the defence lawyer exercise no control over the substantive rules that shape the prosecution or the discretionary decisions

---

[39] An introduction to the literature can be found in Cappelletti *et al.* 1978–9; Schwartzkoff and Morgan 1982; Abel 1982; Nader 1982.

[40] Illich 1977.

[41] Weisbrod *et al.* 1978.

[42] O'Connor and Epstein 1983: 12.

[43] Oñate 1979: 230.

to investigate and charge. Most important, civil litigation and criminal prosecution are not analogous. The accused is always resisting state coercion, with all the tactical advantages that such a posture offers; in many civil cases, especially those with the greatest potential for social change, the legally aided litigant is asserting a claim, seeking to compel action. In civil litigation, legal aid clients face adversaries who have structured transactions with an eye to future legal consequences; who enjoy advantages of experience, information, and credibility; who possess infinitely greater resources, and can benefit from economies of scale. When legal aid lawyers do win cases, especially test cases, they may secure only paper victories: some commentators have estimated that enforcement rates vary from no more than 50 per cent to as low as 10 per cent.[44] Yet how could it have been otherwise? How could anyone ever have expected a few dozen, or even a few thousand, lawyers to effect fundamental social change? The illusion shows the enormous power of the myth of rights in liberal ideology.

When social institutions fail to fulfil their ostensible purposes, social scientists frequently attribute those institutions to the need for legitimation. That is one of several objections to the concept: it preserves the tautological quality of the functionalist paradigm. Everything in capitalist society is driven by the same dynamic; therefore, if a practice does not contribute to accumulation, it must further legitimation.[45] There are also other problems with seeing legal aid as legitimation. What does it legitimate: the programme itself, the legal profession, the legal system, the welfare apparatus, social inequality, capitalism, or the state? In whose eyes do these institutions gain legitimacy: those of actual clients, potential clients, the legal profession, judges, or the public? Why is legal aid needed for legitimation now? And how do we know whether it succeeds or fails?

The available evidence casts considerable doubt on what might well be thought the most plausible hypothesis: that legal aid legitimates the legal system in the eyes of the population most directly affected—clients and potential clients.[46] First of all, most of those eligible are ignorant of the availability of legal aid.[47] An institution can hardly affect the attitudes of those who are unaware of its existence. Secondly, even those who know

---

[44] Katz 1982: 180.   [45] Joel Rogers quoted in Hyde 1983: 379.
[46] Genn 1982: 22.
[47] Koos 1949: 10 (three-fifths of a sample in Rochester, New York); Levine and Preston 1970: 80 (60 per cent of an American sample); Abel-Smith *et al.* 1973: 194 (75 per cent in three poor London boroughs); Byles and Morris 1977: 9 (50 per cent of a North Kensington sample); Zander 1978: 44 (75 per cent unaware of the Green Form Scheme); Report of the Royal Commission on Legal Services in Scotland 1980: 78 (59 per cent knew nothing of legal

about legal aid prefer not to use it: more than a tenth of the respondents in three poor London boroughs declared they never would go to a solicitor for *any* reason.[48] Because willingness to seek legal aid correlates directly with socio-economic status in most countries,[49] those with the greatest reason to be disaffected from the legal system are also least likely to be persuaded otherwise by legal aid. Thirdly, the experience of invoking legal aid appears to impair, rather than enhance, the legitimacy of the legal system. Users find the process slow and incomprehensible, they are unimpressed by their lawyers, and they resent the monetary contributions.[50] Legal aid clients lose their cases with disproportionate frequency; not surprisingly, those who lose are further disillusioned.[51] Also, of course, the (significant) proportion of applicants denied legal aid because they are ineligible do not gain a more favourable impression of the legal system.[52] All this is entirely consistent with other studies of encounters with the legal system: familiarity breeds contempt.[53] Thus legal aid may actually delegitimate the legal system in the eyes of the poor. Many appear to embrace the cynical belief that justice is available only to the rich.[54] Why should we have expected anything else? The theory of legitimation rests on the patronizing assumption that the poor are somehow fooled by legal aid—an institution that we sophisticated lawyers and social scientists know can improve their lives only marginally. It is as though the saying: 'If you're so smart, why aren't you rich?' has been turned upside down: 'If they're so poor, they must be dumb.' However, the acquiescence of the poor in the legal system need not be secured by their belief in its legitimacy. They comply with its dictates because they are compelled to do so, just as their acceptance of the social order is ensured by economic necessity, political powerlessness, and social disorganization.

Perhaps legitimation theory is attractive because it expresses the universal desire of oppressors to believe they are loved by the oppressed.

advice); Cass and Sackville 1975: 68 (only a quarter could correctly describe legal aid in Australia). But see also Report of the Royal Commission on Legal Services 1979: 265 (80 per cent knew of the legal aid scheme and 60 per cent associated it with low-income people).

[48]   Abel-Smith *et al.* 1973: 204; cf. Morris *et al.* 1973: 301.

[49]   Levine and Preston 1970: 94, Abel-Smith *et al.* 1973: 192; Cass and Sackville 1975: 69; Oñate 1979: 233; Royal Commission on Legal Services 1979: 265; Royal Commission on Legal Services in Scotland 1980: 79.

[50]   Paterson 1971: 71; Valétas 1976: 92; Reifner 1980: 39.

[51]   Casper 1978: 237; Zander 1980: 55.

[52]   Valétas 1976: 92; Genn 1982: 33; but see Golley 1982: 54.

[53]   Cass and Sackville 1975: 86; Curran 1977: 235; Sarat 1977: 427.

[54]   Morris et al. 1973: 312; Cass and Sackville 1975: 82; Curran 1977: 232; Oñate 1979: 233.

Legitimation then becomes an effort by those who enjoy the privileges of wealth, power, and status to convince *themselves* that those privileges are justified or, better yet, that there actually are no privileges. Legal reform is one such means: a declaration of rights or a prescription of behaviour that simultaneously parades as description, an implicit assertion that such rights or behaviour actually exist. Welfare programmes are another example: the amelioration of some particularly egregious inequality that serves to distract attention from the overwhelming inequality that remains. In this sense, 'abuses' of the proffered benefit by 'scroungers' and welfare 'cheats' serve the indispensable function of showing that the programme is, if anything, working too well, and that its beneficiaries are not needy, and that further reforms are not only unnecessary but unwise. Thus the 'litigation explosion' shows that we have granted people too many rights.[55] Trivial, rigid regulations show that the state has interfered too much in economic activity.[56] When those patently 'guilty' of crime escape prosecution or punishment, we must be coddling criminals. A huge matrimonial settlement for a Saudi Arabian sheikha shows that divorce law is too generous to women. Mammoth tort judgments show that it pays to be injured. Legal aid shows that we have achieved procedural justice. Test cases and the representation of ineligible or unpopular clients (groups, homosexuals, hippies, racial minorities, aliens) are the necessary 'abuses' of legal aid that demonstrate 'we've gone about as far as we can go'.

This interpretation is at least consistent with the apparent paradox that legal aid programmes are created by the adversaries of its clients. Thus the earliest legal aid programmes were established by the state to defend the criminals it prosecuted.[57] At the turn of the century, legal aid was encouraged by capitalist philanthropists to protect workers exploited by (capitalist) employers and money-lenders. The enormous expansion of

---

[55] Galanter 1983: 4.   [56] Abel 1985a.

[57] Even today there is a correlation between the degree and visibility of state coercion in criminal proceedings and the prevalence of legal aid. In Britain, the following are the proportions of criminal accused represented by legal aid:

Crown Court sentencing—98%
Crown Court Trial—96%
Court of Appeal, Divisional Court—86%
Magistrates' Court adult trial of indictable offences—57%
Magistrates' Court juvenile proceedings—22%
Magistrates' Court trial of non-indictable offences—2%

In Scotland less than 10 per cent of those subject to summary prosecution are awarded legal aid (Royal Commission on Legal Services in Scotland 1980: 102).

legal aid after World War Two was in large part a grant by (male) legislators of assistance to women who were seeking divorces (and child custody and support) from men who had mistreated or abandoned them. Finally, in the last few decades, the welfare state has provided lawyers to enable its beneficiaries to assert claims against it; and capital (through the major foundations it endows) has created public-interest law firms to represent the consumers of products and of environmental amenities against the very enterprises that are overcharging, selling unsafe products, or destroying the environment. Such apparently disinterested behaviour reveals cleavages within the dominant category: monopoly *versus* competitive capital, the national state *versus* local government, high-level policymakers *versus* street-level bureaucrats. The theory of legitimation, however, suggests another perspective: legal aid is an attempt by those who enjoy state power, ownership of capital, and patriarchal domination to convince themselves that those privileges are not being abused through arbitrary action, exploitation, violence, or irresponsibility, and that any abuses are promptly redressed.

Conclusion

It is essential, even if it is very difficult, to maintain the inescapable tension between optimism and pessimism in attempting to understand legal aid. Much of this tension is inherent in the institution itself. Lawyers devote their energies to the interests of property and capital, not because lawyers are politically conservative (though many are), but because only those interests can generate the kinds of fees that the legal profession has come to expect as a result of the monopoly it successfully created. The problems of individual poor clients are too small to attract the attention of lawyers, and it is difficult to aggregate them. Mass-processing a high caseload is the inevitable solution adopted by private lawyers and forced on salaried lawyers by a cost-conscious state. Yet such routine handling has serious drawbacks for both clients and lawyers. Legal aid derives its justification from the powerful ideology of equal justice under law (just as income redistribution derives its justification from the ideology of the market, and equal access to the media during electoral campaigns is justified by democratic ideology); yet each of these limited redistributions also legitimates a system that consistently betrays its promises. Many sociological and anthropological studies have shown that law is an effective means of handling conflict between strangers, but not between intimates; yet because the clients of legal aid lack the political and economic power to negotiate directly with adversaries, they must mobilize law even in disputes with intimates.

The paradox of legal aid is also manifest in the particular functions that lawyers perform for clients. Because the poor lack the property that preoccupies lawyers for private clients, they seek legal assistance primarily in three other areas. The largest by far is family matters. Legal aid lawyers have played an important role in redressing the dependent position of women within marriage and after divorce; and as long as the sexual division of labour persists they may have to continue doing so. However, it is important to acknowledge that these are intra-class controversies and that the lawyer ostensibly representing a dependent woman actually may be acting on behalf of a welfare bureaucracy against an unemployed or working-class man. Secondly, legal aid lawyers discipline the welfare bureaucracy, securing the entitlements of beneficiaries and helping to protect their dignity. Yet these lawyers have little or no influence over the content of welfare benefits, and their efficacy depends on a theory of deterrence that consistently is defeated by what Joel Handler calls the bureaucratic contingency. Thirdly, legal aid lawyers have no control over the content of the criminal law, the sources of crime, the invisible exercise of police or prosecutorial discretion, or the conditions of punishment. We can generalize about the marginality of much legal aid work by noting that it is concerned almost exclusively with reproduction, not production.

Finally, it is necessary to preserve an awareness of this tension between optimism and pessimism when reflecting on how legal aid might be improved. Let me hesitantly advance three suggestions, conscious that these may be applicable more to the United States than to Britain. First, there is something to be said for expanding eligibility to the entire population. Such an extension would make the middle class a powerful constituency for legal aid, advocates for greater funding and enhanced quality. The effect of such a political base can be seen by comparing the National Health Service in Britain or the Social Security programme in the United States, or education in both countries, with programmes directed only at the poor, such as welfare benefits or prisons. Yet there is a real danger that middle-class eligibles will consume a disproportionate share of services, driving out the poor or relegating them to inferior providers. Secondly, I think an argument can be made for mixed programmes that use both judicare and staffed-office models to deliver legal services (such as exist in Ontario, Canada). This would mean an expansion of law centres in Britain and an expansion of judicare in the United States. We know from empirical studies that staffed offices are more innovative in the services they deliver and the strategies they employ. On the other hand, clients appear to prefer private lawyers for many routine services, and the latter often are geographically more accessible (if also more expensive). Judicare programmes mobilize a substantial fraction of the legal profession as another powerful constituency in support of legal aid. Yet there is little control over the quality of the services offered by private lawyers, and mixed programmes can engender competition between salaried and private lawyers for limited funds. Thirdly, I would support the incorporation of legal aid work in the training of all lawyers: a mandatory clinical experience in law school and a mandatory year or more during apprenticeship, working in a staffed legal aid office or for a private lawyer specializing in legal aid. This would expose all entrants to the distinctive legal problems of the poor and sensitize them to the need for legal aid. It would utilize the strong idealism that characterizes many incoming law students (and that quickly erodes under the dual influence of a traditional curriculum and a limited job market). It would effect a major increase in the quantity of services available to legal aid clients, while acknowledging that burn-out may be inevitable in a job that makes extraordinary demands on time, energy, and emotion without offering much in the way of material rewards. It would generate a pool of experienced lawyers who might continue to render legal aid to clients they encounter in private practice. It is readily justified: a couple of years in public service is not much to ask of students who have benefited from state support for some fifteen years and who, for the rest of their working lives, will continue to benefit from the state-conferred monopoly enjoyed by the legal profession.

Legal aid cannot eliminate patriarchy within the family before or after divorce, but it can alter the balance of power between men and women. It cannot transform capitalist relations of production, but it can regulate the market and discipline the welfare state. It cannot eradicate the pain inflicted by the criminal process, but it surely mitigates that pain. It deserves our critical support.

Bibliography

ABEL, R. (1979) 'Socializing the legal profession: can redistributing lawyers' firms achieve social justice', 1 *Law and Policy Quarterly* 5.

—— (1981) 'Why does the A.B.A. promulgate ethical rules?' 59 *Texas Law Review* 639–88.

—— (ed.) (1982) *The Politics of Informal Justice*, New York, Academic Press.

—— (1985a) 'Risk as an arena of struggle', 83 *Michigan Law Review* 772–812.

—— (1985b) 'Law without politics: legal aid under advanced capitalism', 32 *University of California Law Review* 474–642.

ABEL-SMITH, B., ZANDER, M. and BROOKE, R. (1973) *Legal Problems and the Citizen*, London, Heinemann.

BELLOW, G. (1977) 'Turning solutions into problems: the legal aid experience', 34 *NLADA Briefcase* 106.

BLANKENBURG, E. (1975) 'Studying the frequency of civil litigation in Germany', 9 *Law Society Review* 307.

—— (1980) 'Why historical precedents of the Access to Law movement in Germany were not followed up', in E. Blankenburg (ed.), *Innovations in the Legal Services*. Cambridge, Mass., Oelgeschlager, Gunn and Hain.

—— (1982) 'European experience in innovating legal services', 2 *Windsor Yearbook of Access to Justice* 247.

BYLES, A. and MORRIS, P. (1977) *Unmet Need: the Case of Neighbourhood Law Centres*, London, Routledge and Kegan Paul.

CAPPELLETTI, M. and GARTH, B. (1978–9) (and Weisner, J.) *Access to Justice: a World Study* (in four volumes), Alphen aan den Rijn, Sitjhoff & Noordhoff.

CASPER, J. (1978) 'Having their day in court: defendant evaluations of the fairness of their treatment', 12 *Law & Society Review* 237.

CASS, M. and SACKVILLE, R. (1975) *Legal Needs and the Poor*. Canberra, Australian Government Publishing Service.

CHAMBERS, D. (1979) *Making Fathers Pay*, Chicago, University of Chicago Press.

COUNCIL FOR PUBLIC INTEREST LAW (1976) *Financing Public Interest Law in America: Balancing the Scales of Justice*, Washington DC, Council for Public Interest Law.

CURRAN, B. (1977) *The Legal Needs of the Public*, Chicago, American Bar Foundation.

FITZGERALD, J. (1977) *Poverty and the Legal Profession in Victoria*, Canberra, Australian Government Publishing Service.

FRASER, A. (1976) 'Sackville, poverty and the Law', 42 *Arena* 3.

FRIEDMAN, L. M. (1981) 'Claims, disputes, conflicts and the modern welfare state', in M. Cappelletti (ed.), *Access to Justice and the Welfare State*, Alphen aan den Rijn, Sitjhoff and Noordhoff.

DE FRIEND, R. (1979) 'Welfare law, legal theory and legal education' in M. Partington and J. Jowell (eds) *Welfare Law and Policy*, London, Frances Pinter, 43–64.

GALANTER, M. (1974) 'Why the "Haves" come out ahead: speculations on the limits of legal change', 9 *Law & Society Review* 95.

—— (1976) 'Delivering legality: some proposals for the direction of research', 11 *Law & Society Review* 225.

—— (1983a) 'Megalaw and Megalawyering in the contemporary United States' in Dingwall R., and Lewis, P. (eds), *The Sociology of the Professions*. London, Macmillan.

—— (1983b) 'Reading the landscape of disputes: what we don't know (and think we know) about our allegedly contentious and litigious society', 31 *UCLA Law Review* 4.

GENN, H. (1982) *Meeting Legal Needs?* Oxford, Centre for Socio-Legal Studies.

GOLLEY, D. (1982) *Evaluating Eligibility Criteria: a Study of the Legal Services Commission of South Australia*, Canberra, Australia Government Publishing Service.

GOUGH, I. (1979) *The Political Economy of the Welfare State*, London, Macmillan.

GRIFFITHS, J. (1980) 'A Comment on Research into Legal Needs', in E. Blankenburg (ed.), *Innovations in Legal Services*, Cambridge, Mass., Oelgeschlager, Gunn and Hain.

GUTTENTAG, M. and SECORD, P. (1983) *Too Many Women? The Sex Ratio Question*, Beverley Hills, Ca., Sage Publications.

HANDLER, J. (1978) *Social Movements and the Legal System: a Theory of Law Reform*, New York, Academic Press.

HIRSCHMAN, A. (1970) *Exit, Voice and Loyalty*, Cambridge, Mass., Harvard University Press.

HYDE, A. (1983) 'The Concept of Legitimation in Sociology of Law', *Wisconsin Law Review* 379.

ILLICH, I. (1977) *Disabling Professions*, London, Marion Boyars.

JETTINGHOF, A. (1983) 'Clients of the courts', 4 *Nieuwsbrief voor Nederlandstalige Rechtssociologen, Rechtsantropologen, und Rechtspsychologen* 283.

JONES, J. (1940) *Free Legal Advice in England and Wales: A Report on the Organisation, Methods, and Future of Poor Man's Lawyers*, Oxford, Slater and Rose.

KAKALIK, J. and ROSS, R. (1983) *Costs of the Civil Justice System: Court Expenditures for Processing Various Types of Civil Cases*, Santa Monica, Calif., Rand Corporation.

KATZ, J. (1982) *Poor People's Lawyers in Transition*, New Brunswick, NJ, Rutgers University Press.

KING, M. (1976) *The Effect of a Duty Solicitor Scheme: an Assessment of the Impact on a Magistrate's Court*, London, Cobden Trust.

KOOS, E. (1949) *The Family and the Law*, New York.

KRONMAN, A. (1982) *Max Weber*, Stanford, Stanford University Press.

LAZERSON, M. (1982) 'In the halls of justice, the only justice is in the halls', in R. Abel (ed.), *The Politics of Informal Justice, Vol. I. The American Experience*, New York, Academic Press.

LEVINE, F. and PRESTON, E. (1970) 'Community resource allocation among law income groups', *Wisconsin Law Review* 80.

LUHMANN, N. (1982) *The Differentiation of Society*, New York, Columbia University Press.

MORRIS, P., COOPER, P. and BYLES, A. (1973) 'Public attitudes to problem definition and problem solving: a pilot study', 3 *British Journal of Social Work*.

O'CONNOR and EPSTEIN (1983) Balancing the scales of justice: assessment of public interest law, paper presented at the 1983 meeting of the Law and Society Association.

OÑATE, S. (1979) 'Mexico', in F. Zemans (ed.), *Perspectives on Legal Aid: an International Survey*, Westport, Conn., Greenwood Press.

PATERSON, A. (1971) *Legal Aid and Social Service*, London, Cobden Trust.

PIVEN, F. F. and Cloward, R. A. (1977) *Poor People's Movements: Why they Succeed, How they Fail*, New York, Pantheon.

REICH, C. (1964) 'The new property', 73 *Yale Law Journal* 733.

REIFNER, U. (1980) 'Types of legal needs and modes of legalization: the example of the Berlin tenants initiative', in E. Blankenburg (ed.), *Innovations in the Legal Services*, Cambridge, Mass., Oelgeschlager, Gunn and Hain.

—— (1982) 'Individualistic and collective legalization: the theory and practice of legal aid advice for workers in prefacist Germany', in R. Abel (ed.), *The Politics of Informal Justice, Vol. II. Comparative Studies*, New York, Academic Press.

RHEINSTEIN, M. (1972) *Marriage, Stability, Divorce and the Law*, Chicago, University of Chicago Press.

ROACH, J. L. and ROACH, J. K. (1978) 'Mobilizing the poor: road to a dead end', 26 *Social Problems* 160.

ROYAL COMMISSION ON LEGAL SERVICES (1979) *Report*, London, HMSO, Cmnd 7648.

ROYAL COMMISSION ON LEGAL SERVICES IN SCOTLAND (1980) *Report*, Edinburgh, HMSO.

SARAT, A. (1977) 'Studying American legal culture: an assessment of survey evidence', 11 *Law & Society Review* 427.

SCHWARTZKOFF, J. and MORGAN, J. (1982) *Community Justice Centres: a Report on the New South Wales Pilot Project, 1979–81*, Sydney, New South Wales Law Foundation.

TEUBNER, G. (1983) 'Substantive and reflexive elements in modern law', 17 *Law & Society Review* 239.

THOMPSON, E. P. (1975) *Whigs and Hunters*, New York, Pantheon Press.

TRUBEK, D. (1972) 'Max Weber on law and the rise of capitalism', *Wisconsin Law Review* 3.

VALÉTAS, M. (1976) *Aide Judiciaire et Accès à la Justice*, Paris, Ministere de la Justice.

WANNER, C. (1974) 'The public ordering of private relations, Part I: initiating civil cases in Urban Trial Courts', 8(3) *Law and Society Review* 421.

WEISBROD, B. A. with HANDLER, J. F. and KOMESAR, N. K. (eds) (1978) *Public Interest Law: an Economic and Institutional Analysis*, Berkeley, University of California Press.

ZANDER, M. (1978) *Legal Services for the Community*, London, Temple Smith.

—— (1980) *The State of Knowledge about the English Legal Profession*, Chichester, Barry Rose.

8. The Politics of Legal Aid—A Solution in Search of a Problem?[1]

MEL COUSINS

The actual and potential roles of legal aid in overcoming barriers to 'access to justice' have played a prominent part in the literature on this issue.[2] This article examines the development and role of civil legal aid in Western European countries. Much of the debate on legal aid has concentrated on ideological arguments about the role which legal aid should or should not play,[3] and on economic arguments about the financial cost (to the taxpayer/state) or the financial benefits (to the legal profession) of legal aid services. There has been relatively little debate from a sociological viewpoint as to how and why civil legal aid develops or fails to develop, nor as to its role under the advanced capitalism of Western Europe.[4] The debate has tended to be based on preformed (and frequently uninformed) opinions as to the role which legal aid should assume. This failure has led to a fundamental lack of coherence in many of the arguments advanced.

This article begins by outlining some of the limited information which is available on the extent of civil legal aid services in some Western

[1] Richard Abel argues that 'legal aid is a social reform that begins with a solution—lawyers—and then looks for a problem it might solve, rather than beginning with the problem—poverty, or oppression, or discrimination, or capitalism—and exploring solutions'. R. Abel, 'The Paradoxes of Legal Aid' in *Public Interest Law* (Cooper and Dhavan eds. 1986). Criminal legal aid—with its role in relation to the most obviously coercive powers of the State—raises quite different issues from civil legal aid and so is not considered here.

[2] See, for example, M. Cappelletti *et al.*, *Towards Equal Justice: A Comparative Study of Legal Aid in Modern Societies* (Milan & Dobbs Ferry, 1981).

[3] Should legal aid cover only 'traditional' legal advice and representation or should it include work in the area of education and law reform? What areas of law should it cover? and so on.

[4] Some important exceptions to the generally atheoretical debate in this area include Abel *op. cit.*, P. Alcock, 'Legal Aid: Whose Problem?' (1976) *British Journal of Law and Society* 151; P. Morris *et al.*, *Social Needs and Legal Action* (1973); A. Paterson and D. Nelken, 'Evolution in Legal Services: Practice without Theory' (1983) CJQ 229. I would suggest that it is not coincidental that many of the most important contributions come from non-lawyers. On the broader issue of informal justice see R. Abel ed., *The Politics of Informal Justice* (Academic Press: 1982).

European countries. It goes on to consider how and why civil legal aid develops in these countries. In this context, the part played by important interest groups, such as the administration and the legal profession, in the development of legal aid is considered. Some of the justifications put forward for a broader approach to legal aid are then considered and criticized.

The article suggests that the debate on 'access to justice' and legal aid generally has been hamstrung by its emphasis on 'the legal' and its inability to distinguish the (socially constructed) legal from broader issues concerning access to the law. This has led to the already noted failure to try to understand what legal aid does and how it develops and the failure to develop coherent theories and policies on access to the law. The debate on legal aid and legal services, constrained as it has been within the paradigm of the 'legal' can be accused of asking the wrong questions. This article seeks to ask different, and more relevant, questions. Given the exploratory nature of this study, the intention is to consider problems rather than to provide solutions.

The Extent of Civil Legal Aid

The first point to be made is that there is a marked lack of comparable information (or indeed any information in some cases) on civil legal aid in Europe.[5] Unlike other areas of social policy, little comparative research has been undertaken in the area of civil justice, and specifically in relation to civil legal aid. Thus the empirical information upon which a comparison may be made is quite limited. Because of the difference in definitions used in each country and the differing structures of legal aid schemes, it is difficult, if not impossible, to compare legal aid services in terms of outcomes, e.g. the number of persons assisted. The only reasonably comparable figure available is that for state expenditure on legal aid. Accordingly this will be used as a measure of the extent of public provision of civil legal aid.

Figure 1 compares expenditure on civil legal aid in a range of Western European countries as a percentage of Gross Domestic Product (GDP). This gives an indication of the percentage of total national income spent on legal aid. It will be noted that there is a very wide variation in spending between countries—ranging from below 0.01 per cent of GDP in

[5] See M. Cousins, 'Civil Legal Aid in France, Ireland, the Netherlands and the United Kingdom—A Comparative Study' (1993) 12 CJQ 154 and the references therein for some recent studies.

Belgium, Ireland, and Spain to about 0.05 per cent in the United Kingdom.[6] These figures are for 1989, but this divergence has continued, indeed increased, in subsequent years. For example, in 1992 expenditure in the United Kingdom has increased to 0.08 per cent whereas expenditure in Ireland has remained below 0.01 per cent.[7] This means that as a percentage of total national income the United Kingdom spends over eight times as much on civil legal aid as Ireland.

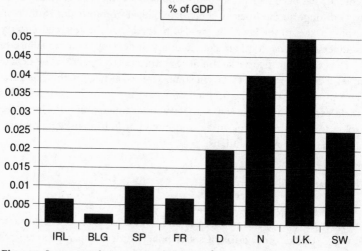

Figure 1: State expenditure on legal aid in 1989[8]

In Figure 2, the expenditure on legal aid as a percentage of GDP is plotted against the national figures for GDP per inhabitant.[9] This compares the proportion of total national income spent on civil legal aid with the average national income allocated on an individual basis. As can be seen, there is little correlation between the level of GDP per inhabitant—which

---

[6] See n. 8 for the sources of these figures.

[7] 1992 figures are from the Public Estimates for 1993 for Ireland and from the Legal Action Group report *A Strategy for Justice* for the United Kingdom.

[8] Figures for Spain (SP), France (FR), Germany (D), and Sweden (SW) are from the report of the French Conseil d'État, *L'aide juridique pour un meilleur accès au droit et à la justice* (La documentation française, 1991); figures for Ireland (IRL) are from the Legal Aid Board, *Report 1987, 1988 and 1989* (Stationery Office, 1991); for the United Kingdom from the *Northern Ireland Legal Aid Annual Report 1989–90* (HMSO, 1991); figures for Belgium (BLG) are from a personal communication from the Ministry for Justice; for the Netherlands from the Netherlands Ministry of Justice. GDP figures are from Eurostat.

[9] The figure for GDP per inhabitant is given in Purchasing Power Standards (PPS) which allows variations in purchasing power between countries to be held constant.

can be seen as a rough proxy for the wealth of the country—and expenditure on civil legal aid, except in so far as none of the less developed countries have a high level of legal aid spending. However, several wealthy countries—Belgium being the obvious example—have a very low level of spending on civil legal aid.[10] Conversely, the United Kingdom, which is only in the middle of the upper EC range in terms of GDP per capita, spends much more on legal aid than any other EC country.

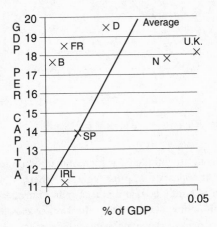

Figure 2: Legal aid spending compared to GDP per capita[11]

A comparison with expenditure in EC countries on other social services, e.g. health services, is instructive. This is set out in Figure 3 and again expenditure on health services (for 1990) is plotted against GDP per inhabitant. There are several points to be noted here. First is the massive nature of spending on health compared to that on legal aid: for example, Germany spends 7.4 per cent of GDP on health care as opposed to about 0.02 per cent on legal aid. Second is the relatively low deviation from the average spending compared to the wide variation in legal aid spending.[12] Finally, and perhaps most important, is the clear correlation between GDP per capita and expenditure on health services which is in marked contrast to the lack of any such correlation in the case of legal aid.

In terms of the services provided by legal aid schemes, it is clear that the vast majority are confined to a very traditional approach to legal

[10] This is also true of the United States.
[11] Figures for legal aid spending are as n. 8. Figures for GDP per capita are from Eurostat.
[12] Health expenditure varies by a factor of 1.5 whereas legal aid spending varies by a factor of up to 15.

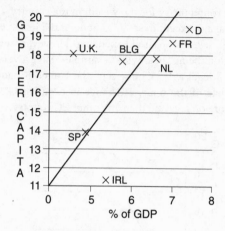

Figure 3: Health spending compared to GDP per capita[13]

services and concentrate uniquely (or predominantly) on legal advice and representation.[14] It appears that most legal aid schemes initially concentrate on the area of family law, and indeed many European schemes are still in this initial 'family' stage.[15] Only the Netherlands and the United Kingdom appear to have developed post-family schemes (although the area of family law matters remains the largest single area in both countries). However, in the Netherlands—under the influence of non-governmental legal aid services—the scheme has developed significantly in the area of welfare law (social security, housing, employment, immigration) while in the United Kingdom—under the influence of the legal profession—the scheme has expanded into areas of law traditionally dealt with by private lawyers.

The Development of Legal Aid

This section considers some of the forces behind the development of legal aid. As with any social service, a variety of theories can be put forward to explain the development of legal aid.[16] In the United Kingdom the social

[13] Figures for both GDP per capita and health spending are from Eurostat.

[14] See Cousins, *op. cit.* n. 5.

[15] The United States is an exception to this general rule as the legal aid scheme there developed out of the War on Poverty programme.

[16] R. Mishra, *Society and Social Policy: Theoretical Perspectives on Welfare* (London: Macmillan, 1977).

administration or Fabian approach has tended to play a dominant role in the area of legal aid as in other social services. This viewpoint tends to an atheoretical approach to the development of services. It seeks concrete reform but often ignores the tensions and contradictions underlying the society within which the reform is sought.[17] Although this approach has come under challenge in recent years, much analysis which explicitly rejects Fabianism can itself be accused of paleo-Fabianism with its emphasis on citizenship and the development of 'rights'.

In the United States, as Alcock shows, the dominant paradigm has been that of functionalism.[18] A functionalist approach seeks to ascertain the role (if any) which legal aid plays in ensuring ongoing coherence and harmony in society. Relevant factors would include the role of legal aid in industrialization/modernization of developing societies, in relation to rising levels of divorce and marital breakdown, in moderating political unrest, etc. This approach assumes, as does the Fabian which can also be accused of functionalism, that law is independent of conflicts in society and can act as an arbitrator between different interests.

Several writers have been influenced by a Marxist analysis from which perspective the role of legal aid is seen as assisting in the legitimation of capitalist society and helping to disguise the class tensions generated by factors such as industrialization.[19] A nuanced Marxist view would in addition consider the ideological and cultural issues involved. However, while this approach has been extremely effective in pointing out the limitations in the role of the law (and legal aid) in a capitalist society, there has been less success in operationalizing these insights in legal practice. While it is easy to see the role which the law plays in supporting capitalist society, it is less easy to find ways of using the law to articulate the struggle *against* capitalism (and even more difficult to find funding for such an approach). In the United Kingdom, for example, the Law Centres movement has frequently combined radical rhetoric with reformist practice.[20]

While, over the last decade or more, new approaches have developed to challenge those outlined above—such as postmodernism and critical legal studies—the legal aid debate has not yet been significantly influenced by such developments.

[17] Much United Kingdom writing in the 1960s and 1970s is within this paradigm, see for example, B. Abel-Smith *et al.*, *Legal Problems and the Citizen* (Heinemann, 1973). However, despite ongoing criticism of its atheoretical approach it remains important: see Legal Action Group, *A Strategy for Justice* (LAG, 1992). [18] P. Alcock, *op. cit.*, n. 4 at 158 *et seq.*
[19] See, for example, P. Alcock, *op. cit.*, n. 4, R. Boure and P. Mignard, *La crise de l'institution judiciare* (Christian Burgois, 1977).

This article seeks to adopt the Marxist influenced approach outlined by Alcock, i.e. 'to locate the social basis of the phenomenon of legal aid in the variety of practices historically involved in its formation'.[21] This approach takes account of the particular class and group interests involved in the creation and development of legal aid. It does not treat any one factor as determinative in the development of legal aid, but rather 'treats all phenomena as the result of the interrelationship of the social factors comprising them, none of them being the sole causational factor, but all together acting as the structural cause of the existence of the phenomena'.[22]

The emphasis here on a comparative approach will tend to underplay the importance of the specific historical and cultural environment in individual countries. These factors will, of course, be of importance in relation to the development of services in specific countries. However, the comparative approach enables us to see factors which are of importance (or which are irrelevant) across countries.

Industrialization and modernization

Proponents of the industrialization theory see the legal system as playing a particular functional role in the development of advanced capitalism. Kerr *et al.* state that:

> the industrializing societies of the modern world have introduced legal systems which encourage economic growth through some protection to private property and individual rights. Rights and obligations of labor, management, and the state are developed through statutes, codes, court decisions, and administrative agencies acting under statutory power. The arbitrary power of the state or its agents is limited by these means. Private law, developed by management and labor organizations as part of a system of industrial relations, is a further limitation on the all-powerful state.[23]

In this context, it is sometimes argued that industrialization and the increasing complexity of society leads to an increase in legal aid as a

---

[20] For the position in France see R. Boure and P. Mignard, *loc cit*, who argue that alternative legal organizations should operate at the interface between the law and the people, to demystify and politicize legal conflicts. However, this approach also seems to have made little headway.

[21] P. Alcock, *op. cit.* at 163 *et seq*.

[22] Ibid., p. 164.

[23] C. Kerr *et al.*, *Industrialism and Industrial Man* (Oxford University Press, 1964). See also the discussion of the role of the law in the development of capitalist society in J. Habermas, *The Structural Transformation of the Public Sphere* (Polity, 1989).

response to the development of a 'lumpen proletariat', the increase in immigration, urbanization, and changes in family structure.[24]

However, the wide variation in state spending on legal aid set out in the previous section would suggest that there is a weak link between the modernization of society and the development of legal aid. Legal aid appears to be functionally weak in relation to the needs of society's over-all development, i.e. while factors such as industrialization and modern-ization do have some effect on the development of legal aid, some highly advanced countries (such as Belgium and indeed the United States) have very low levels of state expenditure on legal aid. Nonetheless, it is clear that no poorer European country has a highly developed legal aid scheme. This might suggest that it is not industrialization or moderniza-tion *per se* which leads to legal aid but rather specific aspects of develop-ment which may vary from one country to another, e.g. divorce and marital breakdown. This is next considered.

Marital Breakdown and Divorce

It has been argued that divorce has had a major impact on the develop-ment of legal aid. This is undoubtedly true in some countries, for example the United Kingdom where the early development of legal aid was inextri-cably linked to the rise in divorce.[25] However, it has further been sug-gested that

the centrality of divorce may explain the correlation . . . noted between the pres-ence of legal aid in Protestant northern Europe (and North America and Australia) and its absence in Catholic southern Europe (and Ireland and Latin America), which, until recently has not permitted divorce.[26]

However, while this explanation sounds initially plausible, further exami-nation shows that it does not explain several features of the development of legal aid. For example, the divorce rate in France at the time of the development of legal aid in the United Kingdom and the Netherlands was comparable to the divorce rate in either of the two latter countries, yet no comprehensive legal aid scheme was established in France until the 1970s (and even then at a very modest level).[27] Belgium, a northern Catholic

[24] See R. Abel, *op. cit.*, n. 4 at 380.
[25] See Alcock *op. cit.*, n. 4; L. Stone, *The Road to Divorce* (Oxford University Press, 1992). C. Gibson, 'Divorce and the Recourse to Legal Aid' (1980) 43 MLR 609.
[26] Abel, *op. cit.*, n. 4, p. 380.
[27] W. J. Goode, 'A Sociological Perspective on Marital Dissolution' in *Sociology of the Family* (M. Anderson, Penguin, 1971); F. Robertson Elliot, *The Family: Change or Continuity?* (Macmillan, 1986).

country, has a relatively high divorce rate[28] but it has no comprehensive legal aid scheme and state spending is at an extremely low level. In addition, divorce has now existed in Italy for over twenty years and was preceded by a long period during which, although there was no divorce, there was considerable marital breakdown. Yet legal aid in Italy is still based on legislation from the 1920s and there has been no marked expansion of legal aid in response to the introduction of divorce.

The failure of a comparatively high level of marital breakdown to lead to a development in legal aid services does not appear to be related to the differences in national divorce procedures. For example, in France all divorces must go before the courts and legal representation is required by law in all cases, whereas in the United Kingdom it has always been possible, at least in theory, to represent oneself in such proceedings.[29]

Thus it appears that divorce may lead to a development of legal aid in some countries but not in others. It appears that it will do so in liberal and generally Protestant countries but not in conservative Catholic regions (or at least that the development in Catholic societies will be much slower). This can be seen within the United Kingdom itself where legal aid developed much later in Northern Ireland with its mixture of conservative Protestant and conservative Catholic culture. It would thus seem that the existence of divorce (and marital breakdown) may or may not lead to a development of legal aid.

Religion

It is noteworthy that legal aid spending is generally higher in Protestant countries than in Catholic countries. The reasons for this are not immediately apparent but it is suggested that they may be related more to general cultural factors which have an indirect effect on political, economic, and social developments than to a specific explanation such as the presence or absence of divorce. This indirect linkage can also be seen in relation to other issues. For example, religion appears to have had an important impact on the development of political rights of women and in the political socialization of individuals. Thus the right to vote was granted to women in Protestant countries in the early part of the century: Denmark (1915), Germany (1918), the Netherlands (1919), the United Kingdom (1928), whereas it was not generally granted in Catholic countries until much later: France (1944), Italy (1945), Belgium (1948), Portugal

[28] F. Robertson, Elliot, *op. cit.*
[29] M. Cousins 'Family Litigation in France' [1993] *Fam. Law* 78.

(1976).[30] A recent study found that people in Belgium, Spain, Ireland, Italy, and Portugal discussed politics relatively rarely and that women were much less likely than men to discuss politics.[31] This compared to a situation in Denmark, Germany, France, the Netherlands, and the United Kingdom where politics were much more commonly discussed and where there was much smaller difference between men and women in this regard.

Political Conflict and Political Violence

In certain specific situations, political conflict may give rise to increased legal aid expenditure. Thus for example, in Northern Ireland, legal aid expenditure has increased due to the violence both because individuals require legal aid in relation to civil disputes arising from the violence and, more interestingly, because funding has been granted to organizations such as the Belfast Law Centre, which provide a constitutional outlet for challenges to the state. The difference in the level of funding provided to the Centre *vis-à-vis* that provided to mainland law centres is marked.[32] Without in any way taking from the quality of service provided by the Belfast Law Centre, one might question whether it would receive the *amount* of funding which it does were the legitimacy of the existing political structures not under threat.

A similar situation can be seen in Germany in the early part of the twentieth century. Here, as is well known, the German government combined a policy of repressing socialist and social-democratic parties with an advanced social policy, including the establishment of comprehensive social security schemes. This led to a demand for advice and assistance in relation to social security which was initially catered for by radical trade unions. This soon led to the establishment by the state of well funded public legal aid services in order to contain such problems within a politically acceptable context.[33]

---

[30] *Women of Europe Supplement No. 27* (Commission of the European Communities, 1988). This report comments that 'while Spanish women were granted these rights in 1930, it is no secret that they rarely had the occasion to use them prior to 1977'. Ireland (1922) is also an exception in that the grant of the right to vote was influenced by the fact that Ireland was part of the United Kingdom until 1921. After independence women 'found it difficult to realise the promise of female enfranchisement', L. O'Dowd, 'Church, State and Women: The Aftermath of Partition' in *Gender in Irish Society* (C. Curtin *et al.* eds., Galway University Press, 1987).

[31] *Women of Europe Supplement No. 35* (Commission of the European Communities, 1991). There was at least at 15 per cent difference between men and women in these countries.

[32] See Cousins, *op. cit.*, n. 5 at 161.

[33] E. Blankenburg and U. Reifner, 'Possibilité de transplanter d'un pays à un autre les experiences touchant l'accès à la justice. Ses limits' in *Accès à la justice et état-providence* (M. Cappelletti, Economica, 1984).

Legal Systems

It is interesting to note that the legal systems do not seem to have a determining effect on civil legal aid. Thus, unlike the situation in relation to
criminal legal aid, there is no clear distinction between levels of expenditure under common law and civil law systems.[34] Equally, legal aid spending appears to bear little relationship to the number of lawyers in a
country. Thus, the Netherlands which has one of the lowest numbers of
lawyers per capita has one of the highest levels of spending on civil legal
aid.[35]

Because of the wide variation in the definition of judicial statistics
between EC countries, it is very difficult to constitute any 'index of litigiousness for Western European countries. However, in so far as the ratio
of lawyers to members of the population might give some indication of
litigiousness, this varies from one lawyer per 498 people in Greece to one
for every 2,500 in the Netherlands and, as we have seen, no correlation
with legal aid spending is apparent. However, one might argue that there
is a relationship between the economic position of any particular national
legal profession and its interest in the development of legal aid. This will
be returned to below.

The Effect of Functional Factors

Thus, in summary, we have argued that legal aid is functionally weak in
advanced capitalist societies of Western Europe, i.e. while factors such as
industrialization, development, religion, divorce, political unrest, etc. *may*
(and frequently do) have an impact on the development of legal aid, they
are not determinative. However, a cumulative absence or presence of
many or all of these factors will be likely to have an impact on the state of
development of legal aid. Thus a poorly developed, Catholic country with
comparatively low levels of marital breakdown and no marked political
instability is very unlikely to have a developed legal aid scheme.

Political and Interest Groups

We have argued above that the role of wide ranging factors such as the
level of industrialization has had an important but not determinative role

[34] In the area of criminal legal aid, most common law countries spend 50 per cent or
more of their total budget on criminal legal aid whereas in civil law systems with their different approach to criminal justice, legal aid spending is generally much lower than spending
on civil legal aid.

[35] See D. McIntosh and M. Holmes, *Civil Proceedings in EC Countries* (Lloyds of London,
1991).

in the development of legal aid. This section looks at the role of political and interest groups as a possible explanation of the different levels of legal aid development in Europe. Again it must be said that there is a lack of available national analysis of the development of services in individual countries which means that many of the arguments advanced here are only tentative and may be considered as a basis for debate rather than a completed theory.

The first point which must be made is that there is relatively little indication that political parties have had any great impact on the development of legal aid. In the United Kingdom, for example, Alcock shows that in the period 1920 to 1942 the Lord Chancellor's Office, the Treasury and the legal profession—rather than political parties—dominated ideological discussion about the nature of legal aid.[36] The initial introduction of a comprehensive legal aid scheme in 1949 was broadly supported by all political parties with relatively minor differences as to the approach to be taken.[37] Indeed it is clear that the Law Society rather than the political parties was influential both in the decision to establish the scheme (so that the Society would be relieved of the responsibility of running the Services Divorce Department) and in the structure of the new scheme (with its heavy emphasis on the role of private solicitors and of the Law Society itself). The legal aid scheme remained tied to the traditional notion of legal services despite many years of Labour party government. In more recent years, legal aid spending, starting from a comparatively high level, has continued to grow at a higher rate—not only in overall terms but as a percentage of GDP—than in most other EC countries, despite fourteen years of Conservative government. This does not ignore the current attacks on the United Kingdom scheme but given the rhetoric of the Conservative governments and their record in other areas of social spending the lack of impact in this area to date is striking. Readers who believe that any Labour government would be spending more than 0.08 per cent of GDP on civil legal aid may care to examine the position in France where the then Socialist government only undertook reform of the totally inadequate legal aid service in 1990 following a series of strikes by the legal profession.

The reason why few political parties see legal aid as a burning issue may be related to an assessment of its (lack of) functional importance. In addition, legal aid is rarely of benefit to a clearly identifiable group or class

[36] P. Alcock, *op. cit.*, n. 4.
[37] E. J. Cohn 'The Political Parties and Legal Aid' (1945) 8 MLR 97 and 'Legal Aid to the Poor and the Rushcliffe Committee' (1946) 9 MLR 58.

of people—other than the legal profession, of which more below—and consequently no group has any clear interest in campaigning for improved services. Because of the diffuse nature of potential users, it is rare for class or social group based campaigns to develop much coherence. Even women's movements have not generally prioritized legal aid, although it appears that in most countries the majority of the users of the service are women. The traditional suspicion of the law and lawyers to be found in trade union circles appears to have contributed to the fact that trade unions have rarely become strongly involved in campaigning for legal aid.

In contrast, the state administrations have played a very important role in the development of legal aid. Generally speaking, administrations are concerned with controlling the cost of legal aid. However, the high levels of spending in both the Netherlands and the United Kingdom can, to some extent, be explained by the role of the respective civil services. In the Netherlands, the Ministry of Justice has adopted a very 'hands-on' role in relation to the management of legal aid services and it also appears to be committed to providing an extensive legal aid scheme.[38] Thus the Ministry has been able to provide a reasonably comprehensive service without excessive costs by carefully managing the delivery of services and by carefully manipulating the legal profession to keep costs to a minimum.[39]

In contrast the Lord Chancellor's Office (subsequently Department) traditionally adopted a comparatively 'hands-off' approach, leaving management of the service to the Law Society which obviously had little incentive to keep costs down or deliver a cost-efficient service. When the Conservative Government decided that legal aid was getting out of hand the knowledge, ability, and structures to control costs simply did not exist, with the result that costs have gone on rising despite the government rhetoric. However, once the Legal Aid Board (which took over the administration of the service from the Law Society in 1988) has acquired the relevant skills and structures, which it appears to be doing, legal aid spending will then be controllable. The question then will be whether the Lord Chancellor's Department and the Board will work together, and

[38]   T. Goriely, 'Legal Aid in the Netherlands: A View from England' (1992) 55 MLR 803.

[39]   For example, by encouraging the development of a quasi-nongovernmental sector which then creates potential competition to the private sector thereby keeping pressure on rates of payment. At the same time the establishment of this sector helped to divert attention from criticism by the more 'radical' law shops. For an assessment of the Netherlands lawshops as reformist rather than radical see R. Boure and P. Mignard, *La crise de l'institution judiciare* (Christian Burgois, 1977).

whether either or both want a reasonably comprehensive legal aid scheme or not. In practice, as the interface between a powerful legal profession and the Government, the administrators are likely to be extremely influential in the future direction of policy.[40] Thus one can see the administration operating with relative autonomy to mediate the interests of different groups in the ruling bloc, i.e. the broader interests in minimizing expenditure with the specific interests of the legal profession in maintaining their legal aid income.[41]

Interestingly, the judiciary have had little involvement in the area of legal aid. Judges do not seem to feel that civil legal aid is necessary to legitimate their actions. This is in contrast to the position in relation to criminal legal aid in common law countries. For example, the Irish and United States Supreme Courts have held that there is a constitutional right to criminal legal aid under their respective constitutions.[42]

The legal profession, as we have seen, has an obvious interest in developing publicly funded legal services and also in ensuring that funds are concentrated in areas of work which are of interest to the profession. This may go a considerable way to explaining the heavy concentration in most countries on providing traditional legal services, i.e. advice and representation in court, rather than any education or law reform role. The role of the profession in the United Kingdom has already been referred to. In the Netherlands, the profession—caught between the Ministry and the non-governmental sector—has played a less dominant role. However, it has achieved a major increase in payments from July 1993. This has corresponded with a sharp increase in the level of contributions to be paid by legal aid clients.

In France, the decision to reform the extremely outdated and underfunded scheme was largely forced on the government by lobbying from the legal profession—including strike action. In addition, in the course of introducing the recent legal aid act, the legislation was amended to give

---

[40] To say that the role of the administrators has been critical in the development of legal aid in the Netherlands and the United Kingdom does not explain why there should have been such a difference between the two countries. This must await further empirical and theoretical consideration.

[41] See N. Poulantzas, *Les classes sociales dans le capitalisme aujourd'hui* (Éditions du Seuil, 1974).

[42] *Gideon v. Wainwright* (1963) 372 US 335; *State (Healy) v. Donoghue* [1976] IR 325. Neither court has established a similar constitutional right to civil legal aid. The only major court decision in this area remains *Airey v. Ireland* (1979) 2 EHRR 305 but this appears to have been a once-off case and there has been no development of this jurisprudence by the European Court of Human Rights. See M. Cousins, 'Access to the Courts: The European Convention on Human Rights and European Community Law' (1992) 14 *Dublin University Law Journal* 51.

the French profession increased control over the provision of legal advice.[43] The French Ministry of Justice appears to have conceded a quasi-monopoly in legal aid and advice to the profession in return for low levels of payments.[44] In Ireland, the representative bodies of the professions which have long shown considerable reservations about becoming actively involved in legal aid[45]—fearing that legal aid might force down charges and bring increased state control—have recently shown much more interest in legal aid.[46] One might suggest that this is not unrelated to the fact that the rapidly expanding number of lawyers is not being matched by a rapidly expanding market for their services.

In this area campaigning organizations are faced with a dilemma: one of the most effective lobbies for legal aid is the legal profession and the involvement of the profession will almost inevitably result in higher levels of legal aid funding; at the same time, the involvement of the profession will mean that legal services are concentrated in traditional areas and that little emphasis will be put on a broader role for legal aid.

The final type of interest groups to be involved in the development of legal aid are specialized legal and quasi-legal groups interested in 'access to justice'. While broader advice groups have become involved in the debate from time to time, these groups have tended to be specialized bodies made up mainly of lawyers such as the *Landelijke Organisatie Buros voor Rechtshulp* and the *Vereniging van Socale Advocatuur Nederland* in the Netherlands, the Legal Action Group and the Law Centres Federation (and its constituent parts) in the United Kingdom, and the Free Legal Advice Centres in Ireland. These groups are generally quite small and do not have any level of mass support. They have been extremely successful in setting the agenda for public (chimerical) discussion about legal aid but have generally been much less successful in influencing the real debate (largely controlled by the state and the legal profession) and the actual delivery of legal aid services. One need only compare the amount of discussion in the United Kingdom about community law centres with the reality of the number of such centres and the peripheral role which they

[43] *Loi No. 91–647 relative a 'l'aide juridique.* This legislation updated the existing provisions and introduced a new legal advice scheme (which did not previously exist in France).

[44] It appears that it was originally intended that a wide range of groups might be involved in providing legal aid. Whether this 'deal' will be sustainable must be open to question.

[45] At present the Irish scheme is provided through a salaried service.

[46] The Irish Law Society has recently approved a governmental proposal that family law solicitors take on one legal aid case on a *pro bono* basis to clear a backlog of cases in return for a commitment to expand the existing salaried scheme to include the participation of private practitioners, (1993) LS Gaz. June.

play in the delivery of legal services. The contrast between the success in articulating arguments (leaving to one side the merit of the arguments) and the failure to influence events reflects the fact that the 'legal aid debate' rarely entered into the realms of political discourse. Ideas such as community involvement, education, and law reform were of little interest to the administration and the legal profession and they largely ignored them. On the other hand, many of the pressure groups showed little interest in trying to understand how they might actually influence events and so they did not do so.

The Netherlands has been the one major exception to this rule in that the influence of non-governmental groups has helped to ensure that welfare law plays a significant role in the Netherlands scheme. There appears to have been a better 'fit' between the needs of the administration and the groups involved: it suited the Ministry of Justice to have an alternative provider so as to put pressure on the legal profession, whereas the non-governmental sector adopted a reformist rather than a radical approach and thus could easily be accommodated within the state services.[47]

Conclusion

We have seen that the two groups which have particular influence in the development of legal aid are the legal profession and the administration in its role of mediating the interests of the constituent groups of the power bloc in capitalist society. The power and economic interests of the legal profession tend to be of particular importance since the specific needs of a powerful legal profession which is unable to generate an adequate (private) market for its services—as in the United Kingdom—may prevail over the more general interests of other groups in the power bloc in relation to a legal aid budget which is in global terms quite small.

The Role of Legal Aid and Legal Services

We have looked at the available information on the extent of legal aid in Western European Countries and we have outlined the forces and interest groups which have influenced its development. In this section we discuss the role which legal aid can and should play. We must first consider what we mean by 'legal aid' and 'public legal services'.

---

[47] This is, no doubt, a superficial account and research at a national level might well reveal more detailed reasons for this pattern.

The Concept of Legal Aid

Legal aid was, in most countries, initially seen primarily in relation to assistance in court with legal advice outside court being left to voluntary organizations.[48] Legal aid was seen as necessary from the point of view of formal equality before the law, i.e. in many cases both parties required legal representation if such formal equality was to be ensured. As many persons could not afford a lawyer, it was the responsibility of the state to provide for such representation. Legal advice was gradually recognized as a necessary part of legal aid services. This only occurred quite recently in some countries, e.g. France (1991). However, in the 1960s, particularly in the United States, a much broader approach developed to the role of legal aid and legal services generally. Access to legal services was seen as necessary from the point of view of a more general principle of equality and in order to ensure equal access to justice—lawyers being seen as a necessary prerequisite to such access. The notion of 'unmet legal need' developed with researchers trying to show that access to legal services was differentiated on a social class basis and that many working class people (including welfare claimants, etc.) had legal problems which were not being catered for by existing legal services.[49] Legal services were seen as an essential part of an anti-poverty strategy.[50] In this context, a broader approach to legal aid—including community involvement in the delivery of services, the expansion of services to include education and law reform, etc., was seen as desirable. Aspects of this broader approach—which in fact contains many different, frequently conflicting approaches—have dominated writing on legal services since the 1960s although with the exception of the Netherlands and, to some extent, areas of Canada and Australia[51] it has not been very successful in influencing the actual delivery of legal services.[52]

The theoretical basis of this approach has been heavily criticized (see below). Nonetheless these arguments have remained as a central plank

[48] E. J. Cohn, 'Legal Aid for the Poor: A study in Comparative Law and Legal Reform' (1943) 59 LQR 250 and 359. N. S. Marsh, 'Legal Aid and the Rule of Law: A Comparative Outline of the Problem' (1959–60) 2 *Journal of the International Commission of Jurists* 95.

[49] See J. E. Carlin and J. Howard *op. cit.* and K. Schuyt *et al.*, *De Weg Naar Het Recht* (Deventer: Kluwer, 1976) reviewed by J. Griffiths (1977) *British Journal of Law and Society* 260.

[50] E. Cahn and J. Cahn 'The war on poverty: a civilian perspective' (1964) 73 *Yale Law Journal* 1933.

[51] See Legal Action Group, *A Strategy for Justice* (LAG, 1992).

[52] While the anti-poverty approach did influence the structure of public legal services in the United States and while the models of service in that country are very interesting, the amount of money spent on legal aid is very small and the public legal services approach appears to have had little impact on mainstream legal services.

for much of the current arguments around legal aid. For example, the Legal Aid Board for England and Wales—which remains committed to a narrow concept of legal aid—utilizes the rhetoric of the broader approach in its definition of access to justice whereby: 'Access is achieved where individuals are aware of their need for legal services and can select and actually obtain legal services of an appropriate quality, at a price within reach.'[53]

In its submission arguing for the establishment of a nationwide scheme of salaried legal services, the Law Centres Federation were content to 'adopt this definition' albeit only 'for present purposes'.[54] The Legal Action Group—stating that the above definition 'echoes . . . much of LAG's approach'—argues in its recent publication,[55] for 'the attainment of equal access to justice for all members of society'.[56] This means that: 'the ultimate policy aim must be that anyone with a legal problem has equal access to its just conclusion so that disputes are determined by the intrinsic merits of the argument of either party, not by inequalities of wealth or power.'

'Access' to 'legal' services: a critique

A detailed criticism of concepts such as 'access to legal services' and 'unmet legal need' was outlined by Pauline Morris in 1973.[57] Given the continuing reliance on such arguments as a justification for expanded legal services, it is worth recalling briefly Morris' critique of this approach. She pointed out that: 'need is *socially defined*. It is important to stress that legal need cannot be viewed in any absolute sense, nor can it be isolated from a mere general idea of social need.'[58] She predicted—and indeed we have seen that this has been the case—that: 'definitions of need likely to be adopted in terms of the service provided will reflect the power and status of those providing the service rather than the definition of those receiving it.'[59] Unsurprisingly therefore:

the definition of unmet legal need currently being used is that of the lawyer—legal problems are those problems for which there is at present a legal solution, and by

---

[53] Legal Aid Board, *Annual Report 1990–1991* (HMSO, 1991) paras. 8. 1–2.

[54] Law Centres Federation, *Review of Financial Conditions for Legal Aid Eligibility for Civil Legal Aid: The Law Centre View* (LCF, 1991).

[55] *A Strategy for Justice, op. cit.*   [56] Ibid. at 111.

[57] P. Morris, 'A Sociological Approach to the Research in Legal Services' in P. Morris ed. *op. cit.*, n. 4.

[58] P. Morris, 'A Sociological Approach to the Research in Legal Services' in P. Morris ed. *op. cit.*, n. 4, at 50.   [59] Ibid. at 51.

a relatively simple head-counting operation which determines how many people have such problems yet do not consult a lawyer, and which discovers to what socio-economic class they belong, it is argued that one can assess at least in crude form, the extent and type of unmet legal need for legal services. This is, of course, a gross simplification; what is necessary, both in the wider field of the social services and in the field of legal services, is to discover whether the relationship between the provision of services and the need (both met and unmet) is congruent with the conceptions of social or legal need held by the community, as well as by individual clients.[60]

She argues that the establishment of 'purely legal' services may simply 'perpetuate the definitional *status quo* (there are certain problems with which one goes to a lawyer)' and will be unlikely to meet the needs of the individual. Thus definitions of need—social or legal—involve not questions of 'scientific objectivity' but *values*.

John Griffiths also pointed out that the definition of 'legal problems' is essentially subjective.[61] The difficulty arises as to *whose* subjectivity is deemed to be the relevant one. On the question of access to legal services, Griffiths is unequivocal:

The concept 'access' should be banished from empirical study of the distribution of legal services because it has no empirical referent. It goes with the concepts of 'need' (for legal services), (serious) 'legal problems,' and 'legal competence' which . . . lead only to one or another of two subjectivities: that of the subject or that of the sociologist.[62]

Thus concepts such as 'access to legal services' and 'unmet legal need' have been shown to involve value judgments rather than empirical assessments. The people making the value judgments have been lawyers rather than individuals seeking access to the law. As we have seen, these sociological criticisms of legal aid theories have largely been ignored. This can be attributed to the fact that legal aid theorists operate almost exclusively within the paradigm of the 'legal' as indeed all lawyers are trained to do.[63] Thus they (the lawyers) see reform of the legal—by way of legal aid and, more recently, by a broader 'legal services' approach—as a solution with-

---

[60] P. Morris, see also P. Lewis, 'Unmet Legal Needs' in P. Morris ed. *op. cit.* n. 4: 'to say that someone has a legal problem is not a description of a state of fact; it is to suggest that he should take a certain course of action.'

[61] J. Griffiths, 'The Distribution of Legal Services in the Netherlands—review of K. Schyut *et al.*, *De Weg Naar Het Recht*' (1977) *British Journal of Law and Society* 260.

[62] Ibid. at 280.

out having properly defined the problem: they mistrust non-legal (socio-logical) approaches. This has resulted in the lack of coherence in legal aid and legal services theories. In addition, we have sent that—in practice—legal aid has much more to do with the economic needs of the legal profession than it has to do with the 'legal needs' of individuals. Thus we need to reconsider the basis of the debate about access to the law.

Access to the Law—Deconstructing the Legal

The law and the legal

The law and the legal system are often seen as the same thing. However, this article will distinguish between the concept of the law(s) and that of the legal—including the legal system, the legal profession, etc. We must first consider what we mean by law. The concept of law from a legal (positivist) viewpoint (and from that of the legal profession) comprehends quite a narrow understanding of law and laws. 'Law consists of data—primarily rules—which can be recognised by relatively simple tests of "rules of recognition"'.[64] One such test is that the rules have gone through 'certain formal stages of a legislative process'.[65] However, others have put forward a much broader understanding of 'the law'. Ehrlich, for example, sees the law as involving not just the norms created and applied by the state (which he refers to as 'legal provisions') but as including also 'social order', i.e. the rules which are actually followed in social life—the real 'living law'.[66] As Ehrlich points out: 'the modern practical jurist understands by the word 'Law' generally only Legal Provisions because this is the part of law which interests him primarily in his everyday practice.[67]

Without attempting to resolve the definitional issue, it is clear that there are many problems which arise concerning rules of law which may or may not be seen as legal problems. This may be because the legal system has not recognized the issue as legal (e.g. many areas of welfare rights) or because the individual concerned does not perceive his or her problem as requiring a legal solution.

---

[63] P. Goodrich describes entry into law school as 'the start of an extremely lengthy process of socialisation into the techniques and languages of an authoritarian hierarchy': *Legal Discourse: Studies in Linguistics, Rhetoric and Legal Analysis* (Macmillan, 1987).

[64] R. Cotterrell, *The Sociology of Law* (Butterworths, 1992), p. 9.

[65] Ibid.

[66] E. Ehrlich, 'The Sociology of Law' (1922) 36 *Harvard Law Review* 130.

[67] Ibid. at 132.

The law can be seen as a rule base over which operates the superstructure of the legal system. While the nominal role of the legal system is to facilitate the operation of the law and to act as an interface between the law and the community, in practice the legal system operates to control the operation of the law (for the immediate financial benefit of the legal profession and the economic and power benefit of the ruling classes). Thus the legal system serves to inhibit rather than facilitate access to the law for those who are not part of the ruling classes. This is not to suggest that the law in itself is an impartial forum. The law has always and, in a capitalist society, will always reflect inequalities in power and wealth. However, my argument is that the legal system simply increases these imbalances. Thus rather than attempting to reform the legal system in order to reform the law, one should try to deconstruct the legal and encourage more direct (uncontrolled) access to the law.[68]

Problems of law

These discussions re-emphasize the difficulty in defining a 'legal' problem. In effect the legal profession—itself a social construction[69]—has appropriated to itself a certain number of the problems which arise concerning the law (problems of law) as 'legal' problems which require 'legal' services. Much of the debate concerning legal aid and legal services has, as we have seen, either accepted the legal profession's definition of legal problems (which in the area of civil law applies primarily to property issues) or has attempted to expand that definition to include problems concerning 'new forms of property' such as social security or other welfare rights. Those adopting the 'legal services' approach have also called for increased community (or public) management of legal services and improved legal education.[70] However, one must question whether it is useful to attempt to expand the legal in this way.

In less 'advanced' societies problems of law were frequently dealt with in an informal way—or, in many cases, property relationships were simply enforced by coercion. As society becomes progressively more 'advanced' the informal methods of dealing with problems of law have tended to be displaced and to be replaced by legal remedies. Equally, under advanced capitalism property relationships are enforced through

---

[68] Currently access to the law is both mediated and controlled by way of the legal profession. While, given the complexity of the law, some form of mediated access is probably a practical necessity in many cases, the aim should be to return control to those who wish to use the law.

[69] See Cotterrell, *op. cit.* ch. 6.   [70] Legal Action Grup, *op. cit.*

the legal process rather than by force. While in an increasingly complex society, law (in the broad sense) will almost inevitably increase in importance—together with the necessity of dealing with problems of law—this does not necessarily require an increased emphasis on the legal.

Thus this approach does not question the differentiation processes in modern society—with the increased emphasis on the role of the law—but rather 'the specific form in which these differentiation processes have been articulated and institutionalised in capitalist societies'.[71] The approach advocated here seeks a:

'permeability' of the relatively autonomous subsystems or cultural spheres for each other: The formalized processes of administration, legislation and jurisdiction would then enter into a new constellation with nonformalized—or not necessarily formalized—processes of communication and will-formation, so that formalized decision processes would become permeable to the need-interpretations, moral impulses, or aesthetic experiences articulated beneath the level of formal organizations.[72]

I would argue that rather than try to convert problems of law into legal problems and then look for access to legal services to assist in the resolution of these problems, one should allow problems of law to remain outside the realm of the legal and find alternative ways of dealing with such problems. This would involve an increased emphasis on political-democratic solutions, on collective responses to problems of law and on an increased civic competence. In practice it would involve alternative forms of dispute resolution such as elected Ombudsmen at local governmental level, patients tribunals to deal with complaints concerning health services,[73] and a greatly enhanced role for democratically controlled advice services (including services for specific interest groups).

Such an approach would emphasize the political, participative, democratic, and collective aspects of problems of law as opposed to the apolitical, representative,[74] non-democratic, and individual manner in which legal problems are channelled through the legal system. Under the present system, as Boure and Mignard point out: *Le légal détrone le politique.*[75]

---

[71] A. Wellmer, 'Reason, Utopia and the *Dialect of Enlightenment*' in *Habermas and Modernity* (R. Bernstein ed. Polity, 1985).

[72] Ibid. at 63.

[73] Such tribunals have been established in Italy. See D. Mezzana ed., *Complice, utente, cittadino* (Movimento federativo democratico, 1991).

[74] See P. Morris, *op. cit.*, n. 4 at 65.

[75] R. Boure and P. Mignard, *op. cit.*

To emphasize the collective and democratic aspects of the law avoids the mistaken effort to equate 'welfare rights' with (legal) property rights. Property rights are the concretisation of the interests of politically and economically powerful groups in society. Welfare rights relate to the interests of groups which are frequently politically and economically weak. One cannot make welfare rights equivalent to property rights by changing their names or the structures of enforcement but only by increasing the political and economic strength of the groups to whom welfare rights attach.[76]

This approach leaves the area of property law, which currently appertains to the legal profession and the legal system, to those interests. The legal system has relatively little (economic) interest in 'non-legal' problems and so there might well be little economic resistance to a non-legal approach in non-property areas of law. However, one might expect a political-bureaucratic resistance to such a political, democratic, and collective approach.

What about those problems which are currently considered as legal problems (or which are on the margins of the legal)? I will outline five specific steps. An initial step must be an increased emphasis on the civic competence of individuals. While proposals for an educational role for public legal services (such as those proposed by the Legal Action Group)[77] are welcome, a much broader approach involving the entire educative system (in the broad sense) would be necessary. However, one might again anticipate resistance from the existing political structures. Gramsci wrote that one of the most important functions of the state 'is to raise the great mass of the population to a particular cultural and moral level, a level (or type) which corresponds to the needs of the productive forces of development and hence to the interests of the ruling classes'.[78] Implicit in that understanding is that the state is unlikely to see it as being its function to raise people to a *higher* level of development.

A second step would be to co-ordinate and expand advice and information services. Such services should not be seen as a bureaucratically organized first step to legal assistance but as one of the primary agents in resolving both problems of law and legal problems with only a limited number of cases being referred to a separate legal aid service. Such services might, as in France, incorporate or be closely linked to services such as conciliation, mediation, and specialized advice services (including

---

[76] In this context the law may play a role.   [77] *Op. cit.*
[78] A. Gramsci, *Selections from Prison Notebooks* (London: Lawrence and Wishart), p. 258.

money and legal advice). This would involve an extensive reappraisal of the type of service currently provided in countries such as the United Kingdom and Ireland, particularly as regards the type and range of services provided and the management and control of such services.

A third step would involve the promotion of *alternative* forms of dispute resolution.[79] This is particularly relevant in the area of family law, small consumer claims, and minor interpersonal disputes.[80]

Fourth would involve the role of organizations representing the interests of their members through collective legal and non-legal action.[81]

Finally, in those areas where legal aid and legal services generally will remain dominant, e.g. property law, personal injuries claims, judicial review, much employment law, some family law, I would see the most important issue as being how to increase the public's involvement in the delivery and control of legal services—including legal aid, the courts, and legal education. Legal services of all kinds are one of the few areas of public service where there is little if any public involvement in the delivery and control of services.[82]

Conclusion

This article has looked at the development of legal aid in several Western European countries and has advanced arguments as to how and why legal aid has developed quite differently within those countries. Fundamental to this argument has been the assertion that the growth of legal aid has tended to reflect the economic needs of the legal professions to a much greater extent than it has reflected the needs of the public or of individuals seeking access to the law.

Much of the debate about legal aid has simply reflected lawyers' opinions as to the role which they should play in solving other peoples' problems, with little, if any, consideration as to whether there are other and better ways in which these problems can be addressed. I have argued that

---

[79] By alternative forms of dispute resolution, I mean more than simply modified court procedures and ADR although simplified court and tribunal procedures are also important.

[80] B. Bastard and L. Cardia-Voneche, *Le divorce autrement: la médiation familiale* (Syros Alternatives, 1990); J.-P. Bonafé-Schmitt, *La médiation: une justice douce* (Paris: Syros Alternatives, 1992): M. Cappelletti, 'Alternative Dispute Resolution Processes with the Framework of the World-Wide Access-to-Justice Movement' (1993) 56 MLR 282.

[81] See, for example, Udo Reifner's account of how German trade unions developed a 'law of the people' approach through collective action in R. Abel ed., *The Politics of Informal Justice* (Academic Press, 1982).

[82] See J. Epstein, *Public Services: Working for the Consumer* (Luxembourg: Office for Official Publication of the E.C., 1990).

the debate about access to the law needs to be seen in a much broader context than a simple debate about access to legal services. It should involve a collective, democratic, and political approach to the issue. The application of these principles to the concrete problems of access to the law involves not only reform of the existing legal system but also, and more importantly, a search for new structures rather than simply improved access to the old.

9. Comparing Legal Aid Schemes in Europe

ERHARD BLANKENBURG

Legal services for the poor have been a latecomer to the growth of the welfare state in most countries in the European continent. While Scandinavian countries, West Germany, and the Netherlands rank highest in the world as far as expenditures for their systems of social security go, only one of them (the Netherlands) has built up an infrastructure of legal aid institutions which could be compared to that in Great Britain, the Commonwealth, and many parts of the United States.

There seems to be an easy explanation for the national differences which lies in the role which lawyers play in common law courts as compared to the civil law tradition. Comparative lawyers like to emphasize that adversarial procedure lays the full responsibility on argumentation and investigation for each party in court on to the lawyers representing their case, while in an inquisitorial procedure the judge has to actively search out the facts and legal arguments for both sides. There is some truth to this argument: many judges in continental courts see their role *not* as waiting for the lawyers to present a case and listening passively to arguments on both sides, but rather as the main actor in court who works on the basis of an extended file for preparing the case and who in court compensates for the weaknesses in argumentation of an inexperienced party by asking questions and searching for evidence on the bench's own initiative. It can be advantageous for a private party in some courts on the continent *not* to be represented by a lawyer, because that can be a way of engaging the judge in compensatory action against an overly clever lawyer on the other side.

But I do not regard such arguments to provide sufficient explanation for the lack of legal aid in many European countries. Procedural representation is only a small fraction of what lawyers do for their clients; consultation, negotiation, and advice how to *avoid* litigation being more important than representation in court. Furthermore: an explanation along the lines of the procedural role of lawyers in the civil law tradition would have to hold true for all countries on the European continent alike, because they do not differ much in their procedural law systems. What we observe with respect to legal aid, however, are great differences from one country to the next: the Netherlands developed a most remarkable legal aid infrastructure during the 1970s, while in Germany it took until 1981 for a modest legal advice scheme (*Beratungshilfegesetz*) to be enacted, and even though young lawyers in Germany, looking for new markets, are discovering legal aid as a possibility for attaining a subsidized clientele, pre-court advice on legal aid is still used to a relatively modest degree. The most longstanding system of legal aid in Europe is certainly that of the United Kingdom, and it is still more expensive than those on the Continent. However, this is mainly due to the extent of criminal legal aid, for the proportion spent on civil legal aid by other European countries has surpassed the level of British expenditure in recent years (cp. Tables 1 and 2).

That levels of expenditure on legal aid cannot be explained by a simple correlation with welfare state levels is demonstrated by the comparisons of the Netherlands with the Federal Republic of Germany (for which I have taken figures of the adjacent state of North-Rhine-Westphalia in order to keep economic and social factors constant). There would be no reasons in economic and social structures to expect any significant difference in legal aid expenditures between these two countries, because both rank on similar levels of economic growth as well as welfare state development. However, the Dutch government spends 14 times more in subsidy per head of the population on legal advice than the German government: 51.3 million guilders legal advice by attorneys and an additional subsidy of 43.0 million guilders for legal aid bureaux in 1989 (cp. Table 1).

There must be additional reasons for the development of legal aid in some countries and not in others. The level of welfare state expenditure cannot be the determining factor: the Federal Republic of Germany ranks high as far as social security expenditures go; it has a high level of expenditure for court-fee waivers, but insignificant subsidy for lawyers' activities outside of court representation. In the Netherlands in the 1970s a number of local initiatives developed, establishing law shops, complemented by a national system of state-funded legal aid bureaux which give first-hand legal advice as well as referral services to a network of 'social advocates', and a considerable part of the Bar is dependent on a legal aid clientele. Research in 1980 identified 10 per cent of the Dutch Bar as being specialized in a legal aid clientele, running law shops which cater exclusively on legal aid subsidy, and 25 per cent of the Bar gaining a considerable part of their income from legal aid clients.

TABLE 1 *Money spent on legal aid in three countries (England and Wales, the Netherlands, and Germany) in 1989*

	England and Wales (£m)		The Netherlands (Gu.m)		Germany [North-Rhine-Westphalia] (DMm)	
Civil (and administrative) procedures	146.0	27%	106.1	46%	125.0	85%
Criminal legal aid	334.0	62%	73.5	32%	15.6	10%
Legal advice and assistance	62.0	11%	51.3	22%	6.7	5%
Total	542.4		230.9		147.3	
Citizens Advice Bureaux/Bureaus voor Rechtshulp	20(?)		43.0		n/a	

TABLE 2 *Government money spent on legal aid in these three countries (European currency units (ECU) per head of the population per year)*

	England and Wales	The Netherlands	Germany [North-Rhine-Westphalia]
Population in millions	50	15	17.5
Exchange rate ECU	0.70	2.31	2.05
Civil (and administrative) legal aid	4.17	3.06	3.48
Criminal legal aid	9.54	2.12	0.43
Legal advice and assistance	1.80	1.48	0.19
Total	15.51	6.66	4.10
Para-lawyer aid	.57	1.24	n/a

To illustrate the range of difference in legal aid infrastructures, I compare figures on government expenditures for legal aid in three countries: England and Wales, North-Rhine–Westphalia in Germany, and the Netherlands, per head of the population, in order to keep the size of the countries constant, and in ECU-currency in order to keep money values comparable. Budget comparisons show considerable differences in government money spent on legal aid. The Lord Chancellor's Department in England and Wales pays ECU 15.51 yearly per head of the population, the Dutch Minister of Justice ECU 6.66, and the German Minister of Justice at the state level ECU 4.10. Splitting by type of aid reveals even greater differences:

— in penal court matters the differences are most significant. England and Wales spend four times more than the Dutch, the Dutch government again five time as much as the German government per head of the population;

— in civil legal aid (that is subsidies for lawyers' fees for representation in court) differences between the three countries are much less dramatic: most of the civil aid is spent on lawyers in divorce procedures (Germany 90 per cent, the Netherlands 70 per cent);

— most complicated are the differences in the institutional infrastructure and consultations. Both England and Wales and the Netherlands pay considerably more on schemes for legal advice than the Germans [ECU 1.80 (UK), ECU 1.48 (N.L.) respectively, compared to ECU 0.19 (D)]; these differences notwithstanding, there is still more para-lawyer aid subsidized in both countries [ECU 0.57 (U.K.), ECU 1.24 (N.L.) respectively] which in Germany is not permitted by statutory law.

Another comparison more relevant to the situation of the legal profession is that of money spent relative to the number of practising lawyers. For simplicity one might here take the indicator of the number of registered lawyers; if we want to get nearer to the reality we should subtract those lawyers who are actually in salaried positions (in Germany around one-third of all registered lawyers) or otherwise not practising (in Great Britain an estimated 25 per cent, in the Netherlands very few lawyers). In terms of actually working on forensic law, Dutch and German lawyers receive about the same average government subsidy, and twice as much subsidy for legal services to a poverty clientele than does an English practising lawyer. But, again, we have to keep the different branches of legal aid in mind.

The bulk of government subsidy for lawyers' work is spent on divorce in Germany (75 per cent) [that is 90 per cent of the 85 per cent civil legal aid] while only 40 per cent in the Netherlands and 20 to 25 per cent in Great Britain [that is two-thirds of the 56 per cent civil legal aid]. Here 62 per cent of lawyers' subsidies goes to criminal defence lawyers, which in the Netherlands is 26 per cent, in Germany only 14 per cent.

More important in this comparison than mere figures are some of the institutional differences. As we know, lawyer densities around the world differ considerably, Anglo-American figures ranking highest (California with more than 300 lawyers per 100,000 of the population being the highest of all). In our comparison England and Wales average highest with 150 barristers and solicitors per 100,000 of the population. West Germany with 77 has one of the highest lawyer densities on the Continent, the Netherlands with 37 one of the lowest. Part of the difference has to do with the degree to which those who have a law degree get registered with the Bar (as is the general expectation in the United States, somewhat less in the United Kingdom) or whether a considerable proportion of law school graduates enter salaried positions in civil service or as employees of corporations (which is the case for about two-thirds of all lawyers in Germany and the Netherlands). In civil law countries usually less than half of all lawyers are registered as advocates, because legal work is largely internalized into management and staff of big corporations and government bureaucracies. Services for which an American corporation or city-government would hire a law firm would be rendered by internal legal departments in their European counterparts.

We might expect high lawyer frequencies in common law countries to correlate with high government expenditures for legal aid. But if there were a correlation to this effect, the Netherlands would form an exceptional case, ranking high as far as legal aid expenditures go, but especially

TABLE 3 *Lawyer density in three countries (1989)*

	England and Wales	The Netherlands	Germany [North-Rhine-Westphalia]
Number of lawyers	76,200	5,500	13,500
Lawyers per 100,000 population	150	37	77
Estimated % of lawyers actually practising	(75%)	(90%)	(70%)

*The percentage of lawyers actually practising can only be estimated in Germany, about 25 per cent are only nominal members of the Bar while actually working in salaried jobs. In the UK 16,562 of the registered 69,748 solicitors are not practising, and 6,266 barristers in 1989. In the Netherlands we estimate non-active members to be about 10 per cent.

Table 4 *Money (ECU) spent on lawyer subsidies (solicitors and barristers per year)*

	England and Wales	The Netherlands	Germany [North-Rhine-Westphalia]
All registered attorneys	10,177	22,117	5,375
Estimate of all attorneys actually practising	13,570		7,660

low in the number of lawyers. (Among the developed countries only Japan has fewer with 10 lawyers per 100,000 population). Thus, the differences of legal aid expenditure among European countries are by no means explained by the size of the Bar, but rather by their traditional policy with respect to the services to be rendered by advocates and in how far they manage to maintain a privileged monopoly keeping other professions out of offering similar services.

Such differences in professional policy might be illustrated by explaining a second difference which is notable in our table looking at para-legal (or para-lawyer) institutions for legal aid. Great Britain and the Netherlands do not restrict the giving of legal advice to lawyers, while German advocates enjoy a privileged monopoly which is defended quite actively against any possible competition, even against journalists, ombudsmen, and the like. (Exempted are a few interest groups which may give legal advice in a specialized area of law such as trade unions for labour law, registered consumer agencies for consumer law, or tenants' associations for rental law matters; and there are some city-states like Hamburg which traditionally run legal advice centres for the poor as local government services.) Citizens Advice Bureaux, like those in Great Britain, which could be considered a competition for lawyers (even administering do-it-yourself divorce schemes) would be contrary to statutory law in Germany, and they would be unlikely to develop in the Netherlands. The British system seems to subsidize competition among different bodies of government as well as legal aid schemes of solicitors turning as many 'legal needs' into actual demand for legal services as imaginable; the Dutch system in comparison is somewhat more restrictive, combining government-subsidized legal aid offices with a fee-subsidizing scheme for lawyers. Both systems have allowed a section of the advocacy to make a living on a subsidized clientele, even though such 'social advocates' earn much lower yearly income than average lawyers (not to speak of corporate law firms).

German law up to 1981 strictly reduced legal aid to a waiver scheme for court and lawyer representation fees (*Prozesskostenhilfe*) which has run into considerable costs in recent years, but it allowed only since 1981 for a modest legal advice subsidy (*Beratungshilfe*) which remains strictly tied to the advocates' monopoly.

It should be added that all three systems have been expanding rapidly. Over 20 years, the English expenditure for legal aid rose from £27 million to £542 million; German overall legal aid expenditure rose from DM 15 million to DM 147 million in 1989 with legal aid subsidies; and the Dutch figures rose from 13 million guilders in 1970 to 231 million in 1989. If we account for the doubling of personnel costs for the judiciary which we experienced in our three countries within the last 20 years as an indicator for inflation (which is certainly a generous estimate, because it includes not only the increase in salaries but also expansion of personnel which courts have managed to achieve), we may consider any increase beyond doubling the service rendered by legal aid schemes as an expansion which is beyond that of the rest of the judicial system.

In Great Britain legal aid expenditure has kept rising steeply, mainly due to the highly subsidized criminal defence programme. The 'green form scheme' for legal advice is being administered under increasingly restrictive conditions. Also many communities have stopped subsidizing law centres and Citizens Advice Bureaux because of lack of funds.

In the Netherlands the very steep rise of legal aid costs in the 1970s and early 1980s has slowed down since 1984/85. Limits to entitlement were introduced as well as higher monetary contributions required from clients. The restrictions coincided with the Conservative government's attempt to reduce welfare spending on the whole. It might be fair to say that legal aid is somewhat more protected from austerity than are the budgets of welfare departments and social insurance, because first they are not as significant in amount as other welfare expenditures, and secondly they are hidden in the overall smaller budgets of Ministries of Justice, which enjoy a general sympathy within the framework of conservative law and order policies. But, while the budgets of our Ministries of Justice are increasing these days more than others, there are tendencies to keep (if not reduce) legal aid expenditures within these budgets. The Dutch government in 1983 abandoned the principle of free legal advice under the legal aid scheme by requiring a contribution of 50 guilders from even the most needy client under the legal advice scheme (with contributions rising as higher income levels are indicated by the means test). Future plans include a scheme of limited admission and maximum ceilings for legal aid expenditures.

In Germany discussions are mainly directed at reducing the growth of civil legal aid for divorce procedures, but even the modest expenditures for legal advice have come under attack because of their growth-rates. We may expect many additional requests in the East German parts of the country as soon as the system of justice starts working after the unification in 1990, as legal needs among former East Germans are enormous and many people fall below the income level entitling them to legal aid.

The pressure under which legal aid lawyers have come as a result of austerity politics are a typical fate of professions which become partly dependent on government subsidies for their services. The mechanism has been studied exhaustively for the health services: with insurance schemes paying for the costs of most extensive treatments, neither patients nor doctors have any incentives to restrict services under cost considerations; unrestrained investment in highly technological medicine has been the result. The other side of insurance coverage of health services is their regulation by collective negotiation systems consisting of medical associations, pharmaceutical industries, health insurance bodies, and government bodies. They form corporate regulatory systems whether labelled 'autonomous professionalism' in some of our countries or 'socialized medicine' in others. In all the countries compared here lawyers are still far from the degree of corporatist dependency that doctors have reached. Even where their fees on the Continent are statutorily regulated, lawyers still work in a rather wide array of non-regulated activities which open the possibility to individually negotiated prices as well as the kinds of services to be rendered. The subsidized sector of legal services is only a tiny fraction of what lawyers do as a whole—that holds true even in England and Wales where assumedly 50 per cent of all forensic income of lawyers is subsidized by some kind of legal aid, or in the Netherlands where some 23 per cent of all lawyers live on legal aid subsidy. Most of the lawyer income which is subsidy-related are regular fees for divorce cases (the Netherlands and Germany) or for criminal defence (in England and Wales, to a lesser degree in the other two countries).

Legal advice for the poor is the smallest sector of subsidized legal services. It provides one of the possibilities for specialization for lawyers among others in the countries where legal advice subsidy is effectively developed but social advocates make only a very modest living. Their ranks are not very likely to attract ambitious lawyers because of the low income prospects. Many social advocates serve only a limited time, attempting to move over into regular law firms or government services (as well as teaching). As a specialization, social advocacy cannot exist without legal aid subsidies. Nevertheless, it has attracted a sufficient number of activist lawyers who have helped to develop jurisprudence in new fields of law and to render rights more effective in employment protection, tenants, and consumer protection, as well as for improving the legal position of welfare clients and immigrants.

The other two branches of subsidized legal services are specializations quite distinct from that of 'social advocacy'. Criminal defence lawyers are usually a law unto themselves, because of the intensive court work and regular contacts with people arrested or under suspicion, which create time-patterns which are hardly to be reconciled with other law work.

Legal aid for civil litigation, on the other hand, is distributed over the entire unspecialized, run-of-the-mill advocacy as a whole; it makes almost every lawyer in our three countries, as far as they are not specialized otherwise, an occasional recipient of government subsidized litigation.

The share which subsidies contribute to lawyer income doubtless increases the dependency of the profession on government policies, as we can presently see when austerity hits a small number of specialized 'social advocates'. When legal advice for the poor depends on government spending, it can within a short time be terminated by government withdrawal. But withdrawal would affect the different branches of legal aid to very different degrees:

— Maintaining a social advocacy specialization is generally the least expensive of all branches of legal aid, but it is also the most dependent on public finance.
— Criminal defence is largely dependent on legal aid or public defence as far as traditional (violence and property) crime is concerned. Duty solicitor schemes have a long tradition in the penal codes or statutory law of all three countries compared—nobody seems to challenge the necessity of public subsidy (and in Germany nobody seems to argue for extending it). While for traffic misdemeanours and 'modern' crimes (of fraud, environmental offences, etc.) there rests a private market for criminal defence independent of subsidy.
— Almost all of the divorce work would be paid for by the parties involved, if there were no recourse to legal aid.

Subsidies for divorce work are defended by the Bar in all countries concerned, but they might be reduced if simplified divorce procedures (do-it-yourself divorce) are to be introduced—but here the lawyers' lobby will be very careful to maintain its involvement because of the considerable remuneration they receive from divorce cases. If policy-makers decide on the shape of court procedures for divorce, they decide at the same time on the desired amount of subsidy to lawyers. The one branch of legal aid which needs support for reasons of public interest seems to me to be legal aid for advice and assistance. It invests in lawyering before problems have become cases in court; it might thus help to avoid litigation as much as it facilitates access to it.

Social advocacy is a specialization within the Bar which could not survive without subsidy. The only alternative, if public interest demands to keep it up, would be internalizing its functions into government services—certainly a solution which would be less sensitive to changing legal needs and most likely less innovative than a subsidized 'Social Bar'.

10. Extract from 'The Evolution of Legal Services in Britain: Pragmatic Welfarism or Demand Creation?'

ALAN PATERSON and DAVID NELKEN

Legal Aid: New Beginning?

For the first half of the twentieth century the burden of providing legal services to the poor in the United Kingdom fell,[1] as it had done in previous centuries, on the legal profession—usually for little or no fee. Curiously this was not a source of dissatisfaction for the bulk of the profession. First, because in the early part of the century the burden was not an onerous one. The prevailing wisdom of the period held that the problems of the poor were individuated—whose solution lay in 'self reliance, independence, thrift and a taste for hard work'. As Leat (1975: 169) has argued:

this emphasis upon individual responsibility in the . . . theory of the aetiology of social problems [entailed] that access to the law was regarded as irrelevant, if not harmful, in that it implied that the problems of the poor lay somewhere other than in the individual.[2]

Secondly, the burden was not shared evenly amongst the profession but was borne disproportionately[3] by the younger members (learning, as some said, at the expense of the poor) and by a few firms who specialized in legal services for poorer clients. Thirdly, because the profession, particularly in England, was able to use its control[4] over the scope and extent of

[1] The burden was partly self imposed, partly imposed by statute. In Scotland the first Act providing for legal representation was passed as early as 1424.

[2] There were dissenting voices who argued not only that the causes of poverty were structural but also that they could be alleviated in part by improving access to legal services. See Leat, (1975).

[3] This moral division of labour (see Carlin, 1966) was in part due to a distaste on the part of many firms for the work of the poor and for those firms who were willing to do it.

[4] The control was not absolute. The Lord Chancellor's Office also played an important role—particularly in relation to proposals for reform. See Alcock, (1976).

the voluntary legal aid scheme to restrict both the numbers of those eligible for assistance and the situations in which they would be so eligible. Thus, even when the burden of providing these services increased during the twenties and the thirties, as a result of legislative changes, it was not merely the Treasury but also the leaders of the profession (see Alcock, 1976: 167) who opposed the calls by some members of the profession for a state-funded legal aid scheme or state-salaried lawyers.[5] In their eyes, the spectre of losing control over the provision of legal services far outweighed any benefits which might accrue to the poor from such an innovation.

In consequence the voluntary legal aid scheme lurched from crisis to crisis in this period until the expansion of the grounds of divorce of the 1930s provided the straw that broke the camel's back. With the impending breakdown of the scheme the feeling grew that state intervention was inevitable. This eventually came with the Legal Aid Acts of 1949. In part, the legislation was due to the election of a Labour Government in 1945 which was committed to the expansion of the welfare state. This undoubtedly helped to overcome Treasury resistance to a long-term state commitment in this area. Nevertheless, a crucial factor contributing to the reforms was the recognition by the Lord Chancellor's Office and the Law Society that the increasing demand for legal services for the poor could no longer be met under existing arrangements which left the profession inadequately remunerated for the work done. The conversion of the profession's leaders to state-funded legal services was essential to the success of the reform—without the co-operation of the profession the new scheme would have been inoperable. In fact the profession's strategy was one of co-option. The Rushcliffe and Cameron Committees which were set up in the 1940s to review the provisions for legal services for poor persons in England and Scotland were both heavily dominated by members of the profession. This went a long way to ensuring that the reports and recommendations which emerged (and which were subsequently enacted) were very much in keeping with the new line of thinking in the Law Society, i.e. legal aid and advice would be available in all courts and to a majority of the population (not just the poor) with a sliding scale of contributions. The services, which would be adequately remunerated, would be provided in the main by members of the private profession willing to take it on, though some state-salaried lawyers appointed (and controlled) by the Law Society might be necessary to pro-

[5] As early as 1905 the Secretary to the Edinburgh Legal Dispensary (now Scotland's oldest Legal Advice Centre) put forward a scheme for State Legal Aid for the Poor.

vide legal advice in poorer areas. Most significant of all, with the exception of criminal legal aid, which would be in the purview of the courts,
the new schemes would be run by the Law Society—'a strong independent agency'—not by the state or by laymen. The importance of maintaining the independence of the profession was accepted on all sides.

In the light of strong opposition by the profession and others to any
form of nationalization (and the profession's history of administering the
existing schemes), the Labour Government, departing from its policy in
relation to the Health Service and the nationalized industries, conceded
that state-subsidized legal services should be administered and controlled
by the Law Societies of England and Scotland (see Abel-Smith and
Stevens, 1967: 327). Nevertheless, the Treasury had the last word. The
new schemes would be phased in gradually. Initially legal aid would only
be available in the intermediate courts, and legal advice and criminal legal
aid would not be introduced until the economic climate had significantly
improved. Until then the existing scheme would just have to limp on as
best as it could. Though branded by some as Stalinist proposals which
would lead to state control of the profession[6] the introduction of state-
subsidized legal services was very much a restatement of the status quo.
Though presented to the nation as part and parcel of the welfare state it
reflected far more a compromise between the pragmatic politics of the
Law Society and the Treasury.

True, the poor were now seen to have legal problems—but their legal
problems were thought of as no different from those of other citizens—it
was merely that they could not afford to pay for lawyers' services. In short,
poor people were seen as rich people without money. The profession continued to control the services that would be offered and to whom, and
the legal needs of the poor were defined in ways which accorded with the
interests of the profession. It should be noted, however, that although the
profession was concerned to exercise market control, the demand for re-
imbursement from the state for services rendered to the poor owed more to
a refusal to carry on acting for nothing in the face of increasing consumer
demand than to a desire for new markets, i.e. demand creation.

Law As A Social Service: Making Rights Effective

In the fifties and sixties legal aid was gradually extended to cover the
remaining courts and a limited form of criminal legal aid was introduced.

[6] See [1949] *Scots Law Times* (News) 30.

The Law Societies quietly forgot their commitment to state-salaried lawyers providing legal advice in poorer communities, preferring instead to push for a legal advice scheme which any private practitioner could operate. These gradualist tactics were not without their critics. During the 1960s liberal lawyers from practice and academia launched a series of critiques against the profession and the 'inadequate' legal services provided to the poor. The thrust of the attacks was that the legal needs of the poor were not being met and that the reluctance of the poor to seek legal assistance was attributable to the deficiencies of the profession. The critics asserted that many interests of the poor, e.g. social security, employment, and tenancy 'rights' had not been transformed into, or not been perceived as legal property rights (see Carlin and Howard, 1965; Reich, 1964; Cahn and Cahn, 1964). This was a direct challenge to the narrow definition of legal reality prevailing amongst the bulk of the legal profession at the time. As Carlin and Howard (1965: 406) observed:

the argument that the poor have fewer legal problems than the rich and therefore less need for lawyers, often merges into the welfare-oriented idea that the problems of the poor are inherently non-legal. This view entails the risk of misconceiving the individual in such a way as to rob him of the dignity of citizenship. . . . We propose that a distinctive characteristic of the poor, and an essential condition of their predicament, is their lack of participation in the legal and governmental process. Thus the answer to the question of whether the poor have legal problems and need lawyers turns ultimately on the strength of our commitment to the extension of citizenship, for enfranchisement necessarily rests on the capacity to participate in and make effective use of the legal order—in our legal system, this means access to competent legal representation.

Closely allied to the 'rights creation' approach was the 'unmet legal needs' perspective. Adherents of this position asserted (and continue to assert) that even the rights of the poor that were legally recognized, e.g. in the welfare, consumer, employment, or criminal law fields, were unenforced or underenforced. This 'gap' between the rights 'promised' by the welfare state and their application in the real world became known as the 'unmet legal need'. The existence and size of the 'unmet need' was established in a number of ways:

(1) Empirical studies which showed that many applicants before tribunals and defendants in criminal cases went unrepresented (Zander, 1969 and 1972) or that working class respondents in deprived areas had a multitude of 'legal problems' of which they were often unaware (they were equally ignorant as to legal aid) and which were rarely resolved

by resort to the law or lawyers (Abel-Smith, Zander and Brooke, 1973).

(2) Legal aid statistics which showed year after year that 80 per cent of legal aid went in support of the 'traditional' area of litigation between husbands and wives rather than on housing, welfare rights, employment, immigration, and consumer problems.

(3) Research on the organization and structure of the profession which showed, *inter alia*, that lawyers' offices were inaccessible to the poor because of their geographical distribution (overwhelmingly situated in the centre of towns and cities) and their restricted opening hours (usually closed at lunch times, in the evenings, and at weekends) and that there was a severe shortage of lawyers specializing in local authority housing, landlord and tenant, welfare benefit, employment, and consumer matters.

In sum, the critics were alleging that the limitations of the legal aid schemes and the actions of the profession, e.g. in the siting of its offices and in effectively defining problems in non-traditional areas as 'non-legal', were combining to deny the poor their birthright in a liberal democracy—equal access to justice and to the law. It should be noted, however, that criticisms of this sort are double-edged; they complain that needs are not being met, but they simultaneously presuppose that the needs in question are legal ones.

The critics' solution to the problem—a commitment to 'making rights effective'[7]—consisted and consists (for it is still favoured by many in the profession) in extending the scope of the legal aid schemes and in improving the access of the poor to lawyers (see Conservative Political Centre, 1968; National Consumer Council, 1970). The campaign to extend the scope of the schemes has met with a considerable measure of success. The consensus over the 'unmet legal need' of the poor amongst pressure groups as varied as the Society of Labour Lawyers, the Conservative Lawyers Group, the National Consumer Council, and the Law Society was such that in 1973 a much improved Legal Advice and Assistance scheme was introduced—though again it is significant that of the competing models it was the Law Society's model which was adopted. (The new Act empowered the Law Society once more to employ salaried solicitors to give legal advice—but as before this part of the Act was never implemented.) In the 1960s and 1970s the scope and coverage of criminal legal

---

[7] The solution has recently been described as the first wave of reform in the access-to-justice movement (Cappelletti and Garth, 1978; Garth, 1982).

aid was expanded (particularly in Scotland). Only in relation to tribunals did the movement falter. Although it was and is accepted on all sides that legally aided representation should be available before the more important tribunals and although the mechanism for achieving this was incorporated in the Legal Aid Act, 1979, legal aid for tribunal cases has still not been introduced and seems unlikely to be so in the present economic climate.

Attempts to make lawyers more accessible to the public in general and the poor in particular have also made some headway in the last twenty years. There has been a considerable expansion in branch offices first in the suburban shopping areas (see Bridges *et al.*, 1975) and subsequently in new towns and local authority housing estates (Paterson, 1981). Voluntary schemes with free advice sessions by local lawyers at generalist or legal advice centres have mushroomed in the same period. Directories with lists of lawyers, their office hours, and the areas of work they normally handle have been published by the Law Societies. Most significant of all: from 1970 onwards neighbourhood law centres with state-salaried lawyers have been set up in the United Kingdom specifically to tackle the legal problems of the poor (Downes, Hopkins and Rees, 1981).

The activities of the reformers of the 1960s and the implementation of their preferred solutions in subsequent years were at one level a rejection of the narrow definition of the legal needs of the poor which had hitherto held sway in the profession. But the Law Societies continued to define how the legal needs of the poor would be met, either by co-option or control. Neither of the solutions favoured by the reformers worked against the interests of the profession and, in particular, the expansion of the legal aid schemes (which were controlled by the Law Societies) provided it with much work. Those who criticized the existing provisions were aware that their proposals would lead to more work for lawyers—but that was not the object of the proposals. Similarly, the improvements in access[8] were monitored by the Law Societies who used (and continue to use) the ethical rules against advertising and the unfair attraction of business to hamper or defeat innovations in legal services for the poor which they disliked (Zander, 1968 and 1978).

[8] The explosion in branch offices was clearly demand creation by different sectors of the profession. The offices in the suburbs tend to be set up by firms who specialize in property transactions, while those in the poorer areas are usually set up by firms who mainly do court work. But the Law Societies have used their powers as enforcers of the ethical rules to control the manning and advertisement of such offices. These developments are a good illustration of the competing groups within the profession (see Bucher and Strauss, 1961; Podmore, 1980).

Nonetheless, to explain the expansion of legal aid in terms of demand creation by the profession would be to mistake cause for effect, because the calls for improved legal access came from a disparate variety of groups with widely different motivations (Garth, 1982: 192). Nor did these groups systematically lobby the government of the day for a planned programme for reform in the legal services field. What did unite them was a common philosophy whose roots lay not so much in sociological theory as in the welfarist pragmatism of neo-Fabian social administration.[9] The assumptions of this approach can be seen in the following passage taken from the Twenty-fifth Annual Report of the Law Society on the operation of the legal aid schemes (Law Society, 1975: 1):

Legal aid is increasingly being thought of as a social service and part of the welfare ideal; its fundamental importance, however, has not been sufficiently recognised in that its function is to ensure that justice—the first of all the social services—is made available to all and is not confined to those able to bear the cost of protecting their lawful rights. The help afforded to those of limited means and the disadvantaged must be seen in the broad context of the role of the law itself, which provides the only foundation upon which the whole edifice of social welfare depends. In so far as the law is not made effective in the lives of all citizens it must fail in its social purpose and weaken all other social measures. Only through a truly comprehensive legal aid system can laws enacted to benefit those in need fully serve their intention. Legal aid is not an independent social instrument; it is an essential ingredient in the administration of justice without which the law must remain partial and socially discriminative. Again, legal aid is being regarded by some as an instrument for social engineering. It is, however, the law itself that serves as the instrument for achieving the social purposes determined by political discussion and debate: the function of legal aid is limited to ensuring that the law when laid down fulfils its intended purpose. The priority that should be accorded to legal aid needs urgently to be reassessed in the light of these realities.

In short, the poor have individual, objective needs for the law which can only be met by resort to lawyers funded by legal aid.

Conclusions

We think that three points emerge from the foregoing account. First, the number of groups whose different interests and ideas must be given some weight in any comprehensive explanation of the evolution of legal

[9] While we agree with Blankenburg (1982: 251) that some of these groups helped to foster a 'supportive subculture' from which new forms of legal services could develop, we have greater reservations with his conclusion that their work provided 'an informed basis' for legal aid policy.

services in the UK must be recognized. These include, more obviously, different groups within the legal profession: the Law Society, the Law Centres' Federation, legal academics, politicians, and civil servants but also, more diffusely, those involved in voluntary and consumer movements only loosely related to access to justice. Instead of seeing the Law Societies as the prime movers in the expansion of legal services, we have shown that their tendency has frequently been to resist new developments until a stage where they can be safely neutralized and co-opted without threat to vested interests. Moreover, the debates between groups within and outside the profession demand to be considered in their own terms rather than from an external point of view which identifies demand creation as a key issue.

Secondly, we have stressed the importance of recognizing that the construction and reconstruction of the problem of current legal need is an important aspect of developments in legal services with its own influence over events. Just as it is anachronistic to explain the earliest methods of providing legal services for the poor in terms of modern debates over access to justice, so it is a mistake not to acknowledge that such debates introduced a new element into the situation. We are not arguing that ideas are unrelated to interests or that ideas are not also weapons of struggle, but we do stress that both ideas and ideals do move people quite as much as self-interest, and sometimes even in opposition to it. To see the growth of a spirit of activism amongst lawyers in the 1960s and the heightened claims-consciousness of claimant groups as a Trojan horse by which lawyers' interests were advanced is to impose a predetermined theoretical framework on what were historically unpredictable events. Even if movements in ideas do have political and economic repercussions, there is no failsafe mechanism by which they can be made to coincide with the material interests of particular groups. Indeed, it is typical for ideas to come to be accepted as conventional wisdom at a point where the material factors that first helped them forth have changed out of all recognition.

It would therefore be a remarkable coincidence if the growth of consumerism and concern over unequal access to law were timed to be available just when the profession was in need of legitimation to extend its reach. In practice, the problem is to discern the unfolding relationship between the changing definitions of (unmet) legal needs and the changing position and strategies of the legal profession.

Finally, as already indicated, we see this account of events as posing real difficulties for the demand-creation explanation of the expansion of legal services. By pointing out where this explanation seems to provide a particularly awkward fit we hope at least to have put the onus of proof back onto the proponents of this theory so as to require them to show which period of the recent history of the legal services movement in the UK their explanation is intended to illuminate. But if our account of the developments in legal services in Britain provides more support for the pragmatic welfarism explanation than it does for the theory of demand creation we must still be cautious. We admit that there can be no 'objective' account of the nature of the problem of access to law which does not involve political and moral action on the 'need' for legal services. Our account of the construction of the 'unmet legal need' shows the continuing capacity of the legal profession in Britain to co-opt and canalize the movement for access to justice in accordance with their definition of the problem. Although we strongly differ from a definition which tailors the meaning of unmet need such that it reinforces existing types of work by solicitors, we also feel ourselves more in sympathy with the movement to expand legal services in more novel forms than are the proponents of the demand-creation thesis.

Moreover, we concede that no theory is ever going to provide a perfect fit to all the possibly relevant facts about this or any other area of social life. More to the point, it must be accepted that what counts as a relevant fact is itself theory-dependent though not to the extent that it becomes possible to exclude, without argument, what critics allege to be relevant but unexplained or ill-explained facts. We welcome the attempt to provide unifying theory in an area which all too conspicuously lacks theoretical development of this sort. Nor do we make any claim that our description of the various factors that seem to impinge on the history of developments in legal services in Britain represents any alternative explanatory theory. We have at most raised some problems for the demand-creation theorists and offered a competing perspective, admittedly less ambitious and perhaps less satisfying but, we think, more in touch with the ambiguities, conflicts, and accommodations of interests and ideals which mark the course of social change. If there is any policy relevance in our argument it is that the funding of further developments of legal services will be more affected by shifts in support for welfare services generally than by changes in the market situation of solicitors. This means that the response to this situation needs to be conceived in terms of current political realities of economic retrenchment rather than the fears of the overextended welfare state now redolent of the 1960s.

References

Abel-Smith, B. and R. Stevens, *Lawyers and the Courts* (London: Heinemann, 1967).

Abel-Smith, B., M. Zander and R. Brooke, *Legal Problems and the Citizen* (London: Heinemann, 1973).

Alcock, Peter, 'Legal Aid: Whose Problem?' (1976), 3 *British Journal of Law and Society* 151.

Blankenburg, E., 'European Experience in Innovating Legal Services' (1982), 2 *Windsor Yearbook of Access to Justice* 247.

Bridges, L., B. Suffrin, J. Whetton, and R. White, *Legal Services in Birmingham* (Birmingham: Birmingham University, 1975).

Bucher, R. and A. Strauss, 'Profession in Process' (1961), 46 *American Journal of Sociology* 325.

Cahn, E. and J. Cahn, 'The War on Poverty' (1964), 73 *Yale Law Journal* 1933.

Cappelletti, M. and B. Garth (eds.) *Access to Justice: A World Survey* (Amsterdam: Sijthoff and Noordhoff, 1978).

Carlin, Jerome, *Lawyers' Ethics* (New York: Russell Sage Foundation, 1966).

Carlin, J. and J. Howard, 'Legal Representation and Class Justice' (1965), 12 *University of California Los Angeles Law Review* 381.

Conservative Political Centre, *Rough Justice* (London: CPC, 1968).

Downes, T. A., P. R. Hopkins and W. M. Rees, 'The Future of Legal Services in Britain' (1981), 1 *Windsor Yearbook of Access to Justice* 121.

Garth, Bryant, 'The Movement toward Procedural Information in North America and Western Europe: A Critical Survey', pp. 183–211 in R. Abel (ed.), *The Politics of Informal Justice* (New York: Academic Press, 1982).

Law Society, *Twenty-fifth Legal Aid Annual Report* (London: HMSO, 1975).

Leat, Diane, 'The Rise and Role of the Poor Man's Lawyer' (1975), 2 *British Journal of Law and Society* 166.

National Consumer Council, *Justice out of Reach* (London: NCC, 1970).

Paterson, A., 'The Legal Profession in Scotland' (Unpublished paper, 1981).

Podmore, D., 'Bucher and Strauss Revisited' (1980), 7 *British Journal of Law and Society* 1.

Reich, C., 'The New Property' (1964), 73 *Yale Law Journal* 733.

Society of Labour Lawyers, *Justice for All* (London: Fabian Society, 1968).

Zander, M., *Lawyers and the Public Interest.* (London: Weidenfeld and Nicholson, 1968).

Zander, M., 'Unrepresented Defendants in Criminal Courts', [1969] *Criminal Law Review* 632.

Zander, M., 'Unrepresented Defendants in Magistrates' Courts', [1972] 122 *New Law Journal* 1041.

Zander, M., *Legal Services for the Community* (London: Temple Smith, 1978).

PART THREE: LEGAL AID IN CRISIS

. . . no Government can make unlimited funds available for any of its programmes, however fundamental they are to the health and well being of society.
. . . Justice is priceless, but it must not be too pricey if it is to be accessible. To be accessible it must be affordable to the individual both as tax payer and litigant.

Lord Mackay of Clashfern, 'Litigation in the 1990s', (1991) 54 Modern Law Review 171.

A CAB [Citizens' Advice Bureau] in North London reported that the local authority was seeking a possession order against a client who had mental health problems. She was in receipt of invalidity benefit, and her solicitor applied for legal aid for her, which was granted subject to payment of a contribution of £24 a month. She could not afford this, and the bureau commented that she would probably end up unrepresented, increasing her chances of losing her home.

A CAB in Essex reported that a 79 year old client who was in receipt of invalidity benefit had been advised by his solicitor to bring a claim against the local hospital following alleged medical negligence. He was granted legal aid subject to a contribution of £50 a month, which he could not afford . . .

The large number of cases that CABx are reported from across the country indicates that there is a serious problem with people not pursuing their case as a result of the very large contributions they are being asked to pay and cannot afford.

National Association of Citizens' Advice Bureaux, Barriers to Justice: CAB clients' experience of legal services, 1995.

11. Rushcliffe Fifty Years On: The Changing Role of Civil Legal Aid Within the Welfare State

TAMARA GORIELY

The last few years have been difficult ones for legal aid. As the Government abolishes the contributory green forms scheme, increases contributions, and holds down pay rates, the President of the Law Society has accused it of crippling a 'once proud public service'.[1] At the same time, the number of cases dealt with by the scheme and the cost per case continue to increase.[2] Legal Action Group has described the current state of legal aid as 'stagflation'.[3] Increased use of legal aid and rising costs are combined with decreasing eligibility, morale, and belief.

Why is it that each year the legal aid scheme appears to deal less well with the increasing demands made upon it? This chapter looks back over the last fifty years of civil legal aid, to chart its varied fortunes within the welfare state. It argues that the changing philosophies of welfare have shaped both the structure of the scheme and the demands made upon it. At the same time as governments have confined direct welfare services to the poor—to the neglect of those of moderate means—they have put greater emphasis on individual 'consumer' action as a means of regulating welfare providers. Thus, the early 1980s saw the expansion of rights enforced through courts and tribunals, though by the end of the decade the emphasis had shifted to internal complaints systems and formal complaints handlers, such as regulators, ombudsmen, and inspectors. Legal aid has failed to keep pace with either development. Private solicitors have traditionally ignored welfare issues; the scheme fails to pay for representation before most tribunals; and the varied advice needs raised by the Citizen's Charter approach have been ignored.

[1] *The Times*, 29 Mar. 1994, p. 35.
[2] Between 1983–84 and 1993–94 acts of assistance rose at an average annual rate of 5.9 per cent while cost per case rose by 10.6 per cent: Legal Aid Board, *Annual Report 1993–94* HC (1994) 435, p. 4.
[3] Legal Action Group, *A Strategy for Justice* (1992).

The welfare state is a difficult concept, as the meanings attaching to the term have changed markedly since the Second World War. In 1945 it was an aspirational depiction of a new kind of state: by the 1960s it was a label applied to specific, central, public bureaucracies.[4] Now it is often used to describe a minor and residual function of a state primarily concerned with other matters. For the purposes of the present discussion, the welfare state is taken to be that part of the state apparatus which takes responsibility for the health, education, housing, and basic income of its citizens, and the physical care of its weakest members. There have been huge shifts in the level at which that responsibility is met: while Britain still attempts to provide adequate health care and education for all, the tendency of the last fifteen years has been to provide income and housing only at a minimal level for the poor. Furthermore, welfare responsibilities are being discharged in an ever wider variety of ways—through direct provision, through simulated welfare 'markets', through contracts with private suppliers, and through the regulation of private sector creditors, landlords, or employers. Whatever the method of provision, government has increasingly put the onus on individual recipients to influence the way suppliers operate, by pursuing their grievances through complaints procedures and tribunals. This raises new challenges for the legal aid scheme, which have yet to be faced.

The Wartime Legacy

1. The spirit of VE Day

Modern civil legal aid developed as part of the post-war reconstruction. Our present paid scheme is based on the recommendations of the Rushcliffe Committee, set up in 1944 at the time of the D-Day landings. Its final report was published in May 1945, the month in which Germany unconditionally surrendered to Allied forces.[5] If we are to understand the thinking behind the legal aid scheme—and the role that legal aid was intended to perform in post-war Britain—we must understand something of the popular mood of the period.

---

[4] Thus, Pauline Gregg points out that the first Oxford English Dictionary entry, in 1955, defined a welfare state as a 'polity so organized that every member of the community is assured of his due maintenance, with the most advantageous conditions possible for all'. By 1964, it was defined as a state 'having national health, insurance and other social services': P. Gregg, The Welfare State (1967).

[5] Report of the Committee on Legal Aid and Legal Advice in England and Wales (1945; Cmd. 6641; Chair, Lord Rushcliffe).

First, it was a time of hope. As *Picture Post* kept reminding its readers, it was time to plan for a brave new Britain. The popular acclaim following the publication of Beveridge's report in November 1942 had forced Churchill to accept that government had to do something about the old giants of want, disease, ignorance, squalor, and idleness.[6] Over the next three years, a multitude of official committees started to design a better country after the peace. The Rushcliffe report was a very small and unobtrusive part of the plans for a New Jerusalem.[7]

Secondly, it was a time of social solidarity. Disaster was no longer individual but something whole communities had shared. As the Home Intelligence reports of the time noted, there was a strong desire for equality, even if it was an equality of misery. In 1942 most people had positively welcomed increased rationing as a way of reducing the 'big bugs' who took more than their fair share of petrol and food.[8] They now wanted equal shares in forthcoming prosperity. The basis of the welfare state was not to be minimum benefits for the few but equal benefits for all. The middle classes were prepared to give the welfare state their support provided it also gave them tangible benefits.

The Rushcliffe Committee started on the basis that legal aid must extend beyond those 'normally classed as poor'.[9] Sir Claud Schuster, Permanent Secretary to the Lord Chancellor, still remembered the hostility of the House of Lords in 1942 when plans had been unveiled for an Army Legal Aid scheme limited to sergeants and below.[10] The opposition had come from every quarter. Hereditary peers had lamented the exclusion of poor subalterns and second-lieutenants, while Lord Addison, speaking for the Labour party, had declared 'it may be thought that the Labour Party has got a bee in its bonnet about the means test. You can say that if you like—we object to it in principle'. This type of language alarmed the Law Society, who worried that an overly generous scheme might cover existing paying clients.[11] The Rushcliffe Committee accepted a compromise. A means test would remain, but would be generous. When the legal aid scheme started in 1950 it covered almost 80 per cent of the population. In return, the Law Society secured a commitment that the means test would not be raised to include anyone with a gross income of over £750 per annum without a mandate from the profession.[12]

---

[6] Sir William Beveridge, *Social Insurance and Allied Services* (1942; Cmd. 6404).

[7] For a full account of this period, see P. Addison, *The Road to 1945* (1975), Correlli Barnett, *The Audit of War* (1986), gives a more jaundiced view.

[8] Addison, id.   [9] Rushcliffe, *op. cit.*, n. 5, para. 127(2).

[10] *HL Debs.* 14 July 1942.   [11] See, for example, PRO file LCO2/2846.

[12] See PRO LCO2/7519.

Thirdly, and most importantly, people believed in public service. During the war, people had accepted an unprecedented degree of state control over their lives. Almost eight million Britons had joined the armed services and 705,000 had become civil servants. Nearly every man and unmarried woman between the ages of eighteen and sixty had accepted some state control over their employment.[13] For many people the work had been hard, drab, and dangerous, but on VE Day all that was forgotten. The point was it had worked. It had won the war—and therefore it could also win the peace. Barnett reminds us that much of the optimism was misplaced: Britain had almost lost the war, and had only won because of American dollars and Russian sacrifice.[14] But these are the comments of the disillusioned 1980s: at the time, people believed that each giant on the road to reconstruction could and should be slain by its own separate branch of the civil service.

The belief in public service may be seen in many different sectors. For example, in 1943 the Cabinet discussed a plan to group family doctors into local authority-run health centres, where they should be paid a salary rather than a capitation fee. The paper commented: 'It is notorious that a doctor who is most successful in securing patients is not necessarily more competent than his colleagues . . . The general principle applicable to public service, civil and military, that exceptional competence or zeal should expect to find its reward in the shape of promotion in the service, must, in our view, apply to the present case.'[15]

Even lawyers had to acknowledge the general belief in salaried services. The Rushcliffe Committee recommended that legal advice should be given from area offices through 'whole-time paid solicitors' employed by the Law Society,[16] while the Society's war-time expedient of employing solicitors to handle divorce cases was to be continued for the poor. However, careful lobbying managed to ensure that divorce clients of moderate means used private practitioners in the normal way. The only difference would be that the state contributed towards the bill.

In 1948 Aneurin Bevan commented that the Rushcliffe scheme gave solicitors too much power: he was 'particularly opposed to any scheme in which a committee of lawyers had to decide whether particular cases should qualify' since an affirmative decision would 'result in the payment of fees to the legal profession'.[17] Bevan considered that compared with his

---

[13] H. Perkin, *The Rise of Professional Society: England since 1880* (1989) 407.
[14] Barnett, *op. cit.*, n. 7.   [15] Addison, *op. cit.*, n. 7, p. 240.
[16] Rushcliffe, *op. cit.*, n. 5, para. 178(4).
[17] Minutes of the Lord President's Committee 5 May 1948: PRO file LCO2/4621.

tough negotiations with the British Medical Association, the Lord Chancellor's Department had given in to the Law Society. Bevan was right: legal aid conceded a greater role for the private profession and its representatives than other schemes of the period. Nevertheless, compared with present provision, the Rushcliffe proposals were heavily oriented towards salaried services. Under 1948 costings, it was envisaged that the salaried divorce department and advice scheme would between them consume 44 per cent of the legal aid budget.[18]

2. Beveridge, public service, and a dislike of lawyers

Beveridge himself had an unbounded belief in the effectiveness of public service. As long ago as 1923, the National Council of Social Service had stressed that there was a need for a place where people could go for independent advice about an increasingly complex and remote social security system.[19] Beveridge acknowledged the problem but rejected any suggestion that advice should come from an independent source. If advice were needed, it should come from within the organization itself. He considered that every local security office should run its own advice bureau 'to which every person in doubt or difficulty [could] be referred'.[20] Beveridge genuinely believed that if the ministry were properly run, by enlightened bureaucrats such as himself, a service could be created which was both efficient and humane. Provided it was decentralized and in touch with local agencies, and that it selected and trained its staff with care, it could serve the public with sympathy and understanding.[21]

Allied to Beveridge's belief in public service was a profound distrust of lawyers. He was opposed to deciding industrial compensation issues through the courts, which he regarded as too expensive, too contentious, and too likely to produce lump-sum settlements. He acknowledged that the lack of legal help available to claimants led to a sense of injustice[22]— but the answer was to change to an administrative procedure, not to provide legal advice.[23] At one stage, Beveridge even suggested that in a rational world the whole of tort liability would be abolished: 'with the inevitable uncertainties of legal proceedings . . . [they] cannot escape something of the character of a lottery'.[24] Beveridge gave little attention to the question of benefit appeals, a subject which did not interest him. In one short paragraph, he recommended that the appeal system should be

[18] PRO file LCO2/4622.
[19] National Council of Social Service, *Annual Report* (1923).
[20] Beveridge, *op. cit.*, n. 6, para. 397.
[21] Id., para. 385.
[22] Id., para. 79.
[23] Id., para. 336.
[24] Id., para. 262.

retained more or less as it was, but should be rationalized and made local and informal.[25]

3. Tribunal representation

The Rushcliffe Committee designed a comprehensive scheme, covering all the main courts, Coroners' Courts, and 'any tribunal where audience is normally granted to barristers and solicitors'.[26] In February 1947 the Attlee Cabinet accepted this proposal without demur. After the August sterling crisis, though, government optimism started to drain away and by November 1948 costings were scrutinized more carefully. Herbert Morrison, stalwart of municipal socialism, was particularly alarmed at the breadth of the legal aid scheme, and argued that tribunals should be excluded: 'I should like to go the whole way and allow no legal aid before tribunals of any description. We ought to work to a position in which a man can appear personally before a tribunal and we could then reserve for the Courts cases in which he should be represented.'[27]

The problem with extending legal aid to tribunals, however, was not so much Morrison's opposition, as the lack of any well argued support for the proposal. The Rushcliffe Committee had made only the barest exami-nation of what tribunal representation might involve, and the Lord Chancellor's Department did not attempt to compile a full list of tribunals until ten days before the legal aid bill was published. When they did, the results were alarming. They found around ninety different types of tri-bunal, thirty of which had been established under post-1945 legislation. They did not know how many cases they heard, or how they operated. It was too late to distinguish between different tribunals: the only adminis-tratively coherent solution was to remove them all from the 1949 Act.

The incident reveals the limited imaginations of the lawyers involved in legal aid policy: tribunals were outside their professional purview, and they had not thought through the many questions they raised. Non-lawyers such as Beveridge, Bevan, and Morrison could see no reason why lawyers should be involved. As far as they were concerned, lawyers should play a minimal role within the welfare state. To the wartime plan-ners, there was no question of citizens needing legal rights against welfare bureaucracies. Similarly, if private employers or landlords needed to be

---

[25] Beveridge, *op. cit.*, n. 6, para. 394.   [26] Rushcliffe, *op. cit.*, n. 5, para. 170.
[27] Letter from Morrison to the Lord Chancellor, Lord Jowitt, 5 Nov. 1948: PRO file LCO2/4625.

regulated, this could be done by an administrative agency.[28] It is worth noting that injustice was not one of Beveridge's giants.[29] A measure of how far things have changed is that it is difficult to imagine a modern-day battle-cry for the welfare state in which the terms 'justice' or 'injustice' did not figure.

4. Marriage breakdown

Despite Beveridge's desire for administrative rather than legal solutions, there was one problem he singularly failed to solve. What should happen to women whose marriage had ended 'otherwise than by widowhood'? White points out that the main role of legal aid was to 'plug gaps or plaster over unresolved difficulties' in the national insurance scheme for separated and divorced wives.[30] Unlike widows, separated wives received no national insurance benefits. Instead, they were left to rely on means-tested benefits or such support from their husbands as could be extracted through the court system with the help of legal aid.

Civil legal aid has been dominated by divorce and marriage breakdown from the start. Indeed, the original 1914 charitable 'poor person's procedure' can be seen as the Bar's response to the Gorell Commission on divorce in 1912. The Commission had highlighted the growing number of 'poor but honest' artisans whose marriages had broken down, for whom divorce was their only hope of respectability. The fact that they could not afford a High Court divorce brought the law into disrepute, and, as Mr Justice Bargrave Deane put it, 'raised the general questions of "a law for the rich" and "a law for the poor" '.[31] Without legitimate remarriage, many lived with the social stigma of adultery, bigamy, or bastardy. The Commission's proposed solution to allow cheap divorce in county courts was vehemently opposed by the bishops, the Mother's Union, and the Bar. Instead, the compromise adopted was to set up a procedure whereby the very poor could receive charitable help from lawyers to obtain a High Court divorce.

[28] For example, the Disabled Persons (Employment) Act 1944 did not permit a disabled person to bring any form of legal action. All prosecutions required the express authority of the Minister of Labour (s. 19(1)).

[29] The words Beveridge used were: 'But want is one only of five giants on the road of reconstruction and is in some ways the easiest to attack. The others are Disease, Ignorance, Squalor and Idleness' (*op. cit.*, n. 6, para. 8).

[30] 'The distasteful character of litigation for Poor Persons' (1975) 3 *Juridical Rev.* 233. See also Sally Hughes, 'The Committee on Legal Aid 1944–1945' (unpublished).

[31] *Report of the Royal Commission on Divorce and Matrimonial Causes* (1912; Cd. 6478; Chair, Lord Gorell) para. 51.

The poor person's procedure was never adequate to meet the growing demand, and under wartime pressures it collapsed altogether. It was replaced by temporary wartime expedients, including command legal aid sections run by the Army, the Royal Air Force, and the Navy, and a service divorce department run by the Law Society. The divorce department had begun in 1942 with one salaried solicitor in Chancery Lane. By 1947 it had grown to twenty-seven units, each headed by a solicitor, based in nine provincial centres, handling both service and civilian cases.

The social disruption of war had caused divorce on a grand scale. In 1935 the divorce rate had stood at 0.45 per 1,000 married couples. By 1947 it had climbed to a peak of 5.6. As a solicitor commented to the *News Chronicle* in 1945, 'the whole fabric of our social life is changing and the attitude towards divorce has completely changed with it'.[32] Although the post-war divorce boom was clearly related to the special stresses caused by wartime separations, it was to have a long-term effect on social attitudes. During the 1950s there were considerable attempts to re-assert family values, and the divorce rate did fall—but it was never to return to anything like the pre-war rate. The lowest post-war divorce rate, in 1958, stood at 1.9, four times the 1935 rate. Since then divorce has risen inexorably, to 13.5 divorces per 1,000 married couples.[33]

The present civil legal aid scheme was set up in response to the divorce crisis. Its main purpose was to deal with marriage breakdown, and this is the task it has in fact performed. Yet both the Lord Chancellor's Department and the Law Society were reluctant to admit this basic fact—preferring instead to use a generalized rhetoric about the rule of law, and 'the need to prosecute a just and reasonable claim or defend a legal right'.[34] Internal memoranda reveal that playing down divorce was a conscious public relations strategy. As the War Office told the Lord Chancellor's Department in 1942, the general ground for the army scheme is 'that it is a "welfare" need, and we do not want to give the impression that the morale of the whole Army will suffer if there is no machinery for easy and cheap divorce'.[35]

Post-War Britain and Growing Disillusion with Public Service

Both the nature of the legal aid scheme and the social role it was expected to perform were moulded by the social beliefs and attitudes of Britain

---

[32] *News Chronicle*, 15 Dec. 1945. [33] *Social Trends* 24 (1994) 38.

[34] Lord Chancellor's Department, *Legal Aid and Advice Bill 1948: a summary of the proposed new service* (1948; Cmd. 7563).

[35] Letter from P. J. Grigg to Sir Claud Schuster, 9 Feb. 1942: PRO file LCO2/2845.

from 1942 to 1945—during the period from El Alamein to the Allied victory, when it looked as if Britain would win the war and could lay plans for winning the peace.

The last half century, however, has seen a growing disillusionment with the ideal of public service. As Harold Perkin has pointed out, Britain is currently experiencing a backlash against public sector professionals, and the institutions that employ them.[36] For the present discussion, it is possible to distinguish three separate periods in the decline of belief in public bureaucracy. The first challenge from the traditional right, occurred during the 1950s. The second challenge, from the radical left, is associated with 1960s and '70s, whilst the third challenge, from the radical right, is a 1980s phenomenon. All three have had increased citizens' need for independent help, to deal with increasingly legalistic welfare services and judicialistic tribunals.

1. The 1950s: the first challenge

(a) The traditional professions re-assert their independence Soon after the victory euphoria had died down, the traditional professions of medicine and the law re-asserted their traditional belief in 'independent' practice. General practitioners and solicitors succeeded in extricating themselves from the salaried bureaucracies that had been planned for them. Neither plans for local authority-run salaried health services nor advice through salaried lawyers were ever implemented. Lack of money gave the legal aid scheme a slow start. When first introduced in 1950, it was confined to the High Court only. It was not extended to the county court until 1956, and did not include advice until 1959. The Law Society seized the opportunity this provided to re-negotiate the Rushcliffe deal, persuading the government that salaried lawyers would be too difficult to recruit and too expensive. The 1959 legal advice scheme bent, if not broke, the words of the 1949 Act by paying private practitioners on a case-by-case basis to give advice in their own offices. During the war, the Law Society had stressed how much cheaper a centralized divorce department would be over private practice. By 1960 it was considered to be ideologically indefensible, and in 1961 it was quietly closed.

(b) Crichel Down, Franks, and the rule of law As the war receded, so did belief in the infallibility of public bureaucracy. By 1955 worries that officials might misuse their power found a voice in the famous Crichel Down

---

[36] Perkin, *op. cit.*, n. 13, p. 473.

incident, in which an aristocratic family had been deprived of their land through bureaucratic bungling.[37] Tory lawyers seized on the affair to argue that administrators should be subject to the control of the common law, with its traditional respect for property and liberty.[38]

Crichel Down led directly to the establishment of the Franks Committee on Administrative Tribunals and Enquiries. This addressed the symbolic issues behind the incident, even though it did not itself involve either a tribunal or a statutory enquiry.[39] The Committee openly asked the question Beveridge had neglected: how can the rights of individual citizens be harmonized with wider public interests?[40] Its reply was that tribunals existed to safeguard individual rights: they were thus part of the machinery of adjudication rather than administration. It followed, therefore, that they should be more like courts. They should be independent of government, have more legally qualified chairmen, follow clearer rules of procedure, produce reasoned decisions, and be subject to rights of appeal. The advantages of tribunals over courts—their 'cheapness, freedom from technicality, expedition and expert knowledge[41]—were purely secondary issues, compared to the over-riding need to be open, fair, and impartial.

Although the Franks Committee was strong on constitutional principle, its lack of empirical data led to a misplaced complacency about how tribunals worked in practice. Its impression of national insurance local tribunals was 'most favourable',[42] national assistance appeal tribunals worked 'satisfactorily',[43] there was 'no evidence' that forms and leaflets were unnecessarily difficult for the average person,[44] and the lack of legal representation 'may often not work harshly in practice'.[45] Thus, many of its recommendations lacked urgency. Nevertheless, the Committee reasoned that if tribunals were essentially courts, it followed that citizens would need legal advice and representation in their dealings with them. It recommended that legal aid should be extended: '. . . there is a good case for extending the legal aid scheme at once to those tribunals which are formal and expensive and to final appellate tribunals. We also consider that any extension of the scheme to cover a wider range of proceedings in courts should be accompanied by an extension of the scheme to other tribunals'.[46]

[37] See J. A. G. Griffith, 'The Crichel Down Affair' (1955) 18 *Modern Law Rev.* 557.

[38] In 1955 a group of Conservative lawyers published *The Rule of Law*, arguing for a review of the decisions of tribunals and Ministers.

[39] *Report of the Committee on Administrative Tribunals and Enquiries* (1957; Cmnd. 218; Chair, Lord Franks) para. 15.

[40] Id., para. 5.

[41] Id., para. 38.

[42] Id., para. 171.

[43] Id., para. 179.

[44] Id., para. 67.

[45] Id., para. 87.

[46] Id., para. 89.

Most Franks Committee recommendations have been implemented. Thirty-five years later, leaving aside a few minor exceptions,[47] this one has not. Although empirical evidence now shows quite clearly that unrepresented claimants are disadvantaged,[48] and numerous committees have stressed the importance of extending legal aid to tribunals,[49] it is not a subject which has seized the imagination of either Conservative or Labour governments. Those Conservative commentators who were most vociferous about the need to subject administrative decisions to the rule of law tended to focus on the rights of the propertied classes.[50] Meanwhile, the trades union movement regarded tribunals as its own preserve, opposing further lawyer involvement and stressing their administrative and informal aspects.[51]

2. The 1960s and 1970s: the Left's challenge

The second challenge to the moral authority of public service came from the left. In 1970 Richard Titmuss identified 'a general protest and liberation movement', forming itself into a myriad of single-interest pressure groups—from students, squatters, and gay activists to tenants, widows, and old age pensioners.[52] Although it was often difficult to say what such groups were in favour of, it was easy to say what they were against—the arbitrary, non-accountable exercise of power, discretion, and moral judgements by 'the bureaucrat of the public welfare system'. A wave of left-wing critics castigated welfare providers for being out of touch with their clients, putting their own interests first, and pursuing essentially bureaucratic agenda.[53] Some, such as Richard White, argued that lawyers had a

[47] Legal Aid covers the Lands Tribunal, Employment Appeal Tribunal, and Mental Health Appeal Tribunal.

[48] H. Genn and Y. Genn, *The Effectiveness of Representation at Tribunals* (1989).

[49] *Royal Commission on Trade Unions and Employers' Associations* (1968; Cmnd. 3623; Chair, Lord Donovan); *Royal Commission on Legal Services in England and Wales* (1979; Cmnd. 7648; Chair, Lord Benson); and Lord Chancellor's Legal Aid Advisory Committee, *33rd Annual Report* HC (1982–83) 137.

[50] One of the most outspoken advocates of subjecting administrative decisions to court action was the Lord Chief Justice, Lord Hewart. When challenged that courts were too expensive, he wrote that 'there are scores of highly competent barristers whose fees are not in any way exorbitant': *The New Despotism* (1929).

[51] Thus, the Trade Union Congress supported a ban on lawyers within National Insurance Local Tribunals and advocated its extension to Industrial Injuries Local Tribunals: Franks, *op. cit.*, n. 39, para. 173.

[52] R. Titmuss, 'Welfare "Rights", Law and Discretion', reprinted in *The Philosophy of Welfare*, eds. B. Abel-Smith and K. Titmuss (1987).

[53] See T. Robinson, *In worlds apart: professionals and their clients in the welfare state* (1978) and I. Illych, *Disabling Professions* (1977).

particular role to play in making welfare services more responsive to the needs of their clients.[54]

In 1968 the Society of Labour Lawyers published *Justice For All* which argued that a legal aid scheme operating exclusively through private practitioners could not meet the needs of the poor:

The existing legal aid and advice scheme is based on the traditional view of the nature of professional services—that the professional man decides where he is to practise and then waits in his office to be consulted. He does not advertise, he does not 'drum up business'. He makes himself available only to those who approach him. The weakness of this system is revealed as soon as it is appreciated that there are large areas with few or no solicitors and a significant proportion of people for whom the service is designed and who need it, who do not make use of it.[55]

The answer was to establish 'neighbourhood law firms' similar to those in the United States of America, in which salaried lawyers set up new offices in the slums and proselytized for their cause. *Justice For All* failed to convince the incoming Heath Government, which rejected independent law centres and instead adopted the Law Society's plans centred on an improved advice scheme (later known as the 'green form scheme').[56]

Undaunted, many involved with the poverty lobby initiated their own improvements. The first law centre was opened in 1970, and by 1979 there were twenty-eight such centres in England and Wales. In 1971 the Legal Action Group (LAG) was founded to encourage lawyers to use the law to help the poor. In 1973 it published a list of all the areas of life where lawyers could offer advice under the newly established £25 scheme.[57] Although it purported to be mere 'information', it was a highly political document which proclaimed a new role for lawyers within the welfare state. The list was broad: immigration, education, welfare benefits, debt, housing, planning, mental health, and complaints against the police were all included. The unifying theme was that lawyers could help the poor in their manifold arguments with large, impervious bureaucra-

[54] R. White, 'Lawyers and the Enforcement of Rights' in *Social Needs and Legal Action*, eds. P. Morris *et al.* (1973). For an account of radical thought on legal services during this period, see A. Paterson and D. Nelken, 'Evolution in Legal Services: Practice without Theory?' (1984) 3 *Civil Justice Q.* 229.

[55] Society of Labour Lawyers, *Justice for All* (1968) 37. The argument received powerful support from one of the first empirical studies of legal services, carried out in Birmingham in 1969, which revealed that over 80 per cent of civil legal aid certificates and advice bills concerned family disputes: L. Bridges *et al.*, *Legal Services in Birmingham* (1975).

[56] Legal Advice and Assistance Act 1973: For an account of this period, see M. Stephens, *Community Law Centres: a critical appraisal* (1991), and M. Zander, *Legal Services for the Community* (1978).

[57] *LAG Bulletin*, May 1973.

cies. Beveridge would have turned in his grave. His belief that if people had a problem with a welfare matter they should go to staff employed by the agency involved had received a direct challenge.

Contemporary legal aid lawyers would have no difficulty recognizing the list of problems. What make the list appear quaintly old-fashioned are the suggestions for action: advice about choice of schools was a matter of 'writing to education authorities'; dealing with homelessness involved contacting social services and the housing department and advising on the 'points system of allocation'; council tenants facing possession summonses were to be 'advised about eviction', while discrimination matters were 'referred to the Race Relations Board'. The fact is that, even as late as 1973, the poor had few legal rights to enforce against the bureaucracies which affected their everyday lives. LAG was several steps ahead of the legislation. It was putting forward a moral argument that the poor *ought* to have more rights against welfare providers rather than reflecting existing legislation. The wartime generation were not necessarily convinced: Titmuss, for example, identified many questionable assumptions lying behind the legalistic approach—that lawyers would be interested in the problems of the poor, and that legal procedures would be sufficiently speedy, cheap, effective, and comprehensible to meet the needs of welfare recipients.[58]

Nevertheless, as the decade progressed, governments slowly accepted an increased emphasis on legal rights enforceable by individuals.[59] At this time, even employers were expected to take some responsibility for the welfare of their employees. Thus there was a substantial growth in employment rights, especially to combat unfair dismissal and discrimination. Davies and Freedland describe the development of 'a new principle' supporting such extensions, motivated partly by a desire to extend welfare provision to those in work and partly by a general concern with the exercise of arbitrary power by large institutions.[60] At the same time, tribunals became more court-like. As the Council on Tribunals commented in 1980, since Franks 'the trend towards judicialisation has gathered momentum, with the result that tribunals are becoming more formal, expensive and procedurally complex'.[61] This time, the movement was spurred by empirical studies. Baldwin *et al.* comment that 'study after study demonstrated that hearings before supplementary benefit appeal

---

[58] Titmuss, *op. cit.*, n. 52.
[59] The Consumer Credit Act 1974 gave debtors more rights against creditors, while the Housing (Homeless Persons Act) 1977 opened up the possibility of judicial review to the homeless.
[60] P. Davies and M. Freedland, *Labour Legislation and Public Policy* (1993).
[61] Council on Tribunals, *The Functions of the Council on Tribunals* (1980; Cmnd. 7805).

tribunals were seen as frustrating and humiliating for claimants', while chairpersons and members doled out 'state bounty to those regarded as morally deserving'.[62] More legally qualified chairpersons were appointed, wing members were better trained, and a right of appeal was introduced.

Despite these developments, many social rights which we now take for granted, such as tenants' security of tenure against public landlords, were not enacted until the 1980s. Furthermore, governments failed to accept law centres as part of mainstream legal provision. In 1976, Richard White joined the Lord Chancellor's Department to write a report on law centres, leading to a brief hope that they might be taken seriously. In the end, though, the report was suppressed for reasons which have never been made public.[63] Although the 1970s were a time of rapid growth for solicitors, and many entered legal aid practice, astute lobbying by the Law Society managed to ensure that the scheme remained a 'judicare' one, delivered in the traditional way, and dominated by the traditional concerns.

3. The 1980s: the Thatcher revolution

The third challenge to the ideal of public service came from the radical right, and is linked to the Thatcher premiership of 1979 to 1990.

Harold Perkin has suggested that the main ideological division of society is no longer between working and middle classes but between public- and private-sector professionals. On this analysis, the Thatcher years can be seen as the revenge of the private sector on public-sector professionals. As Perkin puts it, public-sector workers were 'believed to be parasitic upon the creators of wealth and, undisciplined by market forces, almost by definition inefficient if not actually incompetent'.[64] He argues that many Thatcher reforms affected the working class only indirectly. Their primary purpose was to reduce the income, power, and prestige of the public bureaucracies in which the wartime planners had placed so much faith. Perkin points out that by 1985 all public-sector occupations from top civil servants and hospital doctors to nurses and train drivers (except for police and firefighters) had lost income in real terms.

There were, of course, many ways of cutting welfare providers down to size, including reducing the power of local authorities, centralizing discretion, and contracting out services. One approach was to give consumers new rights. In 1970, Titmuss had referred to a 'paradoxical

---

[62] J. Baldwin *et al.*, *Judging Social Security* (1992) 155. Particularly influential was K. Bell, *Research Study on Supplementary Benefit Appeal Tribunals* (1975).
[63] Zander, *op. cit.*, n. 56.   [64] Perkin, *op. cit.*, n. 13.

alliance' between the 'new Diceyists' of the political right, who wished to reduce administrative empires and the 'welfare rights' campaigners of the left, who also distrusted state bureaucrats.[65] During the early 1980s it was an alliance that proved particularly powerful. In 1980 public tenants were given security of tenure for the first time.[66] In the same year, parents acquired new rights to appeal against local authorities' allocation of school places,[67] while the Education Act 1981 allowed them to challenge assessments of special education needs. The Mental Health Act 1983 increased the possibility of legal challenge to medical decisions, while parents gained extended powers to challenge social services departments who deprived them of access to children in care.[68]

An even greater upheaval occurred within the social security system. In 1980 the Conservative Government implemented previous plans to turn the discretionary allowances of supplementary benefit into legal entitlements. The Government thought that reforms which had originated in poverty campaigners' attempts to make the system fairer offered the opportunity to curb expenditure.[69] At first they succeeded: single payments fell from 1,129,000 in 1980 to 834,000 in 1981. Claimants were often mystified by the changes, and failed to understand how to bring their individual circumstances within the boundaries of the rules.[70] Soon, however, advisers realized that they understood the scheme better than the poorly trained DHSS officers, and could use the rigidity of the rules to gain more money for their clients. One solicitor claimed that, by providing a benefit check for all his clients on supplementary benefit, he could gain additional income for 70 per cent of them.[71] As the new system became better understood, the number of single payments soared, topping 4 million by 1985. This was accompanied by an increase in the number of claims to tribunals, rising from 75,500 in 1980 to 202,000 in 1986.[72] The much criticized supplementary benefit appeal tribunals became increasingly legalistic, culminating in the creation of new social security appeal tribunals in 1984, which finally brought supplementary benefits within the more formal system established for contributory benefits.

[65] Titmuss, *op. cit.*, n. 52.   [66] Housing Act 1980.   [67] Education Act 1980.

[68] See Health and Social Services and Social Security Adjudication Act 1983 and Children Act 1989.   [69] Baldwin, *op. cit.*, n. 62, p. 9.

[70] See J. Allberson and R. Smith, *We don't give clothing grants any more* (1984), and C. Walker, 'Supplementary benefit: the sinking safety net' in *Thatcherism and the Poor*, eds. D. Bull and P. Wilding (1983).

[71] R. Smith, 'Revamping Legal Aid', *Legal Action* April 1989.

[72] Council on Tribunals, *Annual Report 1980–81* (1981); and Council on Tribunals, *Annual Report 1986–87* (1987).

4. Legal aid during the 1980s

Despite attempts to cut much state expenditure, the early 1980s were good years for the legal aid scheme, with a rapid expansion in both the number of solicitors participating and the work done.[73] Although eligibility did not keep pace with increases in incomes, the first actual cut did not occur until 1986, when dependant allowances were reduced. This was followed by the legal aid scrutiny report,[74] leading eventually to the Legal Aid Act 1988, and the establishment of a board to replace the Law Society's administration of the scheme. The 1988 Act allowed for radical reform in the future, but there was little immediate change. For many years legal aid appeared to be insulated from the ideological storm: it was a relatively small amount of money and had the protection of a powerful interest group.

Despite a series of funding crises, the number of law centres in England and Wales slowly increased, from twenty-eight in 1979 to fifty-six in 1991; but they were never taken seriously as part of legal aid provision. With the exception of a mere £3m from the legal aid fund,[75] they continue to rely on local authority and charitable funding. The 1980s also saw the development of specialist 'social welfare' solicitor firms, which were often sited near law centres, employed ex-law-centre workers, and relied on law centre referrals for their clients.[76] This was accompanied by a rise in the number of green form bills for housing, welfare benefits, debt, employment, and immigration work: from 63,000 bills (of 12 per cent of all bills paid) in 1980/81, to 220,000 bills (21 per cent) in 1990/91.[77] Overall, however, civil legal aid continued to be dominated by family and personal injury work.[78] The new social welfare firms tended to be confined to a few geographical areas, particularly Merseyside, which in 1989–90 consumed almost 30 per cent of total green form payments for welfare benefit advice.[79] Baldwin and Hill found that within most legal aid areas there

[73] Between 1980/81 and 1986/87, the number of solicitors' offices participating in the scheme rose from 9,214 to 11,560 while 'acts of assistance' rose from 1 million to 1.5 million: *Legal Aid Annual Reports*.

[74] Lord Chancellor's Department, *Legal Aid Efficiency Scrutiny* (1986).

[75] Legal Aid Board, *Annual Report* [1992–93] (1993; Cm. 735) 20.

[76] See E. Kempson, *Legal Advice and Assistance* (1989); M. Slatter and M. Moseley, *Access to legal services in rural Norfolk* (1986); Law Society, *New Directions in Legal Aid Practices* (1987).

[77] See Legal Action Group, *op. cit.*, n. 3, p. 9, and *Legal Aid Annual Reports*.

[78] See National Consumer Council, *Ordinary Justice* (1989) ch. 3.

[79] See figures obtained by Neville Harris, *Legal Action*, March 1991. At this time Merseyside submitted forty-two green form bills per 1,000 population compared with only thirty in the next highest region, South Wales: Legal Aid Board, *Annual Report* [1989–90] (1990).

were only one or two firms which carried out a significant volume of advice outside the fields of crime or family law.[80]

Social welfare advice under the green form scheme was a drop in the ocean of need. The Civil Justice Review stressed how few tenants or mortgage defaulters received legal help with housing matters,[81] while a study for the Department of the Environment found that ignorance or confusion about benefits played a major part in repossession cases.[82] Genn and Genn highlighted the low numbers of appellants before social security appeal and industrial tribunals who obtained advice. As trade union membership fell, from 53 per cent of the workforce in 1979 to 38 per cent in 1991,[83] almost a third of applicants to industrial tribunals were left without any form of advice.[84]

Legal Aid Now: A Reaction Against Legalism?

So where are we now? For legal aid lawyers the outlook seems grim. The social solidarity of VE Day has all but disappeared. The British public no longer seems interested in an equality of misery, but is prepared to trade the security of a basic minimum for the chance of a great deal more. The reduction in social solidarity has translated itself into a general attack on non-targetted benefits, which has had its effect on the legal aid means test. In April 1993 the contributory green form scheme was abolished and civil contributions were substantially increased.[85]

Legal aid is no longer immune from ideological and financial attack: the Lord Chancellor has taken every opportunity to remind audiences that although 'justice is priceless, . . . it must not be too pricey'.[86] Meanwhile, the Government has attempted to prevent sharp increases in costs per case by freezing legal aid pay rates and introducing fixed fees. So far, this strategy has not succeeded—costs per case continue to grow.[87] Despite

---

[80] J. Baldwin and S. Hill, *The Operation of the Green Form Scheme in England and Wales* (1988).

[81] They found that only 8 per cent of defendants were represented at possession hearings (School of Advanced Urban Studies, *Study of Housing Cases*, 1987) and not more than 1,500 tenants initiated legal action against their landlords, despite evidence of massive disrepair (Lord Chancellor's Department, *Housing Cases*, consultation paper 5, (1987)).

[82] S. Duncan and K. Kirby, *Preventing Rent Arrears* (1983); J. Watts, 'Local authority possession proceedings' *Legal Action*, February 1987.

[83] *Social Trends* 24 (1994) 147. [84] Genn and Genn, *op. cit.*, n. 48.

[85] See Home Affairs Committee, *Legal Aid: the Lord Chancellor's proposals* (1993).

[86] Lord Mackay of Clashfern, 'Litigation in the 1990s' (1991) 54 *Modern Law Rev.* 171. See also speeches of 22 Sep. 1991 and 4 Oct. 1991, and his address to the Consumers' Association, 27 July 1992. [87] Home Affairs Committee, *op. cit.*, n. 85, p. x.

their mounting income, however, the prestige and morale of legal aid lawyers seems at an all-time low. The Law Society's survey of solicitors found that those doing legal aid are in their middle years[88]—the genera-tion who graduated in the 1970s when public service was fashionable. As they celebrate their fortieth birthdays, and worry about mortgages and private school fees, they are casting envious glances at fellow students who went into city firms, and whose income has risen much faster than theirs.[89]

However, with a deep recession in the housing market, and steep falls in conveyancing income, solicitors cannot afford to give up legal aid work.[90] Despite the low prestige of poverty work, it is becoming an ever more institutionalized part of solicitors' practice. For all the Govern-ment's attempts to reduce demand for the green form scheme by cutting eligibility, the number of bills burgeons. This is particularly true of hous-ing, employment, welfare benefit, debt, and immigration bills, which have doubled from 220,000 bills 1990/91, to 466,500 in 1993–94 (or 28 per cent of all green forms paid).[91] The Legal Aid Board's franchising scheme encourages firms to 'target' welfare areas, and develop systematic office routines for dealing with them. By March 1994, significant numbers of firms had applied for franchises in the areas of debt (826), employment (809), and housing (781), though fewer applied for welfare benefits (469) or immigration franchises (177).[92] Once firms receive franchises, they are likely to take these areas of work more seriously, and generate further demands for their services.

Moving lawyers out of the welfare state?

Yet, just as lawyers are becoming more involved in issues of poverty law, the Government seems to be making attempts to move them out, and to stress the advantages of a less legalistic approach to welfare. The steady increase in legal rights of the early 1980s has produced its own reaction against what has been perceived as excessive legalism.

The first and clearest example of the reaction against legalism was to be seen in the social security system. By 1986 the Government regretted the

---

[88] G. Chambers and S. Harwood, *Solicitors in England and Wales: Practice, Organisation and Perceptions. First Report: the Work of the Solicitor in Private Practice* (1990).

[89] For a discussion of the growing disparity between different sections of the profession, see C. Glasser, 'The Legal Profession in the 1990s—Images of Change' (1990) 10 *Legal Studies* 1–11.

[90] For an analysis of the reduction in solicitors' conveyancing income, see Law Society, *Adapting for the Future* (1994).

[91] Legal Aid Board *Annual Report 1993–94* (1994) 93.   [92] Id., p. 35.

power the 1980 reforms had given welfare rights advisers to gain single payments for their clients. In 1988 the policy was changed: single payments and additional allowances were abolished, to be replaced by premiums based on easily identifiable attributes such as age and family status. This new benefit of 'income support' was to be supplemented only in rare circumstances by loans and grants from the social fund working within a cash-limited budget.

As social security appeal tribunals could not be required to keep within the budget, social fund appeals were transferred to internal social fund inspectors, monitored by the Social Fund Commissioner. The new system was controversial, and was widely interpreted as a reduction of legal rights,[93] but it would be too simple to categorize it only as a return to discretion. It has been pointed out that the voluminous guidance given to social fund officers could as easily have been drafted as regulations.[94] Claimants have a statutory entitlement to a review both by the local office and by an inspector. The Commissioner has taken great pains to establish the inspectors as an independent service: she stresses that their function is judicial, and that much of their job is to ensure the correct interpretation of law and directions.[95] Although they examine issues on the papers, the Commissioner stresses that this is effectively a paper hearing which must accord with the rules of natural justice. Thus, claimants are allowed to comment on what the local office says. While the system therefore has some of the advantages of the judicial model of decision-making, it also shares its weaknesses. Dalley and Berthoud found that there was little to choose between tribunals and inspectors on grounds of cost or time taken.[96] Moreover, applicants were frequently confused by the system: they had little knowledge of what was available or how the review system worked, and officers agreed that they were rarely able to present claims in the most effective way. All those involved thought that skilled welfare rights advisers were still enormously important in helping to prepare claims.[97] Clearly such advisers do not need to be lawyers, but

---

[93] Council on Tribunals, *Social Security—Abolition of Independent Appeals under the Proposed Social Fund* (1986: Cmnd 9722).

[94] Baldwin, *op. cit.*, n. 62, p. 10.

[95] Department of Social Security, *Annual Report of the Social Fund Commissioner for 1992/93 on the standards of reviews by Social Fund Inspectors* (1993). Lewis and Birkinshaw comment that they were 'impressed by her efforts to ensure procedural fairness and efficiency in a much discredited scheme'; (N. Lewis and P. Birkinshaw, *When Citizens Complain: Reforming Justice and Administration* (1993).

[96] G. Dalley and R. Berthoud, *Challenging Discretion: the Social Fund Review Procedure* (1992).

[97] Id., p. 121.

they need to be able to understand complex regulations and statutes and work within an essentially legalistic framework.

Those dealing with the social security system today meet a very different organization from that envisaged by Beveridge in 1942. Means-tested benefits, far from becoming the residue of the benefits system, have burgeoned to support six million people (compared with around one million in 1950).[98] Claimants deal with offices 'so severely under-resourced that poor quality work is now the norm'.[99] Although information leaflets have undoubtedly improved, it is rare for claimants to contact staff for advice: indeed, most find dealing with an office 'an unnerving and traumatic experience'.[100] When they appeal, they are faced with highly technical legal documents in which 'improvements in the layout of submissions . . . have been outweighed by the increased complexity of the law involved'.[101] Genn and Genn found that an informal atmosphere cannot compensate for the technicality of the rules: unrepresented appellants, who do not know the rules, are more likely to lose.[102] Around a half of claimants do not attend at all.[103] Beveridge's hopes for a sympathetic institution which could provide its customers with all the advice they needed have been dashed and the need for independent advice is more pressing than ever. Such advisers, whatever their qualifications, must be able to deal with a system bounded by statute, regulations, and directions. Sympathy for the poor is no longer enough.

Single payments are not the only area in which the Government has regretted its own handiwork in increasing legal rights. The Children Act 1989 put much greater emphasis on court hearings in child care cases, giving a wider range of parties the opportunity to be heard and transferring complex cases to the High Court. By 1993 there was not only a large increase in High Court cases, but each case involved more parties, took longer, and cost more, producing concern among judges, MPs, and the Lord Chancellor's Department.[104]

The alarm about the increase in legal aid costs goes wider. The Lord Chancellor stresses that 'recourse to judicial remedies' may not be necessary in all situations. Instead, it would be better to take the 'stitch in time' approach embodied in the Citizen's Charter, under which an informal internal complaints system would put things right more quickly and more

[98] As of November 1992, 5.51 million people claimed income support and 0.47 million claimed family credit: *Social Security Statistics* (1993).

[99] Baldwin, *op. cit.*, n. 62, p. 207.   [100] Id., p. 154.

[101] Id., p. 158.

[102] Genn and Genn, *op. cit.*, n. 48.   [103] Baldwin, *op. cit.*, n. 62.

[104] S. Hughes, 'Suffer the little children', *Legal Action*, June 1994.

cheaply.[105] There has been a renewed interest in out-of-court complaints systems. The 1980s saw a rash of new ombudsmen and regulatory bodies—ranging from Insurance Ombudsman Bureau to OFTEL—which by the early 1990s were experiencing substantial increases in their workload.[106] However, it would be entirely wrong to see this as taking over from the legal systems or, as presently conceived, a realistic alternative to legal aid.

For a start, new complaints systems often generate new demands. Indeed, one of the objectives of the Charter approach is to create more assertive citizens who 'can increasingly put pressure upon those responsible for providing services to deliver them to a high standard'.[107] The first stage seems to be working—citizens appear to be becoming more assertive. As the Audit Commission notes, publication of the service-based charters is one factor leading to the increase in complaints.[108] How far this will translate into improved services (rather than into angry and frustrated consumers) remains to be seen.

There is some evidence that good low-level schemes do reduce the need for more formal schemes,[109] but poor schemes—by promising more than they can fulfil—may increase the use of formal mechanisms, including litigation. An example is the Police Complaints Authority whose complaints have fallen each year since it was established in 1985.[110] This is hardly the result of increased confidence in the police: the British Crime Survey found that one in ten of the population felt that the police had given them grounds for a complaint within the last five years.[111] Instead, 'evidence suggests that, increasingly, complainants are by-passing the

---

[105] Mackay, address to the Consumers' Association, *op. cit.* n. 86.

[106] See the annual reports of the Insurance Ombudsman Bureau, Banking Ombudsman, and Building Society Ombudsman Scheme, and the new regulatory bodies (OFTEL, OFFER, and OFWAT). For a general discussion of these changes, see Office of Fair Trading, *Consumer Redress Mechanisms* (1991), and Lewis and Birkinshaw, *op. cit.*, n. 95.

[107] *The Citizen's Charter: First Report* (1992) 1.

[108] The Audit Commission links the increase in hospital complaints to falling standards, easier access to complaints systems, a general rise in 'consumerism', and publication of the Citizen's and Patient's Charters: *What seems to be the matter: communication between hospitals and patients* (1993).

[109] For example, in 1992 OFTEL reported a small fall in complaints which they ascribe to new complaints handling systems at British Telecom: *1992 Annual Report*. In the early 1990s banks made serious attempts to improve their complaints procedures: C. Graham *et al.*, "Publicising the bank and building society ombudsman schemes' (1993) 3 *Consumer Policy Rev.* 85. Subsequently, the Banking Ombudsman reported a reduction in complaints: *Annual Report 1992–93*.

[110] From 15,865 in 1986 to 11,155 in 1989.

[111] W. Skogan, *The Police and Public in England and Wales: a British Crime Survey Report* (1990).

234   *Tamara Goriely*

existing complaints system to seek a remedy in the civil courts'.[112] This is proving a more successful strategy: civil actions are, it has been estimated, fifteen times more likely to succeed.[113] In the health area, the Association of Community Health Councils comments that, despite the many difficulties and problems of suing, 'complainants are still forced into legal action' to secure a reasonable, impartial response or an explanation of what has happened to them.[114] Since 1986 there has been a steep rise in medical negligence suits dealt with by legal aid—up from 4,542 in 1986/7, to 10,857 in 1993/94.[115] There is a serious danger that, unless low-level complaints procedures can be made to work, current policies towards encouraging greater assertiveness will simply encourage litigation.

Another problem is that even low-level complaints schemes generate needs for information, advice, and support, which at present are not being met. As McCarthy and Simpson point out, many complainants are 'financially poor, are dispirited and unwell; are lonely, isolated and inarticulate; cannot properly read and write; they are sometimes fearful and occasionally angry'.[116] Pursuing a complaint can be a highly stressful activity at the best of times. For many at the bottom of the heap, independent support is vital. Sheffield University's major survey of local government complaints schemes found that although 'virtually all' social services departments complied with government guidelines to implement complaints procedures, these were 'woefully inadequate' as a way of protecting highly vulnerable client groups such as children or the elderly in residential care.[117] Many have stressed the need for independent lay support if children in care are to use internal complaints procedures.[118]

When people are asked where they would go with a problem, they consistently name Citizens' Advice Bureaux (CABx) which have a reputation as being helpful, dedicated, informative, and friendly.[119] At the same

[112] B. Loveday, 'Recent developments in police complaints procedure: Britain and North America' (1989) *Local Government Studies* 25.

[113] See Also R. Smith, 'Is anybody listening', *New Law J.* 12 June 1992, p. 816, and London Strategic Policy Unit, *Police Complaints—a fresh approach* (1987).

[114] *National Health Service Complaints Procedures: a submission to the Complaints Review Committee* (1993).   [115] *Legal Aid Annual Reports.*

[116] P. McCarthy and B. Simpson, 'Effective complaining in local government services' (1993) 3 *Consumer Policy Rev.* 39.

[117] N. Lewis, *et al.*, *Complaints Procedures in Local Government* (1987).

[118] M. Lindsay, 'Complaints procedures and their limitations in the light of the "Pindown" inquiry' [1991] *J. of Social Welfare and Family Law* 432, and V. Plowden, 'Right to Complain', *Childright*, July 1993. McCarthy and Simpson, *op. cit.*, n. 116, stress that independent agencies are a key component in the grivance chain.

[119] Research International, *The Charterline Service* (1992); P. McCarthy *et al.*, *Grievances, Complaints and Local Government* (1992).

time, people are well aware that CABx are 'underfunded', 'shabby' and 'run-down', with restricted opening hours and clogged phone lines.[120] A serious attempt to institute a non-legal response to grievances would necessitate a full review of the advice sector, coupled with a substantial increase in funding. Although such a policy has been long advocated by the consumer movement,[121] it seems as far away as ever. The green form scheme is the only advice scheme in which budgets are not cash-limited. Thus, enterprising private solicitors are more able to respond to new advice needs than already hard-pressed lay agencies.

The institutional arrangements of government do not encourage those in power to take out-of-court arrangements seriously. The Lord Chancellor's Department has had a very narrow focus—the courts, and lawyers' services to represent people before the courts. Other forms of justice—whether tribunals, ombudsmen, or complaints systems—have been developed on an *ad hoc* basis, with little overall planning.[122] Responsibility for lay advice is spread between a number of departments,[123] while improving out-of-court justice is relegated to the occasional committees, whose conclusions, however valuable, are soon forgotten. Any attempt to replace legalistic procedures by fair, workable, informal arrangements would need a much greater political and financial commitment than seems likely to occur.

Conclusion

Practitioners have a tendency to look back on a golden age of legal aid, when funds were generous and needs were met.[124] The golden age existed for practitioners only. For tenants, employees, and claimants, legal aid has always been an inadequate means of enforcing rights.

In 1950 this hardly mattered. The architects of the welfare state— Beveridge, Bevan, and Morrison—saw little role for law or lawyers. Welfare needs were provided by state-run institutions, against which

[120] Office of Fair Trading, *op. cit.*, n. 106, p. 137. Genn and Genn found that many of those appearing before tribunals who could have used Citizens' Advice Bureaux did not do so because they were so difficult to contact (*op. cit.*, n. 48).

[121] See National Consumer Council, *The Fourth Right of Citizenship* (1977) and National Consumer Council, *op. cit.*, n. 78.

[122] See Lewis and Birkinshaw, *op. cit.*, n. 95.

[123] National Consumer Council, *op. cit.*, n. 78, p. 56.

[124] Thus Tony Holland comments that 'there was a time in the 1960s and 1970s when we could put our hands on our hearts and say that the poor received as good a quality service as the rich' ('An open letter to the Lord Chancellor' *Law Society Gazette* 12 Dec. 1990). See also, R. Pannone, 'Enough is Enough' *Law Society Gazette* 23 Mar. 1994.

recipients had few rights, while private institutions were regulated by state agencies. Civil legal aid was intended to deal with divorce only. Since the mid-1970s, however, governments have started to enact legal rights, intended to be enforced by individuals against employers, landlords, and welfare providers. Since 1980 society has come increasingly to distrust its public servants, and to discharge many of its welfare responsibilities through the private market. As this has happened the role of individually enforceable rights has become more central, with new rights in the fields of housing, education, child care, and mental health and a more legalistic approach to social security. Although there has recently been a reaction to what has been perceived as excessive legalism, the emphasis on individuals pursuing their own grievances through formal procedures remains.

Legal aid has failed to adapt to these changes in legislation. It still fails to cover most tribunal representation, despite the fact that tribunals are a well established and extremely important way of dealing with welfare-state disputes, and clear evidence shows that unrepresented litigants are more likely to lose. The newer forms of dispute-processing—internal complaints systems, inspectors, regulators, ombudsmen—require a more varied approach to advice, combining lay and legal skills, which the institutional arrangements of legal aid have failed to encompass. Legal aid is caught within an organizational strait-jacket which requires all advice to be given under the direction of qualified lawyers—and in which over 99 per cent of the budget is paid to private practice. Politicians now emphasize the 'assertive citizen', in which guise individuals are expected to pursue their own grievances though legal and quasi-legal channels, rather than rely passively on state regulators. This is in the face of evidence that aggrieved citizens are often too ignorant, confused, cowed, isolated, poor, or powerless to take on large institutions by themselves. If this approach to social regulation is to stand a chance of working, there is a pressing need to rethink the way advice and legal services are provided.

12. Financing Legal Services: A Comparative Perspective

ALAN PATERSON[1]

Legal Aid Models

There are four principal legal aid models: 'charitable', 'judicare', 'salaried' and 'mixed'.[2]

A. The Charitable Model

Under this approach, meeting the legal needs of the impecunious is considered to be a professional obligation—and usually a gratuitous one. Historically its hallmarks have included:

a. poor funding and inadequate coverage;
b. services provided by 'volunteer' members of the professions, almost invariably (especially in the case of counsel) the youngest and least experienced practitioners, on a part-time basis;
c. services provided on a gratuitous basis with no court dues or expenses being exigible.[3]

Even today there are numerous examples of the charitable model operating both within and without the United Kingdom. The former range from the advice clinics staffed by volunteer solicitors to the free initial

---

[1] I am grateful to the National Consumer Council and the Scottish Office Home and Health Department for support in connection with the research on which this piece draws. I should also like to thank Tammy Goriely, Jon Johnsen, David Kemp, Patrick Moss, Ulrike Schultz, Roger Smith, Wouter Meurs, and Jorn Westhoff for their assistance with aspects of the research.
[2] Zemans, 'Recent Trends in the Organisation of Legal Services' in W. Hascheid (ed.): *Effectiveness of Judicial Protection and Constitutional Order*, 1983 at pp. 388ff.
[3] See Alcock, 'Legal Aid: Whose Problem?' (1967) 3 British Journal of Law and Society 151 and Paterson and Nelken, 'The Evolution of Legal Services in Britain' (1984) 4 Windsor Yearbook of Access to Justice 98. The charitable model also prevailed in France, Italy, Germany, and the United States at the end of the nineteenth century, see Cappelletti and Gordley, 'Legal Aid' (1972) 24 Stanford Law Review 347 and Zemans *op. cit.*

interview offered by solicitors under the ALAS scheme and from 24-hour freephone advice lines to representing clients on a speculative basis.[4]

In the United States, though not in the United Kingdom, there has been a longstanding voluntary commitment to *'pro bono'* work by the really large firms.[5] In the past decade we have seen the emergence of a 'mandatory *pro bono'* movement in the USA.[6] With the decline in federal funding for legal aid it is increasingly being suggested that attorneys should undertake on a voluntary or a compulsory basis one or two cases a year or give up forty hours or so a year to assist in the provision of legal services to the poor. As yet no state has adopted this on a compulsory basis but ten or so smaller jurisdictions have, covering more than twelve thousand lawyers. For lawyers who are unwilling to undertake the obligation or whose specialisms are irrelevant to the poor there is provision for the contribution to take the form of a set financial donation to the programme.

Although the objections to such programmes can be overcome,[7] it must be doubted whether in the present climate mandatory *pro bono* will make the transition to the United Kingdom.[8] In particular solicitors are likely to argue that the fact that legal aid work pays at less than 70% of the private client fee rates,[9] is evidence of a substantial existing *pro bono* contribution. Certainly, the National Legal Aid Advisory Committee of Australia[10] used this argument (legal aid pays at 80% of private client rates

---

[4] See Law Society, *New Directions in Legal Aid Practices*, 1987; Baldwin and Hill, *The Operation of the Green Form Scheme in England and Wales*, 1988 and Genn, *Meeting Legal Needs*, 1982. In a recent survey by the English Law Society it emerged that a minority of practising solicitors (41%) claimed to carry out *pro bono* work. Perhaps ominously, they were mainly older, generalist solicitors. See Chambers and Harwood, *Solicitors in England and Wales: Practice, Organisation and Perceptions*. The Work of the Solicitor in Private Practice: First Report, 1990.

[5] The willingness of one or two London firms to sponsor law centres in recent times may signify the emergence of a similar commitment here. Cynics in North America have pointed out that public interest litigation apart, much of the work done free of charge for clients by American firms turns out to be for clients who could afford to pay in any event, or for charities, e.g. the local symphony orchestra or cancer trust with whom it is good to be associated in public relations terms. In today's competitive times such a verdict may be a little harsh. Why should not the 'new professionalism' encompass links between public service and public relations?

[6] Young, 'The Need for Legal Aid Reform' (1991) 24 Cornell International Law Journal 379; Helton, 'The Pro Bono tradition in the United States' (1991) 141 New Law Journal 69 18/1/91; Gilvarry, 'The Politics of Pro Bono' (1990) 87 (26) The Law Society's Gazette 11/7/90 at p. 6 and 1989 American Bar Association Journal October at p. 52.

[7] Luban, *Lawyers and Justice* Chapter 12 'Some Modest Proposals', 1988.

[8] Gilvarry, *op. cit.*

[9] Aspect, 'Civil Legal Aid Crisis' 1991 Journal of the Law Society of Scotland 1; Bawdon, 'Survey highlights gap in the legal aid/private pay' The Lawyer 15/5/90.

[10] NLAAC *Legal Aid for the Australian Community*, 1990, p. 92.

there) in concluding that it would be neither desirable nor practicable that *pro bono* work should play a significant part in any future strategy for supplying legal services to the poor in Australia. Moreover it is difficult to see how *pro bono* work would have other than a symbolic role to play in meeting the legal needs of the poor in the United Kingdom. The presence of the charitable model in a jurisdiction is unlikely to predispose litigants to choose to raise their actions there. It might however, predispose them not to do so.

B. The Legal Aid/Judicare Model

The second model of legal aid is usually referred to under its American title, the 'Judicare Model', in order to distinguish it from other legal aid models. Under this approach the state funds the private profession to provide legal services to individuals. This model exists in most of the leading industrial countries in the Western world. In some (for example the United Kingdom, the Netherlands, Germany, Norway, Sweden, most Canadian provinces, Australia, New Zealand, and Hong Kong) it is the dominant mode of providing legal services. In most western countries it took over from the first model in the second half of the twentieth century but in a few, for example Belgium, Italy, and Spain, the first model still prevails *de facto* if not also *de jure*.[11]

1. Primary Characteristics The primary characteristics of the judicare model owe much to the version of it which developed in the United Kingdom, where the model was first introduced on a large scale (in 1950). Its features include the fact that judicare is:

1. state-funded: providing access to justice is seen as a state obligation rather than a charitable duty of the profession;[12]
2. independent: responsibility for the administration and award of legal aid is placed in the hands of an independent body, board or court;

[11] It is noticeable that the industrialized countries where legal aid is least developed tend to be Catholic countries where until recently divorce has not been permitted. See Abel, 'Law Without Politics' (1985) 32 UCLA Law Review 474. Certainly, the catalyst for the introduction of the judicare model in the United Kingdom was the provision of state-subsidized legal representation for service personnel seeking divorces during World War II and Abel's data (p. 589) suggest that in most countries family matters represent the single largest category in legal aid programmes.

[12] Lawyers in the UK, and even more in the Netherlands, might well argue that the growing disparity between legal aid pay rates and private practice rates represents a substantial indirect contribution by the profession to the cost of legal services. In Ontario, however, a direct levy of £83 per lawyer brings in £2 million per annum for legal aid work. Smith, 'Canadian Approaches' 1991 Legal Action 8 (August).

3. demand-led: expenditure is open-ended although it is subject to constraints and monitoring before, during, and after the provision of the service;

4. broad in scope: much wider than under the charitable model. Nevertheless some restrictions on coverage exist in that certain types of action may be excluded, e.g. defamation, simplified divorces, and small claims. In the UK it is not available in tribunals and in most countries it is designed to support individual rather than collective actions;

5. subject to multiple eligibility criteria: including means- and merits-testing and an expectation that funding from other sources, e.g. a trade union, are not available to the applicant;

6. contributory: assisted persons are often required to contribute towards the cost of their cases, depending on their means.[13] Until the eligibility cuts in April 1993, only between 10% and 20% of assisted parties in the UK had an initial contribution.[14] One of the significant features in the United Kingdom model (as opposed to the position in many other European jurisdictions) is that the Legal Aid Fund is expected to bear the bulk of the risk of loss if assisted parties are unsuccessful in their actions. However, for successful assisted parties legal aid is a loan, not a grant, and should they be unable to recover the cost of their lawyer from the other side it will be deducted from their contributions and any winnings through the mechanism of the statutory charge;

7. provided by private practitioners: the overwhelming majority of legal aid and advice and assistance is provided by private practitioners. In Scotland there are only three law centres which operate legal aid and nearly a thousand private firms that do so. Nor is advice and assistance used by advice agencies. In England there are no figures available as to the amount of legal aid cases undertaken by the sixty or so law centres there, but the Legal Aid Board Annual Report for 1990/91 indicates that less than a third of 1% of net expenditure under the scheme went to law centres. Research also suggests that advice agencies and law centres account for less than 2% of advice and assistance work.[15] A similar picture pertains in the rest of Europe, although 15% of Dutch

---

[13] Such contributions are less common in criminal cases.

[14] See Legal Aid Annual Reports in the past decade. It appears that a significant proportion of those offered legal aid or advice and assistance with a sizeable contribution refuse to take up the offer.

[15] Baldwin and Hill *op. cit.* p. 56. The extent to which legal aid work in the UK is delegated to less qualified fee-earners or para-legals is unclear. Baldwin and Hill's research, *op. cit.*, p. 50 suggests that law centre solicitors delegate more readily than private firms but there appear to be few equivalents here to the American-style legal clinics staffed by para-legals.

expenditure on legal aid goes to the salaried lawyers in Buros. In New South Wales by contrast the corresponding figure is 42% and in Quebec it is a surprising 71%.[16]

8. open panel: hitherto assisted parties have had a very wide choice of lawyer to act for them in legal aid cases. This is a major advantage over the charitable model, in that assisted parties can be represented by some of the best and most experienced court lawyers in the jurisdiction.

Commentators have tended to see most of the features outlined above as strengths, stressing particularly the importance of state funding; independence; breadth of coverage; risk protection; and choice.[17] Nonetheless, viewed from the standpoint of the profession, consumers, and the Government there are also a number of weaknesses in the model.

(a) The profession's perspective. The principal complaints of the UK profession are that:

1. the coverage of the UK scheme is deficient, for example in not extending to tribunals or defamation actions, and that it is being reduced in small ways by recent and ongoing reforms;
2. bureaucratic hurdles are increasing, necessitating delays, abandonment, or the option of doing work for nothing;[18]
3. there is no payment mechanism which supplies the necessary working capital to support firms through cash-flow problems;[19]
4. the level of remuneration for legal aid work is inadequate. Legal aid rates (in the UK and the Netherlands) are now significantly below the private rates set by the profession and the court. This, however, does not prove that the rates are inadequate. The policy question is what profit margin should be built into legal aid rates.[20]

These drawbacks are said to be causing an increasing number of specialist or sizeable firms to give up doing legal aid, although there are no reliable figures on the issue.[21] Equally disturbing for the public is the

---

[16] Smith, 'Whither the Salaried Sector in England & Wales?' unpublished paper delivered at the ISA Working Group on the Comparative Study of Legal Professions conference at Aix en Provence in 1992.

[17] See Smith and Bailey, *The Modern English Legal System*, 1991 and Zander, 'Public Policy for Legal Services' in Blankenburg (ed.): *Innovation in Legal Services*, 1980.

[18] Baldwin and Hill *op. cit.* p. 53.

[19] In the Netherlands, by contrast, lawyers can receive lump-sum payments in advance (up to twice a year) which reflect the level of legal aid work undertaken by them in the previous year.

[20] Here much depends on whether legal aid is seen as a *pro bono* activity for the majority of the profession or a specialism to be pursued by a minority of firms.

argument that the workload of these firms is tending to devolve to junior and less experienced fee-earners in smaller practices, recreating one of the major weaknesses of the charitable model.[22]

(b) *The consumer's perspective.* A reduction in the quality of service or the availability of legal aid lawyers would be obvious drawbacks from the consumers' perspective. In fact it has already been established that access problems exist.[23] Thus it is clear that there are considerable shortages of practitioners in the UK who are experts in the fields of housing, welfare, consumer, immigration, employment, and child law. Moreover the figures suggest that individuals with problems in these areas are much more likely to consult advice or law centres than private practitioners offering legal aid in the shape of advice and assistance. Paradoxically, therefore, although the *per capita* expenditure on advice and assistance in the UK far outstrips that in Germany, the Netherlands, and Canada,[24] repeated Annual Reports of the Law Societies and the Legal Aid Boards in the UK (and a recent research study)[25] have confirmed that, contrary to original hopes, advice and assistance continues to be used primarily in the traditional areas of family and criminal work (about 65% of Scots cases and 75% of English cases).[26]

Apart from the eligibility criteria, the level of contributions and the statutory clawback—points which we will return to in the Eligibility Criteria section—the other principal concerns of consumers in relation to legal aid relate to its scope. The recommendations of both the Royal Commissions on Legal Services that legal aid should be extended to tribunal representation have been strongly reinforced by the Genn report[27] which graphically demonstrates the advantage secured by those who are represented at tribunals. A further deficiency that has been highlighted recently is the individualized nature of legal aid. As the Opren affair revealed, legal aid does not lend itself to collective actions, for example disaster cases, where many victims are suing the same defender in respect

---

[21] See The Law Society, *Survey of Legal Aid Provision*, 1988 and Holland, 'An Open Letter to the Lord Chancellor' (1990) 87(45) Law Society's Gazette at p. 2.

[22] Research currently being conducted at Warwick University on criminal legal aid appears to bear this argument out. See The Lawyer 1.7.92, p. 1.

[23] See Paterson, 'Evaluating Legal Needs' (1987) 127 SCOLAG 58 and National Consumer Council, *Ordinary Justice*, 1989.

[24] See Blankenburg, 'Comparing Legal Aid Schemes in Europe' (1992) 11 Civil Justice Quarterly 106.

[25] Baldwin and Hill *op. cit.*

[26] The same is true for legal aid. See Smith, 'Financing litigation for the public' unpublished paper delivered to the Hart Workshop, July 1992 at p. 3.

[27] Genn and Genn, *The Effectiveness of Representation at Tribunals*, 1989.

of the same alleged wrong.[28] Provision to deal with this problem was contained in the Legal Aid Act 1988 and in 1992 the Legal Aid Board introduced a system of contractual tendering for firms wishing to undertake multi-party actions funded through legal aid.[29]

(c) The state's perspective. Inevitably western governments are concerned at the increasing cost of providing legal aid through the private profession, particularly since the rise in costs seems often to be running ahead of both inflation and productivity in terms of numbers of cases handled.[30] As we shall see, different solutions to this problem have appealed to different governments. Some have tried the tactic of placing a greater proportion of the funds available into salaried lawyers for cost-efficiency reasons. Others have greatly eroded the fee rates for legal aid work, while others still have followed the UK model of reducing eligibility levels and focusing on improving efficiency and quality controls e.g. through the franchising experiment.[31]

One factor which has hampered rational planning by most western governments is that, despite the open-panel character of judicare, legal aid work is not evenly distributed throughout the profession. In the Netherlands up to a third of the advocates undertake significant amounts of legal aid work but in the UK less than 10% of the firms do 40% of all legal aid work (a third earn less than £5,000 per annum in legal aid fees). In Quebec, less than 20% of the private profession undertake any legal aid at all. Such fluctuations make it difficult to fix an appropriate level for legal aid remuneration (legal aid work done in small amounts is never likely to be cost-effective). On the other hand no researcher has yet demonstrated that doing legal aid work in volume leads to necessary economies of scale. A related problem is whether governments should be encouraging the concentration of legal aid providers. Many legal aid solicitors are already specializing and specialist panels of legal aid lawyers currently exist in England in the fields of mental health and child care law. However, specialist expertise has a tendency to encourage arguments for exclusivity or higher fees. Either development leads to a loss of access to justice.

A final area of concern to the UK Government is the inefficiency in

---

[28] See Levin, 'Opren: Litigation Lessons' 1988 Legal Action (February) p. 5 and NCC (1989) *op. cit.* p. 332.

[29] See Curle, 'Enabling multi-party actions' (1992) 89 (24) Law Society's Gazette at p. 17.

[30] See Cooper, 'A Legal Action Group (LAG), *A Strategy for Justice*, 1992.

[31] See *infra*. One of the major aims of the franchising project is to try to measure the quality of service provided by legal aid practitioners—a task that is not without difficulties. See Paterson, *Professional Competence in Legal Services*, 1990.

administrative terms of the differing rates of remuneration for various forms of legal aid work and indeed of a piecework-based payment scheme. The UK Government has been pursuing an acrimonious debate with the legal profession in England and Wales over the introduction of more block or standard fees. By contrast, in the Netherlands and Germany most payments are in the form of lump sums.

2. Variations on the main theme   As noted above, the judicare model exists in most western industrialized countries. In few are there significant variations on the United Kingdom version of the model, except that few share its scope. The Netherlands is a partial exception. Although legal aid is provided there by private practitioners, mostly in the same traditional areas of law as in the United Kingdom,[32] there is evidence (as we have seen) that a greater proportion of the profession depends significantly on legal aid than is the case in the United Kingdom. Curiously, the award of legal aid certificates is made by state-salaried lawyers working in legal aid offices (Buros) who, having provided initial advice, frequently then refer applicants (if they do not have a lawyer) to private lawyers on their lists on a rota basis. However, in recent times a lively debate has sprung up as to whether Buros should go further and provide representation, perhaps even in competition with the Order of Advocates.[33] Equally interesting is the fact that the Dutch Ministry of Justice provides the option to legal aid lawyers of remuneration in advance.[34] When the work is done, the lawyer sends the account to the Ministry, together with the certificate (from the Buro) and it is paid after deduction of any advance.[35]

Germany has a fairly traditional judicare model in civil matters although its provision for advice and assistance is modest compared with the Netherlands and the UK, despite the more rigorous monopoly on the giving of legal advice which prevails there.[36] The German system, however, is interesting in that legal aid is administered by the courts (whether

[32] See Blankenburg, *op. cit.*, p. 113.
[33] See Smith, 'Going Dutch' 1991 Legal Action May p. 10 and Goriely, 'Legal Aid in the Netherlands' (1992) 55 Modern Law Review 803.
[34] Legal aid practitioners can ask to be paid lump sums every six months based on their turnover of legal aid cases in the previous year, up to a fixed ceiling. Under the current Legal Aid Bill the advance payment system would become compulsory.
[35] See Cooper, *Public Legal Services*, 1983, Blankenburg and Cooper, 'A Survey of Legal Aid Literature in Europe' (1982) 2 Windsor Yearbook of Access to Justice 263 and Schuyt, 'The Rise of Lawyers in the Dutch Welfare State', in Abel and Lewis (eds.) *Lawyers in Society: The Civil Law World*, 1988.
[36] See Blankenburg, *op. cit.* p. 109.

for advice or representation).[37] One factor which might attract a foreign national to sue in Germany is that legal aid there is not restricted to natural persons. Thus legal corporations can be eligible provided neither the corporation nor the 'persons economically interested in it' can reasonably be expected to afford the legal fees.[38] However, legal aid will only be granted to foreign corporations in Germany if there is reciprocity—which would rule out UK companies.

One factor which has inhibited the development of legal aid in Germany is the long-standing penetration of legal expenses insurance there (at least 50% of households have some form of legal expenses insurance policy). Sweden, on the other hand, had until recently one of the most comprehensive legal aid programmes in the world. It provided up to one hour's worth of legal advice to all citizens irrespective of means. General legal aid is provided to individuals who in the eyes of the local legal aid board (consisting of a judge, lawyers, and lay persons) meet relatively generous means and merits tests. There are few areas of legal work which are excluded, the principal ones being the preparation of tax returns and the economic activities of business persons.[39] Interestingly, general legal aid can be provided by private or public lawyers who are in open competition with each other for such work. However, even in Sweden legal expenses insurance is widespread[40] —in part because their legal aid scheme (like most on the continent—including that in the Netherlands and Germany) does not protect assisted parties from paying the other side's expenses should they lose.

This deficiency, perhaps the biggest single difference between the UK model and judicare in other Western European countries, is one which must make any litigant from the UK who is eligible for legal aid cautious of litigating in Europe. Equally, it is a feature which may attract foreign, legally aidable clients with a choice of forums, to litigate in the UK.

[37] For legal advice applicants are required to provide details of their cases as well as their financial situations to a judicial administrator at the district court. If possible the officials will provide the relevant advice, otherwise they will issue a certificate which entitles applicants to ask for advice from any lawyer of their own choosing. Legal aid for representation is handled by the court with jurisdiction to hear the case. See Zemans (1983) *op. cit.*, p. 404, and Blankenburg and Schultz, 'German Advocates' in Abel and Lewis (eds.) (1988) *op. cit.* p. 124.

[38] Hirte, 'Access to the Courts for Indigent Persons', 40 (1991) International and Comparative Law Quarterly 91.

[39] See Olauson, 'Legal Expenses Insurance for Individuals in Sweden' in Pfennigstorf and Schwartz (eds.) *Legal Protection Insurance*, 1986.

[40] Up to 80% of Swedish households are thought to have a legal expenses insurance policy.

3. *Eligibility criteria*   Another factor which might influence potential litigants is the variations in eligibility for legal aid between different countries. The lack of up-to-date information in English makes it difficult to
produce an informed comparison between the financial eligibility tests of
western industrialized countries. Some countries, e.g. the United
Kingdom, the Netherlands, France, Germany, Sweden, and Australia use
detailed financial limits. Others, e.g. Austria, Spain, Italy, and Finland use
flexible criteria whereby those who cannot afford to go to law without
'hardship to the applicant or his family' are eligible for legal aid.[41] Often
there is little to choose between the two approaches. Nevertheless, it
would be wrong to say that in practical terms about the same proportion
of the population is eligible for judicare in most western countries. Even
from the limited information available, it is clear that some countries
(notably the Netherlands, Sweden, and the United Kingdom) established
their programmes to include not just the poor but also part of the middle
classes while others—in part because of the extensive penetration of legal
expenses insurance in Europe—focus primarily on the poor.[42] However,
rising costs have led the former countries to re-examine coverage and
there are signs that some are opting for a transfer of resources to salaried
lawyers (on cost-effectiveness grounds) while others, such as the United
Kingdom, have been cutting eligibility limits or failing to uprate them in
line with inflation.[43] In addition, applicants are increasingly being

[41] See e.g. Abel (1985) *op. cit.* p. 554, Office of Legal Aid Administration, *Who Gets Legal Aid*, Australian Government Publishing Service, 1987, Nousiainen, 'On Legal Expertise and Cost-Free Legal Aid in Finland', (1980) 8 International Journal of the Sociology of Law 165, Colomer, 'Legal Aid in Spain' (1986) 6 Windsor Yearbook of Access to Justice 268, and Lewis, 'Costs and Legal Aid in Europe' (1988) 85 Law Society's Gazette 29 June at p. 50.

[42] In the Netherlands 70% of the population is eligible for civil legal aid, in the UK the fig- ure is nearer to 50% but this is a higher proportion than in Canada or Australia and a much higher proportion than in Norway where only 10% of the population is eligible. See LAG, *A Strategy for Justice, op. cit.* and Johnsen, 'Developments in Legal Aid in Norway' unpublished paper delivered at the Aix conference on Legal Aid, June 1992.

[43] It seems clear that eligibility for legal aid on income grounds in the United Kingdom had fallen from 70% of the population in 1980 to below 50% in 1989. See NCC, (1988) *op. cit.* Glasser, 'Legal Aid Eligibility' (1988) 85 Law Society's Gazette 9 March at p. 11 and Murphy, 'Civil Legal Aid Eligibility 1989 Legal Action October p. 7. The Lord Chancellor's Department disagreed with these analyses but appeared to concede much of the argument by introducing a package of measures which they claimed would increase the proportion of the population who qualified for civil legal aid from 56% to 74%. Michael Murphy's research in 1992 suggested that the decline in eligibility is continuing. See LAG, *A Strategy for Justice op. cit.* Appendix. Murphy's research for the Law Society in 1993 asserted that the Lord Chancellor's eligibility cuts would affect 14 million people. The assertion provoked an out- raged denial from the Lord Chancellor's Department.

expected to make direct or indirect contributions (e.g. the statutory charge) towards the cost of the legal services they receive.[44]

As in the United Kingdom, it is normal for there to be a merits test in the judicare schemes in other jurisdictions. In some, as in the United Kingdom, the legal merit of the action test is separated from the 'reasonableness in the circumstances' requirement, in others the two requirements are integrated.

In the Netherlands legal aid is not granted 'if the application is wholly unfounded[45] or if the matter in question does not justify the cost of providing legal aid'. German judges have to assess whether, on the basis that everything said by the applicant is true, he/she would be entitled to judgment[46] and in Norway the applicant must demonstrate a 'reasonable probability for success'. In France the case must not be 'manifestly inadmissible or devoid of foundation', while Swedish applicants are deemed ineligible if they have no justifiable reason for pursuing a matter.[47] In most Australian states, however, the merit test is simply whether it is reasonable in the circumstances that the applicant should be granted legal aid, although this criterion is usually amplified with legislative guidelines, one of which is often the English 'reasonableness' yardstick of the 'hypothetical paying client' test.[48]

4. Reform: (a) Eligibility review.[49] Ostensibly this review was designed to look at the problem of the increasing proportion of the population in the UK who were ineligible for legal aid. In reality the review primarily addressed the Treasury problem of an uncapped budget which they considered to be spiralling out of control.[50] Not the least curious feature of

---

[44] This, of course, was the major element in the Lord Chancellor's 1993 cuts. Both Germany and the Netherlands now require a contribution from even the most needy clients seeking legal advice and assistance. In the former it is DM 20 (subject to remission by the lawyer), in the latter it is a minimum of 25 Guilders. Blankenburg, *op. cit.* and T. Goriely, *op. cit.*

[45] This is considerably more generous than the probable cause test.

[46] Sometimes described as 'having a good chance of being successful'. In essence the test seems akin to a Scottish plea to the relevancy. See Hirte *op. cit.* p. 113.

[47] Blankenburg and Cooper, (1982) *op. cit.* p. 287.

[48] See OLAA (1987) *op. cit.*

[49] The review commenced with two consultation papers. The first, published by the Lord Chancellor's Department in 1991 'Eligibility for Civil Legal Aid', was followed by a parallel paper from the Scottish Office Home and Health Department in July 1991 entitled 'Review of Financial Conditions for Legal Aid: Eligibility for Civil Legal Aid in Scotland'.

[50] As in the Netherlands and Germany in recent years, expenditure on legal aid in the UK has been running well ahead of inflation. See National Audit Office, *The Administration of Legal Aid in England and Wales*, HMSO, 1992.

the review was that in its initial phase it was not directed at either of the areas which involve the greatest expenditure by the Legal Aid Boards (criminal and matrimonial cases). Ironically, its focus on civil non-matrimonial cases targeted an area where legal aid is arguably at its most cost-effective. In brief the review proposed that contributions should be increased and made to last throughout a case while assessment of means should be made less expensive by adopting a more broad-brush, not to say a cruder, approach. In a purported attempt to tackle the problems of those outside the legal eligibility limits, it was suggested that a safety net should be introduced. Under this system the applicant would spend up to £2,500 of his or her own money (the spending limit) before becoming eligible for legal aid. While this proposal offered assistance to some better-off litigants, the paper hinted that the scheme might also be applied to poorer applicants currently eligible for legal aid but with a contribution (i.e. those above the free legal aid threshold). For them the safety net would be more akin to a tripwire.[51] The Government claimed that the proposal would encourage responsible litigation and settlements. In reality, however, there is no evidence of assisted parties behaving irresponsibly by pursuing their actions. Even those who fall below the free legal aid limit have an interest to be prudent in litigating because of the mechanism of the statutory charge. To suggest that the spending limit would encourage litigants to exercise greater control over their lawyers overlooks the fact that it is very difficult for lay clients to assess the quality of the work being done for them by their lawyer. A more straightforward solution would have been to raise the upper financial limit and increase contributions in line with this.

The near-universal hostility that the safety-net proposal attracted seemed initially to have reduced enthusiasm for its introduction in government circles. However, in April 1993 the Treasury, alarmed by the ever-increasing rise in legal aid expenditure, drove through a series of savage cuts in eligibility for civil legal aid and advice and assistance. In addition, the level of contributions required from assisted parties was greatly increased and extended. The safety-net proposal was not included in the package.

(b) *Value for money.* Whatever the merits of the eligibility review, it is clear that the UK, like many other jurisdictions with the most developed cover, is determined to improve the cost-effectiveness and quality of the

---

[51] The likely effect of the proposal would have been to transfer resources from a large number of relatively small actions to smaller numbers of large ones. See Smith, *Financing litigation for the public op. cit.*, p. 5.

service provided under legal aid. In these countries, e.g. the United Kingdom, Australia, Norway, and the Netherlands, very similar proposals are being considered, as follows:

1. Standard, fixed, or block fees. Germany[52] and the Netherlands already use these and they have been proposed in Norway.[53] In England and Wales proposals that they be used on a widespread basis have provoked mixed responses. The NCC[54] consider that this would be more efficient and more understandable for consumers. The Law Society and the solicitor's profession reacted with extreme hostility to the Lord Chancellor's suggestion that fixed fees be introduced for cases in the Magistrates' Courts, concluding that they would encourage shoddy work or delegation to less qualified practitioners.[55] In Australia most of the legal aid commissions have experimented with such fees in a minor way.[56] While they are thought to enhance the efficiency of legal aid programmes, no research has been conducted to test the argument.

2. Vouchers. This involves an eligible applicant for legal aid being supplied with a voucher providing legal aid which could be cashed in with either salaried or private practitioners. However, the private practitioner may treat the voucher as only representing part-payment for his or her services and request an additional contribution. The NLAAC[57] concluded by a majority that vouchers should not be introduced in Australia. While the private profession supported vouchers because they permit a choice of lawyer, the salaried sector was strongly opposed to them on accountability and practicability grounds. The NLAAC were persuaded that not only might vouchers lead to inequities, because for many applicants the degree of choice would prove illusory, but also that the market mechanism would not work as a check on quality and value for money. Certainly the suggestion that the choices of one-shot clients will provide effective quality controls on private practitioners seems more than a little far-fetched. The limited experiments with vouchers in the United States have proved similarly controversial and inconclusive.

---

[52] Luban, *op. cit.*, 275.
[53] Johnsen, *op. cit.* Instead of being paid on the present hourly basis, the 1991 proposal is that a standard fee of 6 hours should be paid for all cases between 2 and 6 hours. In criminal custody cases a standard fee of 3 hours is proposed, and for simplified trials, 5 hours.
[54] NCC (1989) *op. cit.*
[55] See e.g. Ely, 'Criminal Justice in Danger', 1992 Law Society's Gazette 19.2.92, p. 2.
[56] NLAAC 1990: 153.   [57] *Op. cit.*, 165.

3. Contracts. In Norway there have been several false starts in relation to legal aid reform in the past three years. However, one of the features which has been common to each of the proposed programmes has been the suggestion that there should be experiments in contracting out aspects of legal aid work to private lawyers. These contracts would be aimed at lawyers who want to specialize in a certain field of legal aid work or are willing to handle a substantial amount of legal aid work as part of their practice. Contract lawyers would have a wide discretion to self-certify eligibility for legal aid. In general such contracts would only be offered to lawyers operating or willing to set up in areas where access to private practitioners is problematic. Establishment support for practices being set up in areas of scarcity might be made available in the form of a loan repayable from legal aid work.[58]

Contracting out legal aid work to private practitioners and to salaried offices (Buros) is a proposal which was under active consideration in the Netherlands over the last three years. Originally it was proposed that contracts would offer the opportunity of specializing in legal aid work whilst improving quality and reducing costs. The contracts might vary, e.g. sometimes covering all legal aid work in a community, sometimes for a set number of clients, sometimes for units of work with price discounts for volume, or sometimes for particular types of legal work. The proposals contained disquieting features for the profession, e.g. the suggestion that firms should do 10% of their cases without payment or that they should have to pass on clients to other firms if their quota had been fulfilled. In the event, the resistance of the profession to these proposals has been such that the Ministry of Justice has more or less decided to abandon proposals along these lines. Contracting out legal aid work has actually been tried in parts of Australia—mainly in relation to duty lawyer schemes—with some success, although some have objected that they reduce the clients' ability to select the lawyer of their choice.

The United States has the most experience with contracting out legal work to the private profession. In the main, the contracts have related to indigent criminal work.[59] Despite the substantial body of research findings indicating the serious quality deficiencies of contracting out in

[58] Letter dated 22.2.91 from Professor Johnsen at Oslo University to the author and Johnsen, 'Developments in Legal Aid in Norway' *op. cit.*

[59] Nelson, 'Quality Control for Indigent Defense Contracts' (1988) 76 California Law Review 1147.

the criminal sphere,[60] the Legal Services Corporation decided in the late 1980s that the contract system should be introduced in the civil sphere also, with the work going to the lowest bidder. The research on the pilot projects designed to bring this about has proved to be highly controversial with most commentators concluding that contracting out is proving as problematic in the civil sphere as it has been in the criminal.[61]

The Legal Aid Act 1988 contains provision for contracting out legal aid work in England and Wales. The Legal Aid Board's first foray in this area was an attempt (in 1990) to contract out the duty solicitor work in St Albans, Welwyn Garden City, and Hatfield, but this eventually came to nothing and the proposal has not been repeated. The Board next considered them in relation to the advice and assistance scheme. However, after consultation they came out against contracts in this area because while potentially offering quality control, cheapness, and administrative simplicity they would reduce consumer choice, cause problems in conflict of interest situations, and create major access difficulties in poor urban or rural areas. Nevertheless, a number of these contractual elements have re-emerged in the Board's plans for franchising and also in their new provisions for tendering to undertake legal aid work in multi-party 'disaster' litigation.[62] More ominously, the Lord Chancellor has indicated his desire that franchises should in future be awarded after compulsory competitive tendering.

4. Franchising. Amongst the most advanced plans for ensuring value for money from legal aid suppliers is the English Legal Aid Board's 'supplier development' strategy which has evolved from the franchising project. The project was confined to firms and advice agencies in parts of Birmingham who were prepared to implement certain quality systems. In return for putting these systems in place and operating them, franchise firms receive certain advantages from the Legal Aid Board. Originally it was proposed that all decisions on advice and assistance, ABWOR, and emergency applications would be delegated to the franchisees, and that in addition firms would receive monthly payments in advance representing a twelfth of the firm's earnings from all types of legal aid over the past twelve months. After last-minute negotiations with the Law Society it was agreed that the firms would get four new

---

[60] See e.g. McConville and Mirsky, 'Criminal Defense of the Poor in New York City' (1987) XV Review of Law and Social Change 581 and the studies cited therein.
[61] Weikel, 'Cold Water on Free Enterprise' California Lawyer 9.11.89, p. 33.
[62] See Curle, *op. cit.*

early-payment systems: up to £250 on account for each self-granted emergency certificate, up to £150 on account of each self-certified ABWOR case, the right to be paid at least two hours' worth of costs each time an advice and assistance extension is granted in-house, and 75% on account of costs incurred once a civil legal aid certificate has run for nine months.[63]

The concept of franchising was chosen in preference to tendering or contracting-out since it offered more access to the public with a better guarantee of quality. Originally the Board wanted to pursue economies of scale and suggested that franchise firms should have a turnover of £40,000 a year in legal aid fees and employ supervisors who would not be permitted to supervise more than three categories of work or seven people doing that work. After extensive discussions with the profession and the consumer bodies these requirements were dropped for the purposes of the experiment. However, it is probable that both the Board and the Lord Chancellor's Department presently envisage that the supplier development strategy which is emerging from the franchising experiment will hinge around firms prepared to specialize in and to undertake substantial amounts of legal aid work ('preferred suppliers'). If this line is pursued, possibly in the direction of exclusivity, as the Lord Chancellor has hinted, it may produce considerable problems of access, particularly in the rural areas.

Largely for these reasons the Scottish Legal Aid Board is less convinced as to the merits of franchising than their southern counterparts. It may be therefore that the current proposals of the Ministry of Justice in the Netherlands[64] on this issue will prove more attractive. These include the registration of legal aid practitioners. Registration would be subject to a number of conditions:

— a minimum (about 10) and a maximum number of cases that a lawyer can accept during one year;
— specialization, restricting registration to a limited number of legal areas;
— good office procedures with adequate back-up cover;
— annual reports to the legal aid authorities.

Exceptionally, where there is good reason clients will be permitted to instruct private practitioners who are not registered. Registration will

---

[63] Since Scottish firms already receive some of the advantages provided to franchise firms, if franchising is to be implemented there additional benefits will have to be offered to firms to encourage them to participate in the scheme.

[64] Information derived from correspondence with the Netherlands Ministry of Justice.

be refused if the conditions cannot be met, if the lawyer is over 70, or if the lawyer works much less efficiently than other members of the profession (judged by a series of performance indicators).

C. The salaried model

There are relatively few jurisdictions in the western world (the United States of America and Quebec being the most prominent) in which the third or 'salaried' model of legal aid provision predominates. Nevertheless the model is to be found in a number of other western countries (including the United Kingdom, the Netherlands, Canada, Australia, New Zealand, Sweden, and Finland). The essential difference from the judicare model is that the services are provided by publicly salaried lawyers. The latter are usually restricted in the range of services which they can provide. Thus the staff of the Buros in the Netherlands are generally restricted to providing initial advice to clients before referring them to advocates in private practice. In Australia and the United Kingdom the limits are enshrined in formal agreements, elsewhere the programmes' own priorities ensure that rarely (except in Sweden) are they in competition with the private profession. In the United States of America the Legal Services Corporation salaried programmes are also banned from taking cases to do with school desegregation, abortion, or engaging in political activities such as picketing, striking, lobbying, or working for political campaigns.[65]

D. The mixed model

Even though the experts are divided over the relative cost-effectiveness of the judicare and salaried models of legal aid,[66] there is a remarkable measure of agreement between them that the ideal way forward for western countries is a model that involves a mixture of judicare and salaried elements.[67] In that most of the jurisdictions with salaried programmes also have judicare programmes, it might seem that the mixed model exists widely throughout the world. However, in most countries the two types of programme have developed independently in an *ad hoc* fashion. Genuinely planned and integrated examples of the mixed model, combining the best features of both models with respect to specialist expertise, work styles, client appeal, etc., are few and far between.

[65] See Menkel-Meadow, 'Legal Aid in the United States' (1984) 22 Osgoode Hall Law Journal 29.

[66] Legal Services Corporation (1980) *op. cit.*, Abel (1985) *op. cit.*, NLAAC (1990) *op. cit.*

[67] See Legal Services Corporation (1980) *op. cit.*, Schuyt (1980) *op. cit.*, Zemans (1983) *op. cit.*, Abel (1985) *op. cit.*

In Sweden, Quebec, and the Netherlands the theoretical integration of the two models (the salaried offices assess all legal aid applications and allocate cases to private practitioners) has not worked in practice, partly because they are to an extent in competition with each other. This in turn leads to overlaps in coverage and the costly duplication of expertise. Instead, it is in the United Kingdom, Australia, and Ontario that a division of labour has sprung up which emphasizes the complementary nature of the two models—particularly where the strategic version of the salaried model is in evidence. But even in these jurisdictions developments have been largely unplanned.[68]

Alternatives to Legal Aid

Given the ever-increasing cost of resorting to law, spiralling legal aid bills, and government attempts to curb or rationalize legal aid expenditure, it is hardly surprising to learn that there is increasing interest in alternative methods of funding litigation. One of the most enduring of these is the contingent fee.

A. Contingent fees

Contingent fees are a mechanism which transfers a share in the risks of litigation from the litigant to the lawyer in exchange for an enhanced reward. Typically they involve contracts for the provision of legal services in which the amount of the lawyer's fee is contingent in whole or in part upon the successful outcome of the case, either through settlement or litigation. Usually the lawyers are rewarded with higher fees than they would normally receive if they win, in return for the risk of forgoing a fee if the case is lost. The availability of such fees can help to protect claimants from financial ruin. As such, their existence in a jurisdiction might encourage foreign litigants to raise their actions in the jurisdiction.[69]

Prohibitions on contingent fees are common throughout the world, though there are partial exceptions in Denmark, Japan, the Netherlands, and Spain. Contingent fees are generally permitted in Canada but most

---

[68] An interesting example of a planned mixed model can be seen in some of the better organized and funded public defender programmes introduced in the United States in the last decade. In such programmes salaried and judicare components integrate satisfactorily with work contracted out to private practitioners in the rural areas or in conflict of interest situations. This approach appears to have commended itself to the Australian Government in a recent discussion paper on legal aid, namely, NLAAC, *Funding, Providing and Supplying Legal Aid Services*, Australian Government Publishing Service, 1989.

widely used in the United States. In Scotland, contingent fees are prohibited at common law, though speculative fees (where the legal representatives act for their normal fee if they win and nothing should the case be lost) are acceptable[70] even with an uplift.[71] Similarly, in England and Wales the common law prohibition has been partially repealed by the Courts and Legal Services Act 1990 which permits the use of conditional fees.[72]

In the United States of America, contingent fees are used most frequently in personal injury actions, but are not confined to such cases. In certain areas of law, however, the courts and ethical codes prohibit the use of contingent fees on public policy grounds. These are criminal cases, family cases, and in some states legislative lobbying. Contingent fees may be calculated as a percentage rate, as a fixed fee, or on an hourly basis. In practice, percentage rates are the most common: a typical contingent fee agreement in the United States of America may provide that the lawyer's reward will be 25% of any settlement prior to a writ being issued, a third of any settlement or award made after the writ is issued, and 40% or more if either side appeals. For this, the expenses of the case are usually advanced by the lawyer.

The merits of introducing contingent fees have been keenly debated in the UK on several occasions in the last decade and another inquiry was set up by the Law Society in August 1992.[73] Proponents of contingent fees argue that they permit poor clients to bring their cases to court by transferring the risk of loss wholly or partly to the lawyer. Contingent fees can thus be viewed as 'productivity bonuses' or as an unusual form of venture capitalism.

On the other hand, contingent fees are frequently blamed for excessive awards and unnecessary litigiousness. Neither accusation has been conclusively proved.[74]A more telling argument against contingent fees is that they create conflicts of interest between the lawyer and the client

[69] This is undoubtedly a factor behind the attempts of pursuers in mass disaster cases to bring their actions in the USA. There, the availability of contingent fees and the absence of a 'costs with the event rule' combined with the possibility of high damages awards makes litigation a more palatable prospect than in many other jurisdictions.

[70] Paterson and Bates, *The Legal System of Scotland*, 1986.

[71] S. 36 of the Law Reform (Miscellaneous Provisions) (Scotland) Act 1990 provides that solicitors and advocates can not only charge speculative fees but a percentage increase in the fee to a limit laid down by the court. This measure is designed to compensate lawyers for cases in which no recovery is made.

[72] S. 58 provides for the creation of conditional fees which will involve a percentage uplift on the normal fee if the suit is successful and nothing if the case is lost.

[73] 'Funding Justice and Reducing Delay' (1992) 142 New Law Journal, 1114.

(although most fee systems are open to the same critique). Finally it is alleged that not only do contingent fees lead to excessive fees, since lawyers have superior knowledge of the risks and costs involved, but that they also encourage lawyers to adopt unethical tactics.[75]

In fact, the evidence suggests that the arguments against contingent fees are not insurmountable provided certain safeguards are introduced, such as statutory limits to the percentage fee that can be recovered and how this may be calculated. Despite this, the existence of the 'costs with the event rule' on this side of the Atlantic reduces the attractiveness of such fees to potential litigants since they will still have to pay the other side's costs should they lose. Nevertheless contingent fees do not require start-up costs and are not prone to adverse selection, and if money cannot be found for a Contingent Legal Aid Fund (see below) there is an argument for introducing contingent fees in Europe, with appropriate safeguards, on an experimental basis.

B. Contingent legal aid fund

The fact that contingent fees may be worth experimenting with under certain conditions does not make them necessarily the best alternative to legal aid. There are better contenders for that accolade. One is the Contingent Legal Aid Fund. In 1966 (and again in 1978 and 1992) Justice put forward a proposal, which has since attracted considerable support, that a Contingency Legal Aid Fund (CLAF) be set up to underwrite the litigation costs of persons who fall out with the ambit of the legal aid schemes. This proposal was floated by the Lord Chancellor's Department and the Scottish Office Home and Health in their consultation papers on eligibility for civil legal aid.[76] The CLAF would initially be funded from a government grant, but subsequently from a proportion of the winnings of claimants whose cases had been supported by CLAF. Where claimants were unsuccessful, their costs and those of their opponents would be met by the Fund. The administrative costs of the Fund would be met from a non-returnable registration fee. This scheme, it is argued, would overcome the main disadvantages of contingent fees without losing many of their advantages. (Because the claimants' lawyers would be paid a normal fee, win or lose, there would be no conflict of interest and no possibility of excessive fees.)

[74] See Paterson, 'Contingent Fees and their Rivals', 1989 Scots Law Times (News) 81.

[75] Carey Miller, 'A Case for Considering the Contingent Fee' 1987 Journal of the Law Society of Scotland 461.

[76] *Op. cit.*

Successful claimants would also pay less than under a normal contingent fee arrangement (20% was Justice's suggested figure, but the LCD suggested that 25–30% of a damages award would be needed for the Fund to be self-financing). While claimants would not be subject to a means test (though large corporations would be excluded) they would have to show (as in legal aid cases) that their claims had a reasonable prospect of success. Justice thought that the scheme should not be available to defendants nor apply where a reasonable sum of money was not at issue (the figure proposed was £500) since otherwise the returns to the Fund would be inadequate. However, the LCD considered that a combination of high non-returnable fixed fees and subsidization from reparation actions would enable the CLAF to be used even where damages were not in issue. The attraction of such a scheme to governments is that it is, in effect, an insurance which spreads the risk of loss to other litigants rather than the legal aid fund. The attraction to clients would be that it would cover areas, as well as people, presently excluded from legal aid.

To date only one jurisdiction has any substantial experience of a CLAF—Hong Kong. In 1984 Hong Kong introduced such a scheme as an adjunct to their legal aid scheme for those whose means were just outside the legal aid limits but who were nonetheless unable to afford the services of private practitioners. The Supplementary Legal Aid Scheme (SLAS) is restricted to substantial (over $60,000) claims for death or personal injury. The scheme is administered by the Legal Aid Department; the usual merits test is applied and a more generous means test. Instead of legal aid contributions the applicants are required to pay fees of $1000 (about £80) which are returnable if they are successful. They must also agree to a deduction of between 10% and 12% of any damages recovered (though the deductions can be reduced by up to 50% if the claim is settled at an early stage). Up to November 1990 there had been 297 successful applications to the scheme, representing 67% of all decided applications. It was three or four years before income under the scheme consistently exceeded expenditure. In Hong Kong the start-up costs were met by an interest-free loan of up to $1,000,000 from the State Lotteries Fund. This has now been repaid.

Similar proposals in Western Australia (also backed by the Lotteries Commission) led to the setting up of a 'Litigation Assistance Fund' in 1991. New South Wales and South Australia are also considering such funds. The English Law Society is optimistic that taking advantage of the lessons to be learned from the Hong Kong experience it will be possible for a CLAF to become self-financing in a shorter period in the United

Kingdom. One way to achieve this would be to make speedier cases eligible. The National Consumer Council is also supportive of such a development, especially in class actions or test cases.

Nevertheless, the critics remain unconvinced. Carey Miller argues that a CLAF scheme involves unnecessary bureaucratic controls and administrative costs. The Benson Commission, in a critique subsequently endorsed by the Legal Action Group, argued that a CLAF scheme would be inequitable because poor successful claimants might be subsidizing unsuccessful individuals or even companies. Furthermore, those who have suffered most in personal injury cases, and therefore have the largest claims, would have to pay the most, despite the fact that such claimants tend to be undercompensated as it is. The critics have also claimed that a CLAF would be vulnerable to adverse selection. Thus the success of the scheme would depend on a reasonable take-up. Yet claimants with good chances of success, it is said, would be reluctant to take part in the scheme and those who would be attracted to the scheme would have the weaker cases. Since litigants are rarely so claims-conscious as to know the strength of their own cases, and risk-averse claimants would be attracted by the immunity from paying costs offered by a CLAF,[77] it is likely that this argument is overstated. Nevertheless, as we have seen, most personal injury pursuers/plaintiffs obtain an award of some sort, and solicitors frequently advise clients with strong cases to bypass legal aid in order to avoid delays. If CLAFs are to be set up in different parts of the world, lawyers will be torn between advising clients with strong cases to proceed without cover from the CLAF or legal aid on one hand and suggesting that they apply to the CLAF because they know that the success of the scheme depends on a reasonable take-up by claimants.

C. Legal Expenses Insurance

In many parts of the world the best established alternative to legal aid is legal expenses insurance (LEI). For subscribers who pay an annual premium or membership fee, LEI provides protection by meeting the costs of legal advice or representation during the year. It takes two main forms: group legal services and individual policies. While the former are particularly prevalent in the USA and the UK[78] the latter are more prevalent on the continent of Europe.

[77] The Eligibility Review highlights this point, repeatedly stressing that such a scheme would make litigation almost entirely risk-free. In their eyes this is undesirable because it might encourage reckless litigation and an unwillingness to settle. In reality litigation is already a lottery with many unpleasant side-effects, without the need to insist that the risk of ruin should be retained in the interests of prudent litigation.

[78] Blodgett, 'Prepaid Plans' August 1987, American Bar Association Journal 40.

1. *Group Legal Services:* (a) *The general picture.* Group legal services provide routine and non-routine legal services at reduced or subsidized rates to group members. The exponential growth of such schemes in the US since the 1970s is partly attributable to tax concessions which make them attractive fringe benefits to employees, partly to their appeal to certain sectors of the profession, because they provide a constant supply of legal work, and partly because they are seen as an adjunct of the legal services movement there. Group plans in the US have frequently been aimed at poorer clients who are ineligible for legal aid. As such they provide not only easy access to specialist lawyers but also education on legal matters.

The services offered under these schemes vary quite considerably, but the majority place a stress on preventive law. Consultations to cover routine legal services are comparatively inexpensive and efficient uses of legal expertise, and as such are strongly favoured by the schemes. Representation in court on the other hand, is highly expensive and accordingly less freely available. Typically, the group member and his or her family will be entitled to a stipulated number of hours of advice or representation work from a lawyer, either free or at a reduced rate. Claims which are considered by the lawyer to be frivolous, spiteful, or very unlikely to be successful will usually be excluded.

The schemes may be 'open', 'closed', or somewhere in between. 'Open' schemes are those where the member may select any lawyer they choose to provide the legal services offered in the scheme. 'Closed' schemes are those where the claimant is given little or no choice in the selection of the lawyer who will provide the services. Most group schemes are closed because by insisting that the legal services be provided by staff lawyers or by a restricted panel of private lawyers, the scheme organizers can take advantage of economies of scale enabling greater specialization and expertise to be built up among the lawyers and improved research facilities and machinery to be provided, while at the same time enabling fees to be kept down and the quality of the work monitored. On the other hand, closed schemes largely remove clients' freedom to choose their own lawyers and are liable to provoke accusations of unfair attraction of business from lawyers excluded from the schemes. Nor are they of assistance where the client's dispute is against the organizers of the scheme.

Group plans can also be divided between those in which the insurance is automatically conferred on all members of the group and those where only the group members who voluntarily enrol for the scheme are covered. Not surprisingly, schemes of the former variety have proved more cost-effective in the US than the latter. This is because voluntary enrolment plans have higher marketing costs and present a greater risk of adverse selection.

(b) The UK experience. In the United Kingdom group legal services are also a well established, although little discussed, phenomenon. Principally it is trade unions who have developed such schemes on a large scale. Trade unions view legal services for their members as an important service and (as in Italy) it is one of the strong 'selling' points of union membership. Unlike legal aid, the pursuer has no contribution to pay and if the case is lost the union pays all the expenses.

Indeed, there is some evidence that, in an attempt to boost the attractions of union membership, certain unions apply only a minimal-merits test and will fund litigation which would have very little chance of success in court and which would be refused legal aid for lack of *probabilis causa*. It is clear that a considerable proportion of personal injuries cases in the United Kingdom is funded by trade unions, and the structure of the legal aid schemes contributes to this, for applicants can be refused legal aid if they have access to other facilities or sources of financial assistance. The most common alternative sources of such assistance are trade unions. Although most group schemes in the United Kingdom are closed, both the Law Societies have declared that such schemes do not involve any unfair attraction of business and have granted them waivers of the practice rules against arrangements. However, clients who resent the curtailment of their freedom of choice of lawyer under such schemes have to convince the legal aid authorities that their objection is a reasonable one if they wish to avail themselves of the greater freedom of choice afforded by our legal aid schemes.

Unlike the USA, most group schemes in the UK (and in other parts of Europe)[79] restrict the legal services offered to areas relevant to the activities of the group, and the emphasis is put on meeting the clients' non-routine and more serious legal needs, for example for representation in court. Nevertheless, a few schemes are now offering a 24-hour telephone advice line to group members on any point of law. In 1990 the Law Society and the TUC launched a new scheme entitled UNIONLAW which encourages union members to consult solicitors on non-work related matters. Participating solicitors provide a free diagnostic interview on any legal problem, a written estimate of further costs, and a fixed price for a conveyance or will.

The value of group legal services in civil cases with an international dimension is limited in two ways. First by the narrow scope of most schemes, and secondly because it is unusual for them to provide funding for litigation in foreign countries. Occasionally access to a group legal service may be purchased with an eye to the cost of potential litigation abroad, e.g. joining the AA before going on a foreign holiday. Even here, however, the group legal service is usually being topped up by an individual policy of limited duration.[80]

2. Individual policies: (a) The European picture. Legal Expenses Insurance policies for individuals first appeared in mainland Europe in the 1920s but their significance in the legal services market dates from the 1960s. It is the dominant form of LEI in Europe (although in Sweden and in Italy trade unions are important providers of legal aid). It is estimated that at least 50% of all households in Germany have some kind of LEI[81] and 80% in Sweden, though the figure is lower in other European countries. Predictably, the available evidence suggests that higher-income individuals are disproportionately likely to take out LEI.[82] In contrast to the evolution of group legal services in the USA, individual LEI in Europe has developed along commercial lines. Its aim, like other forms of insurance, is to spread the risk of loss consequent on the happening of an uncertain event. As a result the typical coverage of individual policies in Europe is restricted in a variety of ways—not least in excluding many of the routine legal expenses which are the primary focus of group legal services. Thus in Germany the drafting of wills and other documents, negotiations, representation in divorce, and succession actions are usually excluded. Similar exceptions exist in Sweden.[83] In fact, in most European countries the coverage of individual policies is closely aligned to more general areas of insurance. There is, however, little evidence available as to types of claims experienced by LEI companies. One of the few studies in this area was conducted in Germany[84] and found that 39% of claims concerned traffic violations, another 30% other car-related matters, and 31% other areas (principally consumer, labour law, and landlord and tenant cases).

(b) The United Kingdom. In the United Kingdom individual LEI policies, whether free-standing or 'add-ons' to car or home contents insurance policies, have only been available since 1974. Most policies provide free legal advice by telephone, a free choice of lawyer and, most important in

[79] See Pfennigstorf and Schwartz (eds.) *Legal Protection Insurance*, 1986.
[80] On Group Legal Services generally see Paterson and Bates, *op. cit.* and National Consumer Council, Ordinary Justice, 1989.
[81] Pfennigstorf and Schwartz, *op. cit.*, p. 40.
[82] Blankenburg, 'Legal Insurance, Litigant decisions, and the rising caseloads of Courts: A West German Study' (1982) 16 Law and Society Review 601.
[83] Olauson, *op. cit.*, p. 30.
[84] Blankenburg, 1982, *op. cit.*

this context, they usually offer Europe-wide coverage. For individuals or firms ineligible for legal aid LEI clearly has much to offer, but there are a number of drawbacks. The policies tend to be expensive for the cover offered[85] and the cover offered is limited—most have a financial ceiling on cover and exclude matrimonial disputes, defamation, tax matters, building disputes, and defence of criminal prosecutions involving violence. However, the importance of LEI as a factor for UK-based litigants deciding to litigate abroad is most severely limited by its very restricted penetration of the market. Most people in the UK simply do not have an LEI policy. (A recent survey by the Consumers' Association and the Law Society[86] suggested that only 7% of respondents had any form of LEI). Moreover, its relatively low penetration makes it at risk of 'adverse selection', particularly in the case of stand-alone policies, thus undermining the viability of the market. For these reasons even the Eligibility Review[87] felt unable to recommend it as a replacement for legal aid in the UK—at least for the time being.

Conclusions

(1.) At a time when the welfare state is under pressure throughout Europe spending curbs on legal aid may well become the order of the day. Certainly, the pursuit of value for money and quality assurance in publicly funded legal services is likely to become more commonplace. Whichever route is taken, the English 'preferred supplier' strategy or the Dutch 'registered practitioner' approach, the emphasis on accreditation will be beneficial to international litigators since it will enable them to identify legal aid specialists more easily from abroad. It may, however, entail problems of access in rural jurisdictions and the erosion of the 'free choice of lawyer' principle reiterated as recently as the LEI Directive on Legal Expenses Insurance (87/344). These potential problems reinforce the case for a planned mixed model for the delivery of legal services.

(2.) While the policy of relying on the legal aid system of the chosen jurisdiction rather than one's own to pay the costs of foreign litigation is probably a sound one, it does have certain drawbacks. There is a need for better information systems concerning the scope and availability of legal aid in different countries. Moreover the variations in the scope of legal aid

---

[85] NCC, *op. cit.* (1989).

[86] *Legal Expenses Insurance in the UK*, Consumer's Association/The Law Society, 1991.

[87] *Op. cit.* See also McLeod, 'Cover for cuts' (1993) 90(9) The Law Society's Gazette 3 Mar. 1993 at p. 8.

between countries makes it very difficult for rational actors to select a legal expenses insurance policy to cover the gaps. Equally, greater predictability of legal costs (as in Germany) would help rational planning both by potential insureds and by insurers endeavouring to set a realistic premium for worldwide cover.

(3.) Contingent and speculative fees—possibly even a Contingent Legal Aid Fund—properly regulated could have a residual role to play for those ineligible for legal aid or insufficiently prescient to foresee that they are likely to be involved in international litigation. However, unless CLAFs become more widespread there will still be the problem of paying for the other side's legal costs.

(4.) It should be reiterated that any discussion of the comparative financing of civil legal actions must be viewed in the larger context of the differing remedies and juridical procedures (including fact-finding procedures) available in different countries. For example, an examination of legal aid coverage in Sweden should bear in mind that in that country (1) legal expenses insurance is compulsory for certain matters; (2) trade unions provide a significant measure of cover through group legal services; (3) consumer disputes are usually handled by special tribunals without the benefit of lawyers; (4) courts handle claims for small sums with a simplified procedure, again without legal representation being thought necessary; and (5) administrative disputes are often handled by ombudsmen.[88] It follows that a further complication for the rational litigator of the future will be the success of differing governments in simplifying procedures or in their pursuit of Alternative Dispute Resolution.

[88] See Olauson, *op. cit.*

13. The Current Position

LEGAL ACTION GROUP

Current debate about publicity funded legal services has been dominated both by the Government's concern over the cost of legal aid and by the legal profession's anxiety regarding its level of remuneration. Important as these are, a proper discussion about the future of these services demands an appraisal of several other significant issues too. This chapter offers LAG's analysis of the state of legal aid and of publicly funded legal services generally as they stood in the spring of 1992.

Rising Costs

The cost of legal aid needs consideration. Lord Mackay, Lord Chancellor since 1987, complained in October 1991 to an audience of legal aid practitioners that, 'over the past ten years, the net costs of the legal aid scheme have increased each year by an average of 17 per cent and the cost of each act of assistance (excluding the duty solicitor schemes) by 11 per cent. In the same period, inflation increased by an average 7 per cent each year and the gross domestic product by 9 per cent each year. One does not have to be a mathematician to recognise that such a high increase each year in the proportion of the national wealth spent on legal aid cannot continue indefinitely.[1]

Legal aid costs are rising sharply, both overall and per case. The Lord Chancellor's Department must have been taken to task by Treasury ministers for expenditure which has jumped from £685 million in 1990/91 to an estimated outturn of £907 million for 1991/92 (excluding administration costs), particularly when the public estimate of expenditure for the latter was set at only £698 million as late as February 1991.[2]

---

[1] Speech, 4 Oct. 1991.
[2] *The Government's Expenditure Plans 1991–92 to 1993–94: The Lord Chancellor's and Law Officers' Departments* Cm 1510, HMSO, 1991, p. 1.

Figures for the net cost of legal aid (i.e. excluding contributions from clients and costs in 1991/92 were:[3]

	£m
Criminal	
Higher courts	186
Magistrates' courts	210
Police station advice	54
Court duty solicitors	8
Civil	
Non-matrimonial	161
Matrimonial	115
Interim payments	52
ABWOR	22
Criminal and civil	
Legal advice	95
Administration	
Legal Aid Board	41
Total	944

The combined cost of all forms of criminal legal aid and advice was £472 million, representing 52 per cent of total net expenditure.

A detailed breakdown of bills paid for 1991/92 in respect of all legal aid administered by the Legal Aid Board (i.e. excluding legal aid in the higher criminal courts) shows the distribution of work within the different schemes.

	Numbers of bills paid
Criminal: magistrates' courts	477,000
Criminal, police station advice	549,000
Criminal: duty solicitors (courts)	233,000
Civil: non-matrimonial	127,000
Civil: matrimonial/family	129,000
Civil: interim payments	230,000
Green form	1,230,000
ABWOR	66,000

The 1991/92 figures above represent a 36 per cent increase in bills paid for civil legal aid since 1987/88, an 8 per cent increase in ABWOR bills, a

[3] Legal Aid Board *Annual Report 1991–92* HC 50, HMSO, 1992, from which all figures in this chapter for 1991/92 are taken unless otherwise indicated. Crown Court figures from *HC Answers* 1 July 1992, col. 575.

14 per cent increase in green form bills, and a 17 per cent increase in magistrates' court criminal legal aid. These figures are affected by factors such as the Legal Aid Board's efficiency in processing bills. However, there is no doubt that more people are using legal aid.

The Legal Aid Board is less concerned with the growth in expenditure resulting from increasing numbers of cases than with rises in the cost per case. It considers the latter in its latest annual report, which contains figures for the changing lengths of time spent on the different constituent parts of a criminal legal aid case, as recorded by solicitors in submitting their bills. These figures are more useful than the more generally used figure of percentage increases in cost, which is affected by such matters as changes in the rate of VAT. The table below, taken from a study by the Board, shows the increase in the average time spent on criminal legal aid cases:

	1988 (hours)	1991 (hours)	% increase
Attendance	2.04	2.45	20
Preparation	1.28	1.86	44
Travel to hearing	1.30	1.42	9
	(numbers)	(numbers)	
Letters	7.3	8.9	22
Telephone calls	7.2	8.0	11

One cynical explanation of these figures is that solicitors may be extending the time that cases take in order to maximize their return and compensate for what they see as low annual inflation increases in their hourly rates. There may be some truth in this, but the accusation has been strongly resisted by the Law Society, which rejects the accuracy of the Board's sample of cases. Indeed, some of the Board's other data do not support the case for wholly blaming solicitors for the rise in cost. For instance, the average length of case between the first and last piece of work charged for has increased by almost one-quarter, indicating that cases may actually be taking longer, perhaps because of prosecution or court delays. Furthermore, solicitors are not, overall, spending more time on green form advice. Over the last ten years the average time claimed by a solicitor in a green form bill has remained at around 1.6 hours, against a maximum for all but matrimonial cases (where the limit is 3) of 2 hours.

In its response to the efficiency scrutiny on legal aid, the Law Society suggested six reasons why expenditure has risen: the rise in divorces; increase in property ownership; rising crime and attention to law and order; increasing complexity in the law; rising unemployment causing increased eligibility for legal aid, more debt, family breakdown, and homelessness; and a greater awareness of rights.[4] Each may have some validity.

The Profession and Legal Aid

Legal aid is a significant source of income for the legal profession. The Law Society reported that in 1990/91 solicitors received £571 million in legal aid and barristers £145 million.[5] For solicitors, this represented a 17.5 per cent increase on the previous year. Of the £5.2 billion turnover of all solicitors, legal aid contributed 11.1 per cent. This is roughly the same proportion as five years previously, but close to double the 6 per cent figure for 1975/76 reported to the Royal Commission on Legal Services. (In fact, the proportions are probably slightly lower than those given by the Law Society because its figures for legal aid include VAT and disbursements, while other sources of income do not.)

The Bar is rather more secretive than the Law Society about the total earnings of its members. However, figures released in 1989 showed an even greater dependence on legal aid and public funds. Legal aid then accounted for 27 per cent of the total fee income of all barristers[6]—a proportion similar to that given to the Royal Commission for Legal Services in 1977.

These income figures suggest little change in the legal profession's involvement in legal aid over the last decade. The number of solicitors' offices recorded as receiving a legal aid payment in any one year has also remained roughly constant, at just over 11,000 for the last five years. The Law Society estimates that this represents a payment to 74 per cent of all offices, indicating that some legal aid work is still undertaken by a broad range of solicitors' practices.[7]

Within this overall pattern, however, there are significant variations. First, there are strong regional differences. In 1990/91 legal aid constituted only 3.2 per cent of the income of solicitors in London (including the City), but 19 per cent for solicitors in Merseyside and the North.[8] Second, there are signs that a separate group of specialist solicitors' offices

---

[4] *Legal Aid Efficiency Scrutiny: the Law Society's Response* Law Society, 1976, para. 1.5.
[5] *Annual Statistical Report 1991* Law Society, 1991, p. 31.
[6] Bar Council's Strategy Group *Strategies for the Future* The General Council of the Bar, 1990, fig. 4, p. 18.
[7] As in 5, p. 31.   [8] As in 5, p. 33.

undertaking large amounts of legal aid has emerged. In 1991/92, 1,555 solicitors' offices received £120,000 or more from the Legal Aid Board. Although these represented only 14 per cent of all offices receiving a legal aid payment, together they received 59 per cent of the money paid out by the Board.

Legal aid has thus established itself as being of considerable importance to the legal profession. In 1988, however, the Law Society warned that, because of declining levels of remuneration, there was 'widespread concern that solicitors are ceasing to accept legal aid work or are seriously considering giving it up'.[9] It has repeated this warning since, but as yet solicitors do not appear to be giving up legal aid work in any significant numbers.

Legacies of Rushcliffe

The consequences of the Rushcliffe model of provision, which based legal aid on the existing pattern of legal practice, are still evident. One positive effect of this can be seen by comparison with other foreign jurisdictions. Legal aid in England and Wales is more favourably financed, particularly in relation to crime, than elsewhere. The demand-led nature of the legal aid budget, combined with the commercial drive of solicitors anxious to maximize income, has undoubtedly operated to defend legal aid from a level of cuts which might otherwise have been expected. The experience of Quebec suggests that a service highly dependent on salaried lawyers is vulnerable to a government wishing to hold down costs. Furthermore, lawyers in this country have managed to keep their remuneration rates from public funds significantly higher than in other jurisdictions.

One of the consequences of widespread dependence on private practitioners has, however, been the large-scale neglect of social welfare law. Solicitors continue to use even the most flexible element of legal aid provision, the green form legal advice scheme, largely to subsidize their traditional pattern of work. A report commissioned by the Lord Chancellor's Department and published in 1988 confirmed that 'solicitors have not for the most part seized the opportunity under the green form scheme to develop interests outside those of traditional legal practice . . . It has been the Law Centres rather than the private practice which have sought to use the green form scheme to cover issues outside mainstream legal practice.'[10]

[9] *Survey of Legal Aid Provision* Law Society, 1988.
[10] J. Baldwin and S. Hill *The Operation of the Green Form Scheme in England and Wales* Lord Chancellor's Department, 1988, p. 23.

In consequence, there has been little change in the pattern of green form use. The continuing domination of criminal, matrimonial, and family work is clear. Among green form bills in 1991/92, about 20 per cent of cases related to crime and 35 per cent to matrimonial and family work. As for social welfare law, it still made up only 26 per cent of all green form bills paid. Although four of the five social welfare categories saw the highest increase in green form use—immigration and nationality was up 48 per cent on the previous year, welfare benefits 33 per cent, hire purchase and debt 29 per cent, and employment 25 per cent—this was, in part, an effect of recession. In overall terms, the growth in social welfare law advice and assistance remains slow.

Percentage of all green form bills paid 1990/91

Landlord and tenant, housing	7.6
Employment	2.2
HP and debt	6.7
Welfare benefits	5.6
Immigration and nationality	1.9
Consumer	1.9
% of total	25.9

This low use of the scheme suggests that the unmet need for legal services—taken up as an issue in the 1960s and 1970s, but now unfashionable—should remain a matter of concern. The need for legal services in two social welfare areas, debt and employment, are considered in chapters 5 and 6 [of *A Strategy for Justice*].

Another example of need arises in the field of housing. A consultation paper issued by the Civil Justice Review in 1987 accepted a large measure of unmet need in relation to disrepair: 'The judicial statistics for 1985 show that non-possession housing cases numbered no more than 1,500 in that year, yet the English House Condition Survey undertaken by the Department of the Environment in 1981 shows that in that year 2,796,000 rented dwellings were each in need of repairs costing over £1,000. It is therefore a working assumption of this study that potentially many more than the 1,500 litigants a year might seek a remedy through the courts in respect of a non-possession housing claim.'[11] The research also indicated that, although 78 per cent of a small sample of potential litigants had consulted a CAB, none had been advised to take court action.

Tenants thus make little use of legal advice and litigation to solve problems such as housing disrepair. Subsequent research for the CAB service

[11] Civil Justice Review *Housing Cases* Lord Chancellor's Department, 1987, para. 81.

suggests that lay volunteer advisers are hard pressed to deal with such a complicated area of law. It concluded that 'housing advice falls short of an acceptable minimum standard in a substantial number of cases'.[12] In around half of the cases studied, tenants were referred only to the environmental health or housing department, although, in the view of the researchers, legal action was more likely to be effective.

Solicitors' widespread neglect of social welfare law has been paralleled by government indifference. There still remains no nationally financed scheme for representation in tribunals. Legal aid in one form or another is available only for relatively few hearings—as shown in the 1991/92 figures for bills paid in relation to mental health review tribunals (3,577), certain appeals relating to prisoners (116), and the employment appeal tribunal—really an appellate court (145). By default, advice agencies have provided some representation at tribunals, much of which is of high quality. In the area of social security particular expertise has been developed, but research commissioned by the Lord Chancellor's Department found that it is still the case that only about one in five of those bringing a social security appeal receive any advice, and 'only 12 per cent of appellants at social security appeals tribunals are represented by agencies or individuals with experience of representation or with any special expertise'.[13] The research concluded that representation increased a claimant's chance of a favourable outcome, 'though representation provided by generalist sources of advice has a less profound effect on outcome overall than that of specialists'.[14]

The Absence of Planned Provision

Legal aid is, on the whole, only available where solicitors choose, for commercial reasons, to provide it. The explosion of criminal legal aid has undoubtedly helped in encouraging a limited number of legal aid firms to establish themselves in the poorer areas of the inner cities worst provided for in the 1960s. There is, however, still an overwhelming tendency for criminal practitioners to base their offices near city-centre courts. There is also a dearth of provision in rural areas. A study of Devon and Cornwall concluded that firms in country areas 'lack any obvious expertise in the

---

[12] D. Forbes and S. Wright *Housing Cases in Nine CABx* unpublished, 1990.
[13] H. Genn and Y. Genn *The Effectiveness of Representation at Tribunals* Lord Chancellor's Department, 1989, p. 24.
[14] As in 13, p. 70.

less lucrative areas of social welfare law. There appears to be little pressure for solicitors in rural areas to seek to develop new sources of work'.[15]

Future developments may reduce the accessibility of legal aid even further. If the economy improves, financial institutions may make a further and more vigorous bid to undertake conveyancing. This would potentially affect the commercial viability of the traditional, mixed 'high street' practice and accelerate the existing division of solicitors into those whose practices are based on commercial work, various types of 'niche' practices (such as copyright or entertainment specialists), and legal aid practitioners. The last might then become inaccessible to people living in some suburban or rural areas.

The policies of the Legal Aid Board may be another factor in the encouragement of larger legal aid units. It has developed the idea of franchising—that is, making contracts with the larger providers of legal aid under which the board has more control of quality, in return for more decision-making delegated to the solicitors and the promise of quicker payment. Its original suggestion was that such franchises should only be available to those solicitors' offices with a legal aid turnover of £40,000 or more.

The delivery of publicly funded legal services cannot be left to the mechanisms of the market. There is a need to consider how services should be planned so that all members of society in all parts of the country have an acceptable level of access.

The Divided Profession

Legal aid has operated to sustain Britain's unique model of a divided legal profession. Of the two branches, the Bar received proportionately higher funding from public funds. Its General Council estimates that 'in 1989, barristers earned 10 per cent of fees earned by practising lawyers but 29 per cent of publicly funded fees'.[16] In fact, the total funding of the Bar from public funds was probably a higher percentage, since this 29 per cent appears to include only fees from the Legal Aid Board and the Crown Prosecution Service, and discounts income from other government sources, such as via the Government Legal Service or the Customs and Excise Department.

[15] M. Blacksell, K. Economides, C. Watkins *Access to Justice in Rural Britain: project working paper 6* University of Exeter, 1988, p. 35

[16] As in 6.

Even so, for barristers, legally aided work is relatively badly paid. In consequence, despite a professional duty to undertake legal aid cases recently imposed in the Bar's code of conduct, legally aided clients tend to be the first to suffer if any barrister has a conflict of commitments. [17] Briefs in uncontested or relatively small criminal cases are often returned to solicitors, with the result that legally aided clients may find that their representation is rearranged at the last moment.

The Courts and Legal Services Act 1990 provides the framework for solicitors to undertake work previously reserved for barristers. A recent report from the Lord Chancellor's Advisory Committee on Legal Education and Conduct recommended that solicitors in private practice should qualify for rights of audience in the higher courts.[18] Legally aided clients might benefit from implementation of this recommendation, particularly in criminal cases.

Disparate Provision

The provision of publicly funded legal services is divided in another way. While the legal aid scheme is historically based on, and still largely dominated by, the idea of funding litigation through lawyers, advice agencies have evolved from a very different background. In consequence, many advice agencies are orientated towards a model of advice, information, and counselling ultimately derived from a nineteenth-century charitable model. In addition, some reflect an orientation stemming from an impetus in the 1960s and 1970s towards community action and development. In default of other provision, advice agencies have supplied much of the available assistance and representation in social welfare law. Unless the agencies happen to employ a lawyer (as very few of them do), they exist largely outside the legal aid system. Instead, like law centres, they are overwhelmingly dependent on grant aid from local authorities.

No central government department takes responsibility for the funding of advice agencies, and there is no central information on their total resources, though the CAB service provides information on itself. Core funding from all local authorities for CABx, which totalled £27.5 million in 1990/91, varies considerably. The National Association of Citizens'

---

[17] Amendment inserted into Rule 502(b) *Code of Conduct of the Bar of England and Wales* General Council of the Bar, 1990.

[18] The Lord Chancellor's Advisory Committee on Legal Education and Conduct *Advice to the Law Society on its application for authorisation to grant extended rights of audience to solicitors* LCAC, 1992,

Advice Bureaux reported that, for 1990/91, 'funding from county councils varied from nothing to close to £30,000; funding from metropolitan districts ranged from just over £30,000 to over £560,000'.[19] NACAB itself received a grant from the Department of Trade and Industry of £10.3 million. The Federation of Independent Advice Centres gets no core funding from central government, although it receives a number of individual grants, largely for management training.

The distribution of advice agencies is totally dependent on the funding available, making provision as uneven and unrelated to need as that provided by solicitors. Law centres, of which there were 57 in July 1992, are in a similar position.

The 1986 efficiency scrutiny report was the first enquiry into legal aid to look seriously at using the skills of advice centres. Its most controversial recommendations were that: 'except in criminal cases, initial advice should be given by an advice agency rather than a private practitioner. Family cases should be referred to a private practitioner once it is clear that there is an issue on which legal advice is needed, but other civil cases should be referred only when court proceedings need to be initiated.'[20] These evoked protest from both solicitors and advice agencies, who agreed that it represented an attempt to save money and reduce services.

The idea of using the skills of advice agencies is a feature of the Legal Aid Board's experiment with franchising in Birmingham. Agencies could apply for franchises to carry out green form work alongside private firms. The board's annual report for 1991/92 reported that five advice agencies had been granted a franchise in one or more categories in its pilot project.[21] Incorporation of advice agencies within the legal aid system does, however, lead to potential problems. First, contracts do not help advice agencies to gain reliable core funding, and those under threat of closure are in no position to consider expanding to meet the contract conditions. Second, franchising expects advice agencies to provide the same service as solicitors, which ignores the special contribution of their accessible, non-legal, and more pro-active approach.

Constraints on local authority funding are being felt throughout the voluntary sector, and a number of law centres have been subject to cuts. The London Borough of Wandsworth withdrew its funds in 1990; several other authorities—including Labour-controlled Brighton and

---

[19] The National Association of Citizens' Advice Bureaux *Annual Report 1990/91*, p. 18.

[20] Legal Aid Efficiency Scrutiny *Report*, *Volume 1* Lord Chancellor's Department, 1986, para. 4.7.

[21] As in 3 above, p. 23.

Conservative-controlled Brent—have tried to diminish their law centres' separate identity by way of amalgamating them with their own advice agencies, at the same time placing restrictions on the work they do.

In a more positive light, NACAB was able to say in its annual report: 'it is gratifying that very few authorities decided to limit their grants to bureaux in 1990-91 despite their own internal funding problems.' Nevertheless, there have been closures and NACAB noted with concern 'the combination of community-charge capping and a general squeeze on local authorities'. It reported the closure of two bureaux in 1990/91— North Shields and Hampstead, north London.[22] Since then, at least two more, in Clapham and Balham in south London, have closed.

Independent advice agencies are as concerned as NACAB over their future, with FIAC members as diverse as Harlesden Advice Centre in the London Borough of Brent and Ask Here, a young people's project in Birmingham, recently losing funds.

The proven unreliability of local government funding has encouraged both advice agencies and law centres to look for more consistent central government resources. The Law Centres Federation has promoted the idea of a nationally funded network of law centres. In its 1990/91 annual report, NACAB declared its support for a proposal that 'local authorities should have a statutory duty to plan for and fund advice services in their locality. This should be backed up by a clear recognition of advice needs in the Standing Spending Assessment',[23] against which local authority expenditure is measured by central government.

The Fall in Eligibility

Eligibility for civil legal aid and green form legal advice has fallen substantially from the levels to which it was raised before the Labour Government lost office in 1979. As late as 1986, this development was denied by the then Lord Chancellor, Lord Hailsham, who asserted that cuts in dependants' allowances would be 'practically unobservable' and reasserted that around 70 per cent of the population met the income criteria for grant of civil legal aid.[24]

Much of the debate about levels of eligibility has been conducted with regard to the proportion of the population eligible on grounds of income. No overall figures for eligibility can be given because the Government produces no reliable statistics on savings and other matters relevant to eli-

[22] As in 19 above, p. 18 and p. 5.   [23] As in 19 above, p. 4.
[24] *HL Hansard debates* 18 Mar. 1986, col. 921.

gibility under the capital criteria. The criteria, however, clearly operate to exclude significant numbers of otherwise eligible applicants.

The capital limits for green form, ABWOR, and for most applicants for civil legal aid are now significantly lower than those for income support, whose recipients are automatically eligible for free legal aid. In effect, therefore, those not on income support face more stringent capital limits for legal aid than those receiving income support. The limits are also out of line with the figure for housing benefit or community charge, a comparable form of assistance for those on low incomes. The result is a completely illogical system.

An indication that levels of eligibility are falling is given by the decline in the proportion of civil legal aid certificates for which the assisted person is assessed to pay a contribution. In the ten years between 1981/82 and 1991/92, the percentage of certificates where the assisted person was assessed for no contribution rose from 76.5 to 83.9 per cent. This reveals a pattern in which legal aid is becoming increasingly the province of those in receipt of the lowest levels of income, rather than of those who are just that much better off.

Lord Mackay suggested in a BBC 'Panorama' programme that any decline in eligibility might reflect rising living standards.[25] Consideration of the income limits by reference to state benefits makes this unlikely. In 1979 the lower income limit in civil cases was raised to 50 per cent above the long-term supplementary benefit rate. For 1992/93 the civil lower income limit was £3,060 per annum, less that the equivalent of £3,076 per annum received by a single pensioner on income support from October 1992. The 1992/93 legal aid allowance for a dependant under the age of 11 was £948, only 25 per cent above the income support addition of £756.60 for such a person.

The fall in eligibility has resulted from a combination of the deliberate cuts to dependants' additions in 1986 and the sporadic failure to uprate all allowances. It has particularly affected adults with child dependants: while eligibility for single pensioners fell between 1979 and 1989 from 98.2 per cent to 89.2 per cent, for a couple with two dependent children it plummeted from 75.1 per cent to a bare 33.8 per cent. These figures have been calculated by a statistician at the London School of Economics, Michael Murphy, using government figures on income from the Family Expenditure Survey.

The Lord Chancellor's Department produced its rival statistics in June

---

[25] BBC Panorama interview with J. Rozenberg, 17 Apr. 1989.

1991. These indicate little change—a fall from 73.8 per cent of the population eligible in 1979 to 66.1 per cent in 1990 (69.2 per cent in personal injury cases).[26] To obtain this result, the Lord Chancellor's Department included the effect of a change of rules introduced in April 1990 allowing children to apply for legal aid on the basis of their own income and capital, not that of their parents. This is legitimate in relation, for instance, to personal injury cases, but most potentially legal aided cases concern adults—some, such as matters arising from divorce, exclusively so.

The discrepancy is also due to the Lord Chancellor's Department's less sophisticated use of data. Civil legal aid eligibility is crucially affected by housing costs, which are an allowable expense for a legal aid applicant. A high estimate of housing costs gives a high level of eligibility for groups of the population with incomes of a particular level. The important difference in methodology is that the Lord Chancellor's Department assumes average housing costs of about £100 per week as against Michael Murphy's figure which is around £30 lower. The latter is more in line with actual housing costs identified in other government figures (specifically the Housing and Construction Statistics 1979/89) for people paying mortgages and council rents. Almost all couples with two children are in one of these two categories, suggesting that Michael Murphy's figures can be relied upon, particularly for the group most affected by the decline in eligibility.[27]

A further problem is that relative eligibility levels are inconsistent. Green form eligibility for a couple with two dependent children has, for instance, plummeted from 57.2 per cent of the population in that category to 22.5 per cent—significantly below that of the average for the population as a whole (39.2 per cent) and their own eligibility level for civil legal aid (33.8 per cent). This imbalance may be the result of historical accident, rather than any deliberate intention. However, it exists, and hard-pressed families with young children suffer the consequences of the lack of co-ordination between the different legal aid schemes.

Government pronouncements on the purpose of civil legal aid have, in any case, changed markedly, reflecting less commitment to the scheme. In 1949, the Lord Chancellor's Department confidently asserted the purpose of legal aid to be that 'no one will be financially unable to prosecute a just and reasonable claim or defend a legal right'. By the time of its 1991

---

[26] Review of Financial Conditions for Legal Aid *Eligibility for Civil Legal Aid: a consultation paper* Lord Chancellor's Department, 1991, p. 85.
[27] M. Murphy *An analysis of the differences in eligibility for civil legal aid in 1989* unpublished, copies available from LAG, price £2.

eligibility review, its tone had changed: legal aid had become 'a conditional financial support, provided by the taxpayer, for individuals whose financial circumstances would prevent them from taking or defending proceedings without assistance with their costs'.[28]

Public Awareness

In order to use services, people must know about them. Public awareness of CABx is high—one poll put it at 90 per cent. Knowledge of the legal aid scheme is much lower. In 1990, only 45 per cent of those asked by Gallup to name any scheme which provided help with solicitors' costs mentioned legal aid, and seven out of ten people said that they did not understand the legal aid scheme. Most people who do know about legal aid see it as providing help with criminal charges or matrimonial problems. Few regard it as a general scheme: in the Gallup survey, only 16 per cent mentioned it as helping with housing matters, and only 3 per cent with debt. Other statistics suggest that a similarly low level of awareness exists even amongst those who have attempted to seek help with a problem.[29]

The Rushcliffe report stresses that the legal aid scheme 'should be given proper publicity at all times'. However, the scheme has been advertised on national TV only once—in 1973, before the launch of the green form scheme. Research indicated a dramatic short-term impact: knowledge of the scheme was raised from around one-quarter to almost half of the population. However, a year later, the figure had slipped back to 27 per cent. In addition, the advertising was more successful in reaching the middle classes than the poor.[30]

The legal aid advisory committee commented: 'Experience has taught us that mass publicity for the legal aid scheme, beyond the minimum necessary to explain the scheme to users by leaflets etc., is not good value for money.' It was argued that too much would be spent in reaching people not likely to use legal aid. Instead, it recommended a more selective approach, directed at 'advisory workers' in contact with those having legal problems.[31]

Since then, the Law Society and Legal Aid Board have experimented

[28] Lord Chancellor *Summary of the Proposed New Service* Cmnd 7563, 1948, and Review of Financial Conditions for Legal Aid Eligibility, as in 26 above, para. 1.

[29] Broadcasting Research Department *Citizens' Advice Bureaux: the price of advice* BBC, 1986, and Social Surveys (Gallup Poll) Ltd *Legal Aid Publicity* unpublished, 1990.

[30] Schlackman Research Organisation *An investigation into current awareness and knowledge of the Legal Advice and Assistance scheme among recommenders and potential clients* April 1975

[31] *27th Legal Aid Annual Reports* [1976–77] HC 172, HMSO, p. 82.

with various methods of publicity, including a video in post offices. Leaflets and forms have been improved, with 'Crystal Mark' recognition by the Plain English Campaign for the most recent non-matrimonial civil legal aid form. There has also been more translation into minority languages. However, in a 1992 report the National Audit Office found that 'awareness of legal aid is low, even among the eligible population'. It considered that 'The Board's publicity is informative and explanatory rather than advertising and is more likely to be used by those who have already identified a need for legal services'. Furthermore, it added: 'There is a lack of accurate information about specialist services offered by practitioners, for example in such matters as social security, housing and debt.'[32]

The Legal Aid Board, in the same way as the Law Society before it, has not been effective in ensuring general knowledge of the legal aid scheme. To a limited extent, this has been counterbalanced by the initiative of individual solicitors who have undertaken advertising campaigns—one firm in Liverpool has even paid for radio advertisements on an issue as specific as compensation for one particular industrial disease, vibration white finger. The North Western Legal Services Committee also launched an advertising campaign for personal injury litigation which was then taken up nationally by the Law Society.

Lack of knowledge remains, however, a feature in depressing demand for services, particularly outside criminal and matrimonial work. In Part III we discuss how the question of education and information is approached in other jurisdictions; in this country no institution—be it a government department, the Legal Aid Board, or the Law Society—has ever accepted overall responsibility for the production of information (for instance, a guide to divorce law) on the workings of English law.

Quality, Cost, and Remuneration

Lord Mackay, in his letter setting out the aims and objectives for the newly established Legal Aid Board in July 1988, required it to review 'existing targets and indicators for performance' in relation not only to legal aid administration but also to legal aid practice itself.[33] This has encouraged the Board to look at the quality of work undertaken by legal aid practitioners in a way that would have probably been impossible for the Law Society.

[32] National Audit Office *The Administration of Legal Aid in England and Wales* HC 90, HMSO, 1992, p. 31.
[33] Legal Aid Board *Report to the Lord Chancellor* Cm 688, HMSO, 1989, p. 24.

Control of quality has become a major concern for the Legal Aid Board. From the beginning, it has identified contracts as 'franchises' with service providers as a key means of achieving this aim. 'Franchising', it stated in an early consultation document, 'involves identifying those who can satisfy criteria of competence and reliability, assisting and encouraging them by freeing them from some of the restrictions now applying to legal aid'.[34] Its approach was initially influenced by the techniques of 'total quality management'. In consequence, its franchising specification seeks to detail all the indicators of quality, such as books and training, that should lead to high-quality service provision. The problem is that indicators of quality are not necessarily determinants of it. A practitioner with a wonderful library at his or her disposal may still conduct cases badly or choose to cut corners in order to maximize profits.

The board is now developing the concept of the monitoring of 'transaction criteria'. It describes these as 'a series of points and questions that a trained observer checking a file after the event would use to evaluate what was done and the standard to which it was done.[35] The academic researchers working on the concept for the board have explained that they are seeking to identify a 'competence threshold' which fits modern management thinking on quality—'not perfection but "fitness for purpose"'. 'They raise a potential conflict with the board's involvement in this issue: 'the purposive definition of quality leaves it open to funders of a service in times of budgetary constraint to redefine its purpose so that it requires a low level of performance. All this, of course, underlines the importance of determining *who* is to define the appropriate level of service to be delivered'.[36]

The Law Society believes that quality is simply a reflection of price. One of its arguments against any extension of legal aid payments by fixed fees, as opposed to hourly rates, is that quality will suffer. The Society recently launched a well publicized campaign on this issue—some local law societies even associated themselves with the withdrawal of their members from police station and court duty solicitor schemes in protest at the low remuneration rates for magistrates' court representation proposed by the Lord Chancellor.

Quality, remuneration, and cost, then, dominate much contemporary debate about the state of legal aid and publicly funded legal services. As

[34] *Second Stage Consultation on the Future of the Green Form Scheme* Legal Aid Board, 1989, para. 21.
[35] As in 3, p. 24.
[36] A. Paterson and A. Sherr, 'Quality, Clients and Legal Aid, *New Law Journal* 5 June 1992, p. 783.

this chapter has shown, other issues are also important to those seeking to use those services. These include lack of provision in relation to social welfare law, the effects of a divided profession and divided provision, the lack of an overall strategy for publicly funded legal services as a whole, declining civil legal aid eligibility, and lack of information about legal aid and legal services.

14. Organizing Cost-Effective Access to Justice

GWYN BEVAN, TONY HOLLAND, and
MARTIN PARTINGTON

The current legal aid system is ripe for radical change. At the moment it offers a deteriorating service at ever-increasing cost. In the process it is failing to provide the cost-effective access to justice that enables individuals to secure their fundamental rights.

In this memorandum Gwyn Bevan, a senior lecturer in Health Economics at the University of Bristol; Tony Holland, a former President of the Law Society and senior partner of Foot and Bowden; and Martin Partington, Professor of Law at the University of Bristol, attempt to make sense of legal aid by offering an economic analysis of the present system.

Shorn of legalistic mystique, they argue that its current problems are remarkably similar to those faced by other publicly funded services such as health care.

In particular they say that because legal aid is paid for by a third party, the Government, but is both bought and delivered by the same group of people, lawyers, incentives for costs to escalate are built into the heart of the system. The authors offer a number of proposals to combat this, including:

—Establishing 'fundholders for justice', similar to GP fundholders, who would determine a client's eligibility for legal aid and whether it was the most effective form of redress, before buying legal services from competing lawyers;
—Allowing the Legal Aid Board to negotiate block contracts with selected firms who would be assured a significant volume of work in return for reducing their prices; and
—Making legally aided individuals more cost-conscious by developing the idea of co-payment between the client and the state.

1. Introduction

Legal aid is directed at paying the fees of solicitors and barristers on a massive scale. Public expenditure on legal aid in 1994–95 is forecast to be £1.4bn. If we assume the annual average costs of a qualified lawyer to be £100,000, then legal aid would employ 14,000 full-time lawyers. That is one lawyer per 3,600 individuals in England and Wales. This suggests that the money we spend on legal aid ought to ensure a comfortable income for lawyers, and access for all to basic justice in England and Wales. It currently does neither.

Since 1979, legal aid has been the fastest-growing programme of public expenditure, having increased fivefold in real terms since 1979–80. During the same period, total government expenditure increased by 29%, and Gross Domestic Product by 24% (see Figure 1). Since 1987–88 public expenditure on legal aid has doubled in real terms, whilst total government expenditure increased by 14% and Gross Domestic Product by 4% (see Figure 1). No government can afford to continue to finance a programme which doubles its real cost every seven years.

A rationale for public expenditure on legal aid is to ensure that an individual's access to justice, to secure certain fundamental rights, does not depend on that individual's ability to pay. Amongst the various (unsuccessful) attempts in the past to limit the rate of future increases in expen-

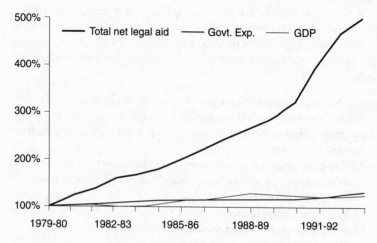

Figure 1: Trends in public expenditure on legal aid, total government expenditure, and gross domestic product

diture on legal aid,[1] the Government has reduced eligibility for legal aid. The reductions in eligibility for legal aid undermine its rationale in a particularly explosive way.

From its introduction in 1949, and during its first decade, about 80% of households were eligible. Subsequently, eligibility was reduced until 1979, when the limits were substantially increased to restore coverage to close to the levels of 1949. Since then, eligibility has been reduced again, so that currently slightly less than 50% of households are eligible.[2] A consequence of this is that there is likely to be a significant proportion of the population who pay taxes but who cannot afford to pay for legal services themselves, and are ineligible for legal aid. Hence their taxes pay for legal aid, and enable others to get legal services which they cannot afford. These individuals may justifiably claim that they are subjected to taxation without legal representation.

The escalation in expenditure on legal aid, and in the costs of legal services, means that only the rich and the legally aided can afford access to justice through legal services. The Government may be a convenient scapegoat for this unsatisfactory outcome, but the root cause is the high and increasing cost of legal services (both privately financed and legally aided).[3]

There must be much better ways of using the vast resources we currently expend on legal aid. The current system puts the Government on the horns of a dilemma: either it seeks to restrain cost escalation by further restriction in eligibility or it maintains the current limited access to justice alongside exponential growth in expenditure. The Government's dilemma over legal aid has close analogies with problems faced by third-party payors (those who purchase services on behalf of their clients as opposed to *payers* who are direct consumers) for health care. The analogous problems in health care have been extensively researched, and resulted in third-party payors developing various innovatory responses as they discovered that they could no longer afford to be passive payers for professional services.

This memorandum offers a framework from an economic analysis of problems with legal aid. Based on that analysis, and relevant analogies

---

[1] These are discussed below

[2] Eligibility to legal aid is typically based on both disposable income and capital. These estimates are based on income only.

[3] Lord Woolf, who is heading the Government Inquiry into an attempt to make justice cheap and simple for the ordinary person, was quoted as saying that: 'We have a very good system of justice—but no one can afford it, neither the state nor the public.' *Observer*, 29 May 1994, p. 1.

from health care, it outlines some possible solutions. It does not pretend to cover all the issues, nor is it based on a review of the literature on legal aid. Its objective is to contribute to debate on ways of reforming legal aid to achieve cost-effective access to justice.

The rest of this memorandum is structured as follows:

Section 2   outlines the case for a radical change to the system of legal aid
Section 3   uses economic concepts to analyse the problems of legal aid
Section 4   describes the different categories which make up legal aid and
            examines how their costs have escalated
Section 5   discusses restructuring the demand and supply side
Section 6   discusses ways of introducing cost-consciousness
Section 7   outlines a possible reformed system of access to justice

2. The Case for Radical Change

There are four reasons for a radical change to the system of legal aid.

First, current arrangements offer the Government some combination of cost escalation and restrictions in coverage: i.e. a worse service at a higher price. This suggests that there is something seriously awry.

Secondly, legal aid makes only a limited contribution in enabling individuals to secure certain fundamental rights. For individuals to be able to do this they need: i) competence to understand that their rights are being abused and that there are means of redress; ii) competence to know how to act; and iii) ability to pay for the processes of securing justice. Legal aid is primarily focused on paying lawyers for iii). The first two points mean that legal services supplied by a lawyer may be neither necessary nor sufficient to ensure access to justice. Legal services may not be necessary, because the case does not require legal expertise or it is not sufficiently complex to merit the use of courts. Legal services may not be sufficient, as people may need help prior to the use of a lawyer: public finance of legal services does not help the most disadvantaged; they cannot present their case to a lawyer without additional help.

Thirdly, to secure justice legal services may be required not because of the intrinsic complexity of the case but because of the complex ways in which the current legal system works: the need for advocacy, for example, is fostered by an adversarial system.

Finally, even where legal services are required this does not necessarily require use of lawyers. Lawyers are essential for some but by no means all legal services. Many other agents provide legal services (e.g. Citizens'

Advice Bureaux, trade unions, etc). Hence paying lawyers for legal services may not be a cost-effective way of using legal services even where these are required. These points mean that reductions in legal aid expenditures on lawyers may or may not reduce access to justice.[4] Furthermore, if the objective of legal aid is that access to justice does not depend on ability to pay, then this raises the issue of those not currently eligible for legal aid. Hence, if more cost-effective means of access to justice can be devised, then the same expenditure would offer scope to make this available to others who are currently not eligible for legal aid.

3. An Economic Analysis Of Problems Of Legal Aid

An economic vocabulary

Having outlined the case for radical change to the system of legal aid, this paper now analyses the cause of current problems. It does so by introducing and using a vocabulary which we hope will prove helpful in two ways. Firstly, giving names to economic concepts will help those who know the law make sense of their own experience.[5] Secondly, using economic rather than legal terms indicates the generic nature of the problems faced by legal aid: exactly the same problems occur, for example, in the field of health care.

We begin with the distribution of property rights for a principal buying service from an agent, where the principal is a sovereign consumer: that is where the property rights over decisions on consumption are vested in the principal, who knows the service he wants and pays at the point of consumption.

The *principal/agent problem* arises when a principal relies on an agent to deliver a service, and there is, between the principal and the agent, both asymmetry of information and a difference in incentives. If incentives are the same, but there is asymmetry of information, there is no problem (as the agent will act in the way the principal would want the agent to do). If incentives are different, but there is symmetry of information, there is

---

[4] There is similar confusion between health and health care. Many factors outside health care influence health and are often more important (e.g. clean water, sanitation, housing, diet, smoking, income); and the impact of much of health care on health is unproven.

[5] As Halsey observed, those who have had no formal training in social sciences know practically all there is to be known. The formal knowledge of these disciplines is nevertheless crucial in transforming individuals' capacity to make sense of their knowledge. See Halsey A. H. (1986) *Change in British Society*, Oxford: Oxford University Press, p. 8. The economic terms given here are intended to provide a way of structuring an economic analysis of legal aid.

again no problem (because the principal can see when the agent is not delivering what the principal wants).

The principal/agent problem can arise from a variety of causes. In legal aid (and health care) two causes combine:

—legal aid is paid for by a third party, and thus the Legal Aid Board (LAB) and the Lord Chancellor's Department (LCD) confront the common problem of insurers who are remote from the services supplied by agents, the problem of *moral hazard*; and
—the legally aided individual relies on the lawyers to decide what services they will supply.

Each of these causes create potential for *supplier-induced demand*, and together are likely to cause serious problems from cost escalation and questions over the value of what is being bought at such a high price.

Principals as Third Party Payors

There is a problem of moral hazard created by insurance. The principal is the insurer who raises finance from individuals according to the insurer's assessment of their risk, but the insurer pays the agent according to the volume of services the agent supplies. The crucial problem here is that the insured individuals lose interest in the costs of services being supplied. We encounter this problem when our car needs to have its body repaired and we are asked: 'Is this an insurance job or are you paying yourself?'[6]

Moral hazard threatens the benefits of insurance as it leads to escalating costs of insured services, which inevitably feed through into increases in insurance premiums.[7] Where the insured individuals may be regarded as knowing what they are getting from the agents they use to supply services, moral hazard may be reduced by requiring the client to pay part of the costs incurred (see below). Where doing this would then mean that the insured individual would encounter a principal/agent problem this may not work: this is because the principal is poorly placed to decide what services are required. In these circumstances the problem becomes one of designing incentives on the agent.[8]

---

[6] This homely analogy was pointed out by Anthony Harris writing in the *Financial Times*.
[7] For example in private health care in the UK.
[8] As for example in US health care. As Evans pointed out, the US has the highest user charges for health care and the most serious problems of cost containment. See Evans R. G. (1987) 'Public purchase of health insurance: the collective provision of individual care.' *Health Policy*, 7:115–34.

Principals as consumers of professional services

The consumer who pays for professional services creates potential for supplier-induced demand: the asymmetry of information means that property rights over consumption are transferred from the principal to the agent; and where the system of incentives pays the agent according to the volume of services delivered, then the agent is rewarded for supplying more services than the principal would ideally want (if the principal understood the choices available, their likely consequences, and their costs and benefits).

Shaw described in a nutshell the principal/agent problem for medicine financed by a fee-for-service system. He pointed out that this meant that he could not knock his shins severely without forcing on some surgeon the difficult question: 'Could I not make better use of a pocketful of guineas than this man could of his leg? Could he not write as well—or even better—on one leg than on two? And the guineas would make all the difference in the world to me just now. My wife—my pretty ones—the leg may mortify—it is always safer to operate—he will be well in a fortnight—artificial legs are now so well made that they are really better than natural ones—evolution towards leglessness etc. etc. etc.'[9]

Paying for legal services

The principal/agent problem and the potential it creates for supplier-induced demand offers one explanation of why the current system of private provision of legal services is so expensive. Lawyers get paid for providing legal advice and remedies through the courts (even where other kinds of advice or other remedies would be more effective and less costly[10]), and typically under the current system, the more work the lawyer does, the more the lawyer gets paid.

The position faced by LAB/LCD is that of the principal/agent problem exacerbated by moral hazard. There is asymmetry of information: as long as LCD and LAB remain passive third-party payors of bills,[11] they are much more poorly informed than a private client about the services supplied. There is an obvious difference in incentives as expenditure by LCD on legal aid is lawyers' incomes from legal aid: LCD can only control

---

[9] Shaw G. B. (1938) 'The doctor's dilemma', *Prefaces by Bernard Shaw*. London: Odhams, p. 237.

[10] This includes, of course, the advice not to proceed with a case through the courts.

[11] A trade union, for example, in its contract with a firm of solicitors, holds the firm to account in terms of whether the fees they charge result in successful cases.

expenditure on legal aid by reducing lawyers' incomes from legal aid from the level at which it would otherwise have been. The system is one which we would expect to lead to uncontrolled increases in expenditure. This is, of course, what has happened. The diagnosis of the principal/agent problem suggests two obvious lines of attack: reducing asymmetry of information, and designing appropriate incentives. We pursue these below. To understand more fully the problems of legal aid, it is necessary to describe its different components.

4. A Description Of Legal Aid

The different categories

The nature of, and eligibility for, each category of legal aid are as follows.

Criminal Legal Aid: available for criminal proceedings in magistrates' courts (where, since 1988, over 80% of indictable cases have been legally aided), and in the Crown Court and above (where nearly all defendants are legally aided). Application is made to the court, and applicants must show that the grant is desirable in the 'interests of justice'. The decision to grant legal aid is made by the magistrate or judge who will use the Widgery criteria.[12] Applicants who satisfy the test of being in 'the interests of justice' may or may not have to make a financial contribution: 90% of applicants are not required to pay (currently the rule is that either they have a weekly disposable income of less than £47 and disposable capital of less than £3,000, or they are on income support). There is no upper eligibility limit. All other successful applicants are currently required to contribute £1 per week out of every £3 by which their weekly disposable income exceeds £46. Contribution from disposable capital of excess of £3,000 is also required.

Duty Solicitor Schemes: there are two statutory duty solicitor schemes: i) for people appearing before a magistrates' court who are otherwise unassisted, and ii) to provide advice and assistance for people detained at police stations in connection with criminal charges. Under both

---

[12] These are from Mr Justice Widgery's 1966 Report and restated in the Legal Aid Act 1988. They are: i) the offence is such that, if proved, it is likely that the court would impose a sentence which would deprive the accused of his liberty or lead to a loss of livelihood or serious damage to his reputation; ii) the determination of the case may involve the consideration of a substantial question of law; iii) the accused may be unable to understand the proceedings because of his inadequate knowledge of English, mental illness, or other mental or physical disability; iv) the nature of the defence is such as to involve the tracing or interviewing of witnesses or expect cross-examining of a witness for the prosecution; v) it is in the interest of someone other than the accused that the accused be represented.

schemes initial advice is provided free of charge regardless of the person's means.

Green Form: this scheme enables a solicitor to give advice on any matter relating to English law up to an initial limit of two hours (for criminal and most civil matters) but up to three hours for advice relating to divorce or judicial separation. This scheme provides for about 43% of all acts of assistance paid for out of the legal aid fund.[13] Those eligible for green form advice are all persons on income support, and any person with a weekly disposable income of less that £70 and disposable capital of less than £1,000 (if there are no dependents). All such persons are entitled to green form advice free of charge. There is no longer a contributory system for green form. It is up to solicitors to assess eligibility of potential clients for green form advice.

Civil Legal Aid: is generally available in connection with proceedings at or above County Court level except for defamation cases. All proceedings under the Children Act are covered by civil legal aid. It is not generally granted for civil cases in the magistrates' court: for these courts there is the other category of Assistance By Way Of Representation (ABWOR). To be granted civil legal aid applicants must satisfy the area office of the LAB that there are reasonable grounds for bringing a case before the civil courts in England and Wales. Those eligible for civil legal aid free of charge are: all persons on income support, and any person with a disposable income of less than £2,382 per year and with disposable capital of less than £3,000. Persons with an income or capital above those limits qualify for civil legal aid if their disposable income is less than £7,060 per year and disposable capital is less than £6,750, but they are required to make a contribution.

Assistance By Way Of Representation (ABWOR): covers the cost of a solicitor preparing a case for and representing a person in most civil cases in the magistrates' courts. It is also available for hearings before the Mental Health Review Tribunals, the Parole Board (for discretionary lifers), and for disciplinary hearings before a prison governor (with the governor's agreement). Those eligible for ABWOR free of charge are: all persons on income support, and any person with a weekly disposable income of less than £63 and with disposable capital of less than £3,000. Persons with an income or capital above those limits qualify for civil legal

---

[13] Acts of assistance are defined for the different categories of legal aid as follows: bill paid for Criminal Magistrates, Green Form, Assistance By Way Of Representation (ABWOR); certificate issued for Civil Legal Aid; person represented for Criminal Higher; person given assistance for Duty Solicitor Scheme.

TABLE 1 *Net and gross expenditure on different categories of legal aid for 1993–94*

Category	Net Exp.(£m)	Net Exp.(%)	Gross.Exp.(£m)	Net Exp.(%)
Civil	544	45	828	55
Criminal Magistrates	192	16	194	13
Criminal Higher	236	20	237	16
Green Form	141	12	146	10
ABWOR	18	1	19	1
Duty Solicitor	78	6	78	5
Total	1209	100	1502	100

aid, if their weekly income is less than £153 and their disposable capital is less than £3,000 but are required to make a contribution.

Lawyers' incomes from legal aid

About 80% of legal aid payment to lawyers goes to solicitors with 20% to barristers.

Data on solicitors' incomes are routinely reported, and their total fees are generally correlated with national income.[14] There were dramatic increases in solicitors' fees in the boom of the 1980s. This masked the loss from the reduced price of conveyancing through legislation which allowed advertising and price competition. The profits firms had made from conveyancing were no longer available to subsidize other work (in particular, legal aid). The slump in the property market and the sharp recession in the late 1980s meant that most sources of solicitors' incomes fell (and for conveyancing the previous fall in price was now accompanied by a precipitous decline in volume). Legal aid then provided a welcome source of work despite problems over its profitability: the proportion of solicitors' income financed by gross fees from legal aid increased by about 26%: from 9.4% in 1989–90 to 11.8% in 1991–92.[15] This, of course, caused escalation in expenditure on legal aid.

Barristers' incomes are not routinely reported. A sample in 1989 estimated that 38% of their incomes came from public funds, with 27% from legal aid and 11% from the Crown Prosecution Service.[16]

[14] Bowles R., Fenn P., Jenkins J. (1992) 'The future of the profession'. *Law Society Gazette*, 13:1 April 1992.
[15] The Law Society (1993) *Annual Statistical Report*. London: Law Society, Table 7.10.
[16] General Council of the Bar (1990) *Strategies For the Future*, Fig.4.

Escalation in expenditure

We now analyse the escalation in costs of legal aid by identifying the cost drivers. Obviously, expenditure on legal aid is the sum across the different categories of the product of the numbers of acts of assistance, and the cost per act of assistance. The LAB pays for civil and criminal legal aid, apart from legal aid for criminal cases in the Crown Court and higher courts which are paid by the LCD. Given the current system, LAB and LCD have control over only part of each. The numbers of acts of assistance will depend on the eligible population, and the rate of take-up by the eligible population. The Government has reduced the population eligible for legal aid, but cannot control changes in the rates of take-up. The cost per act of assistance typically depends on the hourly rate, and the hours billed per act. The Lord Chancellor determines hourly rates, but for much of legal aid cannot control the hours worked. The exception is where standard fees have been introduced.

We have analysed the most recent seven years, from 1987–88 to 1993–94. As mentioned above, during this period public expenditure on legal aid (i.e. net expenditure) doubled in real terms. Figure 2 shows increases in gross expenditure on the different categories of legal aid as compared with GDP. Each of the main categories, showed real increases in expenditure. (ABWOR accounted for only 1% of expenditure.) Figure 3 shows how increases in gross expenditure are caused by increases in volume (acts of assistance) or real increases in price (gross real spend per act of assistance measured by using the Treasury GDP deflator) or both. Of these, two categories merit particular attention.

Firstly, legal aid for criminal cases in the higher courts is the only category where the number of acts of assistance is not subject to supplier-induced demand.[17] Between 1987–88 to 1993–94 the number of acts of assistance decreased by about 26% (see Figure 3). The main scope for supplier-induced demand in this category is in the hours worked per case which will be reflected in the cost per case.[18] Over the same period the real cost per case (i.e. additional to the Treasury GDP deflator) increased by about 130% (see Figure 3).

The other main categories of legal aid show increases in the number of acts of assistance, and this may in part be due to supplier-induced demand. Except for the Duty Solicitor Scheme, each category also shows

---

[17] These cases are determined by the Crown and are virtually all legally aided.
[18] The introduction of standard fees per case, which limits supplier-induced demand applies to about 60% of claims but only 20% of expenditure.

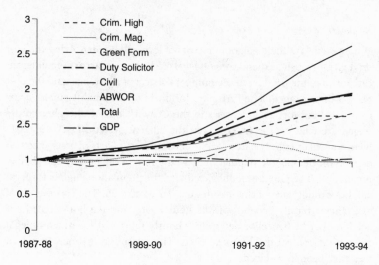

Sources: Lord Chancellor's Department & Legal Aid Board

Figure 2: Increases in gross expenditure on legal aid by category

real increases in price (the cost per act of assistance). The second category of particular interest is the green form scheme, where the eligibility has been reduced dramatically but in spite of this, the number of acts of assistance has increased by more that 50% over the period (see Figure 3).

From legal aid to cost-effective access to justice

The picture that emerges from analysis of legal aid over the seven years to 1993–94 is one consistent with the hypothesis of supplier-induced demand: legal aid provided scope for increases in volume in the numbers of acts of assistance from most categories (except for criminal higher and ABWOR); and for hours per act in all categories (except for the Duty Solicitor Scheme). This analysis:

—Offers an explanation of why LCD's actions so far have been ineffective in containing costs of legal aid.[19] This is because, as explained above, they only address some of elements which drive costs. Experience from

---

[19] They have probably reduced expenditure from the level it might otherwise have reached.

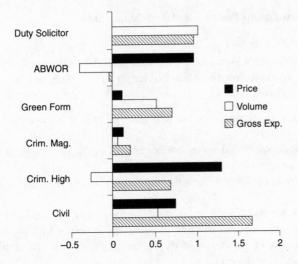

Figure 3: Increases in real gross expenditure, in volume, and in real price 1987–88 to 1993–94

health care suggests that such partial measures are unlikely to succeed in containing the costs of legal aid. [20]

—Offers pointers on how to move from the current system of legal aid to one which is more likely to offer more cost-effective access to justice. This is why we believe that the current budget for legal aid, if used more equitably and effectively, would provide much greater access to justice than current arrangements.

The next three sections consider ways of restructuring the demand and supply side, and of introducing cost-consciousness into contracts for services for justice, and outline a possible future pattern of financing and delivering access to justice.

---

[20] The same applies to US health care which shares the characteristics of legal services in the UK. Green reported in 1986 that since 1960 employer contributions to employee health insurance had been doubling every five years; and that a 1983 survey of the *Fortune* 500 Industrial Companies and 250 largest non-industrial companies found that health-care costs amounted to 24% of average pre-tax profits. See Green D. G. (1986) *Challenge to the NHS*. London Institute of Economic Affairs, p. 42.

5. Restructuring The Demand And Supply Side

A fundholder for justice?

We now consider introducing into legal aid a skilled buyer of services to provide access to justice—a fundholder for justice. This new role might work as follows:

—the fundholder would be the first point of contact for citizens seeking access to justice;

—the fundholder need not be a solicitor, and would have no vested interest in using traditional legal services;

—the fundholder would seek the most cost-effective means of access to justice;

—in many instances the most cost-effective means of access to justice would require new entrants into the market-place of legal services (alternatives to lawyers and the courts, e.g. increased use of ombudsmen and arbitrators);

—for complex cases, the fundholder would require access to lawyers and the courts.

Even if fundholders were created, it would be necessary to reform the supply side because fundholders would be keen to use new kinds of services, but would only be able to choose between services which are currently available and are dominated by traditional legal services. Applying the criterion of cost-effectiveness must also involve a re-examination of the impact of the adversarial system as well as a radical reappraisal of the methods of solution of disputes and the forums for such resolution. We would thus expect these processes to be reformed if access to justice is to be affordable (for example, the courts may have to manage the process of cases and to take a more inquisitorial role). On the other hand, making structural changes on the supply side without reform on the demand side would be unsatisfactory: solicitors would remain the first point of contact with clear financial incentives to stay with traditional legal services.

Who could be fundholders for justice?

The obvious model of fundholders for justice is that of GPs in the NHS who have opted to become fundholders. There is currently no equivalent role in the finance and delivery of legal aid. In contrast with GPs there is no agent with whom all those eligible for legal aid are registered.[21] There is no

---

[21] Requiring people to register with solicitors would almost certainly result in an explosive and unaffordable increase in legal aid.

universal coverage for legal aid, and the eligible population will change significantly from year to year. Virtually everyone uses health care, and in a three-year period most people will see their GP. Most of the population will have no need for legal aid throughout their life. Solicitors are the first point of contact in legal aid and account for most of legal aid expenditure (whereas spending on GP services is small compared with spending on hospitals).[22] We consider in the final section how fundholders might operate and be funded in a reformed system of financing and organizing access to justice. Here, however, we put on one side the practical problems of getting fundholding to work for legal aid, and consider what changes might be made by using the concept of this new role both nationally and locally.

Restructuring the demand side

We propose that the demand side be restructured to change the principals who pay for legal aid:

—from being passive third-party payors of lawyers
—into active buyers of access to justice.

We believe that this will bring two kinds of benefit: those who are currently eligible will get a better service, and more effective use of current levels of spending will enable a far greater number of people to get help from public funds in gaining access to justice.

Experience shows that someone who frequently buys the same commodity can develop into a skilled buyer, in contrast with the individual who makes one such purchase in a lifetime. In contrast with a private individual using a lawyer once, for example, trade unions and insurance companies, which frequently use lawyers in the UK, have contracts so that the lawyers

—are expected to charge significantly lower rates on a case-by-case basis (because they are assured of a volume of work); and
—know that the continuation of a contract depends on their performance (if they incur heavy expenditure on a number of lost cases they risk losing the contract).

This approach transforms the position of a third-party payor for legal services: from being more weakly placed as compared with the private

[22] Per capita spend on the NHS in the UK in 1991 was on average £311 on hospital services, £41 on general medical services (supplied from general practices), and £58 on drugs prescribed by GPs. It is not easy to derive comparable figures of spend on legal aid per entitled individual. One comparison is the spend in 1991–92 of £906m on 3.046m people helped; this gives a spend of about £300 per person helped.

client who pays directly, to being much more powerful than the private client. We see this as a crucial development required in paying for legal aid. We recognize that it entails restriction on the choice by individuals seeking access to justice. However, as we have argued above, this may not be so restrictive, since the nature of the principal/agent problem means that the principal who chooses an agent only once is obviously not in the position of the sovereign consumer. When as individual pays directly for services we naturally expect that individual to exercise free choice. When a third party pays, the right to choice is typically constrained. In the US, for example, firms have sought to control costs of health insurance by contracting with Preferred Provider Organizations (PPOs) who have a panel of doctors from which insured individuals may choose, and these doctors accept scrutiny by the PPO of their utilization of services.[23] The insured individuals may choose other doctors but only get a contribution to the costs if they do so. Restrictions on choice of lawyer may also be applied by insurers in the UK who offer legal expenses insurance.

Hence we propose that:

—LAB would develop contracts with selected firms who would be assured of a significant volume of work and consequently be required to reduce prices;
—continuation of contracts with LAB would be related to performance; and
—those eligible for legal aid would either use firms contracted to LAB, or if they used others receive a contribution to the cost.

It would be essential for clients to be offered choice within the scheme to avoid conflicts of interest: hence this would not remove choice but reveal constraints on free choice. Furthermore, we are dubious about whether free choice in these circumstances offers much, when the individual typically has isolated use of lawyers and is poorly placed to assess their quality. Thus conferring the notional freedom to choose a lawyer has nothing like the same meaning as where individuals are free to choose and know what they are getting. In contrast with the private individual, LAB would be able to assess performance (in terms of court and outcomes) over a run of cases and make comparisons between different firms and different barristers. This development would provide a platform for further changes in competitive tendering for advice (e.g. civil green form).

[23] See also Frech III HE (1988) 'Preferred Provider Organizations and health care competition', in Frech III HE (1988) (ed.) *Health Care in America*. San Francisco: Pacific Research Institute for Public Policy.

In this process, agencies other than solicitors' firms would be invited to tender: for example, Citizens' Advice Bureaux, and other organizations might emerge (employing people with experience of social security, or lawyers who have been unable to find traineeships).

Restructuring the supply side

The restructuring of the demand side, as outlined above, would provide opportunities for new kinds of advice to emerge. New processes of delivering justice would be required to restructure the supply side. Again, this could form part of a process of evolutionary reform. It might begin by re-examining the need for representation in criminal cases in magistrates' courts, and in cases involving custody of children, and divorces. There would always be an option for the judge or magistrate to require representation where cases turn out to be complex and merit this, but the normal course would be to try to avoid this.

The next step would be to examine where the adversarial process is, and is not, efficacious in providing cost-effective access to justice. The savings which can be made by emphasizing the written approach have barely been touched upon. Those savings could be re-allocated to areas where the need is greater. Prioritization of need is far more rewarding than adapting the need to fit outdated methods of delivering justice, which in any event were never invented in the context of the present demands made upon such methods by current society.

Changes in court procedure are being considered by Lord Woolf. He was reported to be recommending a new class of 'procedural judges' who would:

—simplify all civil actions and bring them under a single set of easily understood rules;

—take control of all civil cases out of the hands of lawyers—making it easier for people to represent themselves;

—set ceilings on costs at the outset of each case, and lay down strict timetables for cases to be heard—most within twelve months; and

—seek at each stage to halt or limit the scope of the case by getting the parties to reach amicable agreements.

The reforms indicated above may reduce the unit price of services, but not the volume: problems of supplier-induced demand and moral hazard remain. We now consider how these problems might be tackled.

6. Introducing Cost-Consciousness

Reducing moral hazard

Insurers reduce moral hazard by requiring the insured to contribute to the costs, for example, through:

—a deductible (or minimum) contribution. This may be appropriate for insurance against theft. where the insured has incentives to take reasonable precautions, but once these have been taken the insured cannot be held responsible for the size of the theft. Or:

—co-payments (a percentage of total costs to be shared) are appropriate where the insured can influence total costs.

Of these two, co-payments would seem appropriate for legal aid and, as outlined above, these generally apply. The nature of legal services, however, means that there is a further issue with co-payment. This is because requiring the legally aided individual to pay part of the costs means that that individual then faces a principal/agent problem. This means that it does not make sense to place the burden of co-payment solely on the principal (client) when the agent (lawyer) effectively decides what services will be delivered. Hence remedies to moral hazard may involve the lawyer more than the client.

It is, of course, common in the US for lawyers to bear all the risk under the system of contingency fees: they receive a share of the award if their client wins but get nothing if their client loses.

The indemnity rule on costs has been argued to be a major obstacle to the introduction of contingency fees in the UK, as this means that the indigent litigant, if unsuccessful, faces the possibility of paying costs of the losing side. It is also argued that abolition of the indemnity rule would encourage worthless litigation at the cost of the blameless defendant. Indeed this is an issue in the granting of civil legal aid: costs cannot be awarded against legally aided defendants. The problem raised by the indemnity rule can be addressed in the design of insurance (against the costs of the other parties) alongside contingency fees. The general principle is that of requiring lawyers and their clients to share risk of costs incurred (including their own costs and those of the other parties). This raises complex issues which we believe are resolvable by appropriate systems of risk sharing through co-payments.

Moral hazard can be reduced by:

—extending the requirement for co-payment for cases, so that few services are free at the point of delivery;

—not granting any legal aid for money cases, so lawyers and their clients are only prepared to pursue cases which they are likely to win;

—introducing franchises for firms, which lawyers would forfeit if they take on and lose expensive cases; and

—offering clients who use unfranchised lawyers only a contribution to their costs.

Tackling supplier-induced demand

We suggest here different ways of tackling supplier-induced demand for services in two broad classes:

—high volume and low unit cost, and

—high cost and low volume.

The German system of paying doctors and dentists provides a way of tackling supplier-induced demand for services with high volume and low unit cost. In this system, guidelines are set which fix the total money available for doctors' fees. This system is subject to arbitration, but in principle the system works as follows.[24] Suppose, for simplicity, the fee for each case is the same, then the fee per case each doctor receives is the total sum divided by the total number of cases claimed for in that year by doctors. Thus if each doctor treats 10% more cases than in the previous year, each doctor's income stays the same. The third party therefore decides what it can afford, and the profession, through individual actions, decides the volume of services this sum buys, and the income to each member of the profession.

This system might offer a way of financing parts of legal aid. For Green Form Civil, for example, LCD and LAB might agree a cash limit for England and Wales. This would then be divided between the LAB regions using a population formula (which may be simply in terms of numbers of the eligible population, or be more sophisticated in terms of weighting for likely need for legal aid). Within each region, the cash limit available would then be distributed to lawyers according to the number of acts of assistance.

For complex cases, for example, in the High Court, a different approach would obviously be required. Counsel of any individual party can influence, but not determine, how long and costly a case will be. Contracts for complex cases might be designed to share risk between Counsel and LCD

---

[24] See Abel-Smith B. (1984) *Cost Containment in Health Care*. London, Bedford Square Press, p. 42.

and LAB. Current arrangements appear to be inadequate to an economist, because the LCD and LAB bear all the risk. This provides perverse incentives to Counsel to prolong and increase the cost of cases.[25] Again, oral advocacy is the most expensive form of dispute resolution—lawyers on their feet should always be the last resort in terms of cost.

An obvious approach to contracting for complex cases is to design incentives for shortening cases around a fixed fee. We can consider extending the idea attributed to Lord Woolf of a ceiling on costs. Consider, for example, a case which is assessed at the start to take 100 days of Counsel's time, but may be as short as 50 days, or as long as 300 days. If we assume a daily rate of £1,000, a contract might be designed as follows:

—a fixed fee for £100,000 for the case;
—an abatement of £500 per day for each day less than 100 days;
—additional fees of £500 per day for 100 to 300 days; and
—additional fees of £300 per day for each day beyond 300 days.

The impact of such a contract would, of course, be much greater if each Counsel had the same contract. The impact is diminished if other Counsel are paid risk-free per diem rates, and therefore gain the longer a case drags on. There are also problems in working out what fixed fees might be, and the rates for abatement and additional fees. The purpose of this illustration is to indicate ways of designing incentives to counter supplier-induced demand.

7. A Reformed System Of Organizing And Financing Access To Justice

We now conclude by outlining how, based on the above, a new system of organizing and financing access to justice for civil and criminal legal aid might be developed.

Criminal Higher

Criminal legal aid obviously differs from civil legal aid, as the number of cases is determined by the Crown's decisions to prosecute. There is, however, a difference between the higher courts and criminal magistrates courts: for the higher courts there is a clear need for defendants to be rep-

---

[25] Standard fees are one way of sharing risk between LCD and Counsel, but are not appropriate for complex cases.

resented by lawyers; in the magistrates' courts there is not.[26] This suggests different approaches to these different types of criminal work. For higher courts, the focus would be on contractual design to share risk as discussed above. We propose, however, that legal aid for criminal magistrates courts be distributed and managed as part of civil legal aid.

Civil Legal Aid and Criminal Magistrates' Legal Aid

For civil legal and criminal magistrates' legal aid we propose a system of fundholders for justice. The basic principles of the scheme we propose would be as follows.

The total sum available for England and Wales would be cash-limited. It would be determined by the Government in the Public Expenditure Survey, and would thus be an assessment of what the country could afford (in the same way as spending on hospital and community health services is determined).

The cash-limited sum would, over time, be distributed to the legal aid regions according to their estimated relative needs. Equitable targets would be derived based on the crude population weighted by their likely need for publicly financed assistance in seeking access to justice. These targets may be built up from different components (e.g. criminal magistrates', civil, matrimonial etc.) with different need indicators used to weight the different components. This exercise would be likely to show inequity in the current use of the available funds. We propose that over a defined period actual allocations be moved towards their targets. (This would be similar to the derivation and use of a capitation formula in distributing the cash limit for spending on hospital and community health services).

The legal aid regions would, through their area offices, divide their allocation between a sum for criminal magistrates' courts and for civil legal aid.

The sum for criminal magistrates' courts would be distributed for paying for access to justice at each court on the basis of its catchment populations (again weighted by appropriate indicators of risk). The area offices would set block contracts for cases at these courts. This could be done, for example, by letting a contract to solicitors for cases at each court for each day of the week.

---

[26] The proportion of indictable cases in magistrates' courts which are legally aided has increased from less than 55% in 1980 to over 80% since 1988, with over 94% being legally aided between 1989 and 1991.

For civil legal aid and for advice and assistance (Green Form, ABWOR, and the Duty Solicitor schemes), the area offices would determine fund-holding areas for defined populations. These would be designed to generate a large enough population for managing a budget for all civil legal aid and the skills necessary for effective purchasing of the services needed for access to justice. In 1994–95 public expenditure on civil legal aid, and advice and assistance, was forecast to be nearly £1bn: i.e. £20 per person in England and Wales. Thus an area with a population of about 500,000 would, for example, have a budget of about £10m. This might be a manageable size for fundholding.

The area offices of the LAB would then invite tenders for managing the budget for justice for civil legal aid for each defined fundholding area. This could take various forms, but the principle would be that the organization would provide the combined function of immediate advice, knowledge of which specialist services to use, and capacity to manage a budget for the full range of services. The organization might include no specialist services (with all being bought under contract); most specialist services (with some being bought under contract); or virtually all specialist services (with only a few bought under contract). The optimal design for each area would be left to emerge from the tendering process. It would vary from area to area. Furthermore, since a crucial function of the fund-holders is to develop new and more cost-effective means of delivering justice, the way fundholding would work would evolve over time.

We envisage that there would be national rules on eligibility and levels of co-payment. Access to the initial advice and diagnosis might be free, with some form of co-payment being generally required for specialist services. There would obviously need to be exemptions for people who are clearly destitute: e.g. on income support. Thus we would also propose that access to specialist services depends on co-payment by clients, and that there is no public finance available for money cases.

LAB through its regions and area offices would consider how quality standards would be built into the process of tendering and monitoring performance. LAB would also consider how to handle very expensive cases which are of national interest.

Any person wanting publicly financed access to justice would be required to go to one of the offices run by the fundholder who covers the area.

The basis of the scheme is that the fundholder makes informed choices on behalf of potential clients. If clients want to make different choices they are, of course, free to do so, but would at most receive a fixed sum from the fundholder as assistance in using other services.

The fundholder is thus left to exercise discretion over the use of limited public funds for access to justice. This is a new and crucial role. However, choice lies in facing up to explicit rationing in this way, or not imposing limits on expenditure. We see no alternative to limiting expenditure on legal aid, and hence the need for agents to make rationing decisions. The merits of what we propose are that we believe that it will lead to increased and more effective access to justice within the resources that the country can afford.

Conclusion

We conclude by making three points. First, it seems futile to respond to current problems with legal aid by calling for more public funds to be made available with no change to the current system. Secondly, the problems of the current system are such that radical reform is needed across all aspects of finance and delivery. It is inappropriate: to contract by the hour for spending on such a scale that it employs one in ten of the solicitors in England and Wales; to have systems which create incentives for supplier-induced demand; and to have systems which are constrained to use the lawyers and the courts when there are likely to be more cost-effective alternatives. What we have proposed is intended to address each of these weaknesses. Finally, our proposals are intended, not as a blueprint for the future, but as a contribution to debate about the kinds of radical changes which need to be made to the ways in which legal aid is financed and organized. We hope that others can improve substantially on these initial ideas so that in England and Wales we can return to a system in which access to justice does not depend on ability to pay.